Judith Devlin studied at Dublin, Oxford, the Sorbonne and the Ecole Nationale d'Administration in Paris. She is now a diplomat in Moscow.

The Superstitious Mind

THE SUPERSTITIOUS MIND

French Peasants and the Supernatural in the Nineteenth Century

Judith Devlin

Yale University Press
New Haven and London

Designed by Faith Glasgow
Set in Compugraphic Garamond by Boldface and printed in Great Britain by Bell & Bain Ltd.

Library of Congress Cataloging-in-Publication Data

Devlin, Judith, 1952-
The superstitious mind.

Bibliography:.p.
Includes index.
1. Occult sciences—France—History—19th century.
2. France—Social life and customs. I. Title.
BFL434.F8D48 1987 133'.0944 86-23341
ISBN 0-300-03710-4

Contents

List of Illustrations

'L'histoire positive...l'expression d'une aveugle partialité, le roman consacré d'un parti vainqueur, une fable classique devenue si indifférente à tout le monde que personne ne prend plus la peine de la contredire.'

Nodier, *La Fée aux Miettes*

'Les historiens, s'ils n'ont pas eu tort de renoncer à expliquer les actes des peuples par la volonté des rois, doivent la remplacer par la psychologie de l'individu, de l'individu médiocre.'

Proust, *A La Recherche du Temps Perdu*

Acknowledgements

I should like to thank the National University of Ireland and Somerville College, Oxford, for their support and encouragement, which enabled me to work on this book.

I wish also to record my appreciation to the directors and staff of the folowing institutions: the *Bibliothèque Nationale* and the *Archives Nationales* in Paris; the British Museum; the Radcliffe Science Library, the Bodleian Library and the Taylorian Institute in Oxford; the *Archives Départmentales* of the Allier and Gironde. They resolved many of my difficulties in tracking down material, and were unfailingly generous and resourceful in their assistance.

I am both grateful for the help and impressed by the ingenuity of my editors, Robert Baldock and Faith Glasgow, who wrestled with the problems of a puzzling text and an often inaccessible author. Mary McGeogh, Tina Pryor, Noeleen O'Reilly and Eilis O'Toole, who painstakingly typed various drafts of the text, deserve an accolade for patience (and paleographic skill).

The eccentricities and shortcomings of the book are my own. It would never have been completed, however, without the help and encouragement of my family and friends. My parents remained benevolent even when pressed into active service: the text would never have been produced without their labours and support. To Deirdre MacMahon, Mark and Cliona Leslie, Janet and Oliver Soskice, who were so generous with their hospitality and advice, I express heartfelt thanks and gratitude.

I owe an especial debt of gratitude to Professor T. D. Williams, for his generosity and encouragement over many years. Above all, without the interest, unflagging patience and kindness, stimulating questioning and suggestions of Theodore Zeldin, I would neither have embarked on nor completed this enterprise. It must often have seemed to him like Sisyphus' rock, and if it has finally been pushed to the top of the hill and stayed there, it is largely due to him.

Moscow
July 1986

Introduction

Usually, history deals with the acts and opinions of influential individuals – politicians, civil servants, journalists and intellectuals – most of whom are conscious of the interest they present for posterity and carefully record their own edifying ideas and needs (as well as the less momentous contributions of their contemporaries). They have succumbed to the notion that they 'create' history, that they embody its most significant aspects, that they shape the destiny of mankind. Yet these aspirations, however natural, however typical of our vanity and hubris, are only tenuously connected with the muddle of men's affairs, much less with the complication, obscurity and immense variety of forces which shape human activity. In short, our notion of history is greatly indebted to the heroic rationalism of eighteenth- and nineteenth-century intellectuals, and has hardly been adapted at all to accommodate the evidence of man's perverse irrationality and the emergence into public life of 'the madding crowd'.

That impulse, instinct and feeling are at least as significant as thought, reflection and analysis in accounting for behaviour; that the masses, involved in politics by the efforts of liberal intellectuals in the nineteenth century, have hardly demonstrated a substantial commitment to intelligent debate as opposed to demagogy and spectacle, to reasoned analysis as opposed to myth – all this should give historians pause for thought. It was Proust who pointed out that reality is more complex than our accounts of it usually suggest and that the psychology of ordinary people should be examined by modern historians. With some notable exceptions – Theodore Zeldin, Lucien Febvre, Philip Ariès, Keith Thomas, Jean Delumeau – few scholars have taken up the challenge or concerned themselves, for example, with the divergence between the modern novel (as inaugurated by Proust), which presents man's complexity, and history, which tends to ignore it.

This book sets out to examine the more obscure and puzzling aspects of man's beliefs and behaviour, as exemplified in the superstitious culture of rural France in the nineteenth century. Why France? Why the peasantry? Because France enjoys the reputation of being the mother-country of modern liberal rationality, and to discover the widespread existence within this civilization of a mass sub-culture characterized, on an intellectual level, by irrationality and confusion, and, on an emotional level, by fear and instinct, was a surprise. This apparently medieval outlook seemed incompatible with the modernity which emerged in the nineteenth century and was established when the Great War broke out. How was it to be interpreted? Historians who have examined often identical beliefs in the sixteenth and seventeenth centuries affirm that it should be viewed as an archaic mentality which can be understood by modern man only if it is seen as implying entirely different modes of thinking and feeling. I find this thesis unconvincing – both on formal epistemological grounds and on more pragmatic ones. If we suppose a closed system of meaning and reference, it is hard to see how, logically, we can expect to elucidate it through our own system. More practically, the biological evidence for significant changes in human nature over three or four centuries (much less over one) is less than overwhelming. Finally, the problem of accounting for and identifying a revolution in human nature has never been resolved. The most reasonable hypothesis seems to me to be that the roots of modern culture are to be found in the past and that both its taste for escapism and its anxiety are mirrored in our ancestors' penchant for fantasy and consoling fiction. In short, the superstitious mind appears to me incompatible neither with the reasonable pragmatism of modernity nor with its more disturbing features, and this book attempts to sustain this argument.

I

Popular Religion

Writing of the medieval religious sensibility in classic vein, Lecky observed:

> Nothing could be more common than for a holy man to be lifted up from the floor in the midst of his devotions, or to be visited by the Virgin or by an angel. There was scarcely a town that could not show some relic that had cured the sick, or some image that had opened and shut its eyes, or bowed its head to an earnest worshipper. It was somewhat more extraordinary, but not in the least incredible, that the fish should have thronged to the shore to hear Saint Anthony preach, or that it should be necessary to cut the hair of the crucifix at Burgos once a month.... All this was going on in Europe without exciting the smallest astonishment or scepticism.[1]

Ethnologists and subsequent historians have, similarly, tended to believe that French peasants in the nineteenth century were in the grip of a medieval outlook characterized by tremulous piety and unlimited credulity, and utterly divorced, in its preoccupations and in the sensibility it implied, from modern secular positivism. Modern man, they suggest, is a realist concerned with the material, with the world that is; historical man lived in an exotic world of fantasy, and nowhere is this held to be more evident than in his devotion to religion. But how accurate or illuminating is this view? How assiduous were French peasants in their religious duties? What were their religious beliefs? Do they point to a peculiar sensibility or mentality and do they justify historians' periodization of thought and feeling into the archaic and the modern?

Externals of Official Devotion

The claims of the Church to an unchanging tradition have been, to a remarkable extent, taken at face value. Indeed, the apparent continuity of religious gesture, prayer and image between the Reformation and the end of the nineteenth century is arresting, and has encouraged historians to believe that the everyday life of the Church lay in substantially homogeneous and orthodox popular devotions, in which fear of hell and the desire to go to heaven spurred the faithful to observe prescribed rituals dutifully. Early studies of the practice of religion seemed to justify this picture of naive assiduity at divine worship. Initial surveys yielded a somewhat misleading picture of religious conformity and obedience, at the end of the *Ancien Régime*. Boulard believed that no more than 10 per cent of the population, in any village, failed to go to confession and communion at Easter, and that these individuals were known to their parish priests.[2] Gabriel Le Bras estimated that 95 per cent of the country people fulfilled the obligation of going to church and taking communion at Easter in the eighteenth century, and dismissed refractories as 'des déclassés et des classes remuantes'.[3]

But as more studies were devoted to the historical sociology of religious life, the more evident became the inadequacies, lapses and divergences which the imposing externals masked. Jeanne Ferté, in her study of the Parisian countryside in the seventeenth century, came to ask what presence at mass meant to most of the faithful, who were encouraged to follow their private devotions throughout it. She concluded that the combination of minimal practice with moral laxity indicated 'a more or less conscious materialism which smothered all religious enthusiasm'.[4] Louis Pérouas, in his work on the diocese of La Rochelle, was also struck by what he called the 'diminishing awareness of God', the sense of the mystery of God, which orthodoxy would have led one to expect.[5] Nor, on closer examination, were the statistics as reassuring as they seemed. Le Bras himself uncovered areas of lesser devotion in the eighteenth century – notably the south-west – and social groups more likely to rebel against religious conformity. Michel Vovelle, in his pioneering study of religious practice in eighteenth-century Provence, saw the period between 1720 and 1850 as the 'high point of Catholicism's conquest', but noted a rapid decline of practice in the following period. This was characterized, according to Vovelle, by the birth of 'a whole complex of new attitudes which definitively dispel the impression of a break, caused by the Revolution, between a supposedly Christian *Ancien Régime* and a gradually dechristianised nineteenth century'.[6]

The erosion of traditional practice, which would appear to have started in south-western France in the mid-eighteenth century, was hastened by the Revolution and industrialization.[7] During the Revolution, priests who refused to take the constitutional oath were concentrated in the north, north-west and north-east and in the mountains of the Massif Central – areas which later remained faithful to the Church – while priests who adapted themselves to the régime were to be found in the centre of the *bassin parisien*, the Loire, Dauphiné, Provence, and central France, where practice was subsequently to decline. The inquiry of the Constituent Assembly in 1848 confirmed that Brittany, the Vendée and the Pyrénées were religious, while Saintonge, Aunis, Périgord and the Bordelais in the south-west, Provence in the south-east, western Burgundy and the *bassin parisien* in the centre were described as unsatisfactory. The decline became more acute in the central plains and in Provence and Limousin during the Second Empire, while the lower Languedoc was dechristianized by the early twentieth century.[8] The nadir of the Church's fortunes coincided with the anti-clerical government of Combes, after which they recovered somewhat.[9] But the map of religious practice for France in 1951 reflects patterns already discernible during the Revolution,[10] which prompted Canon Boulard to observe that 'historical research reveals the remarkable continuity of these distinctive communities and of their political and religious attitudes'.[11]

In fact, then, religious devotion – at least orthodox piety – was not a universal phenomenon in nineteenth-century rural France, even in the early years of the century. It had reached its apogée towards the middle of the previous century, and declined thereafter, before industrialization, urbanization or the spread of primary education had taken their toll upon traditional patterns of behaviour.

Attempts to explain the tenacity of religion in some areas and its relative decline in others have pointed to the complexity of traditional behaviour, whose roots seem to be deeply implanted in the past. Urbanization and occupation by no means account satisfactorily for the diversity of religious practice, as the extent of practice varied greatly not only between town and countryside or between different occupations, but also between different towns and, as we have seen, different country areas. The trends of the surrounding countryside influenced urban religious behaviour.[12] Yet both environment and employment seem to impinge to some extent on manifestations of devotion. In the twentieth century, better-paid workers, white-collar workers and wealthier farmers – especially where they are not specialized – often practise their religion more than do unskilled workers and farm labourers.[13] Age and sex are also influential factors, young people and women tending to practise more than adult men.[14] No single variable, however, can be isolated to account for discrepancies in religious behaviour, nor for the rapid decline in practice during the nineteenth century.

Conformity seems to have been a question of habit in sedentary communities. Dechristianization had started in Rouen by 1698, in the opinion of Boulard, on account of a badly integrated mobile population. Le Bras found that soldiers, boatmen, valets and those whose profession led them to interrupt or question custom furnished the first contingent of popular dissenters in the eighteenth century.[15] Charpin, in his study of Marseille, felt that indifference might accompany obedience to religious discipline; curates, answering inquiries about the piety of their flock, frequently bemoaned the materialism and scepticism which sometimes accompanied church-going.[16] The *curé* of Bessuire in 1848 wrote that 'most town-dwellers and country people seem to fulfil their religious duties more through habit than from conviction'. The *curé* of Parthenay felt that 'there is more apparent religion than real religion . . . People are religious on account of fashion rather than from conviction.' The priest at Gençay noted of his parishioners: 'As they know little of the principles of religion, the inhabitants of the district observe their forefathers' customs, and think they have done their entire duty when they have followed the rites of the Church.'[17] To the extent that religion was a custom within a static society, its survival in traditional forms was threatened by the forces of change.[18]

Habit is constituted both of reflex and of tacitly received opinion. Priests often noted that 'human respect' frequently inhibited people's behaviour – as we can readily believe, given the importance of reputation in societies so dependent on personal cooperation and trust – but while on one hand this could simply be a means of enforcing conformity with traditional practices, on the other, radiating out from the tavern or meeting-place of sceptical *petits-bourgeois* and peasants, it could gradually change common attitudes and opinions. Missionaries in the district of Gray (Doubs) in the 1890s noted the indifference of the faithful and their ignorance of Church dogma, and deplored the importance of public opinion in determining manifestations of devotional ardour.[19] Le Bras' final judgement was that practice had 'social rather than properly and profoundly religious meaning. . . . Custom and even local criticism account for seasonal conformity, or, indeed, for religious practice itself.'[20] The weight of custom and public opinion best explains why some groups, like women and children, attended church more than others, and why communities of similar complexion behaved variously. The rapid decline in religious practice in the nineteenth century becomes less surprising in the light of the relatively recent and superficial conversions of the seventeenth-century Counter-Reformation,[21] and of the apparent absence of conscious spiritual commitment on the part of the faithful.

These problems of interpretation indicate the inadequacies of an approach concerned almost exclusively with externals, for its results would point, somewhat misleadingly, to a substantially devout France before the Revolution and an increasingly dechristianized one thereafter. But the term 'dechristianization' itself has had to be called into question. Le Bras, in his last reflections on an area of study which he had largely opened up, felt it was more to the point to ask whether the French countryside had ever been converted. He came to reject the term 'dechristianization' for the reason that 'the "age of faith" is in my opinion a myth'.[22] The survey of formal religious practice does not necessarily throw significant light on popular religious sensibility, as it is concerned with outward gestures – whose significance for the individual can change, as his ideas and cultural climate change, and which are not, in any case, a spontaneous expression of his private beliefs. Evolving habits of religious practice, therefore, do not necessarily correspond to a change in outlook and conviction on the part of the individual. Furthermore, one of the great boons of Church ritual – and doubtless one of the causes of its continued vitality – is that it furnishes forms into which the individual can pour his anxieties and his hopes: it is not as standard and dogmatic as one might at first think. Hence, one can note continuity of religious practice, while it may be translating and corresponding to different needs; similarly, the decline of a custom does not necessarily entail the disappearance of the thought and feeling which found expression in it.

The decline of orthodox religious belief did not herald the emergence of a secular rationalism – even where it was accompanied by the growth of radical politics. Daniel Monnier, when walking one evening in the early 1850s on the outskirts of Lyon, met a middle-aged peasant returning home from work. This man admitted (despite being inhibited by the scepticism he expected to meet in the wealthy town-dweller and his fear of the *curé*'s disapproval) his belief in and fear of the *vouivre* (a kind of flying dragon), in which belief was widespread in Franche-Comté and surrounding areas, according to Monnier. The priest, when discreetly questioned by Monnier, denied that such popular superstitions had any currency in the area, lamenting that the general scepticism extended to orthodox religious belief – a fact which he attributed to the spread of newspapers and extreme political creeds.[23] The anecdote raises the question whether the progress of radical politics and the process of 'dechristianization' were synonymous with the disappearance of seemingly irrational attitudes and beliefs; whether these transformations of social ideals and behaviour were inevitably and simultaneously accompanied by the replacement of an apparently 'mystical' instinct with a modern mentality.

Advanced political ideas excluded neither religious devotion nor belief in and practice of magic, while indifference to or scepticism about orthodox religion could co-exist with fidelity to superstitious rites.[24] François Goguel noted that political and religious geography do not coincide exactly: in the west, politically conservative areas extended beyond religiously devout ones; in the south, regions known for their piety extended into radical areas; the election results of 1877 bore no relation to religious geography. Dr Cavalier investigated belief in spells and associated magical practices in Hérault in the 1860s, and found that it flourished to a greater extent along the coast and in the area of Montpellier than in the mountains – a direct reversal of the pattern of religious devotion and, to a lesser extent, of conservative political affiliations discerned by Cholvy in his study of the area at the start of the century.[25] Cavalier commented:

> Everything would lead one to suppose that such superstitions have persisted above all in remote places, where the disruption caused by business is limited, where travel is difficult and where, as a result, old-fashioned ideas can survive longer in their traditional unaltered form. This is far from the case, however. Around Montpellier, and within a fairly wide radius of it, the areas most tainted by these erroneous old beliefs are in fact those which are the most advanced in every other way.

The vine-growing regions – which most frequently sent their women to work in Montpellier's industries, which had a higher level of education and where 'people are more aware of the common good of the region' than elsewhere – were more superstitious than the traditional mountains, in the doctor's view.

This pattern was not exceptional. The Bourbonnais, which was politically radical and generally agnostic by 1848, was a hot-bed of magical practices and beliefs. Graulle, in his study of popular medicine in the Allier in the 1960s, found that this apparent paradox still held good. 'I'm thinking of one fairly typical farmer, a town-counsellor, very much on the left and anti-clerical, who heals sores and eczema by making signs of the cross and using sacred formulae.' Charente and Charente-Inférieure were also areas notorious for their religious disaffection, but innumerable unorthodox pragmatic religious customs were observed there.[26] Léon Ganachaud, an inn-keeper from Aubérac, grew up in an atmosphere in which religious and political debate was lively. Most of the peasants were sceptical in an earthy way about religion. Yet when asked by his grandchildren whether or not he believed in sorcerers, he responded: 'No, but in all honesty, I would have to say that strange things happen which one has to believe because one has seen them.'[27] These initially surprising inconsistencies of thought and behaviour are doubtless partially explained by a want of systematic reflection, as much as by ignorance, and the correspondingly preponderant role of habit in determining reactions and ideas. Nonetheless, they suggest that growing estrangement from the Church did not necessarily involve the adoption of new criteria of judgement, or the espousal of a new vision of the world, implying new modes of thought. Indeed, the apparently paradoxical co-existence of querulous scepticism with acceptance of tradition, of rationality in some matters and irrationality in others indicates the inadequacy of the conventional classification of thought into archaic and modern, mystical and scientific, and of the supposition that the implied habits of mind are mutually exclusive. In short, they point to the necessity of ascertaining what both religious and magical gestures meant to their practitioners.

Misconceptions about Religion

How much did the rural poor actually know about dogma of religion? How did they view God and his saints, sin and the devil, heaven and hell, grace and redemption? It would seem that the formal religious education of the masses left much to be desired. Since the Counter-Reformation, consistent efforts had been made to evangelize the rural faithful, to develop an orthodox and uniform understanding of religion. Yet the evidence of priests' observations, popular practices and oral tradition suggests that country people knew little of elementary doctrine and preferred self-interested supplication and festive celebration to introspective piety and devotion, to the sobriety and restraint that characterized moral, like polite, behaviour, from the seventeenth to the nineteenth centuries. Despite its deviousness and delight in the distortion of reality, the popular imagination of this period does not appear to have inhabited the unworldly realms of religious speculation or conceived of a transcendental source of privileged knowledge. The supernatural was in fact, more often than not, assimilated to the natural and harnessed to its needs.

Naive faith may have inspired a separate culture, a peculiar cosmology, but that it was truly religious – in contrast to modern secular culture – is not evident. It was based on many vague and unorthodox ideas. The universality and abstraction of theological conceptions appear to all intents and purposes to have escaped the rural poor. Achille Miron, an anti-clerical polemicist from Chartres commented that '...In theory, the Virgin Mary is *one* person.... The reality is quite a different matter. A host of Our Ladies exist, all with special features and virtues; they are so many distinct beings; each has her own appearance, character, speciality in healing or in granting other favours.'[28] This seems to have been true at least of Brittany and the countryside north of the Loire. Around 1890, at Notre Dame de Béron, a preacher attempted to instil into his congregation some notions about God and the divine hierarchy that one would have imagined to be essential to any truly Catholic thought. The priest insisted that no matter where one worshipped, one still honoured the same Virgin. At the exit, an old lady was heard remarking to another: 'Did you hear that old fool maintaining there's only one Our Lady everywhere? As if everyone didn't know that the daughter is here and the mother at Revercourt.'[29]

It is easy to dismiss this anecdote as the inconsequential rambling of a benighted mind, but it does not seem entirely untypical of popular beliefs. Numerous legends referred to similar relationships between local saints. Anatole Le Braz asked a shepherdess from Lan-Karé in Brittany about local cults and was informed that '...In bygone days, Our Lady of Lan-Karé was revered as much as Our Lady of Kernitrou and the one from Cotz-Yéodet. The three virgins were, besides, three cousins.'[30] He also recorded the opinions and tales of a Breton peasant woman, Marie-Jeanne Collorec. The sanctuary of Our Lady of Le Crann was venerated in south Brittany, where Marie-Jeanne lived. In the chapel, the Virgin's life was depicted with some realism: the birth of Christ showed Mary lying in bed, while Joseph anxiously awaited the child's arrival. Despite the explicit references to the Nativity, Marie-Jeanne did not seem to identify her Our Lady of Le Crann with the Virgin Mary. She told a story about Our Lady of Cléden, who came to visit 'Our Lady of Le Crann, her sister' on her feast day. 'My lady Mary of Le Crann is a good saint and an excellent mother, may God bless her!' she is reported to have said. 'There's no disability or misfortune she can't prevent. As sure as you see me here, I owe her my life.'[31]

The devout seem to have thought saints and God worthy of praise because of their readiness to exercise their beneficient powers in this way. The relationship with God, as the source of sanctity and consolation, was sometimes dismissed as irrelevant or unimportant. In 1872, an old woman kneeling in front of the famous Madonna of Chartres, Our Lady of Pity, happened to block a procession. She was invited to make way: 'Come along, move out of the way; can't you see the good God approaching?' 'Huh!' she grunted, 'I didn't come here for *him*, it was for *her*' (pointing to the Virgin).[32] Indicative of the degree of popular ignorance in some areas was the belief of peasants in Finistère that Saint Mathurin of Moncontour could have been God, had he so wanted.[33] It would seem, therefore, that the orthodox model of the heavenly hierarchy was not always appreciated in the nineteenth century.

The divergence from orthodoxy was reflected, too, in the sorts of prayers people addressed to God, many of which were directed to ends of which the Church strongly disapproved. Writing of Brittany before the Revolution, Cambry observed that both men and women were assiduous in their devotion to unorthodox practices:

> In church, people . . . used to recite, without understanding them, prayers which they thought capable of curing every ailment, making the fields fertile, procuring mistresses for themselves, making their enemies waste away. The hope of meeting with success in these projects inspired them with a frenzy of enthusiasm.[34]

How accurate was this affirmation? The researches of folklorists in the last century, and the evidence of popular literature, confirm that prayers were said for all sorts of peculiar ends – both in and out of church.

Unorthodox prayers included love charms. The *Dragon Rouge* (Red Dragon), a chapbook of dubious repute in the countryside, included a good number of prayers for animals, safe journeys, exorcisms, protection from fire-arms and love potions – as well as more dubious enterprises such as casting spells, preventing the consummation of marriages ('nouer l'aiguillette') and 'making a naked girl dance', which did not prevent the catalogue ending with the Pater, Ave, Veni Creator and Credo in French![35] Prayers were addressed to God for the alleviation of all kinds of distress and even for illicit ends. Fear of enemies figures in a number of traditional prayers.[36] A man from Bourbon-L'Archambaut in the Allier, who had something of a reputation as a sorcerer, used to say an 'oraison de la Bonne Dame de Secours Sainte Délice' to preserve himself from spells. He said it secretly, either in the morning or in the evening, when washing his hands. He made a surreptitious sign of the cross, recited three Our Fathers and Hail Marys, and then proceeded to inform God that he had offered these up for the intention of the mysterious 'Bonne Dame de Secours Sainte Délice' so that she might protect him and his animals. By way of explanation, the prayer added: 'Neighbours I dread, envious men and envious women, jealous men and jealous women, sorcerers and witches and all the evil people there are on earth.' It ended with a sign of the cross, made while saying: 'Au nom du Père et du Fils et du Sainte Délice'.[37] Whether the substitution of this apocryphal saint for the 'Holy Spirit' was deliberate or simply an error is not clear; in any event, it pointed to the singular ignorance of the man who said it. Despite the initial precautions, which were typical of magic, the prayer itself was almost entirely religious in vocabulary, however incongruous parts of it were – and this flavour was stressed by the caveat that the rite was effective only if one gave alms to the poor. Yet it strikes one as anything but religious in spirit. But to ask whether it was seen as a religious or magical rite is perhaps irrelevant, for popularly, the distinction between the beneficient and the maleficient seems to have been based as much on the intent as on the content of the rite.

Attitudes to Saints. Popular prayers tended to adapt the liturgical and the biblical to situations where orthodoxy considers their use sacriligious. An example of what could happen to the liturgical prayer was furnished by Nisard in an excerpt from a chapbook entitled *Le Jardin de L'Honnête Amour*. Called 'Invocation which girls who want to marry must make', it started:

> Kyrie, I should like
> Christe, to be married
> Kyrie, I pray to all the saints
> Christe, that it may be tomorrow....
> Saint Frederick, may I have a good husband.
> Saint Bartholomew, may he be handsome ...[38]

According to Mensignac, variants of this invocation were recited by young girls from the area of La Réole (Gironde) who wanted to marry, and they were also known in the Ile-de-France.[39] In it, the saints were addressed much as a child might reproach capricious elders who were depriving it of sweets: the prayer indicates no notion of the distance which was supposed to separate saints in heaven from sinners on earth. These holy figures, far from being models of virtue, far from being concerned mainly with the celestial glory of God (as the blessed were meant to be) and taking an interest in the terrestrial only when it had some immediate bearing upon the individual's spiritual well-being, were seen as somewhat more powerful human beings – knowing the variety of human desires, capable of satisfying them if approached in the right way, and sharing a number of human weaknesses (like meanness and obstinacy).

Hence, perhaps, the imperative summons of a 'prayer to the angels' noted in the Hautes-Vosges by Sauvé: 'N...(here name the angels to whom you're praying) I beg and beseech you to look favourably on my request...and by the sacred names of God, Aagla or Tetragramination, to do what I want.'[40] Whatever peculiar sort of being he might be, the saint's or angel's *raison d'être* was the practical services he could render, the wishes he could fulfil.

Each saint had his own specific powers, and these sometimes tended to obscure all other dimensions of his being. These attributes were all too down-to-earth. Saints were consulted for protection on journeys and against thunder and lightning, for the recovery of lost objects, the punishment of wrongdoers and the discovery of thieves. The remedies they provided were often indicated by their names. Saint Clair (who, according to legend, picked up his head and walked open-eyed after being decapitated) cured eye troubles and restored poor sight. In Normandy, Saint Maclou banished boils, which were locally called 'clous'; Saint Ortaire, being referred to as Saint Tortaire, was consulted for pain and aches ('tortures'); in Berry, Saint Langouret had a chapel, where apathetic, languishing children were brought for relief. Similarly, at Ceaux in the Loudun area, Saint Fort helped weak children when they made the pilgrimage to his chapel and had a gospel said in his honour. Wet-nurses prayed to Notre Dame de Bon Lait (Our Lady of Good Milk), at Moussac-sur-Vienne, Saint-Chartres and Thure. The catalogue included some most unorthodox saints – for example, Saint Sourdeau, invented by the peasants of Vienne, who devoutly applied to him for the relief of deafness. In Normandy, there was Saint Va-et-Vient (Saint Come and Go), to whom one prayed so that an ill person might either recover or die rather than languish on as a burden to his relatives. At Remiremont in the Vosges, Saint Vivra, Saint Languit and Saint Mort (Saint Will-Live, Saint Languish and Saint Death) served the same function, while at Vrémy, one prayed to Saint Maur to speed up the last moments of one's dependents.[41] Sauvé heard a 'prayer' which expressed comparably disedifying sentiments:

> Madame Marie de Molène
> A mon île envoyez naufrage,
> Et vous M. Saint Renan,
> N'en envoyez pas un seulement,
> Envoyez-en deux, trois plutôt,
> Pour que chacun en ait un morceau.[42]
>
> (Madame Marie de Molène
> A shipwreck to my island send,
> And you, Saint Renan,
> Don't only send a single one,
> Send two of them, or rather three
> So we may all have some booty.)

One's first reaction is to smile at the gullibility of the folklorist and his failure to appreciate the ironically charitable afterthought addressed to 'Saint Renan'; but when one has reviewed the variety of human wishes and requests addressed, in prayer and rite, to God and his saints, one becomes less sceptical. Popular prayers and piety as it was preached by the higher clergy were sometimes not just only tenuously connected, but even divorced from each other.

On the other hand, the practicality and functionalism of official religion in its collective manifestations hardly encouraged the development of a refined appreciation of spirituality. Popular pilgrimages, individual or general, for man or beast, health or wealth, were accommodated by the Church (albeit sometimes grudgingly). Pilgrimages for domestic animals were popular all over France at the start of the nineteenth century – a popularity which must partly be ascribed to the belief that the blessing thereby obtained protected animals from illness and accident.[43] Pilgrimages for horses, cows, sheep and the like to trees, wells and cross-roads were still on the religious calendar in eastern Flanders in the middle of the century; while the Bretons of Landernau, according to Cambry, brought their horses to hear mass on the feast-day of Saint Ely.[44] Sauvé recounts how, in Lower Brittany in the later nineteenth century, Saint Ely was offered money, candles and manes to protect the supplicants' horses. On the first of December, the eve of his feast-day, bonfires were lit in many villages. Early the next morning, the horses would be brought to whatever local chapel was dedicated to the saint, where they were made to walk three times around the sanctuary. Water taken from the sacred well was poured over the head and haunches of the horse which, thus baptized, was assumed to be, as it were, insured against accident for the coming year. One Breton prayer which, according to Sauvé, was thought efficacious when recited before the dying embers of the vigil fire, ran:

Seigneur Saint Eloi béni,
Votre assistance nous requérons
A l'effet de préserver de tout mal
Nos juments pleines
Qui sont sujettes à la maladie.
L'étranguillon et la mémarchure
Les empêchent de travailler;
Avec la courbature et la pousse
Moitié prix on ne les vendra.
S'il leur arrive d'avoir le tic
(qui fait ronger le) bois [sic]
on les trouvera trop vieilles avant l'âge.
C'est pourquoi, Saint Eloi, nous vous prions
De garder de malheur nos chevaux.
Ainsi-soit-il.[45]

(Saint Ely, Blessed Lord,
We call upon your help
To keep from all evil
Our mares in foal
That are prone to be ill.
Strangling and lameness

Prevent them from working;
Stiff and broken-winded
They won't be sold half-price.
If they start cribbing
They'll look worn out too soon,
That's why we beg you, Saint Ely,
To preserve our horses from evil
Amen.)

The limited practical and worldly considerations which appear to have inspired this and analogous practices could hardly have been more baldly stated. The saint, as this prayer envisages him, was almost like an underwriter, guaranteeing the value of the farmer's investment – not a figure whose sanctity invited emulation, or whose goodness might also yield peripheral, temporal benefits to the devout.

Spirituality and mysticism were often replaced by materialistic concerns. Habasque contended that, on the pilgrimage of Saint Mathurin, the oxen had even been known to be made to kiss the saint's statue. Broadly similar, if slightly less irreverent pilgrimages were known in most of France, and country people do not seem to have thought it incongruous to solicit saints' blessings for cows and horses, either by bringing the animals to the saint or by praying on the animals' behalf.[46] Jean-Louis Leduc (1766–1841), a vine-grower from Gennevilliers, carefully copied prayers for his sick animals into a notebook. He would seem to have been devout – or at least a conforming Catholic – since he was a member of the Sodality of the Blessed Sacrament (and its treasurer in 1812), as well as church warden of the parish in 1813. It was around this time that he copied down his remedies – many of which were known elsewhere in France – and it seems reasonable to infer that no conscious impiety informed his conduct in this. He included a well-known prayer for horses suffering from colic or *avives* (congestion of the parotid gland), which ran: 'Horse, give its colour, belonging, say it's master's name.... May God cure you, and the Blessed Saint Ely, in the name of the Father, and of the Son, and of the Holy Spirits [sic]. Then say five Paters, and five Aves, kneeling.'[47]

Similarly incongruous was the devotion to Saint Antony, the patron saint of pigs. The annual mass to Saint Antony for pigs was still said in 1900 at Prissac (Indre). One new priest, around 1890, was surprised when an old woman asked for twelve gospels to be said one after the other. When he inquired why she wanted so many, she is reported to have replied: 'Saving your presence, Father, it's that our sow was delivered of twelve little piglets last night and I'm providing for the little ones and their mother.'[48] As though this were not undignified enough, saints were also asked to ensure the success of many common domestic duties. In Brittany, Saint Herbaud (Hervé?) was promised a bullock if he ensured that there was plenty of cream in the milk – which seems like a good deal; two other saints were invoked in the hope of making the dough go further.[49] Saint Geneviève, invoked in Lower Brittany to protect flax from frost, ice and drought, was promised

Et si j'ai du bon lin,
Je donnerai des vêtements aux malheureux.
Je ne ferai pas comme mon voisin,
Qui aime mieux couvrir ses chevaux
Que de venir faire l'aumône.
Pour cette raison, je le trouve un homme cruel,
Et aussi n'est-il pas digne
D'avoir son lin préservé.
Quant à moi, je promets sur mon nom,
S'il m'est donné je donnerai.[50]

(And if I have a good crop of flax
I'll give clothes to the unfortunate.
I'll not do as my neighbour does,
Who prefers to cover his horses
Than go and give alms.
For this reason, I think him a cruel man,
And therefore he doesn't deserve
To have his flax preserved.
As for me, I give my word,
If it's given unto me, I shall give.)

The possibility that the saint might not approve of such a Pharisee's prayer, with its self-righteous meanness and slanderous insinuations about one's neighbour, does not seem to have been considered.

In keeping with the popular distrust of official justice and the concomitant tendency to see religion as a means of redressing the balance in favour of the poor, some saints, especially Saint Peter, were invoked to defend property and punish the unjust and dishonest. Saint Pierre-ès-Liens was supposed to be able to recover stolen objects – if, indeed, he had not prevented the thief from making off with his booty by rooting him to the ground. In April 1824, Jean-Georges Perret of Etobon noted a prayer to this effect: it commanded the robber to remain still until the morning, when the owner would arrive to deliver him to the justice of the mysterious 'Saint Arbre Quacheté qui est le maître de tous les voleurs'.[51] Another prayer for the same purpose, cited by Sauvé, adopted a more peremptory tone:

Peter, Peter, Peter, take, take, take
the power of God over all robbers,
who want to take my goods
or carry away my furniture.
I order you to do it.[52]

Supplication was replaced by command, as though the inhabitants of heaven were recalcitrant minions, a lazy police force that had to be urged into action.

The evidence tends to confirm Emile Sevrin's view of the saints' identity in the popular mind:

> Everything leads one to believe that for most of the devout, at least in this period [nineteenth century], the saint was both a mysterious and a familiar being, both immobile and active, confined to his alcove and to his chapel, one with his statue.... Of course, he was only asked for temporal blessings. The saint of history, the saint glorified in heaven was not thought about.[53]

Telling ignorance was demonstrated by a pilgrim in Eure-et-Loire in 1868. He noisily pursued his devotions with ostentatious indifference to the mass he was disturbing. When reproached with turning his back to God, he countered: 'I amn't here for him', and continued his prayers. A local priest said to a pilgrim who continued his supplication of Saint Maur during the consecration, at mass: 'Le bon Dieu de la messe est là'; to which he received the reply: 'J'viens point pou'l' bon Dieu...j'viens pou l'bon Saint Maur.'[54] If these anecdotes accurately reflect popular attitudes – and they concord with most of the evidence on the subject – they indicate that popular religious activity was anthropomorphic and utilitarian, rather than selfless and spiritual in emphasis. As for the central unifying concept of God as the source of grace and redemption, or the idea of saints as models of holiness who could help man to salvation, these seem to have been remote from popular preoccupations as expressed in traditional, or indeed spontaneous, practices.

Indicative of the materialism of this outlook was the importance attached to the statue itself and to relics – an importance which was not just a feature of perhaps random lore and legends. The saint was one with his statue – indeed, inseparable from it. Ordinary peasants' immediate contact with the figures evoked in sermons, prayers and stories was through these characters' representations in the local church. The realism of ecclesiastical iconography[55] in rural areas tended to confirm the pronounced tendency to appropriate the saint, to humanize and naturalize the supernatural. At Locquenvel, in Brittany, Saint Envel was represented in a fifteenth-century window in labourer's dress. Saint Isidore was usually sculpted either as a country nobleman of the eighteenth century, or in Breton costume, complete with clogs; Saint Fiacre, the patron saint of gardeners, was shown equipped with a shovel, looking decidedly like a robust gentleman farmer or prosperous peasant.[56] At Petit-Rombach in Alsace, Saint Antony, popularly known as the patron saint of pigs, was represented with a pig – the symbol of lust, which was, characteristically, interpreted in a materialistic way.[57] A more or less anthropomorphic view of the saints obtained, a view which, if not actually inculcated, was at least sustained by the Church through its iconography and preaching – in particular, through the legacy of *exempla*. Not surprisingly under the circumstances, statues were invested with the emotional attributes of humanity. They were commonly thought to be prone to weep, move, bleed and wreak vengeance upon the irreverent.[58] In this, they were merely confirming their individuality – for they were thought to be independent persons. The statue of Our Lady at La Loupe cried, when beaten by Prussian soldiers in 1815; while the statue of Saint Joseph, relegated to the seaside, wept abundantly.[59] The material images in the church or chapel were thought to be able to heal, to be susceptible to threats and gestures. Above all, they might be possessed.

Droüart tells of a farmer from the neighbourhood of the town of Moncontour, in Brittany, who was found, one day, putting the statue of Saint Mathurin into a bag. He wanted to bring it to a relative who was too ill to visit the saint. He was persuaded to desist from making off with the object only when convinced that the saint worked no miracles beyond Moncontour.[60] This kind of veneration meant that people sometimes opposed efforts made by the clergy to transport, replace or renew statues, while the movement of relics was more vigorously resisted. An attempt to give the relics of Saint Benedict, then kept at Fleury-sur-Loire, to the Benedictines, who had moved into Solesmes in 1838, provoked popular protest. The local people threatened those who came to remove the relics, and the archbishop had to content himself with sending a small piece of the saint's skull.[61] The relics of Saint Latuin, patron of the diocese of Séez, were preserved in the chapel at Anet in the bishopric of Chartres. In 1842 the bishop of Séez arranged with the bishop of Chartres to take possession of the relics. However, when the Abbé Louvet, vicar-general of the diocese of Séez, arrived at Anet to collect them, he was confronted by a picket of about fifty local men armed with pitchforks and pikes. The bursar, when he attempted to take possession of the relics, was roughly manhandled, and the removal was effected only later, by stealth.[62]

Not that saints viewed such developments with equanimity. On the contrary, they evinced a vindictive attitude, more in keeping with erring humans than with models of virtue. Sometimes they contented themselves with growing so heavy that they could not be moved, but they were often more aggressive.[63] Legends about the vengeance wreaked by irritated saints abounded. Around 1850, at Souvigny, a woman gave a new statue to replace an old one: locals maintained that the old statue reacted by killing two of her horses and sending illnesses as well.[64] In the Brie, Note Dame de Germigny-sous-Coulombs provoked an epidemic when her statue was moved; while Saint Roch caused an epidemic of dysentery after the *curé* and his parishioners banished the saint's statue.[65] Insults were especially likely, according to legend, to provoke a fierce reaction. Saint Anne de Vitry blinded a carter who struck her; Notre Dame des Champs at Arbonne killed a watchman who fired on her; a man returning from the market at Fougeray insulted Saint Yves and cursed – whereat he was paralysed and struck down with fever, being cured only after promising to make amends. At La Garde, a young man scoffed at Saint Maur (whose statue showed him sporting a beard), suggesting that he needed a shave. Soon the young man was suffering from eczema and doctors were unable to help him. Only when many masses had been offered to the irascible saint was he cured. An old woman who had mocked Saint Mirli was struck dumb in punishment.[66] Such stories – which seem likely to have derived from *exempla*, framed to instil respect and eradicate sceptical irreverence – were known throughout France. They reflected an ambivalent view of the saints, and indeed of the Virgin Mary: far from showing mercy or furnishing examples of forgiveness, the inhabitants of heaven were seen as meting out cruel punishments whenever their dignity or vanity was ruffled. But was this really the popular view of the saints? Was it not in the clergy's interest to inculcate healthy respect for religion – if necessary, exploiting fear?

The probable clerical origin of the model for these stories does not invalidate the assumption that they reflected the attitudes of at least some people. They would not have passed into folklore had they held no appeal or been discounted as uninteresting and irrelevant. Popular belief in the vindictive character of saints is illustrated by a story reported by Marcelle Bouteiller. A priest, who was attending a procession in honour of the diocese's saints near Châteauroux, heard an old woman remark to her neighbour: 'L' Bon Dieu, on peut encore le déranger tous le jours, mais ces ch'ti saints, c'est si vengeantieux, qu'il ne faut se risquer à les déranger que le jour qu'ils permettent.'[67] ('You can still bother the Good God every day, but those miserable saints, they're so vindictive that you can only chance disturbing them on the day they allow.')

That the saints were seen as rather ambivalent beings is also confirmed by the belief that they could and did cause illnesses. Many saints were regarded as *batteurs* – apt to afflict the poor with diseases – and a sort of mystical lottery was often held to discover which saint was responsible for a person's illness. Once this was ascertained, a pilgrimage to assuage the irascible culprit was made.[68] Sometimes the experts consulted for this service were prosecuted. In 1828, Pierre-Louis Duflot was brought to trial at Saint Quentin for witchcraft. The mothers of the canton of Saint Simon, whose children were ill, 'in the superstitious belief that their children were "*held by such and such a saint*", that is to say, under the yoke of these saints who were making their anger felt, went to consult the sorcerer, who, tossing six farthings in so-called holy water, told them, for a fee, the names of the saints whose vengeance they had to appease'.[69] In 1864, the Neveu couple were put on trial at Chartres for fraud: they had set themselves up as divines in the area, and the sick had consulted them to learn which saints they had to placate in order to be cured. Many of the witnesses who were called to testify against the couple were grateful for their services.[70] Country people seem to have thought it appropriate, rather than impious, to consult such people.

Around 1915, a missionary met the sacristan of one of the churches in which he preached, in a coach. The sacristan was suffering from cancer, which he called 'la rancune Saint Jean' (Saint John's grudge), and was off on a pilgrimage to placate the saint. When other methods had proved inefficacious he had consulted a sorcerer, who had placed on the table four statues representing 'Saint Crucifix, 'Saint Jérusalem', 'Saint Laurent' and 'Saint Jean'. In front of each statue, he lit a candle. As the first candle to go out was Saint John's, the sorcerer diagnosed the sacristan to be suffering from 'Saint John's grudge' and dispatched the patient to have masses said at his sanctuary.[71] A man who was sufficiently devout to hold the office of sacristan was able to accommodate the idea that saints might harbour grudges, take offence and wreak vengeance – in an underhand manner, to boot – apparently without being shocked or becoming sceptical.

The tendency to reject – or incapacity to appropriate – the highly refined in psychological terms (a failure, perhaps, to appreciate the theological notion of the spiritual) led to a most unorthodox view of the celestial hierarchy. When it was believed that saints could and did do evil, and were no less prone to succumb to avarice, pride and wrath than men, when the divine was understood to be, in nature (if not in power), so similar to the human, it is hard to see much evidence for the metaphysical extravagances once thought characteristic of the popular mind, or to consider that men thought of the supernatural in other than naturalistic terms.

Attempts were sometimes made to punish saints who proved not to be amenable to the requests made to them. When the harvest was bad, peasants of Quercy whipped saints' statues for having allowed hail and frost to ruin the fruits of their labour. The inhabitants of Agonges (Allier), having begged the Virgin in vain to deflect a storm, ordered the sacristan to whip her statue. This practice, and that of throwing statues into rivers, seem to have been not at all uncommon in the sixteenth and seventeenth centuries, and they survived into the nineteenth century. When Saint Joseph ignored the requests of the Little Sisters of the Poor at Charleroi, his face was turned to the wall, and a similar irreverence was imputed to the Sisters in Brittany. In the Minervois, at each new marriage, local girls filed up in front of Saint Sicre's statue and waved a little hatchet at him, saying:

> Grand Saint Sicre, si dans le cours de l'an
> Tu ne me donnes pas un galant,
> Voice pour t'entailler le flanc.[72]
>
> (Great Saint Sicre, if during the year
> You don't give me a lover,
> This will give you a gash in your side.)

Nor was there much compunction about acting on such intimations. At Cocherel in 1789, Notre Dame du Rouget's statue was sawn in two and buried; in the Vaucomtois, Saint Quirin was thrown into a well; Saint Armand was thrown into the Seine at Thoméry when he failed to stop the rain.[73] Michelet affirmed that in many cantons of west Morbihan, 'the saint who doesn't answer prayers is likely to be vigorously whipped'. At Mesquer, according to Gabriel Le Bras, if Saint Gobrien did not cure stomach-ache when asked, his statue was whipped and then plunged into a fountain until the sufferer was relieved.[74]

Even at the end of the nineteenth century, analogous customs were still observed, as is shown in a story read by Colson in the *Annales de Notre Dame du Sacré Coeur* of August 1891. A little house had been promised to some people who, when it failed to materialize, turned to Saint Joseph for help:

> In 1887, a cardboard house was placed at his feet, without his appearing to notice it. This year, on his feast day, we put the house in his arms, *threatening to put it on his head* if the building did not materialise before the end of the month.

In the last week of March, a house of just the kind they had specified was officially planned for them and in due course completed.[75] This appeared to the authors of the original article as a vindication of their attitude, and they appear neither to have felt that their devotion was marred by their irreverence, nor to have understood the nature of prayer and the function of ecclesiastical iconography.

Unorthodox Masses and Rites. It seems reasonable to infer that had the saints not been seen as ambivalent characters, it would not have been thought appropriate to chastise them. Other practices, on the margins of religion, reflect the failure to appreciate orthodoxy's insistence on the virtue of saints. Near Argent (Cher), a fountain was dedicated to Saint Mauvais (Saint Evil), to whom those who wanted the death of an enemy, or of a rival in love, came to pray. Happily, Saint Bon's (Saint Good's) chapel was nearby. The Bretons consulted Notre Dame de la Haine (Our Lady of Hate), whose chapel was near Tréguier, for the same purpose: three Aves said in her honour caused the death of an enemy within a year.[76] Sébillot thought analogous practices to have been fairly common in the south-west. The *messe de Saint Sécaire* – one of a variety of sacrilegious ceremonies – was known in Gascony; it was intended to kill the person for whom it was said, but not many priests could be found who were willing to say it, which is hardly surprising. The ceremony involved a complicated and outlandish parody of the church's liturgy (the texts of the ordinary of the mass were recited backwards). People from Bordeaux affirmed that the ceremony cost between twenty and fifty francs in the Gironde, and it was also expensive in Saintonge. In Bigorre, the *messe de male-mort* was usually said for the death of usurers or inconstant lovers. According to the Abbé Foix, it was much in vogue among malicious peasants in the Landes and threats to have it said were greatly feared.

Mensignac confirmed that belief in the *messe de Saint Sécaire*'s capacity to kill was widespread in the Gironde, and especially in Médoc, while it was also in great vogue in the Landes and in Lot-et-Garonne.[77] When a sharecropper from Saint Saud died after a long illness, his neighbours remembered that a beggar who had been turned away had threatened him with a *messe sèche* and they believed that his death was due to it.[78] Occasionally, priests were asked to say such masses. A cleric from Boulieu is reported to have been requested to say one by a peasant, who was in litigation with a neighbour whom he wanted to die. The priest observed that the mass would be very expensive and would cost twenty pounds. The peasant was ready to pay this; nor, when questioned, did he express any doubts about the justice of his cause. When, however, the priest remarked that God, knowing who was in the right, would kill the guilty party, the peasant retired to talk the matter over with his wife. Indeed, one could spare oneself the expense of a mass because, according to Mensignac, it was enough to light a candle in the first church one came to and, while it was burning recite the Pater, Ave, Credo and other prayers backwards.[79] It is not surprising, then, to find that some masses were believed to break spells and that peasants used to ask their *curés* to say them. There was even a mass which was supposed to counteract the effect of Saint Sécaire's mass and which was reputed to effect the death of the instigator of the first mass. In Normandy, the *messe du Saint Esprit* – another sacrilegious ceremony – was thought to force God to grant the wishes of the person who paid for the mass.[80] In many parts of the Côtes-du-Nord, according to Sébillot, masses to obtain the death of a relative or enemy were still so common at the start of the twentieth century that sermons had to be delivered against the practice.[81] If religion inspired the form of these practices, it did not inform their spirit.

But the ignorance revealed by unorthodox rites should not obscure the social and psychological frustration to which they testified. Seen as an instrument of justice in the hands of the weak, they betray the scepticism in which the law was held. The Bretons had a characteristically idiosyncratic way of dealing with bad debtors and other offenders – they applied to Saint Yves. The saint's chapel near Tréguier was a place of somewhat sinister pilgrimage. According to Sébillot, those who wanted someone to die went fasting to his chapel three times on a Monday, where they shook the statue, saying: 'You are little Saint Yves-of-Truth, I dedicate such a one to you. If right is on his side, condemn me. But if I am in the right, make him die within the time laid down.' A coin was left with the statue, and the pilgrim circled the chapel three times, reciting some ordinary prayers backwards. Anna Bouz, who made the pilgrimage on commission for others, said the *De Profundis* three times for the souls of those who had no one to pray for them. Then, addressing the statue, she announced: 'You know why and for whom I have come; you have been paid; do justice.' The saint was believed to punish the dishonest. In

French-speaking Brittany it was thought that the liar or defrauder could be killed if, during the argument, one threw a coin on the ground invoking the saint. Masses to the saint for the death of an enemy were also commissioned: around 1830, in Côtes-du-Nord, peasants used to threaten debtors who denied that they owed money with such a mass, in the belief that the guilty would be killed by it.[82] Until 1879, the pilgrimage to Saint Yves was made to an old wooden statue in a former charnel house; later, pilgrims followed the statue to the church of Trédarzec, and when the rector removed it they returned to the charnel house, where, in 1908, the practice still survived.[83]

Like so many popular religious practices, this devotion was far removed from the letter and spirit of orthodox religion, which did not envisage the possibility that a saint might be abruptly ordered to kill someone. Yet uninhibited indictments of enemies, however incongruous in retrospect, are to be found in a number of popular prayers. As Jobbé-Duval observed, the adjuration to Saint Yves constituted a primitive form of justice. When courts of law were beyond the pocket of the poor, or where they were felt to be irrelevant to their needs, peasants could have recourse to unofficial or magical justice. In 1901, a pregnant girl from the Dinan area consigned her lover, who had abandoned her, to the mercy of Saint Yves. A rich landowner and former magistrate, whose hard terms had ruined almost all his tenants was, according to Harmonic, 'dedicated' to the saint – as were a man who was found murdered at Hengoat, and a widow who had prevented a sailor from getting work by slandering his wife. Creditors prayed that debtors would pay them or die, and the death of thieves was likewise prayed for.[84] Prayers and devotions of an ostensibly religious or para-religious aspect were, therefore, by no means invariably indicative of flourishing piety.

Attitudes to the Clergy. Small wonder, then, that God's ministers were viewed with distrust. In many parts of the country they were believed to be as powerful as sorcerers, and almost as shady.[85] In 1828 and 1845, attempts to hold ecclesiastical conferences had to be abandoned, as the locals regarded them as analogous to sabbaths, bound to have dire consequences for their welfare. Even more baroque was an incident at the end of the Second Empire: the *curé* of Vichères, furious when the local drunkard (as was his wont) rang the priest's doorbell on his roistering progress home late at night, threatened to cast a spell on the offender, who returned the next morning, sober and frightened, begging to have the spell lifted.[86] The disabused *curé* of La Selle-en-Hermois, in the Beauce, felt that respect for the priest was rooted in fear of his mysterious powers – which included not only all those already mentioned, but the power of curing illness in man and beast. In short, in the estimation of the *curé*, peasants considered the priest to be 'endowed with a power far superior to that of all sorcerers'.[87] According to the anticlerical polemicist Miron, the *curé* was seen as 'at once a man of God and a man of the devil' and was feared more than loved.[88] In the Meuse in 1892, it was popularly thought that when sorcerers came to mass, the priest recognized them, for at the end of the service when he blessed the congregation, they alone turned their backs to the altar. The first child the priest baptized after the death of a sorcerer was 'inevitably destined to replace him', because the priest deliberately omitted certain words in his prayers. When a priest lost his temper one day, because a family had presented him with a child to baptize without telling him in advance, the father drew back, not wanting baptismal water to be poured on the child's forehead: 'You'll make a sorcerer out of him', he told the irascible minister.[89] Religion and clerics, therefore, were by no means exclusively associated with sanctity – or even with virtue. Not surprisingly, perhaps, official religion seems to have been seen more as a practicical than as a spiritual affair.

Orthodox Ideas

Nonetheless, despite the materialism and practicality to which this intellectual confusion testified, the Church managed to inculcate in its erring flock some more or less orthodox ideas – mainly about salvation – as well as a sketchy outline of Christ's life and death. These notions helped to inspire both popular piety and popular religiosity – the tendency to dwell with nostalgic hope on the miraculous transformation of the ordinary, enshrined in the lives of Christ and his saints.

The Popular Conception of God. God, as presented in the folktale and popular verse, was the astute, humorous, indulgent possessor of marvellous powers. He was also the agent of an idiosyncratic primitive justice, imposing harsh penalties on those who offended him and rewarding the deserving. He appreciated hospitality and simplicity above all, and was sympathetic to the poor; but was occasionally inclined to indulge the resourceful if slightly unscrupulous character. Stories of divine vengeance were very common.[90] The intervention of God in history, insofar as it concerns the popular notion of God, seems to have led to his becoming like man, rather than to man's becoming like him. Jesus, whom the Gospels present as compassionate, was seen in one important popular tradition as a rather vindictive individual, sharing human vices much as the Greek divinities did. In one legend, Jesus 'never' forgives a Jew called Malcolm who has hit the Madonna, but condemns him to walk around a pillar on the top of a mountain until the end of the world.[91]

Promethean destinies appealed to the popular imagination. One of the most favoured of all stories was that of the Wandering Jew,[92] Isaac Laquedem, condemned to roam the world until the Last Judgement because of his impiety and cruelty to the suffering Jesus. When Isaac roughly urged Christ, who was resting on his road to Calvary, to move on, the latter responded, according to one chapbook, by cursing his tormentor: 'I go and I will rest; you shall walk and shall not rest; you shall walk as long as the world lasts, indeed until the Last Judgement.'[93] Isaac's lament (which by the nineteenth century had the victim of divine ire well into his eighteen-hundredth year and on his sixth journey around the world) and accompanying portrait were constantly reprinted – so assuring his fame that, from time to time, he was sighted. Around 1575, he met two ambassadors to Madrid, with whom he conversed in Spanish (a comforting instance of diplomatic gullibility). In 1604, two gentlemen bound for the court of Henry IV discussed details of the Passion with him, and on six other occasions between 1609 and 1642 he was seen in various parts of central Europe. An extravagance typical of that age of upheaval and wild beliefs? Near the little town of Serres (Hautes-Alpes), in the early nineteenth century, a justice of the peace, crossing a wood, asked an old woman the way and gave her five shillings to direct him. This sum was the *ne plus ultra* of the Wandering Jew's fortune. The next day, the talk of the area was of this encounter with Isaac of popular fame. 'Several inhabitants claim to have seen this alert old man, weighed down by eighteen centuries and a formidable beard . . . ', added Ladoucette, with the complacency of one whose venerability was not seen to have reached Biblical proportions.[94] A lament and many millions of pictures, published in Belgium, broadcast that Isaac had passed through Brussels on 22 April 1874 at six in the evening.[95] The continued vogue of this legend may be ascribed, in part, to the popular taste for bathos and to the fact that it was a picturesque variation on the theme of retribution.

Divine justice was frequently evoked and, it seems, invoked by the rural poor. It was sometimes so primitive as to be more akin to spiteful punishment than to a sense of righteousness. In the legend of the Wandering Jew, divine violence was surprisingly gratuitous, given that God was supposed to be both omnipotent and entirely good. But it was not an isolated example of divine impetuosity. Local topography provoked popular legendary aetiologies. Stories ascribing unusual features of the landscape to divine ire were quite common. Typical was the story of Jesus who visited the village of Issarlès, disguised as a beggar: displeased with the welcome he received, he engulfed the village.[96] Legends about towns punished by God for the promiscuity and, more often, the inhospitality of their inhabitants were popular in south Brittany and Provence. They sometimes resembled the story of Lot's wife. The people of the townland of Le Bouchet led a life of debauchery, so God decided to annihilate his offensive creatures. However, in justice, he meant to spare the only virtuous person in the area – a poor old woman, whose sole possession was a goat. An angel told her to leave, without looking behind her. However, she felt tempted to cast a last look on the town, which was consumed in fire and sulphur, and for this disobedience, she forfeited her little house.[97]

Like this legend, some stories about divine wrath not only seemed to follow a Biblical model but also conveyed a clerical view of morality – condemning sexual licence and other lapses from divine commandments. The tale of the mason who worked on Easter Sunday and was killed by an angry God[98] is an example of this tradition which, given its form and content, seems likely to have been of clerical rather than of unadulteratedly popular origin. The view of God thus propagated was not consonant with that conveyed in the New Testament: far from being a gentle, compassionate figure, Christ appears as a severe magistrate, preoccupied with his laws to the exclusion of love and mercy.

While one set of stories may have been of clerical origin,[99] others were more obviously popular in tone and emphasis. In these, more room is given to the delineation of character (Christ and Saint Peter having distinctive, on the whole endearing, traits). The punishments meted out by Christ match this more humane image. Christ, in this tradition, generally views men's affairs from a human, rather than from a peculiarly divine, perspective. There is little trace of any preoccupation with man's divine essence and destiny – neither of these ideas being present or investigated to a significant degree. The moral vision propounded through these stories emphasizes the value of humility and generosity, while the poor and weak are usually presented favourably. The function of these tales was to divert and to instruct – classical canons. Christ is usually depicted travelling around France with his rather grumpy, slow-witted friend, Saint Peter, whom he teases and bosses about with undisputed but benign authority. Pierre Lignex of Larrau recounted the following story, which illustrates the relationship that Christ usually bore to Peter in this vein of oral literature:

> One day, Jesus Christ says to Saint Peter: 'I'll give you a horse if you say the Pater without a lapse of attention.' Saint Peter starts: 'Pater noster qui es in coelis . . . but, Lord, with or without the saddle?' To which Jesus replies: 'Either way, you won't get it now.'[100]

A similarly irreverent familiarity, which assimilated supernatural beings to man, was evinced in the Breton legends collected by Luzel. These stories did not necessarily indicate agnosticism but rather observed a literary convention, poking fun not just at pompous or naive piety but at materialism and other human failings too. One Breton tale tells how Christ, accompanied by Saints John and Peter, was labouring in Bas-Léon to convert the locals who still worshipped idols. The three saints were, with one thing and another, having a hard time of it, so they built a house and bought a cow. However, as the cow kept grazing on neighbours' land, Christ instructed Saint Peter to sell it at market. But Saint Peter found that no-one wanted to buy the beast. When he explained this to Christ, the latter exclaimed: 'Old fool! in these parts, you never broadcast the animal's faults at the fair, before selling it and getting your hands on the money.'[101] It is evident that this story was concerned with commenting satirically on local business acumen, as much as with exploiting the incongruous role played by Christ, who, like many popular literary heroes, shows himself to be rather unscrupulous. However, although quick discernment and ready defence of self-interest were characteristic of the secular hero in popular literature, Christ was not usually seen as a sharp operator. Another Breton legend shows Christ and his two companions going hungry and Peter succumbing to the temptation of stealing a little bread from the baker. Christ, however, having seen this, prevents the weak saint from eating his crust by talking to him incessantly.[102]

In popular stories, spiritual elevation was obscured by materialistic ambition. Admittedly, this ambition was usually of an archaic kind, in that the goods desired were first necessities and the manner of attaining them, at least in stories which involved Christ as a protagonist, supposed dependence upon divine munificence. Their heroes were often foolish and incompetent, incapable not only of bettering themselves through their own efforts but even of exploiting the advantages given to them. In one legend from the Bourbonnais, Saint Peter takes pity on a very poor man who begs for his help. The munificent saint furnishes the man with a table which covers itself with a good meal each time one says: 'Table, do your duty'. The man spends the night with an inn-keeper, who steals the magic table and replaces it with a useless one. Saint Peter, however, again comes to the rescue and this time provides the inept man with a donkey which, when spurred, spills pieces of gold; but the donkey is also lost to the inn-keeper. So Saint Peter furnishes his protégé with a stick, which does its duty by giving the inn-keeper and his wife a hiding and forcing them to restore the original table and donkey to their rightful owner.[103]

Many tales concern Christ's coming to the rescue of the poor and weak. He does not usually elevate them to seraphic spheres, however, but acts within the frame of the flawed, familiar world – as the acute social observation of the stories emphasizes. When Christ and Saints Peter and John receive hospitality from a poor clog-maker, according to a Breton legend, they bestow wealth on their host. They tell the clog-maker's wife to continue all day doing whatever she does first thing in the morning; she starts washing canvas and by evening, finds that she has an enormous quantity.[104] A similar tale was told in Huppaye, a Walloon village. Long ago, there lived in the village a saintly old woman, the neighbour of an equally impoverished, but debauched, man. One day, God and Saint Peter visited the area and, being tired, sought repose in the woman's house. 'Certainly, you poor old soul', said she, in reply to their request. 'Let me give you a drop of the hard stuff too, it'll do you good.' Gratefully, God granted her that she might continue doing all day whatever she did first next morning, but she paid no attention to the joker's supposed reward. The following morning, however, she counted her shillings and by evening she had become rich. She told her neighbour of her good fortune. In due course, he offered interested hospitality to the celestial visitors, but met with a Pantagruelian death from urinating all day.[105] This bawdy tale expressed an outlook characteristic of popular culture, according to which God becomes the purveyor of primitive justice, rewarding the deserving (equated with the hard-working and generous poor) and punishing the mean and selfish. The magical and marvellous in the oral literature of France, as it was recorded at the end of the last century, was not so much a gratuitous invention of the imagination escaping the tedium of reality, as some Romantics thought, but rather an imaginary revolution in which the poor man escaped his economic bondage and got the better of those who normally exploited him.

Many popular stories depict the relations between rich and poor harshly; but if the reality evoked is that of the oppression of the weak, the hope instilled by the stories is of future justice, trust in a righteousness which God will ultimately recompense. These rewards are presented in terms not of an afterlife but of immediate material gain. The popular imagination here did not inhabit an idyllic world beyond perception but evoked a transformed actuality, in which the poor and vulnerable came to command power and fortune. Although not a call to arms, the stories were not altogether devoid of positive purpose, since they propounded a popular morality of simple egalitarianism. One tale from the Agenais concerns an old soldier, who had lost a leg during the wars. Sitting in a ditch between Nérac and Agen, he was eating his only bit of bread, when he was joined by a man dressed in white. He shared his bread with the unknown traveller, who told him: 'You can continue your journey. You will lack for nothing today, and before you return . . . to your little house this evening, you will have got enough bread to live on for a month.' The man in white next met three nuns travelling to Nérac by coach. They refused to give him a lift, but the driver made room for him. The mysterious wanderer sombrely announced that the nuns would be dead on their arrival in town, but that the driver's wife, who had been sick for seven years, would have recovered and would be found making soup – another prediction which was realized in fact.[106] This story is not only an apology for charity, but betrays hostility towards the Church.

Animosity towards the rich is sometimes present in popular literature devoted to the topic of charity. In a story recorded by Bladé, Christ, John and Peter turn up begging at a castle. 'A piece of bread', they begin. 'Get the hell out of here, you scoundrels!' responds the lord of the manor. 'You won't get a crumb, good-for-nothings. If you don't turn tail this instant, I'll set the dogs on you.' Christ's reaction is hardly more edifying, for he changes the aristocrat into a donkey, before proceeding on his way. His next stop is a little mill, where a widow offers him and his companions her only loaf of bread. Christ gives her the donkey, which makes the woman's fortune; seven years later, Christ restores the donkey to the castle and thence rapidly to paradise, while the woman is left to enjoy the fruits of the earth.[107] Those, too, who lived not from producing wealth but from serving its producers, creaming off their profits, were the common target of criticism in popular stories: millers, inn-keepers and the like were presented as getting their just deserts in the world of fantasy that resembled reality in so many ways. Finally, if Christ and his companions were usually the agents of change in this world, they also belonged to the promised land that lay beyond life. There at least, the poor man could hope to be vindicated. The theme of Lazarus could hardly fail to appeal to those who were more familiar with want than with abundance and whose chances of enjoying leisure and wealth were so remote. Dardy cites a rhymed account of the glorious destiny of the humble, known in the *pays d'Albret*. Despite the stylization, relations between the rich and the poor are depicted with some realism. Like the lord of the manor punished in Bladé's story, the rich man declares:

> Allez-vous-en d'ici, pauvres,
> Je vous ferai mordre par les chiens.
>
> *Le Pauvre*:
> Si vous pouviez me donner les croûtes
> Qui sont dans vos mains?
> Les petites miettes
> Que mangent vos chiens?
>
> *Le Riche*:
> Mes chiens me portent du lièvre
> Vous autres ne portez rien.
>
> (Be off with you, wretches,
> Or I'll get the dogs to bite you.
>
> *The Poor Man*:
> What about giving me the crusts
> You have in your hands?
> Or the little crumbs
> Which your dogs are eating?
>
> *The Rich Man*:
> My dogs bring me hares,
> You lot bring me nothing.)

There speaks the authentic voice of business-like self-interest. A week later, the poor man dies and is admitted to heaven. A fortnight later, the rich man expires, but Christ tells him that he will burn in five cauldrons of oil and lead, and that he will be damned.[108] Yet it is evident that here, heaven and hell are little more than vengeful human justice, delayed in effect, rather than states of spiritual bliss or torment as the Church suggested. Hope and despair centred mainly on the immediate and tangible, not on the imperceptible, and were confined by the real, without being entirely realistic. God himself was more human than supernatural. One old woman from the south-west even thought that God was nothing more more than a 'good sort'.[109]

The God of Augustine and Anselm was remote from that of the French peasant: God interested him less for his virtues than for his powers, and accounts of divine revelation to man held him mainly in its human and dramatic aspects. The cardinal events of the Gospel, as portrayed in the expressions of the popular imagination, concern the familiar details of human life and occasionally include ribald observations of the cynics and wags present at any public gathering (all the more pertinent in that few events were ever private). The popularity of carols[110] testifies to the appeal of a religious tradition which dwelt on the intimate and human. As Robert Mandrou observed of printed carols, the mystery of the Nativity received scant attention and was not treated with the prim reverence felt to be appropriate among the educated: the supernatural element was largely sacrificed to 'a very "ordinary" presentation'.[111] Pathetic, touching or amusing details were favoured. Carols frequently alluded to the gifts offered by poor shepherds to the child Jesus. Those sung in Gannat, in the Bourbonnais, evoked at some length the culinary contributions of the infant's pastoral visitors: a large piece of cake, a lamb, butter and cheese, a little veal.[112] The same obsession with food emerged in another carol from the Bourbonnais, where one of the shepherds is with difficulty restrained from inviting the holy family to stay with him:

> J'ai du bon vin doux
> Pour ébaudir le Père,
> Du tourton pour le fils,
> Des poix et des noix.[113]
>
> (I have good sweet wine
> To delight the Father,
> Pie for the son,
> Peas and nuts.')

The celebration is virtually secular in form, with its emphasis on feasting and merriment.

A similar naturalism pervaded a mystery plan, the *Mystère de la Nativité*, which was peculiar to Upper Gascony and the Bigorre, where it was performed after the gospel at midnight mass. A child, dressed in a white surplice and sporting cardboard wings, is hauled on a pulley over the chancel, whence he calls to the shepherds (in white capes and holding staffs) to awaken. One sceptical shepherd wants to sleep on and questions the angel's claims:

> Un sort heureux
> N'est pas pour les pauvres bergers.
> Par quel étrange badinage
> Veux-tu que nous obtenions, par un enfant,
> Le sort heureux?

(Poor shepherds aren't meant
For a happy fate.
What silly prattle
Makes you believe a child
Will change our lot?)

The angel's renewed explanations only provoke further questions:

Que dites-vous?
Cela ne paraît pas croyable....
– Que vont faire tous ces bergers?
Voir leur Dieu dans une étable,
Cela me semble belle fable...

(What's that you say?
That seems incredible...
What are all those shepherds off to do?
Visit their God in a byre,
It strikes me as a tall story ...)

Another shepherd worries about the sheep, given the number of wolves in the environs. Yet another complains that the angel (who speaks French, to distinguish him from the simple folk) is incomprehensible, with his strange language.[114] Eventually, after some argument, they all go off to the stable, where Saint Joseph is hardly more sophisticated, or less removed from the concerns of ordinary people. On their arrival, the saint wants to know who they are, thinking that they may be soldiers. The shepherds claim they have a passport from the angel, to which the naive saint replies:

Vous ne vous adressez pas comme il faut,
Pour vous faire faire la lecture;
Je suis un pauvre artisan
Qui ne connaît pas l'écriture.

(You've not come to the right place,
To have your reading done;
I'm a poor artisan,
And don't know my letters.)

The angel intervenes to reassure Joseph, after which a polite conversation ensues, in which the saint apologizes for his miserable surroundings.[115] The principal characters have natural, if not heroic, qualities, being lazy and sceptical to the point of discourtesy, preoccupied to an almost disedifying extent with material considerations (the safety of the flock, the stable unfit for visitors), obtuse or – in the case of Saint Joseph – even rather stupid. Neither the saint nor the event are endowed with other-worldly dignity: on the contrary, everyone behaves in a normal way.

In the Nativity, it was the familiar drama of poverty which was stressed and which appealed, more than the mystery of the Incarnation. Insofar as redemption or salvation entered into it, attention was focussed on the idea that a child born in indigence was a kind of popular king, whose first courtiers and attendants were themselves poor – as though part of the attraction of the story lay in a utopian anticipation of the times when the poor would command. The poverty of Joseph and Mary, and their humiliation at the hands of the slightly better-off, were presented realistically and in some detail in many carols. Their arrival in Bethlehem and unsuccessful attempt to find lodgings, which served to illustrate their want, showed Saint Joseph timidly inquiring about rooms and being repulsed by bad-mannered inn-keepers.[116]

A carol which used to be sung in Moulins on 4 December dwelt on the episode at great length. Saint Joseph approaches an inn beside a watch-maker's, but the inn-keeper pompously declines to house them, with the chilly aplomb of a butler:

Pour des gens de mérite
J'ai des appartements,
Point de chambre petite
Pour vous, mes bonnes gens.

(For people of distinction
I have suites,
But no small room
For you, my worthies.)

They are turned away three more times, before meeting a sympathetic loquacious woman who has no room for them, but who agrees that Mary should rest with her while Joseph finds a place to stay. Having dispatched the saint, the good-natured soul chatters on in a familiar vein about Mary's predicament, like any gossip:

Excusez la pensée
Je ne la puis celer;
Vous êtes avancée
Et prête d'accoucher.

(Excuse my saying it,
But say it I must;
You're expecting
And very near your time.)

Information and sympathy are bartered for a few moments, until the woman's husband shouts to the 'chatterbox' to come in. Reluctantly, the woman leaves Mary to her fate.[117] The characters are plausible and sardonically observed; social relations are recorded realistically, showing the harsh treatment meted out to the poor. The irony and pathos of the situation are emphasized: for Joseph and Mary are not ordinary 'poor folk', but in reality are important people who – were appearances not so deceptive – would receive the servile attentions of the inn-keepers. The mystery of God becoming man is overshadowed by the almost documentary quality of text, which is less concerned with the incomprehensible and the supernatural than with commenting on the relations between rich and poor.

Hostility to the wealthy was sometimes more overt, as in a carol from Montluçon, where two shepherds exchange caustic observations about the three Magi:

Gilbert
C'est merveille que la noblesse
Fasse tant de cas de cet Enfant!
Tous s'en vont disant
Que sa mère est princesse.
Mais est-ce dans une étable
Que se logent les grands? . . .

Michel
La noblesse y est debout
Qui n'ose, morbleu, parler!
Pas plus que Nicolas . . .[118]

(*Gilbert*
It's a strange sight to see the gentry
Make such a fuss of this Child!
Everyone's saying
His mother's a princess.
But do bigwigs put up
In a byre? . . .

Michel
There the gentry stands
Without daring to speak
Any more than any Joe . . .)

The tone of the carol, with its long debate between the shepherds over what to do about the puzzling occupants of the stable and the need to stop them departing for the agreeable Orient with the nobility through dissatisfaction with their reception, is more secular than most. The mood is embittered by the arrival of the Magi and their competition, on unfair terms, for the attention of the mysterious visitors.

Generally, however, charity was dictated not by self-interest but by convention. Carols and analogous songs pleaded for traditional morality and presented Christ and his mother – either implicitly or explicitly – as people who would be sympathetic to the poor and would redress injustices. Thus, in a carol from Poitiers, one of the shepherds at the crib prays to the infant Jesus:

Dissit, fasant sa prière:
'Mon megnon, pré l'amour de votre mère,
Tirez-nous de la misère,
De la taille et de la sau[119] . . .[120]

(He said, in his prayer:
'For the love of your mother, my sweet little one,
Free us from want,
From tallage and the salt tax . . .')

Other songs of the Christmas season, such as those sung at the Epiphany, when children went around their neighbours singing and collecting gifts, appealed for traditional charity.[121] Easter witnessed customs similar to those practised at Christmas and the New Year. During Holy Week, in parts of lower Normandy, children went from door to door singing versions of the Passion and, on Holy Saturday, of the Resurrection. They asked for alms, and if these were not forthcoming or if the inmates pretended to be asleep, the young people sang, tongue in cheek:

Réveillez-vous, coeurs endormis,
Pour prier le doux Jésus Christ
Qu'il vous conduise en Paradis;
Alléluia!
Donnez à ces pauvres chanteurs . . .
Un jour viendra Dieu vous l'rendra
Alléluia.

(Awake, dead souls
And pray the gentle Jesus Christ
That he may lead you to Paradise;
Alleluia!
Be generous to these poor singers . . .
The day will come when God will pay you back,
Alleluia.)

Children collecting eggs on Holy Saturday at Secourt also urged those whom they visited not to ignore them, promising divine recompense to the charitable.[122]

The idea that divine justice finally redressed the inequities of life was a favourite theme in popular songs and stories: some practices even suggest that religion was sometimes viewed as a kind of popular law-court, where the poor could seek the punishment of those otherwise out of the reach of their vengeance. The tendency to idealize in popular religion was largely confined to eschatological expectations of justice and personal dignity, but it hardly impinged upon the person of God. God, the remote divinity, did not appeal to the popular imagination, which preferred to dwell on Christ. He was familiar with human suffering and weakness and his sympathies lay with the poor and virtuous. He was the King of the unfortunate, waiting his time – like the legendary emperors and rulers, Arthur and Frederick Barbarossa, whom folklore proclaimed to be not dead but waiting with their courts and armies in mountains and caverns for the day of judgement. If most popular prayers suggested that the inspiration of religious devotion was primarily practical, in popular celebration its appeal was emotional: it promised the ultimate triumph of the poor, it rewarded the deserving, and transformed reality in marvellous and unimaginable ways.

The Desire for Salvation. Just as this picture of God diverged from the bland or terrifying model proposed by contemporary orthodoxy, so too was popular piety distinguished by original characteristics. It did not abound in gratuitous acts of devotion – expressions of contrition, praise and thanksgiving being strikingly absent from the arsenal of popular prayers – but centred on the preoccupation with salvation. Paradise did not engage men's attention or imagination as did hell, perhaps because preachers found the terror inspired by the latter to be more powerful than the attractions of heaven. Popular hymns about paradise were more anodyne, less vivid than those that evoked hell.[123] In a Breton tale, *Le fils de Saint Pierre*, which Luzel heard in 1870, heaven was rather boringly described as a big garden filled with white angels and happy people who sang God's praises in choirs, walked about among flowers or sat talking under trees of golden apples and fruit. Hell was equally conventional, but less bland. There the hero saw 'a furnace filled with fire' and devils who 'stoked up the flames and, with hooks and forks of steel, restrained the unhappy victims who tried to escape'.[124] Popular iconography observed these conventions, although the devil in popular literature was more often depicted as a figure of fun, or as a stock character, neither strange nor terrifying.[125] The traditional picture of hell[126] was perpetuated in popular iconography until the mid-nineteenth century. Charles Nisard's *Histoire des Livres Populaires* cited as the model for one of the most popular almanacs right up to the start of the Second Empire a *Compost et Kalendrier des Bergers . . .*, dating from 1488. This included the original version of Lazarus' account of hell, or *Peines d'Enfer pour les Pécheurs* (in which a short verse commented on each vice and its vividly illustrated punishment),[127] which was reproduced in the nineteenth-century editions of the almanac. Amidst extremes of flame and ice, with predictable serpents and cauldrons of sulphur, sinners are not even allowed to languish, being tormented by lively, familiar-looking devils.[128] Villon suggested the impact of these pictures on their naive viewers, in a famous poem he wrote for his mother:

> Femme je suis povrette et ancienne,
> Qui riens ne sçay; oncques lettre ne lus.
> Au moustier voy, dont suis paroissienne
> Paradis paint, ou sont harpes et lus,
> Et ung enfer ou dampnez sont boullus.
> L'ung me fait paour, l'autre joye et liesse.[129]
>
> (A poor old dam am I
> Who knows naught; and ne'er my letters knew.
> At my parish church I see

Paradise painted, with its harps and lutes,
And hell where the damned are boiled.
One frightens me, the other gladdens and delights me.)

If the problem of salvation worried the old and the nervous, it was, no doubt, because of the emphasis which priests and missionaries placed on it. The sceptical Cambry, a true man of his age both in his repudiation of religion and in his command of Gothic prose, protesting against this kind of sermon, depicted a Breton mission at the end of the eighteenth century in terms worthy of Walpole:

> ...Dialogues between the skulls of two dead men, between the dammed and the souls in purgatory; darkness, dreadful threats, lugubrious chants, hell in all its horrors, despair, devouring flames for all eternity, serpents gnawing at the heart, tearing at the nerves, icy toads seated upon one's chest, boiling cauldrons... skeletons... all the tricks of the most outrageous deception, produced incredible effects. People rent their bosoms; women miscarried; frightful howls resounded through the caverns ...[130]

For all that we might imagine that Cambry was writing with an imagination rejoicing in the new literary landscape of tombs, yews and mad monks, it would appear that his picture was not so much distorted as exaggerated. At the end of May 1819, the prefect of Seine-et-Loire condemned the missionaries who had just been preaching in his Department for the 'ardour of their oratory' and the exaggeration of the evocations with which they frightened their congregations.[131] Throughout the century, psychiatrists joined this chorus of reprobation. Michéa noted that sermons which presented 'too frightening a picture of the punishments of the next world are the most common cause of true demonopathy'. Baderot noted that in Brittany at the end of the century, sermons were rarely devoted to the happy fate awaiting the good in heaven, as priests exercised all their descriptive powers on the invention of tortures with which to frighten their flock into the pastures of virtue.[132] Gabriel Le Bras affirmed that as a child, he heard many terrifying sermons.[133] Until the Third Republic, at least, the paramount importance of salvation was stressed;[134] accordingly, the devil was introduced in the context of the punishments meted out to the erring by a vengeful God. The devil was the source of man's fall and was ineradicably associated with the torments of hell.

During the Restoration, great efforts were made by missionaries, anxious to reconvert the supposedly Voltairean multitudes, to exploit both the extravagant religious sensibility brought into fashion by Chateaubriand and the traditional imagery of fear through which the clergy were thought to have exercised control over the minds of unlettered men. Hence, missions, preached mainly in towns, were conducted like edifying melodramas, with priests speaking in lugubrious tones, weeping with repentance, roaring with anger.[135] At Romans, in 1821, during the ceremony of making amends (where the congregation confessed their sins and implored God's forgiveness, having meditated upon the fate awaiting the perverse) the church was plunged into darkness; a few candles threw uncertain light upon the emotional preacher, when suddenly, at the climax of his exhortations, the high altar, draped in lurid purple, was dramatically illuminated, revealing a column of priests silently advancing towards it.[136]

Samples of religious oratory from the Restoration indicate that hell, death, the Last Judgement and the consequences of sin were depicted at morbid length and with such insistence as to suggest that preachers derived no little pleasure from their almost hysterical antics. Preachers of the period were informed, in their attempts to define God's justice, by a narrow legalism. Deaf to the objections of Diderot and Holbach, not to mention his own numerous and more obscure contemporaries, Father Girault proclaimed: 'One day, God will take his revenge. Woe! ah! Woe to non-believers!'[137] The author of an anonymous booklet of improving meditations prefaced his remarks with the motto: 'Death and eternity await you... Ite, maledicti, in igne... REFLECT–UPON–IT–WELL'.[138] The bishop of Coutances, describing the mission held there in 1821, gave the text of a preacher's sermon: 'God punishes eternally... he... condemns [the sinner] to terrible and interminable torture!' Since sin offended God infinitely, the punishment had also to be infinite.[139] Thus, God's justice and love were overwhelmed by his desire to wreak vengeance upon his imperfect creatures. Father Guyon, one of the Restoration's chief missionaries, embraced an entirely traditional view of hell, if his sermons accurately reflect his opinions. Doubtless with the philosophers of the eighteenth century in mind, Guyon attempted to prove the moral necessity of hell. 'No religion without hell', he asserted, asking as an afterthought: 'Take away Hell, what becomes of God's justice, of his holiness, his providence?' – without stopping to wonder how they appeared in the light of the bloodthirstiness he attributed to the divinity.[140]

Although missionaries claimed to convince the sceptical by rational argument, in effect they sought to move their audiences emotionally – hence, their vivid descriptions of hell and the Last Judgement. Father Guyon was particularly unscrupulous in this respect. His evocation of hell was calculated to persuade, not through logic, but through fear:

> Imagine a man shut up in a dark tower; the poor wretch has fallen asleep there. Thousands of poisonous serpents lie around him, numbed by the cold and damp... If, at noon, a ray of light falling from the sun warms up these reptiles and brings them back to life, they fling themselves upon their unfortunate victim, enveloping him in their tortuous folds and sinking their forked tongues in his quivering body... Do you hear these howls...? do you see him trying to get rid of these desperate enemies? Can you imagine his despair when he sees that it is impossible to escape from this place of horror? However this is only a very imperfect picture of the torments of hell....[141]

This exploitation of traditional imagery, the appeal to the visual, with rhetorical questions multiplying as the emotional climax approached, were the essence of the melodramatic effect which was favoured by the preachers of the period.[142]

M. Jaisson, one of the principal missionaries at Coutances, preaching on salvation, dwelt at length upon the theme of death. Proud youth might be reduced in a moment to food for worms. He evoked the graveyard: 'Lift that stone . . .; what do you see? A corpse emitting a foetid smell, a mass of worms and corruption! – Answer me now, what is youth?' One was never too young to die; those who were too busy to save themselves now would have eternal leisure to burn in the flames of hell.[143]

Indeed, the whole mission seemed to be devoted to presenting the dangers of sin, the horrors of future punishment and God's relentless justice. Jaisson's sermon was not unique. A similar one was given in Vendôme in 1824, where the slow drama of Death was presented and the congregation was invited to contemplate open tombs and meditate upon the vanity of riches, the ephemeral nature of youth. In Brittany, the missionary, M. de Lammenais, did not confine himself to suggestion but repaired with his congregation to the cemetery, where the ensuing ceremony was worthy of those described by Cambry. A coffin of skulls was placed beside an open grave, and the furious preacher, rather in the manner of Hamlet, interrogated one occiput after another:

> You, who are you? – I am the father of a family, an honest man. – What is your fate? – I am in hell. – Why? – I had children, I neglected to teach them and make them holy; they are lost; God has asked for their souls back again; I am damned.

Then his wife, their child, the bad rich man, the usurer, the devout young girl, who unfortunately liked dancing and pretty clothes . . . skull after skull was thrown into the empty grave. Eventually, one was saved, and after listening to an exhortation to repentance, the trembling procession left the scene, singing the *De Profundis*.[144] Not to be outdone by the illustrious missionary, the *curé* of Saint André at Niort, in July 1819, went to the cemetery accompanied by four priests and three or four hundred women. He too stationed himself beside an open tomb and, grasping a skull, 'gives himself up to furious ranting on this subject: then, turning towards the grave, he cries out: who among you wants to appear before his God? . . . let him descend into this tomb . . . '. His remarks were said to have made the women cry and feel ill.[145]

Restoration missions were usually conducted in large towns, where they encountered the hostility of husbands and the enthusiasm of young women, for whom they provided the excuse of several excursions out of the house each day. The apparently popular celebrations which accompanied the erection of the mission-cross in some prominent place might be explained in terms of the emotional atmosphere – which missionaries encouraged and cultivated – and of the attractions of any form of festivity which involved dressing up and parades. Nonetheless, some people were more permanently affected by these ceremonies. The prefect of Nièvre, in August 1817, reproached missionaries with their too frequent use of sombre images and 'religious terror', their dramatic ceremonies – among them the sermon amid the tombs (which was presumably not uncommon) – which had 'deranged some feeble minds'.[146] The mission of Loch, a parish of some twelve hundred souls, was given by the Lazarists in 1837 and provoked some untoward reactions: five women were reported to have shown signs of madness after listening to accounts of the 'eternal truths'.[147] A sermon provoked the madness of a woman who killed herself, imagining that she was damned.[148] Similar cases were reported by Ball and Voisin.[149]

However, not everyone was impressed with the vision of eternal punishments which were to be their lot. Those for whom religion was habitually a set of conventional social rites, even if they were moved by the priests' exhortations, tended to be affected by a fearful remorse which was transitory. The prefect of Allier felt, in 1817, that tears were more frequent than fear during missions and that the latter sentiment, even when greatly stimulated, was fleeting.[150] While comparative indifference might characterize some reactions, others were informed by anti-clericalism – which was by no means confined to towns. Thus, irascible fire-and-brimstone priests might meet with laconic scepticism or apparently submissive stubbornness. In the parish of Lobé (Ardennes) in 1825, a missionary, Father Baltaux, tried to force a violin-player, whose son had recently been killed by a tree he was felling, to give up his trade. The man pointed out that he had no other means of living; thereupon, Baltaux told him that his son, killed by God's hand, was already in hell, that it was in vain that his father prayed for him and that he and his wife would undoubtedly join their progeny in these nether regions. The following day at the mission, the musician having remained obdurate in the face of these threats, the priest took the violin-player's family as an example of the effects of God's ire. At this, the undaunted musician complained to the local administrators – without success, however, as public opinion was against him.[151] In October 1819, at Saint Lambert (Loire), the vicar of the parish tried to force his parishioners to attend vespers. In the course of his vehement exhortations, he told a smith that if he did not go to church, he would burn in hell in the next life. Whereat the smith replied: 'As for you, you'll freeze!'[152] Camille Marcilhacy reports that an analogously flippant scepticism existed in the Beauce in the early 1860s. One farmer affirmed: 'I don't want to go to heaven, it's too high up, I prefer to go to hell.' Another announced pragmatically: 'Between Paradise on earth and Paradise in heaven, I'd choose the first; because it's more certain, you can get your hands on it.'[153]

Whether or not the effects of such sermons were transient or profound, or indeed even if they were greeted with indifference, prayers for salvation were known and recited – mainly, it would seem, by those perennially devout members of the community, old women – all over France. In the *pays d'Albret*, one morning prayer asked for 'peace and bread, Paradise for the dead'.[154] More common were the little prayers said when taking holy water. In the Bourbonnais one version ran:

Eau bénite, je te prends,
Sur mon corps, sur mon sang,
Si la mort me surprend,
Sers-moi de sacrement.[155]

(Holy water, I take thee,
On my body, on my blood,
If death should surprise me,
Be as a sacrament to me.)

This prayer seems to have been known throughout France.[156] There were many analogous prayers which point to the existence among the rural poor of naive conventional piety, centering on the desire for salvation. In the Pyrenees, they said: 'Blessed bread I want to eat: Not to satisfy my hunger. If I die in the next nine days, it'll stand as communion to me.' Most versions had it that communion, like holy water, would serve as a sacrament – or as an exclusion order from hell.[157]

A number of long prayers, whose central theme was the Passion and man's redemption, were also well-known. While they testify to a measure of piety and some familiarity with the Gospels, they were not entirely disinterested: entry into paradise was one of the advantages to be culled from them. There were three principal texts: the *Or à Dieu*, the *Verbe-Dieu* and the *petite patenôtre blanche*. They were not dissimilar in theme, and individual passages seem to have migrated from prayer to prayer. Their assurances were far from being entirely orthodox – though they no doubt afforded consolation to congregations admonished by pastors like Father Guyon. One version of the Passion promised somewhat sweepingly:

If there are little children in your company
Who know this prayer and say it
In the evening at bedtime,
In the morning when they rise,
Even if they have committed as many sins
As there are grains of salt in the sea,
Paradise will never be denied them.

Gagnon found a version of this account of the Passion, which promised heaven to those who recited it, no matter what their shortcomings on earth had been, in the notebook of a poor woman born in Vienne in 1825.[158] It was also known in the south-west of France, and in the Auvergne, where it ended with the same assurance to anyone who recited it before retiring.[159] This was exactly the kind of practice which the Abbé Thiers, the voice of sensible late-seventeenth-century orthodoxy, had ridiculed,[160] for it rendered the dogma and canons of the Church irrelevant: good deeds and the sacraments might be by-passed by private devotion.

The Passion and Resurrection were central to a widely known prayer – the *Verbe-Dieu*.[161] Surviving versions of the *Verbe-Dieu* suggest that it initially consisted of a long account of the Easter Mystery. The Abbé Paul Bonnin heard a long variant of the prayer from a very old woman in his parish of Saint Thomas de Canal. The grandmother of the folklorist Favraud recited shorter versions of it and other prayers for the dead in 1848.[162] But perhaps the most well-known popular prayer of all was the *patenôtre blanche*. Its status has been variously interpreted, some folklorists inclining to the view that it was the preserve of sorcerers.[163] This view seems to have been first advanced by Lancelin, who affirmed that 'no country sorcerer is unfamiliar with the *patenôtre blanche*, by means of which anyone can enter Paradise; but they all . . . surround it with deep mystery and divulge it only very rarely'.[164] Noting the decline in the popularity of the prayer in the Charente at the end of the nineteenth century, Leproux observed that it appeared to have 'passed into the realm of sorcery', in support of which contention he cited Lancelin.[165] However, extracts from the prayer were frequently recited for frankly devotional purposes in many parts of rural France, while evidence for its use in magical practices is scant[166] – although the allegation that it belonged to the arsenal of sorcerers is plausible, since religious devotions were often adapted for unorthodox purposes. In its complete form, the text of the prayer suggests that it was initially intended to be a conventional prayer for salvation. In the early nineteenth century in the Limousin, the lawyer Juge noted a version of the prayer which he heard the country people recite. It insisted on the physical proximity of the Holy Family and Apostles to the devout: they are represented as the immediate relatives of the person saying the prayer, who is assured of entering paradise if he recites it three times every morning and evening.[167] Almost identical versions of it were heard by the sub-prefect in the arrondissement of Confolens in 1803, and by Lancelin in Normandy in the early twentieth century, while that cited by Gagnon for the Bourbonnais was very similar.[168]

Whatever properties the originals were supposed to have had, the versions we know were taken down by the folklorists mainly from old men and women, who appear to have recited them with the intention of protecting themselves from the dangers of life and death.[169] It is, then, correct to see these prayers as testimony of simple faith and devotion, expressing peasants' cosmological and metaphysical naiveté and reflecting their vulnerability. The ostensible point of saying them was to be saved from the torments of hell. But the idea of salvation was frequently less simple and orthodox than this. Salvation was more often than not associated with bodily safety and preservation from danger, which points to a very literal appreciation of the meaning of hell.

Naive piety appropriated the supernatural in an intimate as well as naturalistic familiarity. In Languedoc, when wood-cutters were tired, they said: 'Mon Diou, sio tiou [I am yours], ou savis [you know it], Adiou.'[170] Morning prayers, which were known in almost every province of France, were quite similar in tone. Berriat-Saint-Prix heard the following one in Maringues in the Auvergne at the turn of the century. It was said on the way to the fields: 'Bonjour bon Dieu, vethi Liabaud, vous sabez che que l'y faut, bon jou bon Dieu, ye m'en vo' ('Hallo, good God, this is Laibaud, you know what he needs, good day good God, I'm off now.').[171] God was addressed in much the same way as an aged relative, and the prayer indicates little of the *mysterium tremendum* which Rudolf Otto thought essential to the apprehension of the Divinity.[172] Many popular morning prayers had the same chirpy familiar tone. Common terrestrial incidents were recorded with the same aplomb as miraculous events, as though there were nothing extraordinary about the supernatural and nothing undignified about the commonplace. Favraud heard the following prayer being recited at Aubigné (Deux-Sèvres) around 1850:

In matin, je m'y lève
C'était pour me laver les mains;
J'aperçois la boune Vierge,
Qu'est dans sa chapelle,
Qui me vouet, qui m'appelle,
Que me défend de cinq mauvaises chouses:

Du sorcier,
Du malin esprit,
De l'ennemi,
De la sarpant,
Et do chin gâté.
Seigneur, mon Dieu, fasez-moi la grâce
Qu'o n'approche pas pu près de moi
Que la belle étele et le soleil.[173]

(One morning, I get up
To wash my hands it was;
I see the good Virgin,
Who's in her chapel,
Who sees me, who calls me,
Who protects me from five evil things:

From the sorcerer,
From the evil spirit,
From the enemy,
From the snake,
From the rabid dog.
Lord, my God, grant me the mercy
That they may come no closer to me
Than the beautiful star and the sun.)

Rouleau recorded a similar prayer fromn the Sologne Bourbonnaise, which was said on the way to the fields. In this, the inhabitants of heaven came down in force to attend to the well-being of the supplicant.[174] Not only are God and his saints neither remote nor confined to elusive spiritual realms, but they are fully involved in the daily problems of ordinary people. Gratuitious praise is not offered to them: few protestations of loyalty, subjection or devotion – such as we find in official prayers – are made. Instead, their attention is directed to man's practical needs, and the physical dangers that beset his life. Indeed, the prayer is more like a list with which a doctor or an insurance agent might be presented, so preoccupied is it with the banishment of earthly worries and so indifferent to the grandeur of God.

The same absence of awe is noticeable in night prayers. One started: 'Din lo let de boun Dieu me fijo . . .' ('I lie down in the good God's bed'), while God, Mary, Saint Joseph and Saint Martha appear as the supplicant's father, mother, brother and sister.[175] This was a well-known prayer.[176] In the Bourbonnais, according to Pérot, before going to bed, many people still recited:

> Quand je me couche, je me couche au nom du bon Jésus. Quatre-z-anges sont dans n'te lit, deux à nout tête, deux à nouts pies, la Sainte Croix pr'e l'mitan (milieu). J'prend l'bon Diou pr'e mon père, la Sainte Viarge pr'e ma mère, Sainte Anne pr'e ma marraine, j'prie ces bons saints quand y mourrai d'conduire m'n âme en Paradis, s'il a plai à Diou.[177]

> (When I go to bed, I lie down in the name of the good Jesus. Four Angels are in our bed, two at our head, two at our feet, the Holy Cross in the middle. I take the good God as my father, the Holy Virgin as my mother, Saint Anne as my godmother. I pray these good saints, when I die, to bring my soul to Paradise, if it please God!)

This prayer was also known in the *pays messin*, Corrèze, the *pays d'Albret* and the Haute Loire.[178] These prayers were quite unselfconscious in supposing that God was on the most friendly terms with the person praying. Even more specific about where God's sympathies lay was the *Pater du Tubet*, which used to be recited in the Pyrenees. It ran:

> Qui [celui] a dormi en male nuit
> Qui a couché en pierre dure
> Notre Seigneur le salue [sauve].
> Notre Seigneur est mon père
> Notre Dame est ma mère
> Saint Jean est mon parrain
> Saint Pierre, mon cousin
> Qui ait ces quatre parents
> Peut dormir clairement (en paix).[179]

> (He who has slept on a bad night
> He who has lain on hard stone

Our Lord will save him.
Our Lord is my father
Our Lady is my mother
Saint John is my godfather
Saint Peter, my cousin.
He, who these four relatives has,
Can sleep untroubled.)

This God looked favourably on the unfortunate, offering them protection.

Almost all of these devotional prayers were concerned with the long- and short-term security and protection of those who recited them. This was sometimes expressed in night prayers, in which God might be depicted as saying:

...Couche-toi
Sans peur, sans crainte,
Sans avoir peur de rien.[180]

(...Lie down
Without fear, without dread,
Without being afraid of anything.)

In an evening prayer, recited around 1880 by Mélanie Odille from Saint Gourson, Christ says: 'Sleep my little one, don't be afraid.' The use of the familiar language of paternity points again to the tendency to assimilate God to man, as well as to his function as a protector of the weak. Another night prayer tried to reassure the devout in the following terms: 'The Blessed Virgin at my side tells me: Sleep, lie down; arise, watch; By my side, have no fear of fire, of sea, nor of the arm of the law.'[181] One is not surprised to find that fire and water are feared, but that a prayer might express fear of the police is disconcerting. However, a number of popular prayers included the exhortation that the devout should be delivered from justice. According to Juge, country people near Limoges often added the phrase 'Deliver us from justice' to their evening or Sunday prayers. They claimed that they meant by this 'the blue uniforms', or police.[182] It was also common in the Confolentais to end one's prayers with this expression, and when questioned as to what was meant, the peasants indicated that not only the police but also gamekeepers and tax-collectors were understood.[183] That country people feared local agents of law and authority as much as they would any unpredictable natural catastrophe suggests that they distrusted official justice and did not share the values and assumptions on which it was based. Poor people's profound fear of secular power speaks of long oppression. Protection and safety, justice and well-being were not thought to be provided in the secular order, which rather served to perpetuate or increase the suffering and vulnerability of the poor. Happily, God and his saints were not remote and indifferent to the concerns of the humble, but dispensed consolation, justice and hope.

Conclusion

Small wonder, then, that the popular God was the child of 'petites gens', a God who punished the arrogant rich and who helped the poor, who appeared to the miserable and charged them with important tasks, who arranged miraculous reversals of fortune; a God who offered protection in life and even solace in death. Apart from this idealism, however, popular religion was marked by a cast of mind that turned to the familiar and practical, rather than to abstract speculation. The religious ideas of poor country people were often confused and frequently diverged from orthodox dogma. Rooted in matters of this world, popular religion had, apparently, little to do with spirituality and holiness. It considered morality almost exclusively in terms of the relation of the rich to the poor, the powerful to the weak. Its appeal was twofold: it lay, above all, in its power to reassure and sustain the anxious and vulnerable, and (through its admittedly disguised radical populism) to compensate the poor for the misery of life. Hence, popular religion was at once more eschatological and more practical than authentic spirituality, and this paradoxical character has inspired accounts of it which have insisted either on the boundless credulity which it implied or on its materialism. It was, however, underpinned by an all-pervasive religiosity – a disposition to seek solace in symbol and myth – which resurfaced in people's reactions to illness, poverty and stress and which, even if ostensible religion itself declined, survived the advent of modernity.

II

Traditional Medicine

Popular medicine showed the same sensitivity to human psychology that is to be found in other branches of folklore. The shortage of doctors in the French countryside and primitive state of clinical medical infrastructure account to some extent for the proliferation of faith-healers of various kinds – although their survival in contemporary France and their apparently consistent popularity in some areas suggest that their appeal is not solely attributable to technological underdevelopment. At all events, in the nineteenth century, most country people appear to have depended more upon unorthodox medicine than upon its academically respectable counterpart. People believed in the efficacy of the inherited prayers and secret rites of healers and sorceresque figures and these were frequently consulted and often respected in rural France.[1] Even in 1963, France was supposed to have over 40,000 faith-healers (but only over 38,000 doctors) and 50,000 consulting rooms belonging to unorthodox practitioners.[2]

Traditional Healers

Who were these characters? Most folklorists have distinguished between bone-setters, who confined themselves to fractures and sprains, faith-healers, who dealt with all sorts of illness by reciting prayers and observing a ritual which had been passed on to them by a relative or acquaintance and who were often believed to have inherited a gift for curing, and sorcerers, who treated illness as a spell which they broke with their magical powers.[3] In practice, however, these distinctions were often blurred. According to Dubalen, the peasants of Clermond and neighbouring areas used to consult a famous spell-breaker, Jacques-Thomas Fournier, who specialized in curing the ill and in warding off hail-storms. He was a small fat man, who claimed to belong to the order of the Hermits of Saint Augustine. For twelve years he went about the countryside, sleeping at inns, collecting offerings in money and in kind for his services. Another man, as much sorcerer as healer, who was famous in the Landes for his healing powers, possessed books and liturgical ornaments and was consulted by the well-to-do as well as the poor. Gipsies and local bone-setters were popular (and even advertized their skills!)[4] Between 1880 and 1907, so many people came from all over France and even from America to a little vilage in Aveyron to see the bone-setter Pierre Broude, that hotels were built to accommodate his clientèle.[5] Some healers, like seventh sons, were held to have inherited their gifts. Only a little over twenty years ago, Eugène Camus, a thirty-six-year-old bone-setter and farmer at Laboret (Allier), claimed to have inherited his gift from his father. His family had been rewarded with this skill, he believed, for having saved the remains of a crucifix during the Revolution.[6]

According to the version of this story heard by Gagnon, one of Camus' ancestors, labouring in the field, had found a broken ivory crucifix which he stuck together. As he finished this task, he heard 'a celestial voice saying to him: "Since you have repaired me so well, in future, you and your descendants will have the power to reset fractured limbs."'[7] An almost identical tale was told about the vocation of the famous bone-setter from Nasbinals, from the Aubrac, Pierre Broude. Broude, who was born in September 1832, became so famous and well-loved that after his death in 1907 a statue was erected to his memory at the instigation of the local senator. According to the legend surrounding Broude, he had repaired a cross 'and at that moment, he had heard a celestial voice telling him: everything you shall repair will be repaired'.[8] A similar story was told about a bone-setter known as Kérambrun. This man's ancestor had, with difficulty and piety, repaired a statue of Christ which he had found when working in a field. That night, he fell asleep beside the restored statue. Around midnight, he was awoken by a hand placed on his shoulder. A dazzlingly bright light filled the room and a voice said: 'As you have reset your unfortunate master's limbs so well, I give the mission of mending your brothers' limbs to you and your kin.'[9]

This story about God's magnanimity illustrates not so much a naive disposition to believe in the supernatural, as the utility and adaptability of legend. Legends, in pre-modern society, were not only a form of anecdote but also a kind of emblem, whose function was to identify and confirm as much as to divert. Legends of this kind were common, and healers seem to have liked to account for their powers by suggesting that they came directly from God. Thus, in the 1880s, when Charles Durand asked a famous healer from the Bordeaux area how he had become a faith-healer, he was told the following tale. The healer had once been a wood-cutter. One wet, windy night, he offered hospitality to an old man, giving him half his dinner and sharing his bed with him.

> In the morning my guest said to me, I have neither money nor gold to give you, but here is a book which will give you more satisfaction than all the riches of this world. – But I said, what would I do with this book? I cannot read. – Open it, he answered me, and read. I opened it and. . . . I read. When I lifted my head the good God had disappeared.

The book which the sorcerer had inherited was, according to Durand, an indecipherable book of spells.[10] It is possible that some old traveller did indeed reward the hospitable wood-cutter with the book and that he, labouring under the influence of similar tales, decided to embroider on it for the benefit of his clients. Equally, the story may have been pure invention (albeit heavily indebted to narrative tradition). In either case, it had the weight of tradition behind it. Medieval preachers, who drew their *exempla* from popular tradition, had suggested in graphic tales that generosity would be rewarded, and even in the nineteenth century, stories about God's sparing the hospitable from the effects of his wrath or rewarding them with earthly goods were still popular. Stories which were told about healers and the origin of their gifts belonged to this well-established tradition, and familiarity made them acceptable. Today the authority of such a tale would be undermined by its implausibility, but historical accuracy was irrelevant to this kind of story, for its purpose was to identify the healer as a virtuous man and competent doctor by placing him in a well-established tradition, and to arrogate to him the authority and prestige of his celebrated forerunners.

However, the credit enjoyed by healers was not attributable in the first place to such stories, which tended only to confirm their authority, but to the utility of the services they rendered. Their good standing was also reflected in more tangible ways. Many were supposed to have become rich, like Guérit-Tout (Heal-All) from the Dunkerque area, or the famous priest near Nîmes who was reputed to earn up to 3000 francs a week, or the bone-setter who died in Gennes around 1890 and left over 500,000 francs. *Voyageuses*, old ladies who visited shrines on behalf of the ill, also enjoyed good standing and sometimes did well by their trade. One old lady made such a good living at this that when she died in 1926 she left a stock of at lest twenty kilos of copper coins.[11] Others, like Pierre Broude, who was twice elected to the town council, were accorded positions of honour in their communities. Attempts to curtail the activities of healers sometimes met with open hostility. When seventy-three-year-old Broude was prosecuted and fined 375 francs in 1904 for practising medicine illegally, the locals were incensed;[12] and a riotous popular protest prevented the authorities from arresting Jacques-Thomas Fournier for fraud.[13] In 1827, near Blesnau in Burgundy, despite all the curate could say against it, there flourished a miraculous fountain, whose patron was the benign (and apocryphal) Saint Bon. The fountain was reputedly able to cure every disease, and Pétrouille, an old *voyageuse*, was among those who were apt to consult it. The administration, however, being anxious to eradicate what it deemed to be fraud – the exploitation of popular superstitions – prosecuted her in Auxerre. Local opinion was hostile to the proceedings and many people testified to her good faith. One elderly peasant affirmed that: 'Pétrouille . . . is a good Christian, and I know nothing about her which doesn't accord with the faith.' A husband

and wife, prosecuted for the same offence at Charters in 1864, were also supported by grateful witnesses, who attributed their cures to them.[14] These clashes between official and popular opinion in court over what was legitimate and desirable indicate the surprising independence of popular judgements: behaviour was sanctioned, irrespective of the recommendations and wishes of the authorities, in accordance with traditional values. The popular view of right and wrong seems to have been long impervious to the rather haphazard attempts to inform or reform it. However, as we shall see, the apparently stubborn attachment to pilgrimages and other forms of traditional therapy may be ascribed partly to the relative psychological sophistication of these rites and to the variety of needs they could meet, rather than to the inexplicable and perverse credulity of the popular mind.

Many healers came from families which had for generations practised unofficial medicine. The Fleurot family from Remiremont had been bone-setters for two centuries and the children of the family amused themselves by dismantling and reassembling skeletons. The Nardin family, in the Vosges, were thought by Kérambrun to be more expert at trepanning than many doctors. In the nineteenth century, some of these clans sent their children to obtain more orthodox training in medical faculties and hospitals. Jollans, a bone-setter from Isère, graduated from the school of medicine of Strasbourg in 1817. Patrocle, a well-to-do farmer and famous healer from Sazaret in the Bourbonnais who was born in 1792, gave his son a formal education, and the boy set up as a qualified doctor at Montmarault – while his father and uncle were frequently prosecuted for the illegal practice of medicine.[15] The difference between illegal and orthodox medicine seems therefore to have been seen as purely one of technique, rather than a metaphysical one as writers like Eliade have contended.

One healer from Hérault was reported by Cantaloube to consult the doctor in the principal town of the canton whenever he had a particularly difficult problem on his hands. The healer used both ancient recipes – such as those drawn from notebooks and chapbooks – and modern techniques like auscultation. He was anxious to suggest that he was also studying academic medicine.[16] This interchangeability between the archaic and the modern, the superstitious and the scientific, suggests that neither the practitioners of popular medicine nor their patients gave much thought to the theory behind their approach, and that the supposedly religious dimension of faith-healing was lost upon them.[17] This is confirmed by the research of H. Graulle in the Bourbonnais who discovered that 82 per cent of the healers he encountered were non-practising Catholics, although most of them relied to a great extent on prayers to effect their cures.[18]

Traditional Techniques

Nonetheless, healers were often at pains to stress the importance of faith on the part of the patient, and indeed of the healer, if a recovery were to be made. An old healer from Indre-et-Loir, whom Dr Blanchard knew, emphasized that trust in God was as important as knowledge of the technique in ensuring a cure:

> 'To succeed', he used to say, 'it's not enough to make the right gestures and to recite the prayers correctly, you have to say them with fervour and conviction. Mrs. R. said that I had cured her husband of colic: in fact I only made some signs of the cross on his stomach and said several prayers in Latin which I did not understand. The Supreme Being heard my prayers and cured him.'[19]

Such modesty was not common, however, and it was more usual for healers to demand that their patients put their trust in the efficacy of the rites. Vigne, from Vialas, when he had asked his clients to describe their symptoms, would say: 'Do you believe? If you believe, you will be healed.' Charcot's investigations into nervous disorders led him to stress the importance of the imagination in determining cures in some cases.[20] Thus, Vigne cured a girl who had long been unable to speak and who presumably had suffered from hysterical aphonia.[21]

Dramatic cures of this kind, which doubtless did much to enhance the reputation of those who effected them, were a striking feature of popular medicine. In the commune of Loirac, in July 1923, a farmer's wife of forty-eight who had stayed in bed for over a year, weeping in a darkened room, unwilling to rise and exhausted by the slightest effort, was treated by a local sorcerer. He came to see her and after 'several magnetic passes' told her to get up, which she did; thereafter the woman went about her business, apparently cured.[22] Symptoms which were caused by shock or by some other emotional trauma were, as Charcot and his disciples realized, more likely to yield to this sort of treatment than were any others. At Saint Seurin-de-Prats in Périgord, a girl of eleven who fell asleep beside a fire and was burnt went blind after the accident. The local doctor believed her to be gravely ill. She was unable to eat, and seemed to be about to die. A woman from the village of Les Granges presented herself, and, making the sign of the cross over the child, recited a traditional prayer to cure burns, known by healers throughout France in the last century:

> Feu
> Perds ta chaleur
> Comme Judas
> Perdit ses couleurs
> Au Jardin des Oliviers.
>
> (Fire
> Lose your heat
> As Judas

Lost his colour
In the Garden of Olives.)

Immediately, the girl felt relieved, the pain ceased, and a few days later she was cured.[23] The recoveries effected by unofficial techniques were sometimes striking. In France, and in much of the rest of the world, the successes of traditional medicine may be ascribed to its occasional psychological relevance. It exploited primarily psychological techniques – as the insistence on the importance of trust or faith implied[24] – which, applied to psychosomatic illnesses and nervous disorders, could work satisfactorily. It would seem likely that the miraculous cure of the burnt child was due to the fact that her chief symptoms – blindness and withdrawal – had been caused by shock and could be treated successfully by traditional techniques. Hence, although it often amounted to a parody of science and involved shameless charlatanism, as contemporaries often observed, traditional medicine was also practised in good faith and to good effect.

The arsenal at the command of healers was comparatively limited and prayers were a significant element in it. These were supposedly secret, but appear in fact to have been well-known, if the number of examples and variety collected by folklorists at the end of the nineteenth century are any indication of their popularity. One of the most popular prayers was that addressed to Saint Appolonia for toothaches.[25] The *Médecin des Campagnes* gives a model version:

> St. Appolonia is seated on the marble stone, Our Lord passing her says, 'Appolonia what are you doing there?' 'I'm here for my head, for my blood, and for my toothache.' 'Return home Appolonia: if it is a drop of blood, it will fall and if it is a worm, it will die.' Say five Our Fathers and five Hail Marys in honour of the five wounds of Our Lord and make the sign of the Cross with the finger on your cheek where you feel the pain and you'll be cured in no time at all.[26]

Oral versions of this prayer were found throughout France. Bidault collected one of them in the Morvan, at the end of the nineteenth century, which differs interestingly from the printed prayer: in it, we do not know that the person talking (we have only the dialogue) is Jesus – which perhaps indicates a tendency towards secularization. Marcelle Bouteiller discovered the prayer (as it is given in the *Médecin des Pauvres*) in the notebook of an old sorcerer; she also found a young woman who, having learnt it from her grandfather, could cite it to her exactly. At Vicq-Exemplet, Jean-Louis Boncoeur unearthed a slight variant, in which Jesus, after enquiring why Appolonia languishes, tells her that 'if it is wind, it will come forth'.[27] This seems to indicate that the literary version – however recondite its origins – became popular, and that the book's influence on rural society was maintained through the reading or memorization of its contents. The fact that some people took the trouble to copy it indicates not only the relevance of its pretensions to popular worries and the faith attributed to the written word, but also that it fitted existing social institutions – namely, the array of obscure healers, bone-setters and sorcerers who seem to have flourished to the detriment of the only marginally less lethal country doctors.[28]

Appolonia was just one of a galaxy of saints to whom such devotions were addressed. Saint John was particularly favoured, especially for eye illnesses and burns. Bidault found a version of a prayer to heal burns in the Morvan, in the late nineteenth century:

> Our Lord and Saint John went for a walk. Saint John said: 'Lord, I hear a child crying' – 'It's a child burning, Saint John, off you go and cure it!' – 'Lord how would you have me cure it, I don't know how to do it!' – 'Go and blow upon it three times, Saint John, and the pain will go away!'

The healer was to touch the patient while he recited this.[29]

Thiers knew a law officer who repeated a similar prayer for eye complaints: in it Saint John, meeting three virgins, asks them why they are there; they are curing a cataract in someone's eye; an invocation to them to cure the patient's eye is accompanied by a sign of the cross and a breath, which is followed by the prescription and recital of three Paters and three Aves.[30] An identical version is to be found in the *Enchiridion*.[31] What seems to be an abbreviated version of this (based on the incantation section) was also used.[32] Canon J. J. Moret, a *curé* of Saint Menoux at the turn of the century, found an old manuscript belonging to a bone-setter from the area of Moulins. The pages were blackened with age and worn at the corners, testifying to long service.[33] It included a less literary variant of this prayer:

> S. Lazare et N. Seigneur allaient se promener dans notre ville. S. Lazare dit à N. Seigneur: 'J'entends un cri.' N. S. dit: 'C'est un enfant qui brûle; allez, bouffez-y trois fois de votre vent, de votre haleine sans prendre vent; l'enfant guérira.'[34]

> (Saint Lazarus and Our Lord were going for a walk in our town. Saint Lazarus said to Our Lord: 'I hear crying'. Our Lord said: 'It's a burning child, go and blow on him three times with your own wind, with your own breath, without drawing breath; the child will get better.')

What is particularly striking about this rendering is the extent to which Jesus has been incorporated into rural France: whereas, in the Gospels, the incidents of Christ's life are recounted with solemnity, so that all his actions seem deliberate and significant, here Christ seems to be wandering around the village in the company of his friend, as might anyone taking a short break from work: in short, he indulges in the idle trivia so common in men and so rare in gods. Perhaps the most arresting feature of the formula is its unhesitating appropriation of the incident: the event happened in 'our' village[35] – hence making it all the more immediate and the prayer all the more efficacious. What could be further from the hidden God of post-Copernican intellectuals?

Prayers of this kind abounded for all sorts of complaints.[36] They probably worked by helping to create the atmosphere which the healer needed in order to make a suitably awesome impression on his patients. The descriptions given by a number of folklorists of the rites of healers and sorcerers suggest that their very obscurity and peculiarity contributed to their mysterious authority.[37] Rocal described the appearance of a sorcerer at the deathbed of an old man called Jendon. On entering the room, the sorcerer threw some salt on the fire, to keep the devil away. He then listened to the dying man's chest, recited a prayer to secure his entry into paradise, then prayed silently, drawing signs of the cross on his patient, placing a sachet on his chest and removing it. Next, he put a bowl of water in each corner of the room, so that the old man's soul could wash in the water and, thus purified, go straight to heaven. As the death-rattle sounded in the dying man's throat, the sorcerer recited the *patenôtre blanche*, accompanying the prayer with mysterious signs made with his left hand. When, finally, the old man died, the sorcerer threw the water out (so that the soul would not dally in the house).[38] The sorcerer's incantations – which expressed the desire that the man be purified of the evil incarnated in his illness, and so go to heaven – accompanied a ritual which mimed this intention. Both fire and salt are age-old symbols of purification, and the preliminary gesture set the tone of the act to come. The sachet placed on the man's chest seems to have been intended to draw the illness out of him.

This sort of miming was common in unofficial medical methods – being evident in techniques such as the well-known way of getting rid of warts and the rites observed during pilgrimages. The methods of the sorcerer Pipète exemplify this approach. He invited his patients suffering from malaria to breathe into a handkerchief or box: the illness was thereby trapped in the object, which was left on the road for some passer-by to pick up (and thus catch the illness) or tied to a branch of a tree or bush, where the evil withered and died.[39] The symbolism of these techniques – with its emphasis on the concrete and dramatic – tended to make the sense of the rite easily accessible. Odenthal witnessed a cure of a Parisian woman suffering from shingles, which shared some of these characteristics. She was staying in a château in the Dordogne and had been ill for three days, when an old woman came to the place and offered to cure her. The offer was accepted and the healer sat her patient and the two witnesses in a darkened dining-room, lit two candles and put some dried herbs in the form of a cross on the table. Then, touching the woman and the cross of herbs, the healer began to mumble prayers. Then she stared piercingly at her patient for some moments in silence. Finally, she gathered up the herbs, made the woman climb on her back and answer 'shingles' to the question, 'What am I carrying?' as she turned to face the four cardinal points. The healer told them to burn the herbs, because the illness was now in them. Odenthal affirms that the woman was cured by this procedure.[40] The performance exploited both the appeal of theatricality and the authority of traditional words and symbols to achieve the desired result. It involved the patient actively in the cure, turned her disposition to believe (apparent in her readiness to participate in the antics) to effective use, and attempted to impress her both by creating an imposingly eccentric atmosphere and by the well-worn technique of staring steadily at her. The sort of success exemplified by this cure would seem to be attributable to the importance, in some illnesses, of the patient's frame of mind in determining recovery; and it indicates that traditional medicine was aware of and exploited this dimension of illness long before orthodox medicine understood it. This is clear, too, in the many pilgrimages into which people channelled their anxieties about their health.

Pilgrimages

Pilgrimages for the relief of illness were commonly seen as a manifestation of flourishing religious belief. In reality, their relation to dogmatic religion was tenuous. In the diocese of Meaux, fevers were the most frequently cited complaint in devotions of this kind, followed by children's illnesses, eye diseases, worries about progeniture, sick cattle and epidemics. Of 275 popular rites centering on saints' shrines, 30 per cent were devoted to children or to the desire to have them, 66 per cent dealt with adults and their worries, while 4 per cent concerned animals. Saints filled the roles nowadays played by doctors, psychiatrists, priests, counsellors and insurance agents: they looked after wives, soldiers, and travellers; protected households against thieves, hail, storm; fire, spells and evil spirits; arranged marriages and cured illnesses.[41] Although apparently striking signs of religious vitality, pilgrimages were usually undertaken with practical considerations in mind. The nineteenth-century clergy of the diocese of Chartres, like their colleagues from Orléans, noted with distress that confession and communion were usually neglected, while low masses were generally ignored as unnecessary accessories. In 1892, one *curé* rather naively exclaimed: 'When are we going to see our pilgrimages to Saint Marcoul, Saint Evroult, Saint Gilles... etc. become once more what they must have been in the past, pilgrimages for sanctification and salvation!'[42] That they had ever had such a character must be open to question; at all events, it seems clear that complaints, rather than saints – and still less, God – were at the heart of the pilgrims' preoccupations.

In the Charentais, innumerable fountains, chapels and churches offered relief to the ill; in Angoulême, the fountain of Saint Augustine, near the Carmelite chapel, was very much favoured in the nineteenth century for the relief of nervous disorders; at Chazelles, girls wanting husbands might apply to the chapel of Saint Blaise; headaches, weakness and rickets were alleviated at Marrillac-Le-Franc. Some places dispensed only one kind of service – the *fontaine du Miracle* at Moutiers and the *Fontaine des Nouailles* at Jauldes were among those to which recourse was had only when rain was needed – while others provided a universal panacea, like the church and fountain of Saint Gilles at Aigues and Puyperous, where pains and fevers might be cured, marriages arranged and rain ordered.[43] At Villeneuve-sur-Allier (Allier), Note Dame de Recouvrance brought still-born babies to life briefly to enable them to be baptized and go to heaven (which was thought to be a more enjoyable fate than going to limbo, where the deserving souls of the unevangelized were sent). In the Department of the Allier, twenty fountains were devoted to fever, fourteen to eye-diseases, three were for illnesses of cattle and two for rheumatism and skin-diseases, while others were consulted for headaches, impetigo, rickets, breast diseases, madness and children's ailments. There were, apart from these, fountains which protected pilgrims against various infirmities, and annual processions to them were a primitive form of preventive medicine.[44]

These pilgrimages sometimes excited the reproval of enlightened onlookers, who assumed that their censure hardly needed justification: the dangers and inefficacy of many popular rites were apparent; the outlook which they implied condemned their devotees to impotence and suffering (and, as some writers pointed out, to political and economic exploitation). *Pardons*, Cambry wrote, with their apparently haphazard, irrational gestures, illustrated the point:

> People go to confession and communion, give alms, observe some superstitious customs, buy crucifixes, rosary-beads with which they touch the demi-god's statue; they rub their foreheads, knees, paralysed arms on miraculous stones; throw pins and farthings into fountains, dip their shirts into them to be cured, and their belts to give birth painlessly, and their children, to make them insensible to suffering.[45]

The practices observed at Saint Clothilde's spring at Grand-Andély, in Normandy, were not unusual. The custom was to jump into the fountain, to which a little red wine had been added and into which the saint's statue had been dipped three times. Children, screaming and scarlet with fever, were plunged into the water, right up until October, often with fatal results. When Boué de Villiers, who observed this practice in 1868, expressed his indignation, he claims to have been almost attacked. Attempts to suppress the pilgrimage there in June 1798 had led to riots and later efforts to the same end had been equally unsuccessful. The anticlerical radical, A. S. Miron, reacted in a similar way to the pilgrimage at Pierrefixte, near Nogent-le-Rotrou. There, the fountain of Saint John the Baptist was said to be able to cure all diseases on 23 June each year. The ill had to soak a piece of linen in the sacred waters, then rub the afflicted part of the body with it. Miron was especially exercised by the sight of many people, including young women, undressing so as to don a wet garment. Before 1848, he had attacked the habit of plunging young children into the fountain, in the local paper, the *Glaneur d'Eure-et-Loir*. 'At last, in 1848, when I was in charge of the administration of the district, I issued a prefectorial edict making this prohibition [to dip children into the fountain] definitive. Several simple folk complained and claimed that their liberties were being undermined, ...'[46] – a perhaps not unjustified contention.

Psychological Techniques: Mime and Catharsis. However, pilgrimages and analogous rites imply a less far-fetched way of thinking when viewed as psychological techniques than when interpreted (with largely irrelevant considerations in mind) as reflecting a naive cosmology. The difference between techniques whose conception is indebted to ordinary experience and which seem to us sensible, and many of the strange rituals of popular religion and magic lies in the fact that whereas the former manipulate things, the latter manipulate feelings, and are therefore unconcerned with the objective causality that is central to materially profitable activity. Pilgrimages all too often did not centre on God, but on man's material and psychological needs, yet they were unlike profane activities because they reflected and tried to satisfy these needs in a deliberately specialized way. In this respect, religious devotions were often disconcertingly like those castigated by the Church on account of their paganism. At Barcelone-de-Gers in 1910, pilgrims suffering from migraine repaired to Saint John's fountain, where they immersed a brand new piece of linen with which they enveloped their temples, saying: 'Saint John, take my illness away and give it to whomever you wish.' Then they proceeded to Roquefort, where a priest read a gospel for them.[47] In this rite, a saint took the place filled, in other cases, by rivers and fountains. Yet the differences between pagan rites and the Catholic practice just cited are less striking than their similarities: function, gesture and word, end and means were all remarkably alike.

The outward resemblances between condemned and tolerated cults were not incidental, but obviously neither complete nor constant; official or quasi-official pilgrimages were not identical with each other, but details which differed appear more like variations on a theme. At the official shrine, the pilgrim usually either attended mass or had a gospel recited while the priest laid one end of his stole on the petitioner's head. He venerated the relic or statue; when there was a sacred fountain, he bathed in it or immersed his clothes in the waters and then donned the damp garments. The rite at the shrine seems to have been shaped partly by the possibilities offered by the place itself, partly by ordained purposes of the exercise. Conventionally, officially sacred fountains were endowed with chapels and effigies of saints; these statues received attentions which ranged from the apparently reverent to the frankly abusive, but which were visually expressive. In peasants' petitions, as in other manifestations of popular religious life, the holy was apt to be treated with the same scant consideration and courtesy that marked social intercourse generally. In Brittany, the saint was frequently pelted with mud, nails or water to induce him to grant a cure. At the church of Saint-Jean-de-Lambelle at Saint Cloud, pilgrims suffering from skin diseases threw handfuls of nails at the statue; while near Lamballe, at the chapel of Saint Laurent, mud was thrown at the saint's effigy for the relief of the *mal de Saint Laurent* (eczema) and the parts of the sufferer's face corresponding to those on the statue on which mud had dried were supposed to heal. The people of Plechâtel, when they wanted rain, repaired to the fountain of Saint Amand: there they drew up water and threw it at the statue's face, adding, in case the point might be lost: 'Saint Amand! rend la ma [moi]'.[48] At Saint Jean du Doigt, however, the saint was credited with greater delicacy of feeling: those who were not cured after an initial pilgrimage returned to throw water at the statue, thereby marking their displeasure; while at Saint Gobrien's fountain at Mesquer, if ablutions and prayers to the saint failed to relieve the pilgrim's colic, the statue was plunged into the water and held there until relief was obtained.[49] The assimilation between god and man, the supernatural and the natural could hardly be more striking (except, perhaps, where the saint was felt to have a penchant for pigs' trotters or to be the jealous recipient of a pound of butter); and it suggests that one should hesitate to espouse the view that peasants' lives were permeated with a sense either of mystery or of the wonder of God. The unknown was often pedestrian and the peasant seems to have been no more in awe of the saint than he might now be of a pathologist. The numerous anecdotes on the theme of irreverent petitioners, who behaved more like dissatisfied customers than devout pilgrims, reflect the naiveté or naturalism which informed these devotions.

To view these rituals in this light is, however, both to ignore their complexity and, to some extent, to misunderstand their function. The pelting of the saint's statue with water or nails was a demonstration or realization, in a limited, rather theatrical way, of what the petitioner desired – not just an amusing, if disedifying, indication of the almost total want of reverent and tremulous adoration which was once presumed to characterize popular religion. In like manner, the familiar rubbings, decorations and less amiable attentions which saints' statues were wont to receive were a form of acting, from which the pilgrim might receive emotional solace. At Trédarzec (Côtes-du-Nord), people suffering from pains touched the offending limb with a little statue of Saint Nicolas which was attached by a string to the door of the church; at Auneau (Eure-et-Loir), the pilgrim rubbed the part of the little statue of Saint Maur corresponding to the area that was giving him trouble.[50] In the Landes at Corbelut, in a grotto called (in that age of pre-Victorian directness) 'las mames' (*les mamelles*), wet-nurses would offer a prayer and suck the stalactites to get more milk, before bringing an offering to the local church.[51] At La Fontaine-La-Guyon, people prayed before an iron cross into which they stuck a nail; and at Christmas, pins were stuck into Saint Sautin's statue to get rid of the mange.[52] These three practices illustrate how contact, imitation and catharsis were typically exploited in pilgrimages. To explain them, commentators have often had recourse to the so-called 'laws of magic', which treat magic as an archaic form of physics. At one level, it may well be correct to affirm that people believed certain objects to contain a kind of energy that could be harnessed to man's needs. However, this perspective places excessive emphasis upon theories which were removed from people's concerns, while ignoring the non-intellectual inspiration of many devotions.

Such devotions appear to have been made in a spirit of concentration and fervour. Prayers and pilgrimages were habits, inculcated at an early age as a way of expressing intense wishes. They betray a lack of curiosity, amounting almost to indifference, about the mechanisms whereby the desires were fulfilled. Paul Sébillot, commenting on the widespread custom of leaving offerings at holy wells, fountains and before statues, asserted that peasants would have been hard-pressed to explain why they did this. Some observed the practice because tradition prescribed it, or because they neither thought nor cared about who received the offering. Others believed that saints occasionally came to collect their booty, while some almost seemed to think that supernatural beings lived in the wells.[53] In Brittany, Saint Hervé was held to have a taste for butter, in return for which he would defend cattle from wolves. At Trefflès, Saint Gertrude was offered chickens; she responded to gifts by curing rheumatism and chronic illnesses. (However, it cannot be presumed that the fowl were a straightforward gastronomic tribute to the saint, since the birds were auctioned off and were supposed to protect farmyard animals.)[54] Souvestre affirmed that honey, chicken, butter and wheat were among the offerings made in Brittany on pilgrimages. They were later auctioned off at the foot of the cross.[55] One possible explanation for these sales, which were quite common, is that sacristans and priests were anxious to exploit the popular notion that the offerings had acquired some sort of magical power through contact with the shrine. However, Rocal cites a strange custom in Périgord, which held a mimed sale of piglets (complete with haggling) to be a panacea for porcine illnesses: the blacksmith who acted as veterinary-surgeon for the countryside around Saint-Saud was said to 'buy' hundreds of piglets each year, according to the ancient protocol.[56]

These practices appear to be linked by the theme of a ritual sale. While the custom observed by Rocal seems at first glance inexplicable, comparisons with the auctions on pilgrimages indicates at least one possible interpretation. On pilgrimages, we presume that the buyers were motivated by the desire to acquire something of materially appreciable value (as is suggested by the anecdote of the man who returned the stick he had bought to the *curé*, complaining that it had allowed his bullock to die).[57]

Those who bought the offerings made to saints might plausibly be supposed to have been actuated by self-interest. In Périgord, the man or woman who pretended to buy and sell piglets behaved as though they were in a similar situation: they were in reality anxious for profit, and acted out the realisation of their otherwise unattainable desire. The Périgordine practice substituted for reality an imaginary situation, in which wishes were satisfied and efforts crowned with success. The search for consolation and satisfaction in fantasy, the evasion of reality, was characteristic of traditional culture, and informed medical and apparently religious practices.

Whatever their origins, however, some rituals at least would seem to have been expressive, rather than mechanistically functional gestures. The relief they gave relied to some extent on the beneficial effects of catharsis. If one of the functions of *ex votos* was to remind the absent-minded saint about the petitioner's request, another would seem to have been to encourage the exteriorization of the worry. In 1897, at the shrine of the blessed Father Montfort near Pierrebrune in the *bocage vendéen*, Gaston Deschamps found an old lady selling pilgrims little wax legs, hands, tongues and feet. 'I asked her what these strange little figurines are used for. She replied... "When a child is slow to speak, you offer a tongue to Father Montfort... When you have a bad leg, you offer him a leg..."' Inside, lots of wax feet, tongues and the ilk were piled up.[58] Deliciously incongruous and illustrative of an engaging naiveté, the practice was, in various forms, common.[59] At the oratory of 'Saint Ermite' at Theneuille (Allier), women prayed for marriage, fertility and the protection of young children, often leaving tangible evidence (in the form of bonnets and nappies, *inter alia*) of their prayers attached to the statue. The gift or offering, therefore, often materially represented the pilgrim's request. During the Great War, they wrote their intentions on ribbons with a necessarily succinct simplicity, which testifies to the cathartic function of the exercise and to the essentially profane nature of the devotees' preoccupations. 'For those whom I love and for myself, I ask for health and happiness', proclaimed one ribbon, somewhat prosaically. More begged for the survival of soldiers. One simply said: 'Saint Hermite, make the war end soon'; while another asked: 'O good Saint Hermite, pray [misspelt] for me and so as my loved one will come back to me as I love him too much and so's I shan't spend too long looking at him [before seeing him again is meant]', naively adding: 'and grant me the grace of going to Paris next year [...]'[60] In short, these prayers were framed quite as though those who offered them believed they were addressing a kind of fairy-tale king, who had the power to intervene in history to grant their requests.

Since commentators have often interpreted these rites in the light of their own understanding of causality, they have been forced to the conclusion that peasants, ignorant of the mechanical interdependencies of nature, attempted to explain and control the world by postulating supernatural beings like man in all things but power, and that, consequently, they lived in a world dominated to a large extent by the extraordinary and fearful.[61] But the aims of many of the religious gestures which we have been examining seem to have been pragmatic and the implied view of the universe was probably beside the point for most pilgrims. Method, in these areas where man's impotence was a function of his ignorance, was not a calculated adaptation of means to an end or a reflection of a theory of natural causality (as it was in technical matters like husbandry), but a rite seen to be tenuously connected with the desired result, and that partly in the mind of the performer.

Healers and pilgrims all stressed the importance of faith in ensuring the efficacy of these rites, an emphasis which suggests that the means employed were seen as being qualitatively different from purely mechanical ones. To this extent, they were understood to be primarily techniques for manipulating feelings and then, through them, for adjusting things. These techniques had to be all the more carefully executed as the relief they afforded depended on the degree of attention and intensity with which they were performed. Leproux identified a number of conditions which were observed in almost all devotions of this kind. The first and most often stressed was the necessity of implicit faith in the efficacy of the proceedings. The pilgrimage would be undertaken early in the morning; the fasting, silent pilgrim made his way to the sacred fountain or statue, where he would leave money, bread, a ribbon or pin and perhaps a lock of hair or a patch of clothes, as a tribute to the saint or to remind him of the pilgrim's request. It was considered prudent to drop something on the way – presumably to symbolize, as the tying of ribbons at the shrine might do, that the infirmity was thereby left behind. The pilgrimage usually ended either with a reading of the gospel or with mass. The pilgrim returned home, if possible by another route, and might then eat, drink and pay for his meal[62] – doubtless reflecting the notion that the rite renewed the pilgrim, who could return to enjoy life freed from his earlier afflictions. The pilgrimage indicates not so much a confusion between physical fact and personal feeling, as was once felt to be the case, but a tendency to express publicly private emotions and wishes. This gave disturbing experiences a social status and enabled people to find relief in conventional behaviour and narration. If the prestige of miracles and the popularity of these pilgrimages are anything to go by, visiting shrines would appear to have been one way in which peasants sought relief from the pressures of their lives.

Pagan Rites

Some pilgrimages excited livelier disapprobation and interest than these superficially pious devotions – namely, those observances of apparently pagan inspiration, which are usually seen as evidence of nature-worship and of the French peasant's pre-historic sensibility. Worship of the hawthorn both exemplifies the phenomenon and indicates why scholars have difficulty in explaining it. A great number of irrational beliefs and practices surrounded the plant. In Burgundy, people who carried a sprig of hawthorn were supposed to be protected from lightning and spells, as the hawthorn had derived sacred properties through having furnished the material for Christ's crown of thorns.[63] In Saône-et-Loire, it was said to be not unusual to find mothers praying to the hawthorn in spring for the restoration of their children's health.[64] In Morvan, at Monthelon, in 1880, an old woman called Jeanne Chanlon earned her living by doing novenas for the sick. As she lived far from the church, she occasionally prayed at the foot of a hawthorn tree and thought that she had, in that manner, saved the lives of many people.[65] A similar readiness to dispense with officially prescribed rites and to find in the immediate environment a vehicle for devotion, in blithe ignorance of any impropriety, was evinced in the custom of country-people from the north of the Ardennes, who used to sing:

> Aubépine, mon bien
> Je te cueille et te prends,
> Si je meurs en chemin,
> Sers-moi de sacrement.[66]
>
> (Hawthorn, my fortune,
> I gather and take thee,
> If I die on the road
> Be a sacrament to me.)

Similar prayers for eternal salvation were common throughout France – although they were usually recited while taking holy water at the church, or on some other appropriate occasion, and hence seemed passably orthodox or even devotional. Even more incongruous is the prayer collected in the Hautes Vosges by the folklorist Sauvé in the late nineteenth century. In it, the hawthorn was invoked to cure sore eyes by the power of God: 'Hawthorn, God blesses you more than any other flower and root. In the name of God, flower, I command you, if you are white, to whiten [soothe the inflammation].'[67] Delcambre, in his famous study of witchcraft in eastern France in the seventeenth century, found a version of the same healing prayer in late sixteenth-century Lorraine – an indication of the surprising efficiency and accuracy of memory and transmission in pre-modern, oral culture.[68] This curious mixture of an apparently pagan cult of nature with naive piety, applied to unorthodox ends, was not an exceptional phenomenon. The senior clergy traditionally inveighed against these practices (although some of the less exalted seem to have contributed towards their popularization), in which prayers were recited to the accompaniment of practical and fanciful rites by an eccentric, if not always shady person who was supposed to know the 'secret' and was not infrequently considered to be a sorcerer. Yet these official anathema were ignored and the distinction between the orthodox and the pagan seems to have been lost on many country people – at least where para-medical practices were concerned.

One recipe for curing fevers from the *pays d'Albret* illustrates this: in its general form and taboos it resembled pilgrimages which individuals undertook in order to rid themselves of various ailments and which the Church tolerated, but its object was not some consecrated shrine but a hawthorn bush. 'You must leave your house through a door', read the instructions, somewhat unnecessarily, 'with bread and salt, which you bring to the hawthorn. Once at the bush, you must hail it thus:

> Farewell, white bush
> I bring you bread and salt
> And fever for the morrow.

Stick the bread on to a forked branch of the hawthorn, throw salt on it, leave by another way than that you took when coming and don't enter the house by the door you left by. If there is only one door, enter by the window.'[69] It was usual, on private pilgrimages, to take one route to the shrine and a different road home, indicating liberation from old afflictions, and to leave some token at the shrine (as an offering or as a symbol of the illness one was leaving behind).

The use of salt (and accompanying benedictions) was common in popular healing and apotropaic rites, perhaps because of its function as a preservative. The invocation to the hawthorn, however, resembles prayers addressed to rivers, known in Brittany and the Nièvre. To see this rite as a form of adoration of nature diverts attention from its cathartic function. That this was its primary role seems clear, as many of its elements recurred in other healing practices that are unrelated to any form of nature-worship. The gestures it prescribed were designed to make explicit the expulsion and leaving behind of illness. While it is not clear why healing powers should have been attributed to the hawthorn, the important point to bear in mind is that these practices constituted not so much the cult of the hawthorn but the expression of a desire for health and safety. The fact that holy water or a sacred fountain or boxwood blessed on Palm-Sunday or a variety of other objects might be, and often were, substituted for the hawthorn, suggest that the plant itself was not the object of the exercise; and that in a devotional sense, it was not hallowed, but was rather a pretext for the most important aspect of the rite – the expression of a limited range of feelings and aspirations. The hawthorn and many other ordinary objects conventionally acted as emotional outlets and stabilizers, for which popular lore furnished some summary justifications. This was obviously an elastic and complex function, which was distinct from although co-existent with its ostensible purpose – that of practical, tangible efficacy.

A singular practice, found in Brittany by Sauvé, illustrates a similar apparent reverence for nature. Twin apples, linked by their branch, were kept to protect the house and its inmates from the effects of storms. As the wind grew stronger, prayers were addressed to the gales, and the apples were taken out of their box and passed round to the accompaniment of strange prayers. 'Good and delicious fruit', started the first invocation in sycophantic vein, 'look upon us with pity; you control the weather . . . '. Another proceeded: 'Now that we are fortunate enough to have you in our midst, we ask Saint Mathurin from Ponthou in your name, that from so pitiless a scourge we may be, like you, preserved.'[70] This rite seems to have been unique, although its spirit is not so far removed from other invocations we have examined. However, the reverence it expressed for the fruit is as startling as it is unusual – although were one to substitute a saint's name for the apples, one would be confronted with quite a conventional prayer. Now, while there is nothing very odd about appreciating apples, it is strange to address them in terms usually reserved for God and his saints. Should one then assume that this represents an extension of religious attitudes and values to the domain of nature?

Form and Meaning. The substitution of an apparently incongruous element in an otherwise familiar and common pattern of expression, whether in speech or behaviour, is disorientating. Yet we have found this substitution is characteristic of invocations to nature and of allied practices, although the sense of the standard pattern appears to be, if not dislocated by the variation, at least distorted or stretched beyond its original intention. One possible explanation is that the substitution of one element for another in an otherwise standard prayer did not, as is commonly assumed, change the primary meaning of the rite for its practitioners. For the importance of finding a pattern in practices of this sort is to suggest that meaning in this area is to be derived not just from investigating references to things and ideas, but also from examining the fact that certain situations provoked typical responses, whose form and content were furnished by tradition, rather than free and various expressions of ideas and feelings. We often tend to look for the meaning of things by referring to an accepted system of values, thereby assuming that the context is to be taken for granted, that its contribution to meaning is incidental. But if we considered meaning in this instance to be determined not by the act's references but by its form and function, then the invocation to fruit would not be isolated from its context (namely a prayer of otherwise conventional form for safety) and consequently, not necessarily taken to be its central, most important aspect. Why was the prayer recited? Not to adore apples, but to ask for protection. It was primarily a vehicle for expressing desire and fear, not an act of homage to fruit – the latter having apparently been slotted into a role often taken by Saint Hubert.

Variation of specific terms in prayers and acts often disguised a fundamental similarity of form and inspiration, which indicates that what was retained was more important than what was rejected and, consequently, that these rites were primarily a calculated outlet or channel for feelings.

Illness and anxiety. The inspiration of prayers, pilgrimages and magical rites lay as much in the need to be delivered from anxiety as in placid, mechanistic utilitarianism or functional theory. Emile Guillaumin observed of the prayers of poor farmers in the Bourbonnais, who feared having their harvests ruined by storms: '...During storms country-people are afraid of seeing their year's labour ruined, their income and food lost ... In these monents of great distress, they become humble and fearful, they implore, they beg.'[71] While prayers and the ilk reflected an anthropomorphic theory of causality, they also formed a psychological technique. Reverence and devotion may have complicated such gestures, but they were only accessory features. The necessity of eliminating a worry and its cause were of primary importance, and the rites not only point to a peculiar view of the natural order, but also betray considerable psychological sophistication. They frequently dramatized the theme of expulsion or catharsis, or exploited the somewhat hypnotic, reassuring effect of litanies, repetition and prolixity, and by stressing the need for accuracy and uncomfortable or awkward acts, diverted attention and provided some respite from the illness. That the individual's antics were supposed to honour God, a saint or some other creature or thing, who would be moved to grant relief, has tended to overshadow the fact that real relief might have been procured through the observance. The granting of the request appears to have been incidental to the perpetuation of the practice. People had recourse to it whether or not the ideas on which it was based were borne out by what subsequently happened, and this suggests that it was found useful, independently of its explicit external object. True, excuses for the failure of the rite could always be found, without calling the system into question – often, there were so many conditions to be fulfilled and the acts themselves were so complicated that mistakes in their execution might easily be made – but there would have been little motive for discovering them had no benefits, other than the declared material ones, attached to the rite.

Animism. So when we approach evidence of apparent nature-worship, such as that collected by Sébillot, we should be wary of supposing the prevalence of pagan beliefs and rites – not only for the reasons indicated by Van Gennep (principally, that isolated practices cannot constitute a cult), but also because mystic communion with and pious adoration of nature were very rarely gratuitous: prayers were not addressed to rivers, bushes or fountains without the pilgrim having a request – and these were usually codified, as each shrine had its speciality. Nor were the requests often framed in such a way as to flatter or tempt the perspicacious being who was the object of such devotions. The river Arroux, its tributaries and the Loire were, according to Sébillot, visited by villagers who wished to be cured of fevers. For three consecutive days before sunrise, they would repair thither, throw a penny into the water and announce: 'Arroux, je t'apporte mon malheur, donne-moi ton bonheur', or 'Bonjour Loire, donne-moi ton bonheur, et je te donnerai mon malheur'.[72] As a discerning river would be unlikely to be enticed by such an offer, it seems reasonable to suppose that assumptions about the river's sensibilities were not, as the theory of animism would implicitly have us believe, at the heart of this practice. Instead of looking at the pecuniary tribute as an offering to the spirit of the river, we might see it as a material sign of the misfortune which was to be banished, a way of emphasizing the wish expressed in the greeting. A similar rite in the Nièvre may also be interpreted in this way. There, the sufferer from fever might visit a spring before dawn; kneeling beside it, he would recite: 'Source, je t'apporte mon malheur, donne-moi ton bonheur.' Then, Sébillot comments, he would throw 'a small coin over his shoulder, as an offering to the divinity' and return home – all this without being seen.[73] Although Sébillot is unreserved about the significance of throwing the coin, one may question his judgement on this point. Popular therapy often recommended symbolically parcelling the illness up, or representing it and leaving it behind one on the road or at the shrine, or even burying it.[74] The intention of prayers was also often made visually explicit, or materialized.[75] The throwing of the coin may perhaps belong more properly to this set of practices than to that suggested by Sébillot. In any event, the cathartic nature of the rite is made clear by the invocation. Through the use of symbolism, the individual could satisfy his desire by acting it out, by realizing it allegorically.

In Brittany, where boils were called *clous*, it was common to offer the saint who specialized in curing them an indefinite number of nails, leaving them at his feet, in a hole in the wall or, at Saint Laurent-en-Sion (Loire-Inférieure), on the altar. The affliction was, as it were, left behind. It might also be washed away. The lake of Saint Andéol (Lozère) was believed to be capable of curing all illnesses on the second Sunday of July each year. The afflicted had to go round the little chapel on their hands and knees and then bathe. Those suffering from eczema flung their shirts and trousers into the water. Others waded as far out as possible, throwing money, cakes, fruit and cheese into the water.[76] The pilgrim washed himself because, under certain conditions, the water was supposed to be able to cure him. The pilgrim participated in and helped to achieve the cure: bathing was an active, almost flamboyant, image for being cleansed from illness.[77] In much of France, it was believed that the dew of the morning of 24 June cured the mange. In the Landes, the sufferer repaired to a field of oats before sunrise, undressed and walked through the field, saying:

> Cleanse me well, fresh dew. – Feel how scabby I am. – See how my whole body, from top to toe, is covered with the rash. – Deliver me please, in this hay, – From pustules and the itch, which cause such misery; – For if you grant me a quick cure, – I'll give you praise, night and day.[78]

The dew was to clean the sufferer through powers which it acquired at a particular time.

That people believed this is naturally arresting, and quite understandably entices the scholar into investigating the para-scientific model of the world which it implied. But people may not be aware of the systematic coherence of their actions, so that other motives for their behaviour have to be found. Where a traditional observance filled an otherwise insatiable material need, it is easy to see why people had recourse to it – there was little else they could do. Yet this would fail to explain why, for example, after the advent and popularization of official medicine, French peasants still frequently applied to faith-healers and innumerable other practitioners of supposedly scientific or miraculous medicine. In short, the forms taken by healing practices are not explained by pointing to technological underdevelopment, given the continued popularity of magic despite the efficacity of modern medicine. However, if one admits that people sought relief not only from physical illness but also from fear and anxiety, emotional as well as material strain, then one sees that the medicine had to fulfil two functions. Since it is easier to manipulate feelings than physical phenomena of whose laws and nature one is ignorant, we should not be surprised that the answers, while irrelevant to the material problem, showed some psychological refinement, being both accessible to the unsophisticated mind and, by making the patient actively express himself rather than treating him as a passive object of inquiry, consoling. Depending on the rite, the patient might express his desire verbally, as in the invocation to the dew just cited; sometimes, he would be called on to mime the cleansing, or to represent, in some fairly obvious way, the expulsion of his illness and return to a new life of health. It seems reasonable to suppose that the psychological relief afforded by this participation in the cure, as opposed to the more detached approach of clinical medicine, accounts for part of the apparently enduring appeal of popular therapy. We might then dissent from the view that the cult of nature or of God lay at the heart of these rites, preferring to see in them primarily psychological techniques for dealing with the pressures engendered by material needs.

Miracles

Miracles, however, appear to distil the irrationality discernible in unorthodox medicine; yet they too are best understood in the light of psychology and psychiatry. Like so many other popular prodigies, they tended to take a predictable form and there were few varieties of them. They almost always involved the sudden restoration of health, usually after a pilgrimage to a religious shrine, and were seen as a celestial reward for this devotion. Rocal's tales from the Périgord illustrate the kind of cure which might be expected. Pinalis, an old man from Les-Farges-de-Saint-Saud who was immobilized by severe rheumatism, decided to see if a visit to the fountain of La Goutte at the nearby village of Bourneix would help. He asked his children to hoist him onto a horse and trotted off hopefully. He returned cured, according to witnesses who were alive in Rocal's time. Garrein, the sacristan of Champs-Roman, told Rocal:

> I had dreadful pains. I could no longer work on my forge. I walked on crutches for three weeks. In the end we 'questioned the saints'. We saw that it came from Saint Avit. My father-in-law did the devotions, he went to get me water at Les Jalaynes fountain. I rubbed myself with it. You're not going to believe me but I swear it's true, the next day I was completely cured and I was thumping away at the anvil at work.[79]

These anecdotes are quite representative. How did they come to be believed?

The answer seems to be twofold. In the first place, there were genuine cures – in the sense that people suffering from nervous disorders, which took an apparently physical form (as is classically the case in hysteria), were sometimes relieved of their symptoms in the dramatic way ordained by miraculous tradition. Secondly, people were emotionally disposed to lend credence to these phenomena – irrespective of the apparent corroboration of actuality. Fantasy played an important part in popular culture, not least because through it man was regaled with utopian prospects all the more alluring in that they were unattainable in reality. Miracles and visions, like some forms of popular violence, flourished in the context of need and misery, as an affirmation of the inadequacy of the existing order. Small wonder that some people attempted to escape the demands which necessity, family and community placed upon them. Since ease and comfort were not realistic or familiar ambitions, at least until the latter part of the century, people tended to look not so much for a practical amelioration of their material lot as for more modest remissions from occasional miseries and to dream of extravagant reversals of individual fortune.

The momentary resuscitation of dead babies seems to have been a surprisingly popular kind of miracle in France in the nineteenth century.[80] Children who had died before receiving baptism were brought on pilgrimages to the chapel of Notre-Dame-des-Faisses (*faisse* meaning 'swaddling band') at Ribiers (Hautes-Alpes), where a mass was celebrated for their resurrection: during this they were supposed to come to life and be baptized. This ensured that they would go straight to heaven and enjoy eternal bliss. Ladoucette, who recorded the custom, noted that these miracles occasioned great interest and general excitement, but that the custom was successfully eradicated by two priests.[81] Saintyves, in his study of the practice, mentioned six such miracles in the nineteenth century. In July 1890, when the Abbé Andrieu visited the sanctuary of Saint Ours, he was told that a child had been brought to life there a fortnight earlier. 'Trustworthy people assured me that the still-born child had his arms folded on his chest and that, suddenly, he stretched them out along his body.' Signs of life could be less dramatic. In 1825, a still-born child was baptized because some drops of blood which appeared unnaturally on her were taken to indicate revivication. In 1850, a still-born child moved his tongue to the edge of his lips and gained colour in the sight of his parents and the Mother Superior of a local convent, and was forthwith baptized.[82] It was believed that at certain sanctuaries, Our Lady might grant this favour, when solicited according to an established ritual.

Since parents who observed this practice were likely to be moved by an intense wish to have their prayer answered, and as tradition led them to expect imperceptible rather than dramatic resuscitations, it is not surprising that their most trivial impression or the slightest apparent twitch from the child might be interpreted as the sign of life for which all were hoping.[83] In May 1863, a little girl born at Passy died before she could be baptized. Her father and two neighbours carried her to the chapel of Notre Dame de Mont Provent at Châtillon-sur-Chises (Haute-Savoie), where a child had been brought to life briefly in 1820. On their way, they stopped at the chapel of Notre Dame des Grâces, to warn the Virgin about the miracle for which they were going to ask and to invoke her protection. On arrival, they put the child on the steps of the altar, lit two candles, and as one woman held a phial of holy water with which to baptize the infant, they began to pray. After half an hour, 'colour came back into the little girl's cheeks, a little foam came out of her mouth, and she shook her head several times'. She was baptized and expired on the spot. 'At that very moment, a phenomenon happened which impressed the witnesses deeply, the two half-burnt candles suddenly went out, of their own accord.'[84] This account of the miracle was given mainly by the father, with the help of the *curé*. It is striking that although the story was supposed to illustrate an exceptional, prodigious phenomenon, the merciful suspension of the natural order by divine power, the event, as it was described, in fact followed a regular, rather conventional pattern. The shrine, the rite and prayers, the reactions, were all prescribed; even the mention of the extinguished candles, symbol of death, followed a literary and liturgical convention (popular hagiographies frequently alluded to nature's participation in prodigies, in conformity with socially recognized symbolism, so that their significance should not elude the obtuse multitude). As for the central event, the child's recovery, that too resembled earlier miracles: no dramatic or unusual demonstration of life, but a conventional manifestation – minimal movement, return of colour. It is beside the point to observe that these signs lend themselves to naturalistic interpretations. What is more interesting is the form taken by the parents' grief – sadness on account of the loss of the child being translated into fear that it will never get into heaven – and the elaborate ritual followed to assuage it. The pilgrimage, followed at least in some cases by the miracle, sign of God's mercy and favour, testified to the parents' own ultimate justification and consolation as well as to their present good fortune. After the miracle, the parents would be at the centre of much local gossip, fuss and congratulation, which – along with the belief that the child was now in happier realms – did not so much compensate them for their misfortune as turn it into an unassailable triumph over suffering. Belief in this kind of miracle was all the less extravagant, in that not only was no astounding natual phenomenon needed to constitute it, but it could also transform grief, inasmuch as suffering provokes a sense of its own pointlessness. In cases of excessive grief, belief in the possibility of miracles could rescue men from a sense of being hopelessly overwhelmed by misfortune.

Another reaction to the strains and demands of poverty seems to have been to withdraw from normal life altogether. Such was the response of the fantasists whose sudden cures, or re-integration into society, were apt to be described as miraculous. Contrary to what was once thought, country people were no more exempt from neuroses engendered by pressure than were city-dwellers. The few doctors who before the Great War devoted their attention to the mental health of their poor rural patients noted the prevalence of nervous disorders among them. Dr Réné Belbèze, whose study of the subject was based on eight years of observation in a rural community in Tarn-et-Garonne, estimated that about 30 per cent of the local country people suffered from a more or less pronounced form of depression. The illness reflected the sufferer's inability to adapt to his surroundings and was caused by poverty, overwork and fear. Deprivation engendered permanent depression and discontent, as well as a feeling of social inferiority and a sense of the futility of effort. The anxiety of Belbèze's rural clients was typified by a fear of responsibility that was rooted, in the doctor's opinion, in 'the ever-present fear of the "master" who will demand an account of what has been done, of the terrestrial "Lord" and even of the heavenly "Lord"'.[85] Dr Terrien specifically devoted himself to the study of hysteria among the peasantry of the Vendée. Psychosomatic disorders, resulting in particular in motor malfunctioning, were, he affirmed, common. Like his colleague Boismoreau, he felt that alcohol, poor hygiene and superstition, as well as intermarriage, were important factors in causing this form of illness. He adduced evidence of its mimetic nature. When he fixed a hollow splint on the leg of a young girl from Saint-Fulgent who was suffering from coxalgia, six of her companions began to develop similar symptoms and arrived limping in his surgery, announcing their fear of suffering from the same disability as their friend. Psychotherapy cured them, announced Terrien without specifying what he meant. Similarly, a thirty-five-year-old farmer began to become preoccupied with his elderly neighbour's paralysis. 'One day,' he explained, 'I felt a weakness in my legs. Was it fatigue? Was it something else? I don't know. But I got the notion that I had been stricken by the same illness as my neighbour; the idea sank into my mind, I thought about it constantly, I was afraid, the more I studied my legs, the more certain I became that they were becoming paralysed. I could no longer sleep at night with worry. After about a fortnight, I could no longer stand. Soon I found it impossible to pick myself up when I fell.' He was finally reduced to crawling out on all fours to supervize the labourers in the field.[86]

Not surprisingly, people describing such behaviour – especially when it ceased as strangely as it began – found difficulty in explaining it. Hysterics and neurotics were not, traditionally, thought to be responsible or to have any control over their state, but they could allege a variety of socially acceptable explanations. The most common was to suppose that a jealous neighbour had cast a spell on the sufferer: to discover the offender, it was merely necessary to examine one's relations with one's associates and remember who had shown signs of anger or resentment in recent weeks. This was a comfortable solution, in that the afflicted did not have to feel guilty, but could in good faith blame someone else for his distemper. Indeed, the belief that some people could hurt others by casting a spell on them encouraged the predisposed to develop appropriate symptoms. When a farmer's wife, who had stayed in bed for five years and whom the doctors had given up as a hopeless case, suddenly rose from her couch and quickly regained her former health under circumstances which Boismoreau unfortunately does not relate, local opinion diagnosed a spell.[87] This case was not unprecedented: there are scattered references to farmers' wives and female farm servants (whose lot was notoriously demanding) retiring to bed for prolonged periods, following the malediction of an unpleasant neighbour or beggar, or sometimes for no obvious reason, and suffering from symptoms which refused to yield to treatment until suddenly some healer wrought the desired result.[88]

It is evident that many miracles which occurred at shrines involved people who suffered from what we would now recognize to be nervous disorders, or from illnesses which were determined by the sufferer's state of mind. Charcot was the first established doctor to draw attention to the phenomenon of hysterical paralyses. These, he contended, were usually caused by a traumatic experience and were subject to sudden cures – being analogous in this to the miracles recorded at historic shrines. One of the first cases of this kind which he analysed concerned a young woman from Basses-Pyrénées, whose partial paralysis and blindness he ascribed to the fact that she had been raped. He also explored the syndrome with the aid of hypnosis: through this, he found that he was able to persuade a young hysterical girl that her right arm was paralysed; to get rid of the contraction, he hypnotized her a second time and made the opposite suggestion.[89] In these experiments, Charcot popularized a new and successful method in modern psychiatry, a method which in many ways resembled traditional techniques, in that it furnished the neurotic with a framework in which to act out his illness and cure. Bernheim, Liébault's disciple in Nancy, was even more preoccupied than Charcot with the therapeutic potential of hypnosis when applied to nervous disorders. He described several cases of hysterical aphonia and paralysis which were cured by suggestion. Twenty-one-year-old Pauline B., who worked as a file-sharpener, consulted Bernheim early in September 1884 for pains in her right leg which made it impossible for her to walk. This woman, whose marriage had been marked by her husband's violence and drunkenness and by consequent sickness, seems to have developed the symptoms of paralysis in reaction to the strains and difficulties of her life. Indeed, hysteria may have been commoner among women than among men because it was a kind of retreat, a form of escapism accessible to the vulnerable. Again, Bernheim found that suggestion was able to cure the woman. This procedure was quite simple. In the case of a woman who refused to work or walk because of pains in her legs, Bernheim hypnotized her: 'I said to her: "You are healed; you are at home. Get up, do your housework. Work since you are cured!" and indeed, she got up and walked very well, took a broom that was brought to her, swept and made no more complaints. When she woke, she walked very well.'[90] The quasi-Biblical affirmations, the magical manoeuvring through which the doctor assumed control of the patient, the game in which both healer and patient participated, resembled the rites of the sorcerer and traditional healer with their mixture of imposing mystery and authoritarian gesture – and, like them, appealed to the same psychological impulses. The parallel did not escape contemporary doctors who were quick to observe that miracles usually involved hysterics, who were cured by suggestion.

Modern historical research seems to confirm this contention. Sigal, in his analysis of the 102 miracles which occurred at the shrine of Saint Gobrien at Rheims between 16 April and 24 August 1165, noted that 50 per cent concerned disorders of the nervous system, and more exactly, paralysis. 75 of the 185 miracles attributed to Saint Martin involved paralytics, according to Gregory of Tours. At Argenteuil in 1674, 21 out of 43 miracles also concerned people suffering from paralysis. This kind of proportion was not the invariable rule however, as Sigal shows. He instances the file on the canonization of the cardinal of Luxembourg at the end of the fourteenth century in Avignon, where only eleven cases of paralysis were mentioned among the 145 cures obtained.[91] Dr Diday, in his examination of the miracles of Lourdes, affirmed that nervous illnesses were those which yielded most frequently to the miraculous waters. According to one of the doctors employed by the episcopal commission, the diseases most commonly cured were headaches, weakening

1. The Wandering Jew (ATP)

SAINTE GENEVIEVE DE BRABANT.

CANTIQUE
DE SAINTE GENEVIEVE.

Sur l'air : *Que devant.*

APPROCHEZ-VOUS, honorable assistance, pour entendre réciter en ce lieu, l'innocence reconnue et patience de Geneviève ; très-aimée de Dieu ; étant comtesse de grande noblesse, née de Brabant étoit assurément.

Geneviève fut nommée au baptême ; ses père et mère l'aimaient tendrement ; sa solitude prenait d'elle même, donnant son cœur au Sauveur tout-puissant ; un grand comte fit qu'à la suite, dès dix-huit ans, fut mariée richement.

En peu de temps s'éleva grande guerre ; son mari seigneur du Palatinat, fut obligé pour son honneur et gloire, de quitter la Comtesse en cet état, étant enceinte, d'un mois sans feinte, fait ses adieux, ayant les larmes aux yeux.

Il a laissé son aimable Comtesse, entre les mains d'un méchant intendant, qui la voulut séduire par finesse, et l'honneur lui ravir subitement ; mais cette dame, pleine de charme, n'y voulut consentir aucunement.

Ce malheureux accusa sa maîtresse d'avoir péché avec son écuyer ; le serviteur fit mourir par adresse, et la Comtesse fit emprisonner ; chose assurée est accouchée, dans la prison d'un beau petit garçon.

Le temps fini de toutes ces grandes guerres, ce seigneur s'en revint en son pays ; Golo s'en fut au-devant de son maître, jusqu'à Strasbourg accomplir son dessein ; ce [illegible] lui fit accroire qu'un adultère sa femme avait commis.

Etant troublé de chagrin dans son âme, il chargea Golo ce tyran, d'aller au plutôt faire mourir sa femme et massacrer son petit innocent ; ce méchant traître, quittant son maître, va d'un grand cœur exercer sa fureur.

Ce bourreau à Geneviève si tendre, la dépouilla de ses habillemens, de vieux haillons lui fit vêtir et prendre par deux valets forts des et très-puissans, l'ont amenée, bien désolée, dans la forêt avec son cher enfant.

Geneviève, approchant du supplice, dit à ses deux valets, tout en pleurant ; si vous voulez me rendre un grand service ; faites-moi mourir avant mon cher enfant, et, sans remise, je suis soumise à votre volonté présentement.

La régardant, l'un dit : qu'allons nous faire ? Quoi ! un massacre ! je n'en ferai rien, faire mourir notre aimable maîtresse ! peut-être un jour nous fera-t-elle du bien. Sauvez-vous, dame, pleine de charme, dans ces forêts qu'on ne vous voie jamais.

Golo qui a fait grâce à sa maîtresse, dit, je sais bien comment tromper Golo ; la langue d'un chien nous faut par finesse, et la porter à ce cruel bourreau ce traître infâme, dedans son âme, dira, c'est celle de Geneviève au tombeau.

Au fond d'un bois dedans une carrière, Geneviève demeura pauvrement, étant sans pain, sans feu et sans lumière, ni compagnie que de son cher enfant ; mais l'assistance, c'est le bon Dieu qui la garde en tout lieu.

Elle fut visitée d'une pauvre biche, qui tous les jours allaitait son enfant, et tous les oiseaux chantent et la réjouissent, l'accoutumant à leur aimable chant : les bêtes farouches près d'elle se couchent, la divertissent elle et son cher enfant.

Voilà son mari qui est en grande peine, dans son château consolé par Golo ; ce n'est que jeux, que festins qu'on lui mène ; mais tous ces plaisirs sont mal-à-propos : car dans son âme, sa chère dame, pleure sans fin avec un grand chagrin.

Jésus-Christ a découvert l'innocence de Geneviève, par sa grande bonté, chassant dans la forêt en diligence, le Comte des chasseurs s'est écarté, après la biche qui est nourrice de son enfant qu'elle allaitait souvent.

La pauvre biche s'enfuit au plus vîte dedans la grotte auprès de l'innocent, le Comte aussitôt faisant sa poursuite, pour la tirer de ce lieu promptement, vit la figure d'une créature qui était nue auprès de son enfant.

Apercevant dedans ce lieu obscur, une femme couverte de cheveux, lui demanda ; qui êtes-vous, créature, que faites-vous dans ce lieu ténébreux ? ma chère amie, je vous prie, dites-moi donc s'il vous plaît votre nom.

Geneviève, est mon nom d'assurance, née du Brabant où sont tous mes parens ; un grand seigneur m'épousa sans doutance, dans son pays m'emmena promptement : je suis Comtesse de grande noblesse ; mais mon mari fait de moi grand mépris.

Il m'a laissée, étant d'un mois enceinte, entre les mains d'un méchant intendant, qui a voulu me séduire par contrainte, et me faire mourir semblablement ; de rage félonne dit à deux hommes de me tuer moi et mon cher enfant.

Le Comte ému, reconnaissant sa femme, dedans ce lieu la regarde en pleurant : quoi ! est-ce vous, Geneviève, ma chère dame, que je pleure il y a si long-temps ; mon Dieu, quelle grâce, dans cette place, de rencontrer ma chère bien aimée.

Ah ! que de joie au son de la trompette, voici venir la chasse et les chasseurs, qui reconnurent le Comte, je protestes à ses côtés sa femme aussi son cœur ; l'enfant ; la biche, les chiens chérissent, les serviteurs rendent grâce au Seigneur.

Tous les oiseaux et les bêtes sauvages regrettent Geneviève par leur chant, pleurent et gémissent par leur doux ramage, en chantant tous d'un ton fort languissant, pleurant la perte et la retraite de Geneviève et de son cher enfant.

Ce grand seigneur pour punir l'insolence et la perfidie du traître Golo, le fit juger par une sentence, d'être écorché vif par un bourreau ; à la voirie, l'on certifie que son corps fut jeté par morceaux.

Fort peu de temps notre illustre princesse resta vivante avec son cher mari ; malgré les chères et les tendres caresses, elle ne gémissait qu'au Sauveur Jésus-Christ ; dans sa chère âme, remplie de flamme, elle priait Dieu tant le jour que la nuit.

Elle ne pouvait manger que des racines, dont elle s'était nourrie dedans le bois ; ce qui fait que son mari se chagrine, offrant toujours des vœux au Roi des Rois, qui s'intéresse, de sa princesse qui suivait si austèrement toutes ses lois.

Puissant seigneur, par amour je vous prie, et puisqu'aujourd'hui il nous faut quitter, que mon cher fils, ma douce compagnie, tienne toujours place à votre côté : que la souffrance de son enfance ; fasse preuve de ma fidelité.

Geneviève à ce moment rendit l'âme au Roi des Rois, notre Dieu tout-puissant ; Béni de tout son cœur et son âme, poussait des cris terribles et languissant, se jetait par terre lui et son père, se lamentant, pleurant amèrement.

Du ciel alors sortit une lumière, comme un rayon d'un soleil tout nouveau, dont la clarté dura la nuit entière ; rien n'a paru au monde de plus beau ; les pauvres et les riches, jusqu'à la biche, tout suit Geneviève au tombeau.

Pour conserver à jamais l'innocence de Geneviève accusée par Golo, la pauvre biche veut par ses souffrances, le prouver par un miracle nouveau, puisqu'elle est morte, quoiqu'on lui porte, sans boire ni manger sur le tombeau. FIN

EPINAL, chez PELLERIN, Imprimeur-Libraire

SAINT JACQUES DE COMPOSTELLE.

LA GRANDE CHANSON DES PELERINS DE SAINT JACQUES.

QUAND nous partîmes de la France,
Au grand deuir,
Nous avions quitté père & mère,
Tristes & marris:
Au cœur avions si grand désir
D'aller à saint Jacques.
Avons quitté tous nos plaisirs
Pour faire ce voyage.

Nous prions la vierge Marie,
Son fils Jesus,
Qu'il lui plaise donner sa sainte grâce,
Qu'en paradis nous puissions voir
Dieu & monsieur S. Jacques.

Quand nous fûmes dans la Saintonge,
Hélas! mon Dieu,
Nous ne trouvâmes point d'eglise
Pour prier Dieu:
Les Huguenots les ont rompues
Par grand'malice,
C'est en méprisant Jesus Christ
Et la vierge Marie.
Nous prions, &c.

Quand nous fûmes au port de Blaye,
Près de Bordeaux,
Nous entrâmes dedans le barque
Pour passer l'eau:
Il y a bien sept lieues par eau,
Bonnes me semble;
Marinier, passe promptement,
De peur de la tourmente.
Nous prions, &c.

Quand nous fûmes dedans les Landes,
Bien étonnés,
Nous avions l'eau jusqu'à mi-jambe,
De tous côtés:
Compagnons, nous faut cheminer
En grand journée,
Pour nous tirer de ce pays,
De si grande rosée.
Nous prions, &c.

Quand nous fûmes dedans Bayonne,
Loin du pays,
Changer nous fallut nos couronnes
Et nos louis,
Afin de passer par ce pays
De la Biscaye;
C'est un pays rude à passer,
Qui n'entend le langage.
Nous prions, &c.

Quand nous fûmes à Sainte-Marie,
Hélas! mon Dieu,
Je regretais la noble France
De tout mon cœur,
Et de tout mon plus grand désir
D'être auprès d'elle,
Aussi de tous mes bons amis,
Dont je suis à mal aise.
Nous prions, &c.

Quand nous fûmes à la montagne
Saint-Adrian,
Au cœur me vint une pensée
De mes parens:
Car quand ce vint au départir
De notre ville,
Sans dire adieu à nos amis,
Fîmes à notre guise.
Nous prions, &c.

Entre le peuple de victoire
Fûmes joyeux
De voir sortir de ces montagnes
Si grande odeur:
De voir le romarin fleuri,
Thim & lavande,
Rendîmes grâces à Jesus-Christ,
Lui chantâmes louange.
Nous prions, &c.

Quand nous fûmes à Saint Dominique,
Hélas! mon Dieu,
Nous entrâmes dedans l'église
Pour prier Dieu;
Les Augustins nous ont montré
Un grand miracle,
De voir le Crucifix suer,
C'est chose véritable.
Nous prions, &c.

Quand nous fûmes dedans la ville
Nommée Sion,
Ici chantâmes tous ensemble
Une chanson:
Les dames sortaient de leurs maisons
En abondance,
Pour voir chanter les Pélerins,
Les enfans de la France.
Nous prions, &c.

Quand nous fûmes hors la ville
Nommée Saint-Marc,
Nous nous assîmes tous ensemble
Près d'une croix,
Où il y a un chemin à droite
Et l'autre à gauche,
L'un conduit à St-Salvador
L'autre à M. St. Jacques.
Nous prions, &c.

Quand nous fûmes au mont Etuve,
Eûmes grand froid,
Et avions si grande froidure
Que nous tremblions:
A St-Salvador sommes allés
Par notre adresse,
Les religieux nous ont montré
Dont nous avons la lettre.
Nous prions, &c.

Quand nous fûmes au pont qui tremble,
Gens étonnés,
A nous voir entre deux montagnes
Si oppressés,
Et sous les ondes de la mer
En grande tourmente,
Compagnons, nous faut cheminer,
Tous saisis d'épouvante.
Nous prions, &c.

Quand nous fûmes dans la Galice,
A Rive-Dieux,
On voulait nous mettre en galère,
Jeunes & vieux;
Mais nous nous sommes défendus
De notre langue,
Avons dit qu'étions Espagnols,
Et nous étions de France.
Nous prions, &c.

Quand nous fûmes à la Monjoye,
Fûmes joyeux
De voir une si belle église
Dedans ce lieu,
Du glorieux ami de Dieu,
Monsieur saint Jacques,
Qui nous a tous bien préservés
En faisant ce voyage.
Nous prions, etc.

Quand enfin nous fûmes à saint Jacques,
Hélas! mon Dieu,
Nous entrâmes dedans l'église
Pour prier Dieu,
Aussi du glorieux martyr
Monsieur saint Jacques,
Qu'au pays puissions retourner,
Et faire ce voyage.

Nous prions la vierge Marie
Son fils Jesus,
Qu'il lui plaise donner sa sainte grâce,
Qu'en paradis nous puissions voir
Dieu & monsieur S. Jacques.

FIN.

A Toulouse, chez L. ABADIE cadet, et Comp.e fabricant de papier à tapisserie, rue du Taur, 8.e section, n.° 16.

3. Saint James of Compostella (ATP)

2 (*facing*). Saint Geneviève de Brabant (ATP)

4 (*overpage*). Extract from the *Almanach des Bergers pour l'année bissextile 1892* (ATP)

ALMANACH
DES
BERGERS
Pour l'année bissextile 1892
Par MELCHIOR GRIEFFER, Astrologue.

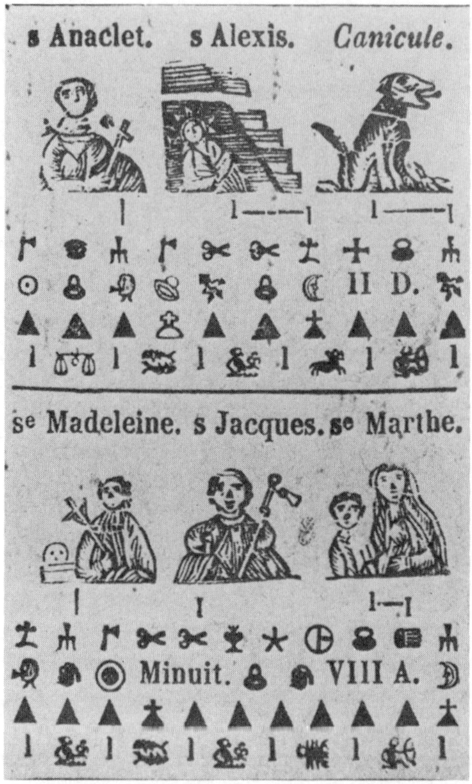
s Anaclet. s Alexis. *Canicule.*
II D.
se Madeleine. s Jacques. se Marthe.
Minuit.
VIII A.

L'ASTROLOGUE.
Je suis le Maître Spectateur
Du temps et de son bonheur.

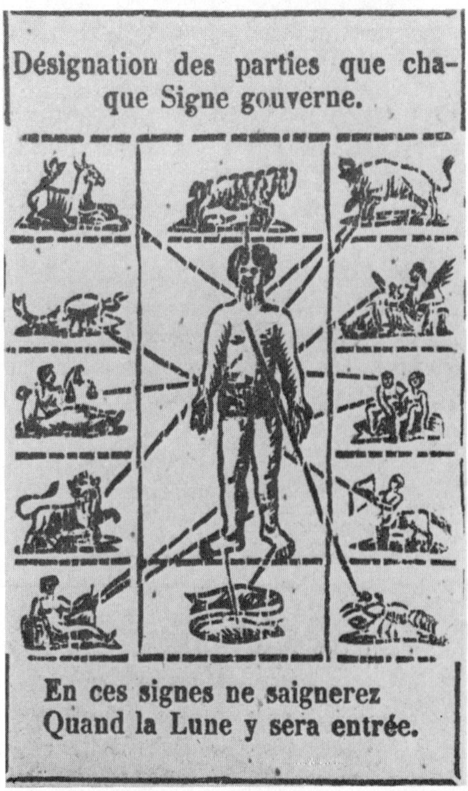
Désignation des parties que chaque Signe gouverne.
En ces signes ne saignerez
Quand la Lune y sera entrée.

eyesight, general or partial paralysis and general or partial debility. In the second category came organic lesions, where cures were less rapid. Diday himself found cases of paralysis slightly more common than muscular contractions and amauroses (gradual loss of eyesight without there being any apparent lesion), all of which – with one exception – were cured instantaneously. Other complaints (ophthalmia, ulcers, fever, eczema) were less common, and healing less rapid. He cited the case of a child suffering from coxalgia (a gradual inability to walk and refusal of food) which was cured at Lourdes and acclaimed as a miracle; this he compared with a similar case observed at Lyon, where the child recovered when threatened with an application of red-hot irons.[92]

Miraculous cures in modern shrines like Lourdes often involved temporary paralyses of this kind. A dramatic early case, which typified this kind of miracle, was presented by a Madame Rizan, a sixty-year-old widow, who had suffered from general weakness and partial paralysis since catching cholera in the epidemic of 1834. In 1858, she has spent the better part of the year in bed, and in the autumn she was thought to be dying. The left side of her body was entirely paralysed and she was too weak to move. On 17 October, she was given, as was her wish, a bottle of Lourdes water. As her confessor, the Abbé André Dupont related:

> ... After having said her rosary devoutly, she drank of this water and had the afflicted parts of her body bathed with it. She was cured before ten minutes had passed. She got up, dressed and walked about without any support. Everyone came running up at the rumour of this sudden cure and wanted to see her, touch her and speak to her. All left the place praising God and convinced that the water from the miraculous spring of Lourdes had wrought this cure.[93]

Madame Rizan's case had all the elements of a classic miracle – prolonged suffering followed by a dramatic cure, apparently inexplicable in natural terms but carefully prepared by a prescribed ritual of hope and prayer. There were dozens of similar incidents. In 1899, a postal sorter, Gabriel Gargam, had been paralysed from the waist down and was unable to eat normally as the result of an accident. The railway company involved had paid him enormous sums in compensation. Despite his lack of religious faith, Gargam went on a pilgrimage to Lourdes. He observed the rite which this involved, by going to confession and communion (for the first time in fifteen years) in the grotto. At the blessing of the sick, he was helped to sit up; as the bishop blessed him, Gargam exclaimed: 'I am cured', stood up and followed the bishop.[94] Paralyses, contractions and disabilities of traumatic origin seem to have accounted for many of the miracles recorded at Lourdes. A sixteen-year-old farmhand caught typhus. A week after her recovery, she began to feel weak and paraplegia set in. The girl, sure that the Virgin Mary would cure her, repaired to Lourdes, where she was able to emerge unaided from the miraculous baths and declared herself to be fully restored. A girl of twenty-one suffered from anorexia and aphonia, and became unable to walk. She coughed up blood and her doctor decided that she was suffering from tuberculosis. She asked to be sent to Lourdes, and her subsequent sudden recovery was hailed as a miracle on her return to Saint Cécile.[95]

Lourdes rapidly became the most famous shrine in France, and the number of marvellous cures that took place there, as well as the enthusiasm with which they were greeted, belie the assumption that reason was supplanting or had supplanted superstition in the minds of ordinary people in this period. Apart from the fifty-five instances in which divine intervention had been authenticated by the relevant clerical authorities, the *Annales de Notre Dame de Lourdes* recorded about six thousand cases where remarkable improvements had been observed, between 1858 and 1914.[96] Furthermore, Lourdes was not the only shrine at which miracles occurred: there remained all the old traditional centres, whose renown was gradually eclipsed by that of Lourdes. The bishop of Montauban wrote a letter on 24 November 1865 testifying to the sudden and supernatural cure, in the village of Castel-Sarrazin, of a woman who had been paralysed in the arms and legs for thirty-two years. According to the *Univers* of 12 September 1880, Madame Colombon, a widow from Avignon, had lost the use of her legs, tongue and reason following a serious illness two years earlier. A neighbour gave her a bottle of water from the miraculous fountain of Saint Gens, hermit of Le Bausset and one of the most popular saints of the area, who was invoked especially for the relief of fever and colic. Madame Colombon took three mouthfuls of the water and was, with each mouthful, relieved one by one of each of her infirmities. The mayor of the commune of Perruel (Eure) claimed, on 10 June 1866, that a miracle at Saint Clothilde's spring – which had a long tradition of marvellous healing – had enabled a woman to walk again. At the sanctuary of Notre-Dame-de-Pitié, at Bray, on 8 September 1802, Amélie Gibierge of Chemilly suddenly recovered the use of a paralysed leg.[97] It would seem likely, despite the fragmentary evidence, that the illnesses cited here were caused by some psychological disturbance such as hysteria.

Newer shrines such as La Salette also knew a temporary vogue. One of the first miracles to be proclaimed there concerned Victorine Sauvet, a twenty-year-old servant from Lalley, who was working in Marseille. Shortly after learning, to her great distress, of the death of some of her relatives, she suddenly went blind. A doctor who examined her could find no reason for this and believed that, correctly treated, she would recover. Victorine, however, devoted herself to prayers and thoughts of novenas at appropriate shrines. She was allowed to return home to her family, whence she went to La Salette, where a novena had been said for her at her request. On her arrival there, she recovered her sight.[98] Again, the recovery is perfectly explicable in natural terms.

What is arresting, however, is people's thirst for unnatural explanations – or more exactly, for the exceptional – and the general excitement with which miracles were greeted. What accounts for the continued appeal of shrines and the prestige still enjoyed by miracles, in an age characterized by the extension to the countryside of the benefits of scientific culture in the form of education, medicine, improved communications and agricultural techniques? Thomas Kselman has suggested that the very advent of modernism provoked a spiritual crisis among the peasantry of nineteenth-century France, which was expressed in the millenarian religiosity of Lourdes.[99] However, there is little evidence to sustain the contention that the response to Lourdes was a reaction to the strains of modern scientific culture, rather than a concentration of once diversified religiosity on a well-marketed and accessible shrine. One explanation for the vogue for miracles might be that they were interesting, a welcome break from the monotony of life in remote, patriarchal communities. They also vindicated the humble sufferer, giving him a prestige and importance he would not normally have enjoyed. Another reason would seem to be the unique relief and legitimation of feeling and behaviour which many forms of popular medicine – and in particular, miraculous cures – afforded the ill. The poor were subjected to greater stress than the wealthy, and had fewer sources of material consolation at their disposal. Pilgrimages, healers and sorcerers were available, however, and these furnished a valuable pretext for the expression of feelings and ideas – anxiety, lassitude, anger and rebelliousness – whose acknowledgement would normally have been considered reprehensible or which would otherwise have remained inarticulate. Popular medicine – which allowed for self-deception and, in an intolerant society, for self-indulgence, which did not hold people responsible for their aberrant behaviour and ideas – anticipated modern confessional psychiatry, which was perhaps more indebted to it than is realized.

III

Apparitions and Prodigies

One of the most arresting features of pre-modern popular culture is its penchant for presages, extraordinary visions and creatures. How can one explain this? The first characteristic of traditional visions is that they were far from being as idiosyncratic and haphazard as they seemed. Contemporary doctors, studying hallucinations, stressed their fantastic quality, and believed this to be true of folklore also. However, both the place and the timing of traditional apparitions, as well as their general nature, were often predictable. Faure wrote that 'demons don't appear just anywhere. Mystical experiences don't happen just anywhere. They require not only appropriate rites but also appropriate sites.'[1] Despite the comparative informality of traditional French rural culture in the nineteenth century, fantastic apparitions and events tended to be located in places set apart, isolated from everyday life, as Nicole Belmont has pointed out.[2]

The tendency to differentiate between natural settings in this way not only reflects man's vulnerability in a hostile environment but also points to the cultural complexity of visions. To describe their aberrant experiences, men could draw on an enormous repertoire of legendary creatures and phenomena, all of which had their specific properties and haunts. As there was nothing demeaning about encounters with legendary beings – quite the contrary, in some cases – people readily described their interesting visions. Indeed, they could also justify their opinions and actions by claiming to have witnessed an extraordinary event, which might excuse their behaviour or lend weight to their allegations. As usual, the variety of uses of folklore – description, diversion, deceipt – ensured the proliferation of stories which drew on it.

Werewolves and Monsters

It was believed, in many parts of France, that sorcerers could turn themselves into animals and that under that guise they roamed the countryside at night. It was not unusual to claim to have encountered a werewolf (a sorcerer disguised as a wolf) or some other magical or legendary beast.

The sorcerer was thought to be impelled to become a werewolf. In order to do so, however, he had first to acquire the skin, which, when donned, would enable him to transform himself into a wolf. To this end, he was believed in Gascony to go to a crossroads at midnight, spread a sheet on the ground and return at dawn to collect the devil's tribute. Once equipped with his skin, the sorcerer would journey forth at night, to curl up in ditches and under trees, waiting for children to feast off and passers-by to frighten. If the traveller were not intimidated by the werewolf and said, 'take off your skin', the sorcerer was obliged to become human. Equal combat then ensued: if the werewolf won, he gained his liberty and relinquished the skin for ever, the loser then being obliged to assume it.[3] Other legends held that one could become a werewolf merely by picking the skin up off the road: one was then obliged to lie in wait at night for travellers in the hope of provoking a fight, for if the wolf's blood flowed, the charm was broken.[4]

What sustained such beliefs? On the one hand, legends of this kind often identified the werewolf, and therefore furnished a means of slandering a neighbour with whom one was on poor terms.[5] But the readiness to believe that malevolent creatures lurked beyond the confines of the village seems to have been common, and was expressed in a rich bestiary of fabulous animals. It reflected not only people's appreciation of the dangers of their environment and their ignorance of nature, but also a tendency to exaggerate the fearful – both to divert and to admonish listeners.

It is also possible to see in these legends a peculiar account of a form of mental illness. Some legends described the werewolf's antics as a form of compulsive behaviour. At the start of the nineteenth century, overpowering impulses were seen as a characteristic of monomania. Only towards the end of the century were obsessions studied as separate entities. Psychiatrists nonetheless chronicled delusions which bore some similarity to the phenomenon of which so many legends purported to tell. Sentoux reported the case of a man who thought he had turned into a bull, in punishment for his sins. '... If he refrained from grazing, it was from self-respect, because he thought that his friends and family had not noticed his metamorphosis... At the sight of a meadow, he felt a desire, a need, a hunger of the most intense variety, and, had he dared, he would have eaten with rapture.'[6] Calmeil even devoted a long article in the *Dictionnaire Encyclopédique des Sciences Médicales* of 1870 to lycanthropy. He distinguished three main forms which the affliction could take: some sufferers were depressed and misanthropic, letting their hair and nails grow, wailing that they were possessed by the devil, sleeping little, sometimes crawling and attacking those who approached them; they would claim to have spent the night on the rampage, perpetrating various acts of cruelty – murder, disinterment of corpses – sometimes in the company of a pack of wolves. Others, who had similar ideas, were very agitated and excited; they sometimes ran away from their homes and wandered around fields at night, sleeping in haystacks when morning came. Finally, there were really violent lycanthropes, who tried to behave like wolves; at night, incapable of resisting their impulses, they attacked animals, children and even adults, and crawled around their commune howling. To substantiate his analysis, Calmeil cited a number of cases, drawn from the sixteenth and seventeenth centuries. The illness could have been provoked, he thought, by poisoning, and was to be observed especially in remote, half-savage mountainous and afforested areas. Shepherds, wood-cutters and those who lived in extreme poverty and solitude were most disposed to develop such symptoms.[7]

More surprisingly, the annals of psychiatry even furnished two cases of lycanthropy dating from the early nineteenth century. Brierre de Boismont cited the case of a mason who, in the autumn of the Year XII,[7a] being obsessed by melancholy ideas and visions, ran away into lonely fields and places where he howled like a wolf, gobbled food up in an unnatural way, and tried to bite people. The crisis resolved itself on the eighteenth day, observed the doctor phlegmatically, with a violent fever.[8] In 1824 another, more gruesome example came to light: the district court of Versailles, in that year, examined the case of a twenty-nine-year-old man called Antoine Léger. The previous year, he had left his father's house in preference for a wood where, after a week of wandering, he installed himself like an animal in a cave. A little girl came upon him there and, believing himself to be a wolf, he killed and devoured her.[9] Apart from the mentally disturbed, other human inhabitants of forests likely to frighten people who encountered them were children who, having been abandoned by their parents, had become quite wild. A young girl, who was found in the area of Châlons-sur-Marne in 1731, had lived in the woods with another child whom she had killed; the famous 'wild man' studied by Itard was a boy who had lived for some years in the mountains and woods of Aveyron, before being captured at the approximate age of twelve in the Year VII.[10] Jean-Roch Coignet alleged that his step-mother, who had seven children of her own as well as six step-children, had rid herself of his little brother and sister by leaving them in a wood, where, after three days, they were rescued by a miller.[11] But cases such as these seem too exceptional to have had a profound impact upon the collective imagination or to have shaped its expression in a significant way.

Man's fear of his natural environment, and in particular of the wild animals which threatened him, seems likely to have impinged to a greater extent on both the conscious and unconscious workings of his mind. Wolves were still numerous in the remote countryside at the end of the eighteenth century and in the early nineteenth century. In January 1796, and again in 1798, they devastated part of Eure-et-Loir; in November 1799, the justice of the peace for the canton of Orgères noted that they were causing terror and panic everywhere. Over five thousand wolves were killed in 1797, according to an official estimate; in 1806, the corresponding figure had dropped to 1926. Travellers in this period commented on these dangers: Cambry observed of the commune of Locmaria, which was surrounded by forests, that its 'cattle were devoured daily by wolves . . . ', and in the canton of Cus, in the Oise, wolves caused considerable damage. Grégoire noted that they were still very common in the Vosges: in the Year VI (1798), he affirmed, 108 beasts were killed in Meurthe, and 150 in the department of Vosges. After the First Empire, wolves were so numerous that battues had to be organized to make some areas safe.[12] Tiennon Bertin remembers that, as children minding sheep, he and his sister spent much of their time worrying about the possible appearance of wolves which were supposed to roam the nearby forest. Even towards the end of the century, wolves still survived in parts of France: in the winter of 1890, wolves appeared in the commune in the Ambérac, in which young Léon Ganachaud lived: one snowy winter night, two wolves made off with the family dog, while two others took two sheep. After this the children were not allowed out in the evening on their own, and when his thirteen-year-old sister was dispatched to look after the sheep, their parents were afraid and told her keep away from the wood. The winter of 1870–71 was famous for its wolves, which prowled about farms looking for food in the bad weather. In the 1880s, wolves were still active in Sancerre, and were hunted in the Vosges, Brittany, Périgord and the two Charentes. Only by the end of the century was the problem resolved: whereas in 1883, 1316 wolves were killed in France, according to bounty figures, by 1900 the figure had dropped to 115.[13]

This threat seems to have registered in the popular imagination in two ways. Dangerous animals tended to assume fantastic dimensions, to be transformed into legendary creatures, the objects of horrid fascination (so long as they were remote) or of fear. The *Bête de Gévaudan* furnished a classic model of this process. One of the many prints representing the beast showed a creature more like a griffon than a wolf devouring a disinterred corpse near a peaceful rusticated village, and an intrepid huntsman firing on it.[14] The real animal had appeared near the little town of Langogne in June 1764 and by October its eleven victims included two men, as well as several children. It had killed a woman in her garden in the hamlet of Estrets, and it (or the band to which it belonged) went on to kill about fifty people before hunters managed to rid the area of the threat. Its immense renown was due partly to the work of printers and hawkers of broadsheets, and it quickly became legendary, not only because of the fear inspired by its great size and ferocity, but also because it fitted easily into a well-established imaginative tradition and could be seen as a realization of ill-defined and complex as well as conscious fears.[15]

The people of Lozère had been terrified by its appearance – indeed, they were not even sure that the animal was a wolf, as wolves usually attacked humans only surreptitiously and in winter. Various suggestions were made about its identity: some thought that it was a hyena escaped from the fair at Beaucaire; some held it to be a large monkey (an opinion backed up by a report that it had been seen fording a river on its hind legs, and wading like a human being); while others inclined to the view that it was the offspring of a bear and a wolf, which had made its way across from the Alps. Rumours multiplied: it became a monster, an apocalyptic beast created by God to punish the Gévaudan (an interpretation espoused by the bishop of Mende in his pastoral letter at Christmas in 1764). The local nobleman, M. de Labarthe, wrote to a friend: 'You would laugh to hear all they say about it: it takes tobacco, talks, becomes invisible, boasts in the evening about its exploits of the day, goes to the sabbath, does penance for its sins. Every man and woman has his own story about it.' Descriptions of the animal varied greatly and stories assimilating it to legendary horrors abounded. It was really a witch and was therefore invulnerable. Another tale credited the beast with witticisms – in the tradition of the medieval *fabliaux*. The day after it killed a fourteen-year-old boy at Mazel-de-Grèzes, it appeared at the window of his home, where preparations were being made for the funeral, to see what was happening inside; it disappeared when the father went to kill it. From this tale grew the belief that the curious animal looked through windows into houses to see what was going on. A boy who claimed to have wrestled with it said that its belly seemed to be buttoned up – from which people concluded that it was a werewolf (in a waistcoat). A woman going to mass, at a time when the wolf had been seen about, was accompanied by a hairy man who suddenly disappeared: the deduction that the beast was really a werewolf was lent much weight by this circumstance.[16]

The tendency to invest really dangerous animals with mythical attributes, which was evident in the stories told about the *Bête de Gévaudan*, marked the folklore of legendary animals. Peasants were sometimes apt to describe their encounters with unusually large or frightening animals in legendary terms. To move from affirming, as did one old man to Dr Ellensberger, that one had seen a serpent as big as a partridge to claiming more exotic meetings presented little apparent difficulty. In many villages, stories about enormous snakes which guarded treasures, were known: at Mauprévoir, shortly before the First World War, a group of schoolboys were frightened by what they thought was the *Serpent de la Garonne* of local lore; and in the same commune, a young woman said her father had seen the fantastic serpent of Chez-Monteau. In the area around Loudun and Richelieu (Indre-et-Loire), an often repeated story recounted how a young girl died of fright on seeing a basilisk that was supposed to haunt the neighbourhood and which the peasants of the locality thought was depicted on the capital of the church at Claunay. Another dragon was thought to figure in the carvings of the church of Saint Savin: this was the dragon that had once lived in the ruined castle of La Fraudière, near Rille, which according to legend had been killed by a soldier returning from the army. Ellensberger heard four old men talking about this story;

they maintained that, centuries earlier, the animal had been photographed and that its portrait was on view in the church. The peasants from the banks of Gartempe, on the other hand, thought that Saint Savin's dragon represented their own local monster, and one farmer admitted that every time he went to town he went to have a look at it.[17] The existence and persistence in legend, anecdote and art of mythical or fantastic animals, betrayed the fear which nature sometimes inspired.

At least some of these creatures served practical purposes – for example, discouraging children from wandering into dangerous areas. In the Ardennes forest lived an ogre, 'the red man', who in one legend tries to lure to their death two young girls who have lost their way crossing the forest. The *male bête*, like the wolf in Red Riding Hood, ate children who dallied in the woods collecting nuts, and his exploits usually resembled the real ravages of the wild boar or the wolf. In the Pyrenees, the 'wild man', a creature that was both hirsute and fleet of foot, lived off roots and milk stolen from shepherds. Bladé gave an account of how an old peasant claimed to have seen 'the green man' – a mythical being who guarded birds – as a child, once when with his father and again, when alone.[18] In some places, genii were held to inhabit the mountain peaks and to determine the weather; in Dauphiné, it was believed that invisible beings charmed travellers, giving them vertigo and causing them to fall to their death. The *vouivre*, a winged snake or dragon, which boasted a magical garnet instead of eyes, was supposed to live near or in fountains, and many stories were told about it in Franche-Comté and Bourgogne. Other legendary animals which might be encountered included the *bête havette* which was known in Brie for its long hooked teeth; the *bigourne*, which in Angoumois devoured indulgent husbands; the *birette* which decimated flocks of animals in Berry; the *bête farrigaude* in Hurepoix and the *farramine* in Picardy and the Beauce.[19]

These creatures could excite real fear, if one is to believe the testimony of George Sand. Around Nohant, where she grew up, legends abounded about a creature which was variously known as the white dog, *bête havette*, *bigorne*, *vache au diable*, and which in Berry was called the *grand' bête*. It was usually thought to resemble an enormous dog, although some women and children who claimed to have seen it said it had horns, eyes of fire and heterogeneous animal attributes. A group of children who had been stealing firewood thought they saw it as they came out of the forest, and affirmed that it looked like a bullock and a hare. When George Sand was about ten, she found herself detained at nightfall by a storm on a farm near her home which was supposed to be haunted, and where the *grand' bête* had been seen only the previous night. It was expected to reappear before dawn:

> I can still see the preparations for combat; men arming themselves with iron forks and sticks; the share-cropper taking his long single-barrelled gun down from over the fireplace and loading it with blessed bullets; his old mother . . .

> starting to pray with her daughters-in-law and her servants before a coloured picture of some general or other of the Empire who was taken by them to be a benign saint . . . And then the doors and windows were closed and the shutters bolted . . . We had to start listening for the beast's approach.

To the writer's disappointment, however, her tutor arrived, armed only with an umbrella.[20]

If stories about meetings with legendary animals perpetuated men's ignorance and fear of their natural environment and tended to discourage adventurous exploration of mountain-tops, deep woods and remote wildernesses, they also reflected a taste for frivolous diversion in the exotic and grotesque. News of monsters and prodigies often satisfied a need for escapism. Mountebacks had long exhibited strange animals and men whose dimensions or features were abnormal. Broadsheets exploited this interest in the strange, recounting with gusto the exploits of various rapacious beasts, of more or less legendary attributes.

In 1811, a broadsheet printed at Chartres represented the 'Figure de la Bête Féroce qui ravage les alentours d'Orléans' and showed a wolf covered in fish-scales and of enormous dimensions, chasing its prey through dwarved woods, having rather eccentrically neglected its previous victim, whose hat, hands and torso lie strewn on the earth in the background. The beast had killed a wood-cutter's wife near the village of Baugency, despite the efforts of her family to save her, as well as an incalculable number of other people. Furthermore, its scales rendered it invulnerable. The accompanying verse asked:

> Qui pourrait de sang froid
> Entrer dedans ces bois
> Sans une tristesse extrême,
> En voyant les débris
> De ses plus chers amis
> Ou de celle qu'il aime?
>
> (Who could be self-possessed
> Entering these woods
> And not greatly distressed,
> On seeing the scraps
> Of his dearest friends
> Or the girl he loves?)

It went on to express the hope that the Almighty would deliver them

> From the teeth
> Of this horrible monster
> And by his holy hand
> May he heal straight away
> All these poor victims.

Around 1819, in Dôle, Delavau published a picture of a 'terrible monster' which had ravaged the area around Dompierre, that became a classic print during the Restoration and July Monarchy.[21]

During the nineteenth century, the vogue for political and criminal news had gradually eclipsed the taste for extraordinary stories. The tales of the *Bête de Gévaudan*, of *Mérénas*, *Animal Amphibie* and *Dragons Volants* were reissued only for want of other material.[22] Nonetheless, they were printed with remarkable frequency. One broadsheet dealt with 'a new monster' which had been discovered in 1816 by a Cypriot pirate ship and brought home by an English merchantman. The beast was depicted as having two heads, four arms and, more prosaically, four legs.[23] The appearance of another extraordinary being, a 'marine monster', was recorded in a broadsheet reproduced by Garnier. It announced:

> On the 7 April 1810 a dreadful storm raged along the coast from Boulogne to Le Portée. The waves were such that they threw up on the sand an animal whose nature it was to live on land as easily as in water. This amphibious animal went into the village of Le Portée, where, trying to hide, it entered a fisherman's cabin and terrified him.

However, 'attracted by the smell of buried corpses', the discerning animal proceeded to the cemetery where it 'exerça des ravages'. These picturesque details were complemented by a dirge, which outdid the introductory narrative in outlandish and pathetic details. On arrival, the animal consumes four fishermen and, having dined off a mother and her four offspring, is killed while examining the gastronomic possibilities of the graveyard. A picture proclaiming 'Marine Monster' accompanied this items of news and showed a wolf-like beast, with nether regions covered in dragon scales and shaped like a halberd, eating a victim beside an open coffin and grave.[24]

Did people believe these prints? To judge by the reaction of Madame Bonnard, who was baptized in July 1690 and lived near Roanne, they were inclined to do so. In her commonplace book, she described at great length the portrait of a marine monster, which had been sent to her in early February 1794 by a friend in Roanne. This beast was even more extraordinary than those we have examined so far: it had a human face and wore a regal crown with crosses on it; its body was covered with standards, cannons, bombs, cannon-balls, barrels of gunpowder and various 'engines of war'; it had the front feet of an eagle, and the back feet of a bear. It was forty-eight feet long and eighteen feet wide, and had been found between Guernsey and Jersey (which the lady, who showed no lack of business acumen or shrewd sense in most of her diary, was able to locate accurately).[25] Not that the modern period lacked extraordinary creatures: the Amphibious Beast of Cette, which was first described in a broadsheet in 1817 (although it was – according to Séguin – modelled on a print published in Lyon in 1811), enjoyed great vogue. Luzel found a version of it, printed in Brest, which showed a dragon-like creature swallowing a man, whose minute legs alone remained visible. According to the broadsheet, the animal had arrived in Cette 'on 4 March last' on a stormy night, and had eaten 250 people (freshly buried or born) before being killed by a detachment of the army, stuffed and sent to the Department of Natural History in Paris.[26]

Monsters began to make their appearances in more exotic climes during the July Monarchy – possibly reflecting the somewhat greater safety of the physical environment in France – but interest in them appears not to have diminished to a significant extent. *Mérénas*, the Amphibious Animal and the marine monster of Algeria kept the tradition alive. According to broadsheets about the latter, French soldiers on guard at a palace on the coast of Algeria kept disappearing every night between eleven and twelve. 'Nothing more was found at their post but their rifles; the sentry box was knocked over. Hence, terror soon spread among the whole army.' Eventually, however, two soldiers saw the monster, which was amphibious, thirty feet long and fed only on the flesh of Frenchmen.[27]

As the century advanced, monsters became somewhat less discriminating, and more and more remote. In 1849 and 1851, Causserouge, in Bordeaux, published two pieces about a *Lion des Déserts d'Afrique*, which was half-fish, half-beast and which retired periodically to the sea, 'après s'être livré sur terre à de sanglantes razzias'. In 1848, a Parisian hawker sold the story (based on the seventeenth-century prototype) of 'the fish-man, who has just been landed at Cadiz'. An early approximate version of King Kong ('Shipwreck and distressing situation of a woman') met with extraordinary success; and in the 1850s and 1860s, sailors' struggles with Alaskan bears on icy coasts became popular.[28] Anything which extended the limits of the familiar world – with its monotony and poverty – appealed to people who could harbour no hope for a change in their destiny. The adaptation of legends to contemporary settings may be explained, to some extent, both by man's sense of vulnerability and by his need for diversion.

Hallucinations

What accounts, however, for the prevalence and popularity of tales about extraordinary visions? Obviously, men's physical environment impinged on their imagination. Forests, misty bogs and nights unilluminated by electricity were conducive to strange visions, and people interpreted their reactions to physical phenomena with an inherited vocabulary. Furthermore, the greater prevalence of illness and delirium meant that hallucinations were probably more common in the last century than now, and they furnished people with a range of disconcerting images which seemed to corroborate the authenticity of traditional beliefs. Part of the explanation for the interest people had in this area of experience and for the importance they attached to it is probably due to the fact that it was relatively common. Many tales of encounters with mythical beings were retrospective commentaries, which suggested that unsettling or unnerving experiences were disagreeable because one was dealing with evil. A person who claimed to have seen a will-o'-the-wisp was held to have encountered a potentially evil force, and the fear he felt was therefore justified. Sometimes, as though to emphasize the point, the threat which these visions posed was explicitly illustrated, and the experience assumed a legendary character.

Late one night, a man from the village of Courmont, in Franche-Comté, was returning home through an area noted for its will-o'-the-wisps. He saw one approach and then follow him to his cottage. 'He suffered nothing, and his house was also undamaged, but the next day he found his hens burnt and killed by the will-o'-the-wisp . . .'[29] Such rhetorical flourishes were commonly appended to stories of this kind. A tale told in 1880 to Carnoy by M. Guilbert from Englebelmer (Somme) included a similar addendum. One summer night, a man was returning home by moonlight. He heard something accompany him. At first he saw nothing, but after a time he was surrounded by a white beast, which whirled around him, undisturbed by his baton blows. When they finally arrived at the village, the animal turned into a man, but disappeared so quickly that the victim could not recognize him.[30] The fact that naturalistic explanations of such experiences readily present themselves to the modern reader is beside the point: for the challenge posed to traditional culture by man's experience of his environment was not simply a pragmatic or functional problem but a psychological one also. All societies require that its members should come to terms with their environment both practically and emotionally. The central problem in visionary experiences was psychological, and it was with this dimension that folklore attempted to cope. What was at issue was not so much an explanation of natural phenomena as an interpretation of the feelings elicited by nature. The man returning home at night was afraid and the story justified his emotions: what mattered was to be able to digest the experience, and this he was able to do by recounting it, describing his feelings in legendary terms, justifying his timidity by suggesting that he had encountred a criminal neighbour in disguise.

Illness, over-indulgence in alcohol and overwork might prompt frightening illusions or hallucinations, and tradition furnished an adequate vocabulary for expressing what one had experienced. An old woman from Béruges told how a farmer, returning at evening from a fair at Poitiers, saw horses dancing around in a clearing. He was so frightened that he rushed home and lay down with a high fever. Anatole Le Braz was told two stories about sightings of *l'Ankou*, or the personification of death in Breton legend. A young man who saw the *Ankou*'s cart one night died of fever two days later, according to a tale recounted in September 1890. In another, a poor day-labourer, coming home late at night after a long day's work and a *veillée* where wine had flowed freely, met the *Karrik an*

Ankou. He almost developed a fever as a result of this unpleasant encounter. The next day, he heard the death knell sounding for a wealthy farmer, near whose home he had seen the legendary cart. In the Deux-Sèvres, one legend concerned the ferocious 'red wolf'. At Villefort, Ellensberger met an old man who claimed to have seen it. He had been digging his potato field one hot day, and as he sat down for a moment to rest, he saw something red come towards him. He lay down and the beast – which had bright eyes, a ruffled coat and was foaming at the mouth – passed over him.[31] Another man appears to have interpreted a characteristic hallucination of an alcoholic by drawing on witchcraft beliefs. He was a tavern-keeper, and no sooner had he felt ill-disposed to grant twenty-six shillings credit to a sorcerer than he was attacked by rats which would have devoured him had he not told his customer to forget the debt.[32] One man even went as far as to accuse another in court of having cast a spell on him. In the commune of Chanceux, near Tours, the Avril family were believed to be sorcerers, and their young cousin Berthau, after consulting a sorcerer, attributed his persistent headache to a spell they had cast on him. He alleged, to support his accusation, that his acquaintance, Godeau, had also been bewitched by Avril. Godeau had visited the sorcerer and had found him reading a book. 'Would you be wanting to harm me?' Godeau asked. Avril replied: 'I'll play a trick on you.' On his way home, Godeau found the field near his home flooded with water, despite the fact that it was August and the weather was very dry. The water was so deep that he was unable to enter his home until dawn, when the flood disappeared.[33]

The reasons why this sort of story was considered by people like Berthau to be convincing are worth examining. Not only were they consecrated by tradition, but they accommodated a wide range of human experience and helped men to come to terms with it. This was as true of occasional aberrations and physical disorders as it was of mental illness. Around 1910, Anatole Le Braz heard the story of a Breton wood-cutter, who thought he had encountered the fairy Viviane. He had been poaching one night in the forest when he was seen by the gamekeepers and shot in the leg:

> He fell; and he prepared himself to be killed there and then, rather than give himself up, when, suddenly, a kind of very dense fog descended between him and his attackers, covering everything, earth, trees, guards and the wounded man himself. And he heard a voice coming from the fog, a soft voice like rustling leaves, whispering in his ear: 'Escape, my son, the spirit of Vivane will protect you until you have crawled out of the forest.'[34]

The circumstances and imagery – with its references to fog and rustling leaves – evoked in the story make it hard to escape the conclusion that the intrepid poacher lost consciousness after being shot. What is interesting about the tale, however, is how the poacher's experience was appreciated and rendered. The cosmological implications of belief in fairies has been of more interest to academics than it ever appears to have been to actual believers, who emphasized that belief was inspired by personal experience more than theory. Stories such as these described unusual experiences and the statements they made about the physical structure of the world were incidental to their purpose.

Thus, an old man – aged about eighty-eight in 1840 – from the parish of Arfeuilles (Allier) was subject to nocturnal hallucinations, which he and those around him took to be a legion of devils. The old parish priest, who described his affliction, assured the reader that the victim 'reasons well besides, is full of common sense, piety and virtue'.[35] Unlike his urban counterparts, the old man did not regard his visions as hallucinations: he had recourse to a notion in some ways akin to that of mental illness to explain them – namely that of a trial or suffering inflicted on him. He and his friends believed his constitution to be under attack, rather than diseased, and in such cases the patient was supposed to fight back.

Legend even enabled him to engage in a sort of mythical combat against his imagined afflictions, which sometimes helped to allay them. A peasant from the Ardennes was reported as explaining how his cows had been charmed; when this spell had been broken, he had found that the sorcerer had chosen him as a target for his malevolence:

> Two or three times a week, during the night, I'd soak my nightshirt and sheets with sweat; it was unbearable. One night, when I was resting on my left side, I seemed to feel an invisible hand, of unusual strength, wanting to turn me over to my right side. I flung myself on my invisible enemy and . . . I didn't catch him. I lay down again on my right side, but without going to sleep again, fearing that some misfortune was about to befall me. . . . I felt . . . the same hand strike my shoulder. Just at that moment, I had the idea of naming the person I suspected of tormenting me in this way aloud, and of threatening to kill him, if ever I met him. I had guessed correctly, for I heard my enemy, the scourge of my nights, escape by the chimney. Since then, I haven't been troubled.[36]

Tradition, through beliefs about witchcraft, furnished models of battles between the sufferer and the evil which he felt to be assailing him – a conflict that was usually, but not always, played out in the imagination, rather than with actual violence. There were some therapeutic advantages – apart from consolation – to be derived from this culture which accommodated illness and aberration within its conception of reality. It had developed a mythology which allowed man to describe and thereby to attenuate the effects of unpleasant experiences.

Fairies and Elves

If one sees the folklore about fairies and goblins as being rooted in man's real inner conflicts and problems, it becomes less difficult to account for its prevalence. The Comte de Résie thought that belief in fairies was widespread throughout France at the turn of the nineteenth century. In Saintonge, peasants thought that *fades* and *bonnes filandières* could be seen, carrying spindles, as they went on their way through the countryside at night. They were supposed to be able to foretell the future. In the South of France, the cult of fairies greatly resembled that of nymphs and other pagan deities. These similarities struck Alfred Maury, who was able to prove that modern fairies were the descendants of *Fata* and shared many of the attributes of the Fates.[37] Their functions and habits were various: in Normandy, they inhabited isolated fountains and rocks, coming out only at night. In Brittany and Auvergne, they often lived in dolmens. Some were malevolent: the *ondines* of the Moselle attracted travellers to the water's edge and then flung them in to drown. The Breton *corrigans*, in some versions, drew those who were crossing the moors late at night into their magical dances. *Huards* followed travellers, screeching at them. The *drac* of Languedoc and Provence was usually thought to be a kind of dragon, but he attached himself to young children and tried to make them lose their way. Other creatures were reported to be harmless – or even helpful: in Lorraine, the *sotret* curled young girls' hair; in Normandy, the goblin swept the house out and did the housework; the *sollèves* of the Alps gardened.[38] In the parish of Arfeuilles, people believed in a dwarf, who groomed and fed horses and rode them on barns and rooftops.[39] In Berry, people also believed in the *follet* who looked after horses: some were good and others evil. They were supposed to take horses galloping in the pasture-lands at night, and to knot the animals' manes to make stirrups so that the little elves could ride them. Horses with tangled manes were once thought to be the best and most lively mounts and the mares were sought-after at market as good brood-mares.

Despite the fact that these goblins were supposed to run away when men appeared on the scene, many people, according to George Sand, claimed to have seen them and furnished the same colourful descriptions of them: they were fat and short, with a cock's red comb, fiery eyes and claws instead of nails.[40] The phenomenon of uniform descriptions of mythical beasts is not unusual[41] and seems to spring from the fact that people used a conventional vocabulary to describe vague and strange experiences.

In the Alps and the Pyrenees, similarly helpful dwarves lived in the mountain grottoes, dancing in the meadows and protecting the grazing-lands. They were sometimes called 'les servants', because they helped shepherds. However, they expected to receive recognition for their aid, and it was thought wise to leave some food – a little milk and cheese – for them. A legend from the *pays de Vaud*, quoted by Sébillot, illustrates the point. A cowherd's young assistant disobeyed his orders and left nothing for the *servants*: a mysterious storm followed some nights later and the ungracious herder's animals were found the next morning, crushed to death at the bottom of a chasm.[42] Several legends referred to the necessity of pacifying fairies and goblins through regular or ritual tributes of this kind. In Brittany, and elsewhere, when a woman was giving birth, a meal was prepared and laid out in the next room, as fairies were supposed to come for the birth of the child. In the Pyrenees, on the eve of the New Year, a feast was prepared for them, so that they would bring prosperity to the household in the year to come.[43]

The reasons for the ambivalent attitude to fairies lay, in Maury's view, in the nature of their pagan models and in the attitude adopted by the Church towards belief in them. They thus became associated in men's minds with revolt against or hatred of Christianity, and were sometimes seen as colleagues of the devil. This official attitude, however, did not stop placatory rites creeping into the liturgy in some areas. Until the seventeenth century in the church at Poissy, a mass was said to preserve the neighbouring countryside from the anger of evil fairies; while the curate of Dorémy, in the fifteenth century, was alleged to have sung the gospel beside a local tree, to keep bad fairies away.[44] Although ritual gestures (like the custom in the Pyrenees of preparing a New Year dinner for fairies) point to a tendency to conceive of imaginary beings in anthropomorphic terms, they were nonetheless differentiated from ordinary gestures, not only by the timing and ceremony they involved, but also in their intended effect, which was psychological rather than physical. The difference between the reality of the fairies and everyday experience – which is confirmed by the marginal religious practices cited by Maury – suggests that the purpose of such customs was not so much practical as psychological. The propitiation of evil, the desire to enjoy good fortune informed these practices. In Brittany, fairies were believed to preside over the destiny of the newly-born child, through the talents and gifts of happiness or bad luck they gave it – a theme that was frequently evoked in fairy-tales.[45] In the context of parents' anxiety about the future, rites to assuage fairies appear as an imaginatively attractive means of crystallizing and then dispelling worry and stress.

Complementing this psychological function was the consoling and reassuring dimension of fairy-folklore. In Finistère, in the middle of the nineteenth century, fairies 'came especially to console orphans who had very unkind step-mothers . . . '. In Léon, it was said that 'the *fées* served to guide unfortunate people, consoling them with the promise of a happy and victorious future'.[46] This belief was, it is hardly necessary to reiterate, reflected in fairy-stories, whose perennial appeal was in large part due to the deprivation and vulnerability of the audiences to whom they were addressed. But whereas more or less formal tales appear to have been treated as inventions (if not as gratuitous fictions), attitudes to folk-beliefs and tales concerning them were more complex. Fairies and dwarves furnished an alibi of kinds to those who needed one: they both reassured people and helped them to conserve their self-esteem. One of the most widespread beliefs in Brittany about *corrigans*, goblins and fairies was that they stole children and replaced them with deformed mites. Hence, in Dinard, not long before Evans-Wentz wrote his book on fairies, a woman of over thirty years old, who was no bigger than a child of ten, was thought to be a changeling. He also heard a story involving just such an incident which purported to be about people who were still alive. A woman from Kergoff had a very strong and pretty boy as her first child, but then

> ...She noticed one morning that he had been changed during the night; there was no longer the fine baby she had put into bed in the evening; there was, instead, an infant hideous to look at, greatly deformed, hunchbacked and crooked, and of a black colour. The poor woman knew that a *fée* had entered her house during the night and had changed her child.

The woman had three other children – two of whom were also deformed and disturbed. These two were also identified as changelings. In the country, according to Evans-Wentz' informer, fairies who came at night to leave changelings always brought hunchbacked children. That abnormal children were the subject of this myth seems to be further suggested by the numerous Breton legends about how to verify one's suspicion that one had a changeling on one's hands. If eggshells filled with water were disposed in front of the fire in such a way as to appear to the child like small pots of cooking food, he would be surprised into speech – and thus betray his demonic nature.[47] These beliefs and legends furnished a way of dealing with the complex emotions – and particularly those which society would normally have tended to condemn – which a mother might feel towards a child who was ill, retarded or otherwise unusually dependent on her. They tended to justify any impulse of rejection she might have and to release her from the sense of guilt she might feel. Beliefs such as these furnished a world into which people could pour their painful experiences, explain them to themselves and to those around them, and by evading the responsibility for their actions, avoid the inconveniences of being excluded from the rest of the community.

Some *corrigans* and dwarves were believed, in Lower Brittany, to cause nightmares and to trouble men and women with obsessing spirits.[48] A woman from Kerallan, near Carnac, a Madame Le Rouzic, told Evans-Wentz a story which illustrates this point. A young girl went to the sabbath held by *corrigans*. When, on her return, she was asked where she had been, she said: 'I have travelled over water, wood and hedges', and related what she had heard and seen. Subsequently, the *corrigans* came to the house at night, dragged her out of bed and beat her. Upon hearing the uproar, Madame Le Rouzic's grandfather, who lived in the same house, got up and found the girl lying on the floor. She asked him never to question her again, averring that she would be killed by the fairies if she betrayed their secrets further.[49] As Evans-Wentz suggests, the girl was emotionally disturbed and the belief that one could go to sabbaths and have extraordinary experiences, or be punished and suffer for revealing what was involved, enabled her to describe her experience – however approximately – in a way that was understood by and acceptable to people around her. Belief in the reality of fairies and the ilk amounted to little more than the persuasion that disturbing experiences are real. The difference between modern and archaic attitudes in this respect have much to do, on the one hand, with socio-political attitudes and, on the other, with the way language is used. Here there are also points of similarity, as one school of psychiatry has helped to propagate a mythology through which the patient can attempt to talk out his illness.[50]

Mischievous, house-haunting spirits were still believed to exist in Lower Brittany, in Normandy and in Berry. Résie affirms that Norman peasants were particularly afraid of these little elves, but Evans-Wentz found that his witnesses (at the start of the twentieth century) had no strong belief in fairies, although they thought that dwarves and *corrigans* still existed. Fairies were usually relegated to the time of the witnesses' grandparents, when they were last supposed to have been seen. Paul Sébillot found only two people who had caught sight of them: one was an old woman from Saint-Cast, who was so afraid of them that she would never pass a field known as the *Couvent des Fées* at night.[51] In Berry, when George Sand was writing, however, the distinction between fairies and elves does not seem always to have been clear. Thus, while in some legends goblins were supposed to annoy housewives and make them commit stupid mistakes, in other versions, 'the dwarf who likes to mix and knot the yarn women spin is a female spirit, a bad fairy. In my childhood, I heard an old woman say, on such occasions: "The *knotter* has got at it!" and she would make the sign of the cross with her hand to banish the devil.'[52] Gestures of this kind, even though they were probably an habitual reflex rather than considered, were nonetheless one way of diminishing or even banishing the irritation caused by error or accident.

To be able to attribute nocturnal absences from home, or a disorderly arrival there, to forces independent of oneself was convenient – apart from the fact that it was one way of describing what one's adventures had felt like. Breton dwarves were supposed to appear at crossroads to attack travellers; others lived in lakes or ponds and amused themslves by playing tricks on people who were out after dark. Some legends had it that goblins might even turn themselves into black horses or goats, and as it was dangerous to meet them, people who saw the metamorphosis were supposed to be terrified.[53] In the Marche, spirits were thought to guard the dolmens, where treasure was buried: if one happened to wander near the monuments at night, one was likely to be thrown from one's horse and sorely beaten. One story quoted by Sand described how a treasure-hunter saw a dwarf jumping up and down in front of him, and was dragged into his 'magnetic round', where he was made to spin like a top. When the dwarf diverted his attention to make a stone turn instead, the man was able to leave, unobserved. But he was still so giddy that he could barely stagger home, where he collapsed at the door from fatigue.[54] The appeal and relevance of such stories in a society in which undernourishment alternated with great drinking binges – especially at fairs and festivals – seem evident. The convenience of this imaginative tradition was that it could be mobilized to excuse one's behaviour – whether caused through laziness, lack of concentration, drunkenness or foolhardiness. It also betrayed a tendency, which recurred throughout traditional culture, to ascribe personal misfortune to the malevolence of someone else or of a different creature.

Ghosts

Belief in ghosts also exemplifies the complexity of legendary beliefs of the rural poor. In the context of the intrusion of the fantastic into ordinary life of peasants, the question that concerns us is how one can reconcile claims to have seen and heard ghosts, and traditional ritual reverence towards them, with the contention that there was no great difference of mind and sensibility between people who could accommodate such ideas and modern man. Jean Delumeau has suggested that such attempts are misleading, since in the past, 'life and death did not always seem to be separated by a distinct division'. An animistic view of the world obtained.[55] Folklore about ghosts was marked by a duality of conception which may be explained by the influence of the Church.

Influence of the Church. The anthropomorphic mode of conception which informed some practices and beliefs about the dead is striking – even if it does not justify the assumption that death was not clearly distinguished from life, or indeed the contention that the natural was felt to be permeated with supernatural or marvellous beings.[56] Ghosts, in the popular mind, were usually like men, not in appearance but in their supposed habits and predilections. In this, the traditional view of phantoms needs to be distinguished – as Professor Delumeau has observed – from the once official religious one. For François Lebrun, and the folklorist Camille Fraysse on whom he bases his opinion, 'a ghost is a dead person who, unable to settle his scores with God definitively, . . . comes back to earth to haunt the places where he lived, to ask his relatives for prayers and masses, in order to facilitate his admission into the kingdom of the blessed'.[57] Ghosts of legend were indeed sometimes tormented souls who came in quest of relief to the living in the hope that they would pray for them. Various practices were admitted by the Church as being effective for this purpose: indulgences were attached to the recital of certain prayers at certain times, and the faithful could compute the length of time by which they were reducing the sufferings of the soul in purgatory – plenary indulgences were especially valuable (and correspondingly difficult to gain), earning long remissions like seven years and seven quarantines. Such doctrines were reflected in legend.

One story in Berry concerned a nobleman, Jean de la Selle, who lived deep in the desolate wood of Villemort. One evening, he and his share-cropper Luneau were returning from market with six hundred pounds by the *Gagne-aux-Demoiselles*, which was supposedly haunted. M. de la Selle fell asleep on the journey, but Luneau guided his horse. When they arrived home, the money was missing, and Luneau, swearing they had met no-one on the way, affirmed that the money must have been stolen by the phantoms. The nobleman accepted the explanation, although he could ill afford to do so. Some years later, M. de la Selle was again returning from market – alone this time, as Luneau had died some months earlier. By the *Gagne-aux-Demoiselles*, an enormous white creature appeared to the nobleman, jumped up behind him onto his horse, and made the animal gallop madly across the bog. M. de la Selle had the presence of mind to say:

> 'If you want prayers and masses said, let your wishes be known and, on my honour as a gentleman, you shall be satisfied.' Then M. de la Salle heard a strange voice over his head saying: 'Have three masses said for the soul of big Luneau and go in peace.' Immediately the ghost's figure disappeared the grey became docile . . . He thought he'd had a vision; nonetheless he ordered three masses. But imagine his surprise when on opening his case, he found in it not only the money he'd got at market, but the six hundred pounds.[58]

Stories about the restless souls of the damned – of those who had committed a great sin, who had been excommunicated, who had died without baptism or without proper funeral rites – were numerous throughout Europe, according to Stith Thompson. Also popular were tales about ghosts who returned, either – like Luneau – to make restitution for some wrong done in life, or to punish erring relatives on earth. Malicious ghosts, in Thompson's view, were more common than good ones: thus, dead wives returned to protest about the riotous living of their husbands, and lovers attempted to carry their sweethearts off to the grave.[59] The burden of most of these tales was moral, however – by implication, they preached the prudence of honesty, sobriety and piety – and in this they differed from much of the rest of folklore about the dead, from which ethical preoccupations appear to have been absent. The ecclesiastical view of the dead lived on in popular culture as a source of edification and literary diversion, rather than being profoundly rooted in men's sensibilities.

Popular Naturalism. For legends of this kind were unlike the stories told about actual sightings of ghosts, which seem to be related to independent popular lore about the dead. Professor Delumeau, basing himself on Le Roy Ladurie and Edgar Morin, suggests that there were two ways of believing in apparitions of the dead: the 'horizontal' vision, which was naturalistic and traditional, and which implied that the dead person lived on; and the transcendental conception of theologians.[60] The distinction is useful, not only because it points to a real difference between official and popular perspectives, but because it throws into relief the naturalism of popular thought. The notion of spirituality – indeed the very idea of the supernatural, of a realm independent of the natural – were concepts elaborated by intellectuals, rather than characteristic of or thoroughly assimilated by the traditions of the countryside. They appear to have been essentially foreign to it. As priests frequently regretted, the hallmark of popular concepts was naturalism.

Paul Sébillot's catalogue of practices of apparently pagan derivation which surrounded the dead indicates that death was sometimes seen more as a change of place rather than – as the Church suggested – a transformation of nature. The destruction of the body in death does not always seem to have been appreciated. The dead were buried with all sorts of belongings which they had found useful or enjoyable in life, presumably on the assumption that they would be able to avail themselves of them after death also. In Cornouaille, the dead were carefully buried with their teeth, so that they would not lose time at the Last Judgement looking for them. This practice may also be related to the belief that the dead were thought to be likely to want to eat in the other world: in Auvergne and Creuse, corpses were equipped with a loaf of bread and a plate; around Dinan, they were given some bread to eat on the journey to heaven. Around the start of the twentieth century, an old man was buried with cakes and a flagon of wine. In Puy-de-Dôme, Bordeaux and the Gironde, wine was put in coffins along with the corpse: one old man remembered that his father had given him strict instructions not to forget to place a bottle of wine beside him when he died. In Saintonge, the dead person was buried with his walking-stick or crutch, while little children in Yonne and Bresse were buried with their toys and sweets respectively. One comfortably-off old peasant from the Côtes-du-Nord, around the start of the twentieth century, wanted to have his big cotton umbrella beside him in his coffin, so that he could use it as a sail when his coffin made the journey across the underground sea to the other world.[61] Anatole Le Braz thought that the Bretons looked on death as a journey, a departure to another world, rather than as a change of condition.[62] The striking feature of this corpus of beliefs about the dead was not its supernaturalism or spirituality but its naturalism and materialism. In this perspective, death was, above all, a separation.

Most anecdotes about sighting of ghosts – as opposed to legends – were told by people who claimed to have seen friends, relatives or neighbours. 'This man will claim to have seen his grandmother, another his uncle, his aunt or his father-in-law, a husband his wife in the form of a moving tongue of fire, a wife will have heard her husband's shade, a housekeeper will have seen that of her young mistress', wrote one commentator from

Arfeuilles in 1840.[63] Not only could stress and fatigue provoke visions of this kind but – more interestingly – people were sometimes impelled to interpret vague experiences, which could just as easily have been considered in a different light, as contact with dead relatives. Evans-Wentz found that belief in ghosts was strongly rooted among the Bretons, and a number of people told him how they had seen the dead. Jean Couton, from Carnac, was returning from a funeral one winter evening with a woman who had been related to the dead person, when the woman saw the ghost of the person they had just buried. She asked her companion if he saw anything, but he did not. She told him to touch her, and as he did so, he clearly recognized the dead person.[64] Naturalistic explanations of this incident can be imagined – the stress associated with the death and the funeral, fatigue, the hour and season prompted an experience which the woman interpreted as was natural within that cultural context and which her companion saw through suggestion. What arrests us is that this kind of explanation was not retained by the people involved.

The reason for this may lie as much with psychology as with culture. Some traditional practices and beliefs may have diminished the sense of loss and helplessness caused by the death of a relative or friend. Jean Couton told Evans-Wentz that he believed 'that after death the soul always exists and travels among us'. Eugénie Le Port, who was known as a seeress according to Evans-Wentz, and who had been subject to visions from childhood, frequently saw the ghosts of people she had known, and even saw funerals of those who were going to die before long. She too affirmed that 'we believe that the spirits of our ancestors surround us and live with us'.[65] In the seventeenth century, Thiers condemned the practice observed by those who, 'when someone has died in the house, erect crosses at the crossroads, so that the dead person will be able to find his way home, when he wants to return, or when he goes to the last judgement'.[66] The Bretons – who seem to have had the richest and most idiosyncratic folklore about death – were said to refrain from sweeping their houses at midnight for fear of disturbing the dead and thereby bringing misfortune on the household.[67] Similarly, in the Bourbonnais, one way of keeping evil spirits out of the house was to put the brush across the door when one went out.[68]

Other practices reinfoced this belief in the proximity of the dead. In some remote parts of the district of Quimper, Morbihan and Côtes-du-Nord on 1 November, pancakes were cooked to make a meal for the dead who were supposed to return then.[69] One woman, brought up by an aunt in the Confolentais, was brought at the end of October to a *veillée des anciens*; she wrote many years later a somewhat romanticized account of the occasion, which was, she affirmed, the most frightening one of her life. The hostess, an old woman, was dressed in antique finery; most of the guests were elderly women, and all their effects appeared antiquated – one old man sported the attire of an eighteenth-century squire. The yard was filled with old-fashioned carriages. They proceeded to eat a magnificent dinner off silver plate, by candlelight, reminiscing about their dead families and relatives and drinking their health.

> ... When the meal was over, joints and the remains of all the dishes were left on the table for the supper of the long dead, and more wine and bread was brought, for the old woman was afraid that there wouldn't be enough.
>
> After that, a good fire was made, and the best seats were drawn up in a semi-circle around the hearth ...
>
> Prayers were recited aloud for the souls of the departed and then everyone withdrew to leave the room for the dead who were going to return.[70]

According to Résie, the custom of offering food to the souls of the dead was still practised on certain nights during the winter, in the Auvergne, Manche and Languedoc.[71] That of placing chairs near the fire at midsummer and in November so that the dead could keep warm was also known in Brittany. The separation from the dead was not, then, irrevocable – it was still possible to help them, to express the affectionate memory in which they were held. It may be helpful to see customs concerning encounters with the dead as having a psychological function, as offering some consolation – whether people were aware of it or not – as well as the hope of ultimate reunion.

While part of the folklore of ghosts concerned tormented souls, the rest was more domestic and individual: the legendary and religious (magic seems to have little to do with ghosts by the nineteenth century, at least in the countryside) was balanced by the anecdotal and personal. People who claimed to have seen and recognized dead people do not seem to have associated their ghosts with the active, usually suffering souls of legend. Their encounters were simple – confined to a brief vision, glimpse, impression of the dead, or to overhearing or having a short conversation with them. One must ask whether the tendency to draw consolation from encounters with the dead, which Professor Ariès dates at the birth of Romanticism, did not always exist in the traditional folklore of death.[72]

Omens

Peasants were sometimes ridiculed for their belief in omens, which was taken as proof of the irrationality of their outlook.[73] Lévy-Bruhl, who considered belief in omens at some length in *La Mentalité Primitive*, concluded that they were a typical expression of irrationality. The evolution towards rationality was gradual, he felt: hence, rather than being mutually exclusive, primitive and logical thought could – in the intermediary stage – co-exist in one mind. As an example, he cited the instance of contemporary farmers, who, although superficially aware of the physical conditions necessary for a good harvest, nonetheless, he asserted, continued to believe that it was also due to the good-will of supernatural powers.[74] Lévy-Bruhl suggests that the world of the peasant was permeated by mystic powers which mysteriously dictated the course of events. The need to introduce the notion of power (necessarily mysterious, if not mystic) was due to his insistence that omens were traditionally seen not just as signs but as causes. The evidence does not appear to bear him out.

Some presages were little more than primitive weather forecasts. Based on the observation of nature, they seem to have been intended as approximate guides to rather than unshakeable axioms about nature. Early mushrooms were a sign of a bad year ahead; lots of may-beetles assured a plentiful supply of chestnuts later on. The *Almanach du Cultivateur* for 1834 published a number of prognostications of varying degrees of plausibility and sense: number thirty-six assured the reader that 'when the flame burns straight and still, sign of good weather'; thirty-seven observed, rather unnecessarily, that 'if one hears the sound of bells from afar, it's a sign of wind', while another affirmed that odours became stronger before rainfall. Crows clamouring in the morning indicated bad weather to come later on in the day – as did hens which rolled in the dust more than usual, bees returning in swarms to their hives at evening, and frogs croaking more persistently than normally. Some of these observations are still believed in the countryside and many seem to be quite accurate impressions.

Omens properly speaking, however, are considerably more difficult to explain, for they relate man's destiny to natural phenomena in an apparent relation, if not of causality, at least of obscure dependence. The medieval Church and the Counter-Reformation clergy repeatedly condemned belief in omens, sometimes in terms reminiscent of their comrades-in-arms of the early Enlightenment. Various edicts of the sixteenth and seventeenth century ordered punishments for observing practices associated with such beliefs, but all to no avail. '...What could be more futile, more useless, more trivial, more ridiculous', Thiers was still able to ask towards the end of the seventeenth century, when these beliefs were waning among the educated, 'than to regulate one's steps, deeds, behaviour and life, according to events and meetings which have no certain cause, which result only from chance, and to which a good as well as a bad meaning can be given?' His catalogue of superstitions was presented in a way which could not but reinforce his contention about the arbitrary and meaningless character of omens and the stupidity of anyone who could lend credence to them.[75]

Nonetheless, some order is evident in and some distinctions can be drawn between omens, of which there were two large classes – those which purported to offer a practical guide to men's conduct and those which, through an elaborate form of symbolism, supposedly enabled vague predictions to be made about the destiny of the individual in the community. Belief in both kinds seems to have been quite general in rural France, even around the middle of the century.

Presages as a form of Advice. If one examines auguries involving time, one sees that within this category one can distinguish between beliefs derived from astrology, and others which were more characteristic of popular lore. In Quéras, people believed in inauspicious days, and this persuasion seems to have been quite common throughout France. 'Fear of Fridays is to be found in the Ardennes', observed Nozot. People born that day were supposed to be able to give effect to all their evil intentions without being discovered. If someone was buried on a Friday, another death in the family was sure to follow within six weeks. If one married on a Friday, one would die during one's honeymoon, and changing one's shirt on that day was just as dangerous. Certain times and days – especially Fridays – were still feared in the Bocage Normand, when Lecoeur was writing. Conversely, other times were considered propitious: if one bled one's horses on Saint Philip's or Saint James' feast-day, they were sure to keep in good health for the rest of the year; it was advisable to wait until the moon was on the wane before gathering apples or making cider, when it was also good time to work the land.[76]

Many of these dicta were reiterated in the cheap almanacs which were sold to country people by pedlars and which preserved, in debased form, the astrological beliefs of earlier generations. An *Almanach du Bon Laboureur*, dating from the early July Monarchy, worked its way through the seasons and months, reviewing various ancient beliefs and quoting sayings in an intricate, ponderous manner. 'Bref', announces the author, 'c'est une chose très assurée que la Lune qui se renouvelle devant le lever de la Poussinière, est très dangereuse pour les fruits [sic].' It continued with a list of 'critical days for those who fall ill, with propitious days'. This informed the reader: 'Sixth, to be feared. Seventh, good. Eighth, there's no danger . . . Twelfth, there's danger of death until the fifteenth.' Its detailed advice on propitious times for agricultural labours was barely comprehensible: 'Les semences se doivent faire quand la Lune est dans une des lignes mobiles, comme le Bélier, l'Ecrevisse, la Balance et le Capricorne, ou quand elle est dans un trine ou sextile de Saturne, principalement si cette Planète est dans un aspect favourable. . . .'[77] What a barely literate rural reader would have made of all of this, one can only guess. It seems unlikely that the book would have been consulted for practical purposes, given its obscurity and the established calendar of farm work.

Traditionally, almanacs – which were to be found among the ancient Egyptians, Greeks and Romans – used hieroglyphs to convey the same sort of information[78] and in the first part of the nineteenth century, the *Messager Boîteux* continued this tradition. This almanac printed symbols to predict the weather and to indicate propitious days for different activities: thus, an eye meant 'Bon traiter les yeux', while a hand with long nails meant that one could cut one's nails; an axe stood for 'bon couper du bois' and a fork for 'bon fumer la terre'. The system, as Nisard observed, was complicated and the calendar itself incomprehensible unless one had read and studied the introductory key, from which he concluded that these almanacs could not have been addressed to totally illiterate people.[79] Nonetheless, they enjoyed enormous vogue from the early seventeenth century[80] – when they first entered the catalogues of the popular printers[81] – until the latter half of the nineteenth century, when they were replaced with anodyne publications with a more modern format and officially sanctioned content (such as *Le Grand Double Almanach, dit de Liège*, published in Paris and Troyes by Casterman in 1858).[82] Although these works were primarily addressed to and bought by people who lived in a predominantly oral culture, how far they were actually understood and absorbed remains largely a matter for conjecture. Michelet, when he considered this subject, noted with characteristic discernment:

> People had just one book (or two), and they were greatly attached to it, as is the peasant to his almanac. This unique book inspired confidence . . . the beloved book was really an elastic text, which let the reader elaborate on it . . . It stimulated, awakened initiative. The solitary mind reading through, often between the lines, saw, found, created.[83]

Some facts bear out Michelet's suggestion that the book was a status-symbol to which inventive attitudes were adopted, a means of dreaming, as much and possibly more than a text by which the reader was guided. What was actually written in the work was not necessarily of primary importance, once some suggestive or diverting nugget had been extracted from it. At all events, the data of astrological derivation which almanacs furnished, although apparently similar to popular beliefs, must nonetheless be distinguished from folklore. The information in almanacs was a corrupted version of what had once been regarded by the educated élite as a system with scientific pretensions; the discarded remnant of a branch of high culture, the extent of whose assimilation into folklore – while difficult to assess – does not appear to have been profound.

Most of the popular indications about inauspicious and propitious days which have been recorded seem to have concerned religious feast-days, and the customs associated with them are more akin to the debris of para-religious practices than to presages properly speaking. Thiers indicated many of them: it was best to graft trees on the feast of the Annunciation, and to bleed horses on Saint Stephen's feast-day. Bread cooked on Christmas Eve would preserve cows from many illnesses, if they ate it mixed with their drink. Other customs apparently included not allowing horses out of their stables on the feast-day of their patron-saint; not sowing wheat on Saint Leger's feast-day (lest it should become light); carrying wheat which one was going to sow in the tablecloth that had been used on Christmas Day, so that it might grow better. Important liturgical seasons had equally eccentric prescriptions attached to them. Lest some misfortune should occur, housewives were inconveniently recommended to abstain from doing the laundry during the Ember days, Rogations, the octave of Corpus Christi, when *Tenebrae* were being sung, on Fridays, and from Christmas until the Epiphany. Similarly, it was thought unwise to spin between the Wednesday of Holy Week and Easter Sunday, or on Saturday afternoons, lest one should spin ropes with which to tie the Saviour or lest Christ – who was supposed to be resting at these times – be disturbed.[84] These beliefs are best considered in the light of misunderstood religion, to which men applied erratically when so moved by mood or circumstance and with the perennial inconsistency of human nature.

Presages as a Form of Fortune-Telling. Omens which exploited symbolism pose similar problems of interpretation. Belief in presages of this kind was widespread throughout France, according to Résie, and especially strong in Normandy and Saintonge. Owls were among the most commonly feared omens: screech-owls, bats and owls indicated the death of a member of the family on the roof of whose house they sat. In the Limousin, people liked to hear the cricket singing on the hearth, as they thought it brought good luck. The spider was supposed to be useful in stables, because it allegedly purified the air. A nest of swallows under the roof-ledge was also a sign of prosperity. To see a spider meant that one would come into money; if a log fell in the fire, or if a sleeping dog turned its nose to the door, then someone was going to call.[85] Indicative of social attitudes was the belief that if a woman began to talk before her husband or at the same time as he, bad luck was likely to follow.[86]

It is difficult to know how consistent or selective people were in reacting (or indeed precisely how they reacted) to these signs. Were one to take the catalogues literally, one would be led to believe that a great deal of time was spent attending to and interpreting a wide variety of detailed phenomena. Popular testimony on the subject suggests that the attendant circumstances – the setting and people's frame of mind – as well as this ample folklore, were influential in shaping people's responses to phenomena. Tiennon Bertin recounted how, when he was a young man, one snowy December evening just at bedtime, he and his wife heard a cock crow. Traditional lore had it that a cock which crowed between sundown and midnight was a sign of misfortune. They did not stop to think that the bird, locked up for weeks in the dark, had gradually lost its sense of time. '... We were upset, because, as children, we had seen our relatives become uneasy in similar circumstances. Besides, in the unbroken silence of the winter night, this noisy crowing was eerie ...' Their reaction was fashioned by their cultural environment – by their particular predicament of youth, poverty and insecurity.[87]

Juge affirmed that weak-minded people were terrified by comets and eclipses, while Monnier and Vingtrinier suggested that comets were still commonly regarded as portents of disaster by the uneducated. Meteors, according to Souvestre, were thought in Brittany to have preceeded the outbreak of cholera there in 1853. In the Bocage Normand, comets were still believed to herald war and famine: it was said that armed horsemen could be seen fighting each other on red clouds before great revolutions, and that this phenomenon had been observed before the revolutions of 1789, 1830 and 1848.[88] In crises, the poor instinctively seem to have allowed their anxiety to express itself in elaborations and renewals of traditional imagery and myth. In the winter of 1870–71, when the French were losing the war with the Prussians, Tiennon Bertin recounted how alarming rumours about the imminent arrival of the German troops caused terror in his area. Then bad weather and an epidemic of smallpox compounded the sense of disaster:

> As though to give all these ills the meaning of divine punishment, the sky was often stained with red clouds, or, on one side of the horizon, would become entirely purple, to the point where one would have said it was a shroud of blood. It was simply a matter of atmospheric phenomena to which no attention whatever would have been paid in ordinary times; but it added to our lugubrious frame of mind. The red sky heralded murderous battles; it was the blood of the wounded and dead which stained it thus. The terror grew; people talked of the end of the world as of a very probable thing. Besides, every Sunday, in his sermon, the priest stirred up these ideas of divine vengeance and horrible calamities; he seemed almost pleased about the universal misfortune, that man, almost congratulating himself on his parishioners' anxious faces . . .[89]

In this account, there was nothing inevitable about the interpretation of the red sky as an omen of disaster: it was the context of calamities and apprehension which led people to attend to it; the cultural environment which led them to see it as an image of their woes, a confirmation of their sense of foreboding.[90] The sky was seen as an emblem, not as the cause, of the crisis: its significance was not immediately apparent, but was suggested by the circumstances. Similarly, the girl who wanted to day-dream about a future husband, a man who wanted to avoid going on a journey, a woman who was anxious about the welfare of her children or about the family fortunes, all could draw on a rich set of images with which to confirm their feelings – rather in the way the ancient Greeks had procured the kind of dreams they wanted.[91]

In his comments on his own experience of omens, Tiennon Bertin evinced a tendency to dismiss superstition as the apanage of youth, as a set of beliefs and practices from which the adult man liberates himself. This relegation of superstition to the realm of childish (and often of senile or female) error is to be found in other popular commentators upon traditional culture.[92] Yet it was accompanied, in some cases, by a disclaimer to the effect that the writer or speaker himself had nonetheless experienced one or two strange happenings, which made him disinclined to dismiss everything he had learned as a child.[93] This points to a need to distinguish between collective traditional lore, about which, in general, one might be sceptical or to which one might be indifferent, and private mythology, which was shaped by one's background and which tended to reinforce tradition. The reason for assigning superstition to children, the old and women may be linked to the important role played by elderly people and women in educating the young, in initiating them into the values and beliefs of their culture. But its dismissal is also indicative of a certain detachment from their imaginative inheritance on the part of the most powerful members of society.

Yet this too is predictable. The supposition that young adults in traditional rural France adjusted themselves to their background, without examining it critically, adapting or partially rejecting inherited values, is open to question. Inherited beliefs are rarely accepted *in toto* by the adult, but are frequently either amended or allowed to fall into abeyance until some critical juncture arrives, when ideas which were previously regarded with indifference or scepticism are suddenly revived. Thus, one might not believe everything one was told, but some observations might seem significant in the light of experience. In the case of presages, some images appear to have resumed the pain and anxiety of a difficult period thus to have become emblematic of suffering and misfortune.[94] This point where individual intuition and inherited culture coincided seems likely to have constituted the key area of personal belief in the collective imaginative legacy, which nourished tradition and helped to ensure its authority and continuity. One way of describing belief, then, would be to see it as a disposition to accept as helpful and apposite, in the characterization of experience, an inherited or traditional vocabulary. In this perspective, attitudes towards omens were more complex than those suggested by the alternatives of credulity and scepticism, literal and symbolic interpretation: what omens furnished was not a description of the world and its workings, but a demonstration of man's vulnerability in the world. Omens were a way of enabling man to present his condition and to understand his feelings about it: they constituted a physical imagery which helped him to crystallize and manipulate his own reactions to the world, by affording pretexts which tended to provoke or clarify latent feelings and could be used to indulge others – whether of apprehension, hope, reluctance, or foolhardiness.[95] He was thereby enabled to recognize or escape the uncongenial dictates or probabilities of reality. In this, omens were more akin to a psychological technique than to an archaic mechanical theory.

Conclusion

The frequency with which traditions and stories about encounters with extraordinary phenomena and creatures were told suggests that they fulfilled an important role in pre-modern culture. In a society which was vulnerable to physical disaster and which lacked analytical vocabulary, legends enabled people to describe their feelings about and reactions to their social and physical environment. In formalizing fear and hostility in a collective mythology, tradition enabled divisive and corrosive impulses to be expressed harmlessly. A threat, which often sprang from man's own instincts, could be attributed to dangerous creatures or circumstance – it remained external. Legends about extraordinary creatures and phenomena helped to reassure men who lived in isolated vulnerable communities, and this must account, to some extent, for their persistent popularity in pre-modern societies. However, if it played a positive role in rural culture by helping people to express and exorcise their anxieties and regrets, this legendary vocabulary instilled a tendency to intellectual deviousness and reinforced the deeply-rooted popular rejection and distortion of reality: in this, it merited the anathema which the Enlightenment heaped on it.

IV

Witchcraft and the Sense of Injustice

Belief in spells and witchcraft occupied a prominent place in the traditional culture of the countryside more on account of the possibilities it furnished for expressing and justifying one's feelings than on account of the satisfaction afforded by its theoretical assumptions and explanations. It has been argued that the appeal of witchcraft was essentially intellectual – in that it proposed a variety of remedies for problems that were insoluble in a technologically backward society. In support of this contention, early commentators pointed to the fact that there was a kind of abstract definition of witchcraft; the general scope of the sorcerer's activities, the identification of the wizard and witch were conventional commonplaces. The argument implied by this objection contends that people believed in witches because witches were believed to exist, that the system was self-confirming. There is some truth in this observation. Is it then, correct to conclude that witchcraft was a kind of explanation, a theory of causality, in that it saw certain phenomena as individual instances of a general system or regular pattern of laws? The central objection to this approach lies in the fact that witchcraft, far from having this kind of systematic regularity, was in the first instance an accusation, upon which all its subsequent characteristic elements (the consultation with a counter-sorcerer, the use of prayers, counter-charms and, ultimately, reprisals and violence) depended. Witchcraft was not always invoked as soon as someone met an old woman on a road, or in every case of illness or misfortune. Only when the individual felt his bad luck to be unnatural and excessive did he start to think of witchcraft as the possible source of his troubles. He would then examine the events in his recent past, in the light of consecrated beliefs, and the similarities which he found between his own life and traditional paradigms enabled him to identify the moment when the spell had been cast. Witchcraft, in reality, was not so much a theory which explained certain regular phenomena, as a charge brought in retrospectively and occasionally. To contend that witchcraft was a kind of self-confirming explanation for natural catastrophes, which in a more general sense can be accounted for in terms of the scientific and technological limitations of the milieu in which it flourished, is not only to ignore the historical evidence of these beliefs and practices (about which we learn mainly through trials or anecdotes, not through theoretical exposés), but also to evade the whole problem of understanding why it persisted, by affirming that it explains itself. But this evasion, no less than comments about the needs of backward societies, is confronted with the difficulty of explaining both the ultimate decline of such beliefs, and their apparent independence of technological change.[1] Why, if the system were self-supporting, did the evidence of experience cease, rather than continue, to confirm tradition?

The difficulties which arise from considering witchcraft abstractly and which have led commentators to lay undue stress upon its theoretical assumptions, its explanatory and practical functions – or even to consider it as a theory in some way assimilable to the kind of 'theories' in intellectual vogue in Europe since the seventeenth century – indicate the need to alter the perspective. The very adaptability of the magical rites of which witchcraft formed a part suggests that we should see them not so much as a kind of theory but more as a vocabulary. In rural France in the nineteenth century, magic furnished people with a way of expressing and sometimes of overcoming disorientating feelings, of satisfying their dreams: as practised, it was a psychological technique with social rather than scientific overtones. As more recent research has indicated,[2] the classical presentation of witchcraft, which starts by describing the sorcerer's attributes, puts the cart before the horse. In fact, in most specific cases of supposed witchcraft about which we know, the story starts not with the sorcerer but with the person who thinks a spell has been cast upon him. The explanatory nature of witchcraft, as so many commentators have observed, was indeed important, but less from the perspective of a theory of nature than from that of a theory of society and human nature. Witchcraft, starting as an accusation of a criminal offence not punishable by law, provided a social theory of misfortune and the means whereby the victim might both undo the damage done to him and avenge himself. Its secular and social nature was of cardinal importance, and it indicates that the transition to a 'modern' mentality – in which suffering is often attributed to the mismanagement of resources by the directors of society and salvation is sought in political and legal reform – is not as radical as the proponents of the idea of the mythic mentality would lead us to expect.

Responsibility for Misfortune

The first stage in any individual case of witchcraft was a growing sense of anxiety, when the pressure of illness or bad luck led people first to suspect that a spell had been cast on them and secondly, to try to identify the sorcerer. The Abbé Foix indicated that the stress caused by long illness – 'maladies de langueur' – were especially characteristic of unnatural disease, and real misfortune usually lay behind the suspicion of foul play. The cause of these sufferings was sought not among things but among people: someone with whom one was on bad terms or a person of dubious repute whom one had recently met were liable to be suspected as the author of one's ills. In any case, 'what's beyond doubt is that someone has something to do with it'.[3] The psychological roots of this kind of interrogation cannot be divorced from their social and economic context, which was such that men were vulnerable to disease and misery. However stoical or resentfully apathetic peasants seemed to observers, in the face of their difficult lives, their pent-up frustration should not be ignored, for the violence of their sporadic reaction to critical suffering is otherwise difficult to explain. The individual, in turning to witchcraft, seems to have felt that things were not as they should be or could normally be expected to be. He and his family gave themselves over to speculation about what could have caused his plight. He might decide he had been bewitched, despite some initial scepticism, because of his need for hope and release.[4] The initial suspicion of witchcraft and speculation about the possible identity of the witch were originally rooted in the peculiar anxiety of excessive, unrelieved suffering. 'They worry, they mull over it, and look at what is happening around them with distrust. The talk continues; soon, one name is mysteriously on everyone's lips. . . . '[5] The concept of causality implied by this process was closer to the notion of responsibility than to that of mechanistic interdependence (of which it is often misleadingly presented as being the archaic equivalent), in that it saw criminal irresponsibility on the part of another member of the community in the exercise of powers, albeit mysterious, as being at the root of unusual misfortune.

Witchcraft beliefs are important and interesting, not because they illustrated a false conception of natural laws but because, on one level, they were statements about social rather than physical realities, and on another, they cast light on people's feelings and how they coped with them. Witchcraft – as opposed to magic – was concerned primarily with receiving gratuitous or excessive misfortune, which was seen as an essentially human problem, reflecting the nature of social relations in impoverished communities. The suspicions aroused by witchcraft expose the tensions that bedevilled traditional life. Neighbours, friends and relatives were frequently suspected of having cast the spell, as were those whom the victim felt he had treated badly, in contravention of traditional norms or legal contracts – such as the poor, to whom charity was owed, travellers who deserved hospitality, rejected lovers, and employers or servants who had been ill-done-by.[6] This etiology of the charm emphasized the importance of the sorcerer's social position in relation to his victim, and the feelings which were thereby engendered. Indeed, even the means of harming – whose mechanics were, albeit, mysterious – stressed the primacy of social relations in the origin and effective expression of the hatred and envy which lay at the heart of witchcraft.

One of the most widespread magical beliefs in rural France in the nineteenth century was the persuasion that the witch or sorcerer could, with a glance, ruin his enemy by making him ill or by hindering his agricultural labours. This was an ancient and common notion. It was to be found, according to Mensignac, mainly in Brittany, Normandy, the Auvergne and among the Basques – although evidence suggests that it existed also in central and eastern France.[7] Mahé affirmed that the peasants of the Morbihan thought that the evil eye caused dangerous illnesses and that they thought of it in naturalistic rather than supernatural terms: '... They seem to think it natural and to imagine that some people's eyes give out miasmas or pestilential fluids which are carried on the wind, by which means the contagion is spread afar....' This notion, however strange it sounded, resembled in the antiquarian's opinion, that of naturalists and magnetizers.[8] Indeed, while one may suspect Mahé of having expressed the idea of the spell in the scientific, or quasi-scientific, terms that were familiar to him (that miasmas were the means whereby contagious diseases were transmitted was the theory that governed many seventeenth- and eighteenth-century ordinances in time of plague, and this idea was still evoked in the cholera epidemics of the mid-nineteenth century), his comment casts interesting light on popular beliefs. It suggests that the spell was seen more as a natural than as a supernatural phenomenon, not necessarily involving the divine and diabolical superstructure elaborated by Christian theologians. If Mahé is to be believed, the spell, for some people, belonged to this world of dissension and misery, rather than to an exotic domain controlled by occult mysterious beings.

The spell was the vehicle of the witch's or wizard's evil intentions, and it was often realized in a material, deceptively familiar form or in an immediately perceptible way (as in the hateful look or curse), rather than mysteriously. In the Basses-Pyrénées, it was commonly believed that a person could cast spells by spitting on his victim; while in the Gironde, the sorcerer could charm people by spitting on the doorstep of their house.[9] Camille Gagnon cites the case of a sorcerer from Combrailles, who would go to his victim's house when there was no-one at home, take a bucket of water, over which he would mutter imprecations, and finally stab the reflection of his eye in the water, while wishing blindness on his enemy.[10] In eastern Flanders, it was believed that the sorcerer could cast a spell on his victim by touching him.[11] At Charbonnières-les-Vieilles in Auvergne, magical illness was thought to be caused by a toad slipped under the victim's door or bed, with the intention of making him *sécher* – die slowly and painfully; and at Beaux-Malatavarne, some people were supposed to be able to *donner le mal* (cast a spell) by looking at their victims.[12] The father of the folklorist Schély's mother-in-law, who lived in Strasbourg-Neuhof in the latter half of the nineteenth and early twentieth centuries, thought that if one left hairs lying around, 'evil people could use them to hurt others'.[13] In the way it was transmitted, the spell was broadly assimilable to an infectious or contagious illness, and reflected popular ideas about the etiology of disease.[14]

The sorcerer could also cast spells through his gifts or praise. La Kerzéas, who was thought by her neighbours to be a witch, met a woman who had just bought some piglets at the market at Pont-Croix. 'They're fine little beasts for the price', La Kerzéas observed, examining them attentively. That evening, the animals fell ill – which suggested to their outraged owner not that they were a poor bargain but that the jealous witch had cast a spell on them. At Claix, in the Dauphiné, a neighbour was reported to have gone to see twelve piglets and to have remarked: 'They're grand wee creatures, but I've my doubts whether you'll raise them.' The next day, they were languishing and it was surmised that the neighbour had cast a spell on them out of envy. Expressions of admiration and desire – even an attentive look – were feared, as they hid conscious or unconscious jealousy of good fortune.[15] As an explanation of misfortune, witchcraft offered a figurative commentary on social and economic relations and reflected the tensions generated in small groups by relative wealth and poverty. To attempt to see it purely as a kind of primitive science, rather than as an expression of social and economic frustration in a pre-political society, is both to render it almost incomprehensible and to pose the problem of explaining how anyone could ever have believed in it (or stopped believing in it).

An unusual gift, or one which was received just before the crisis, might also be suspect.[16] In the canton of Chabanais, around 1910, a family of farmers lost both father and son within a few weeks; almost immediately after these deaths, the daughter and the farm-servant fell ill with the same symptoms. The consulting doctor seems to have diagnosed tuberculosis, but when his treatment was unsuccessful, the servant's mother intervened. A man from a nearby village had told her that his brother had cast a spell on the afflicted family, and that the entire household would die. A much-favoured diviner of the locality was consulted. On inspecting hairs from the heads of the sick people, he announced: 'You're the victims of a spell cast on you, through fish that you were given two months ago.' (This gift had in fact been received.) The inmates were suitably impressed. They had all been intended to die, but he would be able to save them: they were to apply a hot brick, previously plunged in vinegar, to the affected part of the anatomy, three times a day for three days; immediately after this, the patients were to drink home-made brandy, 'and you'll have nothing more to fear'. He offered to inflict whatever vengeance they wanted on their tormentor. 'We wouldn't like to wreak vengeance on him', replied the stalwart members of the family, 'but he should be taught a good lesson.' In three days, he would be punished, promised the spell-breaker – prudently adding that he forbade them to ask after their victim. Happily for the counter-sorcerer's reputation, it was learned that when the first victim's widow uttered the sorcerer's name, the delinquent was afflicted by a violent attack of nose-bleeding.[17] That witchcraft beliefs owed more to materialism than to the fickle fantasy of unfettered imagination is evident in this incident. The spell appears to have been seen as a kind of poison, contained in a substance the family had consumed. The prescribed therapy does not seem to have been primarily mystical, but again material: the spell had been cast by means of a fish and could be eradicated by drinking brandy and by a sort of poultice. The view of nature here implied was coloured not so much by mysterious supernaturalism as by ignorant naturalism. Here, counter-magic worked both as a kind of justice – punishing the guilty sorcerer and setting the world to rights – and as a form of medicine, like the techniques of folk-medicine when no foul play was suspected. Similarly, a woman who went around shouting 'Heal me!' was supposed to have been put under a spell by one of her neighbours who had given her an apple. The psychiatrist Hélot devoted a study to hysteria in young girls from the area of Le Havre in the 1870s. In each case, their families attributed their behaviour to a charm. One girl thought an apple given to her by an old widow had been the means of casting the spell on her; another attributed it to a gift of sweets; in two other cases it was thought that wine the girls had been given to drink had enabled the sorcerers to cast their spells.[18]

These theories revolved around the notion of ill-will and envy; they reflected social discord, as they inculpated neighbours, relatives and, sometimes, outcasts. In May 1954, a neighbour was suspected of causing the inexplicable illness of a child whose mother had found a crown of feathers in her eiderdown. Rumour had it that the neighbour possessed books on magic, and the angry father wanted to report him to the police for his criminal activities. In the same region of Armagnac, bordering on the Landes, a grandmother was suspected of having cast a spell on her grandchildren the previous year – a not uncommon attribution of responsibility.[19] When a nine-year-old girl from Le Havre suddenly became averse to work and to her religious duties and began to have convulsions and hallucinations, poor relatives, with whom her immediate family got on badly, were suspected of casting a spell on her. This was confirmed when the *Grand* and *Petit Albert* were discovered in their house after their deaths.[20] According to one of Van Gennep's correspondents in Vaulx-Milieu, illness was at one time attributed to people with the evil eye, 'to neighbours, or even to people met by chance'. Van Gennep remarked that throughout France, 'the inhabitants of one village readily accuse those of the neighbouring village of sorcery, but deny they practise it themselves'.[21] This kind of attitude is comprehensible in the light of the common rivalries which radicals like Perdiguier and Nadaud recorded and deplored, and which surfaced at ritual fights and games. In specific cases, poor relatives or neighbours, or people one had met who had reason to harbour a grudge, were usually accused of casting the spell. A folklorist from the Embrum area remarked that charms 'were caused by bad deeds; for example, a housewife, who had refused hospitality to a beggar, attributed her child's illness some days later to an evil spell supposedly cast on her by the beggar who had been turned away'.[22] Illness and misfortune were often seen as a punishment for failing in one's social duties; in this perspective, witchcraft was a weapon of the poor, one of the few means of retaliating against the injustice of the relatively wealthy.[23] Without the context of often strained social relations, those witchcraft beliefs which centered on the origin of the spell would be incomprehensible.

The spell was seen less as the gratuitous irruption of mysterious supernatural powers into the ordinary world than as a consequence of prevailing conditions in the familiar world, of man's responses to poverty and ill-treatment. The sorcerer was frequently poorer than his victim. When misfortune followed on the heels of a luckless beggar, it was often attributed to a spell cast by the unfortunate person resentful of his victim's refusal to give alms.[24] Lack of charity in all its forms might be punished by the magical dispenser of rough justice. A woman from Nancy who fell victim to a fatal disease believed she had been charmed by a neighbour whom she had refused to visit.[25] A girl from Saint Bénil (Hautes-Alpes) had received a retainer from a merchant of Grenoble to whom she was bound to go in service. She repented of this idea, however, and neither took up her job nor restored the money which the merchant had sent. Some time later, when sitting by the fire with her sister, something fell down the chimney, hitting her violently on the shoulder. It was the merchant from Grenoble who, to avenge himself, had come to cast a spell on her. Thus she interpreted her experience and the local people ascribed her mental illness to diabolical possession, even going as far as to organize an unsuccessful exorcism.[26] To have recourse to the explanation of witchcraft might, as Keith Thomas has suggested, be a way of evading the guilt and moral opprobrium which the victim felt he had incurred by his shortcomings, and attaching them to the sorcerer instead. Sometimes the sense of having infringed traditional laws induced the victim to make his peace with the sorcerer, rather than seeking to bring him to justice. In the 1880s, in the canton of Cambrai-Est, a carter ascribed his horses' inability to pull their load to a quarrel he had with a witch. He went off to make his excuses, whereat the witch directed the loading of the cart which moved off without problem.[27] Witchcraft was thus sometimes seen as a way in which the least fortunate members of society (*cagous*, shepherds, beggars) might avenge themselves on the fortunate who failed to fulfil their social obligations.

The suspicion that sorcerers actually cast spells through occult rites did not exclude a common tendency to see the charm as an act caused spontaneously by an angry or displeased delinquent. Expressions of lively annoyance were thus sometimes feared. Laborde affirms that, in 1935, the proffering of ill will was still greatly feared in the Béarn. A famous witch threatened a woman one day, to the effect that her husband would have reason to regret comments he had made about the sorceress; when, some time later, the man fell ill, the witch was thought to have avenged herself.[28] Van Gennep cites a case from the Hautes-Alpes, in which a woman was supposed to have stopped her neighbour's cow's milk because she had been insulted.[29] Verbal abuse and fisticuffs seem to have been a common feature of rural life and the former was especially resented in a society where one's reputation and the neighbourly help and companionship it ensured were vital. When witchcraft was ascribed to ill-will, expressions of envy and resentment were naturally regarded with distrustful suspicion. At Cap-Sizun in Brittany, La Kerzéas, a notorious witch, asked the captain of a boat, which had just come into the harbour with a fine catch, to give her some fish. He refused. 'Au lieu de *kurzenned* [eels]', the old woman is reported to have replied, 'vous ne prendrez que des *spinegued* [dog-fish]' – and until the end of the year, the boat caught only dog-fish.[30] This story (which illustrates the stereotyped character of this kind of anecdote, with its plausible setting, unnatural – almost Biblical – speech, and penchant for the dramatic) incidentally indicates the popular attitude to the reporting of events. Literal fidelity to historical fact was less important than the aesthetic interest and moral of the story, which here encouraged generosity, if only out of prudence.

When more closely examined, what is unfamiliar and ridiculously implausible about these ideas is not so much the view of human nature and society which they implied, but the idiom in which this view was expressed. What should arrest us about the spell, in the first place, is not the sometimes exotic figuration through which it was made manifest, but the intention which it was thought to express and give effect to. Belief in witchcraft, both in its essential premise – that there was something wrong or morally objectionable about extreme misery – and in its tendency to see fellow-men as ultimately responsible for excessive suffering, seems less strange and incomprehensible than was once thought.[31]

Upon suspecting that his misfortunes were caused unnaturally by a member of the community, the victim tried to identify the culprit more specifically. Recent events of the victim's past were examined for significant evidence: had there been a quarrel? an unpleasant encounter with someone he suspected of wishing him ill? a venomous look? or even a meeting with a reputed sorcerer? Had someone lavished unwanted praise on him, in his good fortune, or sent him an unsolicited gift? If the victim could think of no recent quarrel in which the hatred of an enemy had made itself apparent, he searched among other equally natural and ordinary circumstances of his life, in order to discover whether a spell had been cast and to see if he could name the culprit. Tradition identified various mundane situations as potentially dangerous from this perspective. Thus, it was imprudent to allow a sorcerer to touch you, unless one reciprocated by touching him or saying to oneself: 'I'm on my guard'.[32] Looks, gifts, certain encounters could all, as we have seen, account for the victim's misfortune. These persuasions led to baroque, if occasionally tragic, reactions. In Ardres in Pas de Calais, during late September 1835, a sick man met an old lady who greeted him. He imagined that she had cast a spell on him, and attacked her in her house the next day, wounding her seriously.[33] Since the man's suspicions inserted themselves into a general tendency to attribute illness to a witch's spell, his act is not as marginal or irrelevant to social history as one might suppose. A veteran of Austerlitz who could not get rid of vermin, attacked his neighbours at Carney (Marne) because he thought they had cast a spell on him. In this, he was simply inspired by the common belief that the sorcerer could cover his victim with lice by looking at him.[34]

In some cases, his neighbours might help the victim to elaborate the story. Suspicion would crystallize around the local who either fitted the stereotype of the witch or wizard most exactly, or who was already regarded as an occult malefactor. In Normandy, a former soldier who enjoyed a reputation as a kind of magician, which he had acquired as a result of his taste for books, found himself accused of having caused the loss of the entire herd of a local farmer with whom he was on bad terms. His reputation as a fully-fledged sorcerer was thereupon established, and when, some time later, some locals whom he had plied with drink and tobacco subsequently fell ill, he was held to have been responsible.[35]

Consultation with the Counter-Sorcerer

There were more formal methods of identifying the culprit: one could consult a counter-sorcerer. This consultation, in the opinion of Jeanne Favret-Saada, is usually the first social manifestation of witchcraft in the modern Vendée, and it seems to have been the first practical step in imputed affairs of witchcraft in the nineteenth century also. The counter-sorcerer was often an important figure, as the frequency with which people had recourse to him in affairs of witchcraft suggests. He introduced a degree of formality and hence of convention and, in a sense, of legitimacy to the proceedings. He also helped to transform feelings of resentment and revolt into reactions tolerated by society. Rebellion against one's fate, unwillingness to accept one's destiny as natural or inevitable frequently took what one might be tempted to call an archaic judicial form,[36] whereby the existence of a crime was confirmed and the guilty party identified and punished. The unofficial dispensers of primitive justice, who frequently were far from being respected members of the community, never seem to have cast doubt upon the accuracy of their clients' speculations. On the contrary, they sought to confirm and clarify them. (As contemporary ethnologists were wont to observe, they often exploited the suspicions and imagination of the afflicted in order to reinforce their own authority.) Witchcraft furnished remarkably standard techniques, around and through which the patient or client elaborated the story which satisfied him through its conformity either with the facts as he saw them, or with his wishes. One of the counter-sorcerer's favourite techniques was to show the culprit in a mirror or in a bucket of water to the victim.[37] At the start of this century, a sorcerer from Limoges had recourse to this method, enabling a family from Le Croissant to see the face of a young man who had avenged himself of the rejection of his suit by one of the daughters by casting a spell on the whole family. In the village of La Judie (commune of Saint Maurice-des-Lions), a woman whose gravely ill husband lived and worked with his brother, was shown her sister-in-law when she consulted the local diviner.[38]

These culprits are typical of one class of supposed delinquents: drawn from the family or immediate neighbourhood of the victim, they indicate that the essence – as apart from the methods – of witchcraft lay in the all too human jealousies, rancour and tensions generated within close-knit poor communities, in which discomfort and competition for bare necessities were a frequent source of ill-will. Thus, in 1829, a farmer called Poirier from Maine-et-Loire, whose wife and livestock had fallen ill, sought an explanation for the misfortune under which he was labouring. Suspecting a spell, he consulted a diviner in Angers, with a view to discovering the culprit. He was told that if he prayed before a carafe of water he would see his tormentor. Such is the power of suggestion that Poirier imagined he saw his brother-in-law, whom he forthwith killed.[39] This case is – apart from the tragic ending – by no means exceptional. The technique whereby diviners replied to their clients' questions in a vague way, which put the onus of precise identification on the patient, was standard practice. In one sense the purpose of these consultations was to confirm the suspicions or the diagnosis which the victim was well on the way to formulating independently. Consultation of the diviner or spell-breaker enabled the victim to bring in a definitive judgement, which sometimes won a considerable measure of social approval. Poirier's identification of the sorcerer, rather than being self-evident in the light of objective experience, was a personal one, which seemed to be supported by a socially accepted system. The utility of the diviner in this area lay in the fact that, while no-one understood quite how his methods worked, certain procedures – such as the consultation of the diviner and acting on his instructions – were recognized by the community as appropriate and justifiable in view of the individual's suffering. Witchcraft therefore served to give social sanction to the individual's impulses and intuition.

There is no evidence to suggest that the nature or premises of the counter-sorcerer's techniques were, to any significant degree, the object of popular inquiry or critical interest. On the contrary, such curiosity was discouraged as dangerous. This indicates not, as Lucien Febvre seemed to think, limitless credulity or complete want of a sense of the impossible, but indifference and ignorance. The sorcerer was supposed to have been initiated into a knowledge which most men did not care to acquire, and people seem to have trusted him in his field much as they would now trust a doctor. Thus his affirmations were often believed, especially since they were apt to seem plausible or to confirm the individual's analysis or understanding of his experience. This coincidence is, of course, hardly surprising, when the affirmations issued not from the counter-sorcerer but, albeit without his realizing it, from the victim.

In the early nineteenth century, the *curé* of Réallon (Hautes-Alpes), having affirmed that he did not believe in magic, told the former prefect Ladoucette that one of his relatives saw in a mirror the person who had committed a theft in his house; while he himself, anxious to know if his great friend in the Indies was still alive, consulted a sorceress. She 'had a bowl of extremely clear water brought to us, and stirred it vigorously. When the water became still, I distinctly saw in its crystal-clear depths the features of my friend.'[40] The priest interpreted his impressions in the light of his worries and hopes, and magic thereby helped him to relax. In an incident cited by Trébucq, a young woman's attack of hysteria was suspected as being due to a spell cast by an old neighbour. A counter-sorcerer was called in, who administered a potion and held up a mirror to the girl, asking her if she recognized her enemy. She affirmed that the enemy was her neighbour and promptly recovered. In these cases, it is evident that the counter-sorcerer's job was not to provide unexpected answers but to play a formal, almost figurative, role. The Vendéenne cited by Trébucq had identified her witch before the ceremony: the healer merely enabled her to confirm her suspicions. As her case makes clear, the counter-sorcerer provided a *mise-en-scène*, which enabled her worries to be expressed with dramatic formality and then resolved. It legitimized her feelings, reassured her and provided a socially acceptable confirmation not just of her suspicions but also of her behaviour and anxiety.[41]

Another way of discovering the guilty person was to torture the responsible sorcerer in effigy: this would force him to reveal himself and would make him suffer so much that he would be obliged to lift the spell he had cast. To do this, it was usual to seek the advice and expertise of a counter-sorcerer – although some people might, like the anguished father cited by Meyrac, imitate the usual rites independently.[42] A man who lived at Warcq specialized in this: he would come at night to the afflicted family, sacrifice a year-old lamb, hang its liver in the chimney and pierce it with a big iron needle. This rite was supposed to ensure that the witch would fall ill instantly, and she was supposed to be likely to die as a result of it.[43] Similar beliefs existed in Alsace and Lorraine, in Saintonge and in Haute-Garonne. In the Gironde, Mensignac found a recipe for casting this sort of charm: a veal heart, stuck with crossed pins, was hung in the chimney, while the counter-sorcerer recited: 'I ask God for the body of such and such a person (name the person) to dry up little by little, as this veal heart will, and for him to die.' This supplication was to be followed by several Paters and Aves.[44] One should not be too taken aback to find such ruthless sentiments expressed without any apparent sense of incongruity in a prayer to the Christian God and associated with orthodox prayers – the notion of a merciful divinity whose dignity was never ruffled by spite, the desire for vengeance, ribald or rabelaisian humour seems to have been more characteristic of official than of popular religion.

The technique of boiling or drying animal innards was seen as hurting only the guilty person, who was clearly felt to have merited his torments.[45] His sufferings might oblige him to come and ask for mercy.[46] The person unfortunate enough to interrupt such a ceremony was held to be the sorcerer, compulsively seeking out the place of his torture. Thus, a traveller who came upon a number of inhabitants of Champoléon (Hautes-Alpes) – whose livestock and harvests were afflicted with spells – boiling up stolen new nails and a black cock in vinegar in an earthenware pot, was nearly killed by one of their number, who was armed and lying in wait behind the door for the arrival of the sorcerer. Only with difficulty was the man able to persuade them of his innocence.[47] The allegedly guilty ran the risk of being rudely punished. The spiritist Piérart was told of a man from the district of Avesnes who, having prescribed an operation to lift a charm off horned animals, was himself vigorously assaulted by two farmhands when he went to investigate the outcome of the baroque proceedings. These had demonstrated the same strange mixture of apparent piety with what the Church would have castigated as sacrilege, in that the operator was obliged to boil his black hen with nails only after making a forty-day novena and when he was in a state of grace.[48] The eminent folklorist of the Nivernais, Achille Millien, recounted the story of how a charm-breaker, having diagnosed a spell on a herd of cattle, ordered the owner to boil an ox's heart with nails, which would force the culprit to appear. A man arrived to borrow something, only to be greeted by the counter-sorcerer inquiring of the victim: 'What suffering do you want me to inflict on him? that he should lose an ear or drop dead?' To which the generous farmer responded by requiring only the delinquent's ear.[49]

Exacerbation of Tension. It was quite commonly considered, by contemporary officials, that the counter-sorcerer's implicit identification of the guilty part fomented local feuds, bitterness and quarrels to no small degree. This sometimes even resulted in physical attacks and convictions for assault.[50] The injunction to avoid one's guilty neighbours and the tendency to be suspicious of those thought to be sorcerers were not uncommon.[51] Some counter-sorcerers were aware of the dangers of being too specific in their identification of the sorcerer and tended to be circumspect when pressed on this by curious clients. In the low-lying area known as the Sologne Bourbonnaise, a farmer concluded that his good milk-cow, which appeared to have more or less given up the ghost, was under a spell. In that persuasion, he consulted a sorcerer who made the unfortunate animal consume some blessed candle and cinders from the Christmas fire (to which great protective virtue was traditionally ascribed) wrapped up in a cabbage leaf, which had the happy, if surprising, effect of curing the beast. The farmer, however, desired to know who had cast the spell, whereat the sage delivered himself of the somewhat sybilline clarification that the farmer would recognize the guilty person by a 'sign', while prudently refusing to divulge a name. The perplexed farmer did not forget the matter, for when some days later he saw a poor old woman making her way through the village, emitting frequent loud cries and affected with an incurable hiccough, he decided that she was the 'bad neighbour' and that her shouts were the sign to which the counter-sorcerer had referred.[52] The person who filled the description given by the counter-sorcerer proved to be an old woman – indicating yet again the role of stereotypes, where a more immediate suspicion had not developed, in accusations of witchcraft.

This habit could lead to serious friction when some victims, not unnaturally, wished to remonstrate with these disagreeable neighbours. In Montluçon, in 1875, a baker called Pajot was tried for his fraudulent activities in the area of Cérilly. Pajot, who had inherited a missal from a *curé* and had built his new-found fortune (derived from the practice of sorcery) upon possession of this imposing tome, was uninhibited when it came to naming the culprit. Thus, he accused of sorcery one Gilbert Dormet, who farmed his own land with the help of his brother-in-law and who found himself the object of local loathing, as a result of Pajot's remarks during his visits to the ailing cattle of the district. Near to Dormet's farm was the impoverished establishment of two young sharecroppers, Venaut and Collin, who at Christmas asked Pajot to cure their herd. These two had moved in the previous November and were on poor terms with their immediate neighbours, Dormet and his brother-in-law Gabillat. Pajot said that the unsympathetic farmers were responsible for their troubles – an accusation which the sharecroppers believed – and discouraged them from speaking to Dormet. Similar incidents occurred throughout the neighbourhood. The consequent isolation into which Dormet and Gabillat were plunged was not free of incidents. Another neighbour, Gilbert Arnaud, believing Dormet and Gabillat to have cast a spell on his herd, frequently fought with Gabillat, boxing and insulting him; as Gabillat explained: 'he called me a robber and a sorcerer', and alleged 'that . . . I stole my neighbours' milk by magic'. Dormet and his family were also called 'bad neighbours' and 'sorcerers' (a revealing equivalence), and Arnaud had even gone so far as to say that if he ever learned that Dormet had cast a spell on his cows, he would kill him. Nor was Dormet the only person to suffer from this kind of accusation: Pajot wended his insouciant and profitable way through the lower echelons of Cérilly society, sowing dissension among the poor and afflicted.[53]

Primitive Justice

Being slandered was one thing but the consequences of counter-sorcerers' accusations could be tragic, as the miserable, naive or unbalanced reacted violently to what they learned. Jean and Pierre Joseph Teulié were prosperous farmers from the lowland commune of Lapenne, in Ariège. In 1846, their flock of sheep fell ill, and since their neighbour's herd was well, they deduced this was no natural contagion but a spell cast by their shepherd, Joseph Séguy. Séguy laughed at this accusation and attempted to reassure his employers by predicting that the neighbour's animals would soon be unwell too. When this proved to be exact, the brothers were convinced of his malevolent powers and turned to traditional methods of disposing of him. They had masses said to make him wither away and die, and when this proved ineffectual, consulted an old woman, who told them that Séguy would fall ill and lift the spell if they burned a shepherd's crook at both ends. This singular enchantment they accompanied, before a fire, with earnest prayers to God – but the Almighty remained deaf to these, as to previous entreaties. They dismissed the shepherd – to no avail – then reappointed him on the assurance that he would cure the animals. But when these continued to languish, they murdered him.[54]

Van Gennep reports that in the Auvergne and Velay, it was thought that in order to recover the milk which a witch stole, one had to beat and ill-treat her, and that this belief was acted upon throughout France.[55] The evidence suggests that this affirmation is exact. Meyrac was called, in the Ardennes, to a woman called 'La Morouaine', a reputed witch and healer from the area of Gespunsart. He found her bathed in blood, beaten up by an irate patient who felt that his failure to recover from a skin disease could be ascribed to her and that a sound beating would force her to cure him more promptly. The choleric client, having subsequently been cured by some miraculous water of her prescription, became one of her most ardent admirers, apparently undisturbed by the fact that he had almost killed her.[56] Nor were such persuasions always eradicated by agencies of progress, like military service: when Doctors Cabanès and Nass wrote a history of poisons and charms in 1903, one of them claimed to have served on a jury examining the case of a young soldier on leave, who had used force to make a neighbour lift a spell supposedly cast on his father's herd.[57] Rabaud in a little book on popular superstitions, gave several examples of such attacks at the turn of the century. In July 1902, in the commune of Beauvais (Tarn), a man called Bertrand and his son were shot in the night by one Lanzeral, who believed that Bertrand had made him ill by casting a spell on him. A counter-sorcerer from Castlenau d'Estrefonds had revealed this to him for twenty francs.[58] Violence seems to have been a common feature of traditional witchcraft: those who believed that a spell had been cast on them and who thought they knew who was responsible, felt quite justified in imprisoning the putative witch or sorcerer, threatening her or him with torture (usually by burning) if the charm were not broken on the spot.

In one rare case, we catch an explicit glimpse of the victim's state of mind prior to the crime. In 1832, in the Aube, the wife of a peasant called Mignot was dying. Her husband, suspecting she was charmed, consulted a diviner, who confirmed the diagnosis and enabled Mignot see the guilty sorcerer, one Edmé Jacquier. Mignot resolved to try to frighten the tormenter into breaking the spell by sending him a threatening letter:

> Fais et delibairé à Racine, le 13 mai 1832. Sorcié et majisie, si tu notts pas ce que tat mie cheus nous dissis à 8 jourre, tu vairat ce que tu na pat corre vus: tue et sorsié, mais fis de sorcire: je dejat chairce la droje, je la traivraie; toute la familes, vous périré ce mois ici, à la fille; vou seré brulé tous: je ne peu pas t'an rageté: tu mourat. Aidde de la mors.
>
> (Signed and sealed at Racine, on 13 May 1832. Sorcerer and magician, if you don't remove what you have put on our home within the week, you will see what you haven't yet seen: you are a sorcerer and moreover the son of a witch: I've already sought justice, I will find it: you and your whole family will perish this month one by one; you will all burn; I cannot save you: you will die. Death's Assistant.)

But Mignot's wife died and he tried to burn down Jacquier's house[59] (the burning of an enemy's property was a pre-modern form of protest).[60] Here was an indubitable desire for vengeance, although it was sought only when the sorcerer had shown himself to be incorrigible. In the first instance, Mignot was preoccupied with saving his wife and hoped to intimidate Jacuier into curing her. It is clear, too, that Mignot thought himself justified.

Frequently, torture was used for similar ends. It seems to have been common practice to kidnap suspects, imprison them in the victim's house and attempt to extort a confession of guilt from them by threatening to burn and abuse them. Sometimes the alleged sorcerer would satisfy his tormenters by acknowledging his guilt and pretending to break his spell; but often he maintained his innocence and was murdered as a result. Mensignac tells the story of a peasant from the district of La Réole, who asked a diviner to advise him on his daughter's long, inexplicable illness. The sage informed him that her sickness came from a *mal donné* and that only the person who had cast it could remove it. The father swore vengeance and, on his return home, observed his family and neighbours carefully for some days, with a view to identifying the sorcerer. Finally, he came to suspect an old woman who lived nearby; when she came to make neighbourly enquiries about the child's health, she was locked into the house by the father and mother and was threatened with being thrown into fire if she did not instantly remove the spell. The woman, like many before her, decided that her only chance of survival lay in assuming her role as witch, so she approached the child's bed, touched her and made various impressive gestures, with which she claimed to have lifted the charm. Luckily, she was allowed to return home.[61]

The case is a typical example of the circumstances in which witchcraft came to be suspected, and of how such suspicions were confirmed by the counter-sorcerer, who served not so much to inform as to legitimize or give a certain authority to these suppositions. It indicates that supernatural aspects of witchcraft were overshadowed by more natural considerations: the account of suffering given in accusations of witchcraft centered not so much on the witch's mysterious machinations as on the fact that an elderly neighbour had wilfully caused the illness; it was not so much a supernatural account as a social and human one. The response was certainly immediate and all too terrestrial. In 1826, when Jeanne Forcheriat, a day labourer from Récharq (Landes), was suspected of causing a child's illness, the parents Jean Juzau and his wife Françoise enticed her into their house, where they forthwith accused her of being responsible for their troubles. When she denied the charge, she was put on a lighted fire and escaped only by promising to cure the child. In July of the same year, at the village of Saint Paulse (Landes), a confession of guilt was extorted from Marie Lasalle by one Pierre Lavielle, who was persuaded that she had cast a spell on his cousin and who placed her on burning straw until she promised to cure the girl.[62] The number of cases of this kind that were reported in the official press, or of which we have some other kind of record, is surprisingly large;[63] and they display a striking degree of uniformity, given that these practices were prescribed and regulated by an oral tradition which the authorities had been attempting to eradicate, albeit erratically, since the Counter-Reformation.

These crimes reflected traditional beliefs and hence were not as eccentric as one might initially believe. It was most unusual for the courts to indicate any mental deficiency on the part of those they were trying. In the absence of such evidence, we are led to the conclusion that only a relatively small number of assailants were insane.[64] Dr Costedoat, who conducted one of the few studies on the subject, went further than this in asserting the social nature of this kind of crime: 'Crimes against sorcerers ... are sometimes, but only exceptionally, the work of isolated madmen, who attack their persecutors, mistakenly believing them to be powerful magicians. Leaving these rare cases aside, attacks on sorcerers are the work of groups ... '[65] It is true that such groups were occasionally punished by the official courts; but the law ignored popular culture and this resulted in judgements which, viewed from the village, must have seemed erratic. Crimes which were inspired by the same beliefs and intentions – which were in the context of popular cultue broadly similar – received widely different treatment in the courts. Attacks on witches ranged from indirect maiming (which was no less reprehensible than a direct attack, given that it was believed that magical techniques were just as efficient as more immediate ones), to threats, abuse, torture and murder.[66] Sometimes, the victim of the spell thought he had killed someone, but was not brought to court, because officials had not allowed for the prosecution of offences based on premises which were dismissed as ridiculous. Others, who had killed where they had intended primarly to frighten, were convicted of murder; while more, who had planned murder, received relatively lenient sentences from judges who ascribed their actions to superstition and ignorance. The identification of a person as a criminal by the courts – while illuminating official legal attitudes – does not necessarily reflect his position in his own milieu.

Public Attitudes to the Sorcerer and his Victim

To see these cases as shedding little light on society in general, as illustrative only of criminal marginalia, assumes (as the nineteenth-century moralist was wont to do) that the criminal is not only a reprobate, but exceptional in actions and ideas too.[67] The man who attacked the sorcerer generally acted according to the beliefs of those around him and obeyed a sense of justice shared by them: he was not necessarily an outcast. In assaulting the witch, he was usually supported by his family and often also by the local community. Peasants showed little sympathy for sorcerers – as opposed to healers – and often appear to have regarded them, not the persons punished by the official courts, as the real criminals. In this perspective, the victim was acting in self-defence in trying to get the sorcerer to lift the spell. He might do this symbolically, thus escaping the attention and censure of state lawyers, or he might use violence which marked him as a criminal in the eyes of the state. But his relation, in either case, to his own environment remained the same, and he was no more or less typical of it because the law had seized him.

The general attitude to magical crime was neither that of automatic condemnation nor of immediate approval. In 1839, in Valensole (Basses-Alpes), a farmer killed an elderly woman whom he thought to have cast a spell on his farm, causing the death of eighty-six sheep and pigs. Various neighbours, when interrogated, expressed neither horror nor revulsion at what had happened, but appeared to be convinced that the widow had indeed been a witch. One man ascribed the demise of his animals to her, and affirmed that he would believe in witches and sorcerers all his life. The widow's daughter thought she had killed her baby and caused the illness of her second child. Not that the old woman had done anything to dispel this reputation. Indeed, since she lived by begging, she may have even exploited her magical renown in the hope that, in the absence of spontaneous charity, fear might provide for her subsistence. At all events, her somewhat misanthropic remarks were hardly calculated to induce sentiments of benign tolerance towards her. When a woman refused her the widow's mite, the old woman threatened the uncharitable person with loss of her livestock and, by an unfortunate coincidence for the widow, the animals subsequently fell sick. She was ultimately killed because, when reproached by her murderer with having caused the illness of his beasts, she predicted that more would perish.[68]

Passivity sometimes amounted to tactit collaboration with and approval of the assailants' acts. In March 1834, in the commune of Vergnoz (Isère), Annette Rumilier became mentally ill. Her partial recovery was attended by the suspicion that an old widowed beggar-woman, Marie Chevalier, who was generally thought to be a witch, had caused her illness by casting a spell on her. Annette's family and neighbours agreed with this verdict, but to make sure, Annette consulted a counter-sorcerer in a neighbouring hamlet. He informed her that she must build a big fire, boil a cauldron of water and old shoes and place a chair beside the fire: the first person to sit in the chair would be the culprit and would break the charm only if placed on the fire. The following day, the beggar-woman arrived at Annette's house and sat beside the fire. Since this meant she was the witch, she was tortured and, as she was unable to cure her alleged victim, she was driven from the house, beaten up in front of the whole village and finally flung into a gorge. No-one in the place came to her aid – a lapse that cannot be attributed to cowardice: on the contrary, her death was seen as a benefit to the community and the mayor refused to draw up the act of accusation against Annette's guilty family.[69] The passivity of the villagers would seem to have reflected genuine sympathy for the witch's tormentors[70] and some hostility for the agents of official justice who wished to bring them to court. Implicit condemnation of the witch appears to have lain behind the unwillingness demonstrated by the inhabitants of the commune of Charance to come to the aid of an old beggar-woman, Féron, in 1836. She was generally believed to be a witch – an impression she did nothing to dispel. She was wont to receive the charity of the family of a farmer, whose sons, she somewhat tactlessly used to predict, would go mad. When one boy fell ill, as she had prophesized, the locals concluded that she was responsible and would lift the spell only if tortured. She was duly lured to the farm and placed on a fire until she agreed (although maintaining her innocence) to restore the boy's sanity. After this, having been flung out of the house, she was left to die of her injuries by the villagers, who were said to hate and fear her.[71]

Passive connivance between those officially regarded as criminals and their neighbours, who seemed to regard not the attacker but his victim as the real criminal, was an occasional and significant feature of popular witchcraft. Lynchings and ill-treatment of their magical pariahs by entire villages were recorded. In 1837, during the grape harvest at Verzenay near Reims, a wine-merchant arrived from town to see how the harvest was turning out, to find a man being beaten up by a crowd while the village looked on. The individual was supposedly a sorcerer who had caused a child's illness and had stolen the milk and eggs from his neighbour's farms by magic.[72] Similarly, Ladoucette, writing of the Hautes-Alpes, told how, in 1802, a woman who was accused of casting spells on herds and men was hung by locals who thought she gained new strength from contact with the earth; while another witch, an old beggar-woman, was allowed to die almost without succour in the same area. He also reported the case of a woman some generations earlier, who, having received no invitation to a marriage-feast, swore vengeance and was burned to death by a number of people anxious to forestall her retribution.[73] Piérart recounts that an old woman was burned near Beaumont (district of Avesnes) in 1835, on the public square in the presence of the local authorities, who made no attempt to stop the proceedings.[74] In the same period, an old woman, Delik Kerlaër from the commune of Plogoff, being supposed to have the evil eye, so terrified the local population that they decided one night to set fire to her house and she died of burns.[75] These attacks, although they were exceptional – mainly because they were public rather than private – indicate that the motives and methods of lone assailants did not necessarily isolate them from society, but sometimes reflected the beliefs and values of traditional culture.

The preoccupation with vengeance which traditional witchcraft beliefs and practices evinced, indicates that people thought naturalistically, if not rationally. It also had drawbacks: the vulnerable and suffering were virtually obsessed with finding someone to hold responsible for their misfortunes – a reaction by no means peculiar to pre-modern societies, but often groundless and dangerous. Myth legitimized their speculations and their subsequent actions. The lack of realism of these mental operations is striking. Excessive misery seems to have provoked a retreat into the world of the imagination, where traditional symbols might reinforce private and sometimes public prejudice. That people were ready to collaborate in these enterprises points to the tenuous emotional stability of some communities, to a persistent tendency towards escapism.

Conclusion

There is ample evidence for the existence of witchcraft in the nineteenth century, where it appears to have flourished mainly as a form of counter-magic, as a response to a supposed initial crime. It explained misfortune in social and psychological terms, in that it ascribed the effects of the spell (disease, death, loss of prosperity) to the ill-will or jealousy of a neighbour or relative. It sought to put the situation to rights by what masqueraded as a form of primitive justice – establishing the criminal's identity, insisting that he undo the evil he had effected, and, where this proved impossible, punishing those held to be guilty vindictively. If witchcraft is considered as reflecting strained relations between men in a poor, traditional society, as relieving and justifying people's anxiety and anger, rather than as being primarily preoccupied with explaining and controlling the physical structure of nature, it becomes easier to understand why it was such a common feature of peasant cultures and why the evidence of reality did not always contradict magical beliefs. Counter-magic obviously reflected the tensions generated by the social obligations imposed by a subsistence economy. However, in its implicit (if in fact disingenuous) condemnation of envy and resentment and its view of the natural destiny of man (that of relative health and well-being), it ostensibly implied an archaic ideal of a society at once fraternal and hierarchical, from which the vices of jealousy and greed and the extremes of suffering born of poverty were absent. But this primitive idyll was flawed. For witchcraft in fact constituted an arsenal of practices and habits of mind which justified self-deception, fabulation and violence directed at the vulnerable. It enabled those who in fact fell short of the ideals celebrated in traditional society to pose as the victims of those they had hurt: it created a vested interest in the shared lie and encouraged the retreat into myth.

V

The Possessed

If one of the functions of folklore was to voice an otherwise inarticulate range of experience, implying an outlook not necessarily inconsistent with practical materialism, why were the claims of children to have seen the Virgin Mary taken seriously? What made ordinary people believe the ravings of lunatics who thought they were possessed by the devil or they were God's annointed prophets?

Social Attitudes to Madness

Anthropologists and psychiatrists have shown that attitudes to madness have varied at different times and in different places. Ruth Benedict, in a famous essay entitled 'Anthopology and the Abnormal', insisted that normality was a relative concept. Some cultures valued and honoured behaviour which we would consider abnormal: 'Any society, according to its major preoccupations, may increase and intensify even hysterical, epileptic, or paranoid symptoms, at the same time relying socially in a greater [. . .] degree upon the very individuals who display them.'[1] To know if their wishes would be fulfilled, Crow Indians stimulated hallucinations which were both shaped by and interpreted through their culture; while among the Balahis in Northern India, people who could induce trances in which the Gods spoke to them were consulted in cases of prolonged or dangerous illness.[2] The trances of Siberian shamans and of the *zârs* of Sudan, which were also exploited for medical purposes, were carefully studied and imitated by neophytes. However, in the opinion of Leiris, neither artifice nor pathology alone provide an adequate explanation of possession. The phenomenon was more complex, as it was also a way of expressing and banishing tension and dissent, encouraged and largely shaped by society. Women were more apt to be possessed by a *zâr*, especially when abuse or poverty depressed or angered them. Possession provided an alibi, enabling the possessed to speak and act as they would not normally do. Fun was poked at social and religious values; mimicry, too, often marked displays of possession; complaints about the contemporary world were voiced. Some people sought relief from illness during these sessions; others enjoyed their liberating and festive dimensions.[3]

Ancient Greece adopted a similar approach both to mental illness and to impulses and emotions which were deeply unsettling. Commenting on what he called 'prophetic madness', E.R. Dodds observed: 'The Greeks believed in their Oracle, not because they were superstitious fools, but because they could not do without believing in it.' The dicta of the Apollo reassured man of the Archaic Age, compensating for his ignorance and sense of insecurity. Likewise, the Dionysiac ritual was principally cathartic, enabling man briefly to express his irrational impulses and escape the constricting expectations of society: '... Its psychological function was to satisfy and relieve the impulse to reject responsibility, an impulse which exists in all of us and can become under certain social conditions an irresistible craving.' The repression or failure to recognize the symptoms of emotional pressure would have been intolerable for the individual and ultimately dangerous for society.[4]

In hierarchical societies, in Bastide's opinion, collective hysteria enacted the revenge of the oppressed; in colonized countries, the indigenous population expressed its hostility to the values imposed on it and condemned the colonizers; in monarchies, crises of collective possession attempted to wrest power away, if only briefly, from political authorities; in American societies, hysteria was a means of catharsis; while in South America, outbursts of this kind among the lower classes could no longer confirm and celebrate society's organization, but challenged it and relieved men of strain. Bastide held that this was also the case in Western societies:

> Our trances in the West constitute a *refusal* of language ... Our western trances ... are a means of release, exaltation, intoxication, they belong to the realm of *game* ... Contemporary western trances are a form of protest against or *challenge* to the world of rules, norms and values. They are a revolt against society. Politics are not of secondary, but of primarily importance to them.[5]

In short, outbursts of possession were not erratic, marginal aberrations, of little significance to the student of society, but were encouraged and formalized by the prevailing culture as a means of dispelling or diverting inclinations and feelings which were potentially corrosive, or of expressing feelings which could find no other outlet.

Traditional attitudes in France in the nineteenth century seem, in many ways, to have been closer to this approach than to that of contemporary psychiatry. Although traditional French culture was considerably less formal and elaborate in its treatment of abnormal experience than many cultures, this was perhaps inevitable in a society whose élite not only subscribed to different ideas but was also explicitly bent upon eradicating and replacing traditional beliefs. Possession seems to have acted, to some extent, as a safety valve: not only was it sometimes caused by stress, but it was also used either to escape obligations or to express disaffection. The idiom of popular aberrations should not be taken too literally: for while it was often derived from religion, its cosmological and metaphysical implications were, if not irrelevant, at least secondary to its psychological and sociological import.

Influence of Culture on Delirium

That culture influenced mental illness in nineteenth-century rural France in a number of ways was evident to contemporary doctors. Some disorders seemed peculiar to rural culture to some early psychiatrists, who concentrated more upon the ideas expressed by the ill than upon the character and mode of manifestation of the symptoms. The differences were largely illusory, being due to the fact that ill country-people drew on the imaginative heritage of the countryside, rather than on urban culture, to describe their feelings and to account for them.[6] In turn, their experiences were often seen as confirming the relevance of these traditions. When the ill claimed to have seen the devil, when they furnished conventional descriptions of him, they enriched and reaffirmed imaginative tradition. 'When I was a child', wrote Gabriel Le Bras, 'the devil was a familiar character. I have known men who fought with him. I know houses where he knocked on the door.'[7] In the Bocage Vendéen, according to Dr Boismoreau, belief in the devil and fear of hell were important elements in men's consciousness. 'The devil', he affirmed, 'has nothing mysterious about him.'[8] Since the eleventh and twelfth centuries, iconographic tradition, in both ecclesiastical sculpture and printed image, had insisted on the devil's hybrid appearance, equipping him with horns, wings, claws and tails, and had stocked hell with flames, cauldrons and serpents.[9] Descriptions which visionaries furnished were normally in the classical mould. One fifty-six-year-old woman, whose sight was impaired, imagined she saw a 'tall and black' devil.[10] An hysteric in the wards of the Salpêtrière, who was told by the almoner that she was possessed, began to have visions of the devil and described him vividly:

> He was tall, with scales and legs ending in claws; he stretched out his arms as if to seize me; he had red eyes and his body ended in a great tail like a lion's, with hair at the end; he grimaced, he laughed, and seemed to say, 'I shall have her!'[11]

A Breton baker who saw the devil beside his shop, to his terror, asserted that 'he was all black with big horns and big teeth', although 'he had ... hardly any time to examine him, as he quickly took to his heels from fear'.[12] A twenty-nine-year-old woman from Tarn, who had become ill while nursing her aunt, had hallucinations, seeing rats, grasshoppers, horned and helmeted 'devils wearing pelts'. The devil usually either conformed to the classic image complete with horns, tail and 'eyes like braiziers' – or appeared as a threatening man or animal, like a dragon or a snake.[13] Macario cited the case of an elderly woman, who was praying fervently one summer night at the foot of a country cross when the devil suddenly appeared beside her. He wore an enormous hat which covered his face and 'a large dark tunic', which left only his forked feet visible.[14] Thereafter, she was plagued by his visits until another old woman advised her to throw a bucket of water on him and this trick worked. If the devil's mien was rather unusual, the manner of his manifestation was not: legends to the effect that the devil appeared at midnight at crossroads abounded, and in some versions he came to wayside crosses. Nor was there anything unprecedented about the torments he inflicted. The reality of the woman's visions were not doubted by her friend, who rather collaborated with her in dispelling her obsession. Witches in the Hautes-Alpes furnished identifications which drew more on folklore than on iconographic tradition. To one woman, he appeared as a good-looking man, dressed in red and white; to another, as a black cock, and later as a pale young man with a hoarse voice wearing a long tunic; another saw a black dog and then an old negro, dressed in black, to whom she sacrificed a black hen every year on 1 May. Marguerite Coyffrier from Arrieux saw the devil as a black cock, then as a black cat, and finally as a red-haired man aged between thirty and forty, wearing a short grey tunic and a black cloak, whom she invoked to avenge herself on her enemies.[15] These descriptions helped to reinforce common legends and bolstered the imaginative world of tradition.

The influence of culture on delirium was also evident in the common interpretation of mental illness, according to which madness was sometimes caused by witchcraft. Just as people drew on religious imagery to describe their feelings, so too they might derive their vocabulary from sorcery. Dr Boismoreau observed that the peasants of the Bocage Vendéen saw nervous disorders as 'the result of a spell'. A young man suddenly developed epilepsy, with acute and prolonged attacks, 'during which he abandons himself to incoherent talk, senseless deeds. It's a spell, G. is mad . . . Old Chouans . . . and pious old ladies tacitly agree that he's possessed. Two months later he improves and then is cured. The illness was a spell: it was bound to last as long as the sorcerer had decreed it should.'[16] These attitudes were to be found in other parts of France as well. The father of a young maniac treated by Doctors Marie and Violet assured them that his son's indisposition was due to a spell, and the father of a young farmer from the Nièvre, who imagined that a spell had been cast on him, paid sorcerers a thousand francs to cure his son.[17] In 1908, a man whose family believed him to have been charmed by a local sorcerer was admitted into the asylum at La Roche-Gandon. His mother, after many fruitless visits to doctors, had been cured by this character, who had also treated the father for what was alleged to be anemia, to no effect.

They had refused to pay what the sorcerer demanded, and concluded that he had retaliated by causing the son's illness.[18] The fact that the mentally ill often drew on a vocabulary they shared with normal people to account for their symptoms helps to explain why their descriptions and interpretations of their feelings were so often accepted in traditional communities.

Functions and Forms of Madness

Escaping Responsibility. Esquirol remarked on the striking suggestibility of demonomaniacs and the numerous pretexts for eccentric behaviour with which traditional culture furnished them: '... A shock, the fear of having been charmed, an angry or threatening look, a vehement sermon, the force of example, are enough to make an attack of demonomania break out. Possession is often caused by nothing more than the sorcerer's glance.'[19] It was not uncommon for apparent possession to be brought on by fear and guilt, by the hysteric's conviction that he had failed to live up to society's expectations of him. The convenience of possession was, however, that the burden of guilt was shifted from the person whose behaviour had in the first place been open to criticism to the sort of vulnerable person often suspected of crime, in traditional society.

Threats and imprecations seem to have provoked disturbed behaviour all the more readily in that society tended to vindicate the mentally ill, rather than the persons they accused of wronging them. Beggars who were refused charity were particularly apt to be put in the wrong in this way. In November 1846, at Claire-Fontaine near Rambouillet, a servant refused alms to a beggar and was then threatened by the man as he withdrew. That evening, everything in the house was said to move and the servant was seized with convulsions on the spot where she had turned the man away.[20] In 1906, Fanjoux treated a thirty-eight-year-old woman, D., who ascribed her mental illness to a similar encounter. Some months before her marriage, a gipsy had arrived at her door, asking for charity. D. refused and the beggar responded by touching her clothes and making magic signs, thereby casting a spell on her. Years later, the gipsy met D. again: she renewed her spell and extended it to the entire family; she gave D. a piece of paper on which she had written: you will regret what you have lost. D., who was then ill, decided that the gipsy had taken her soul. When she turned another beggar away from her door, she regretted this too, concluding that the beggar had been none other than Christ, come under this disguise to rescue her. The local *curé* tried unsuccessfully to exorcise her. A chemist (who sounds more like a sorcerer) whom she consulted, gave her a powder and told her to kill a black hen at midnight and sprinkle the blood over the house, without telling anyone. The remedy was useless because she could not keep the secret. Eventually, she was committed to the asylum.[21]

Guilt and fear quite often precipitated nervous disorders. A beggar-woman whose plea for help was turned down told the person who rejected her request that she would die within six months, which she did – from fear, according to the doctor who reported the incident.[22] In June 1837, a hawker, who tried to earn a living by displaying a showcase of wax statues of the Virgin and Child and various saints, went begging in the poor part of Lormes (the suburb of Vieux-Château). A young girl turned him away rudely and he walked away muttering mysterious threats. 'That instant, the young girl...felt giddy, soon lost her head, began singing and talking in the most incoherent way and, in short, giving every sign characteristic of madness. The rumour that the beggar was a sorcerer spread immediately. The young girl's state was attributed to the strength of his spells. The poor devil, fortunately for him, was then going about a much less credulous part of Lormes, where he met sensible people who protected him against the populace. No one doubts that without their intervention', added the laconic journalist, 'they would have resorted to desperate measures against him.'[23] Beggars were not the only scapegoats, however; relatives or friends who had been offended were just as vulnerable to the accusations of the mentally disturbed. In this, the manner of thinking and proceeding of the ill was not significantly different from those who were presumed sane. A young woman presented herself at a Parisian hospital with a paralysed leg. The normal symptoms of paralysis were missing and the doctors decided that she was hysterical. She was therefore hypnotized, the suggestion was put to her that she would use her leg, and when she awoke, she was found to be cured. She returned with her arm, then her hand and then her neck paralysed. She was hypnotized again and made to recount her past history. It emerged that her father was a village sorcerer. When she fell in love with a young man and left her father, the old man cursed the young couple. The daughter, impressed by her father's magical powers and knowing the many acts of witchcraft which he had performed, fell ill. The charade was played out by the doctor, as the account cryptically states, and the girl was cured.[24] It is interesting to note what made for the success of the treatment: the doctors provided a ritual framework, within which she could recount or even act out her experiences and which served as a prestigious device enabling her to recover, to give up he neurotic behaviour without losing face. Her explanations were accepted rather than challenged; she could, without being humiliated, express and relieve herself of her worries and, thus unburdened, resume her ordinary life. The similarities of this approach to exorcism (which equally exploited the cathartic possibilities of a kind of theatre of illness) on the one hand and with psychoanalysis on the other are notable.

Not dissimilar reactions were sometimes provoked by arguments with lovers. One such case – first observed by Esquirol and much cited thereafter by psychiatrists – concerned a wool-spinner from the countryside, who, naturally, had often heard stories about sorcerers. When, at the age of thirty-seven, she was about to marry, she discovered that her husband-to-be was having an affair with someone else. She broke off with him and a year later married someone else. 'The man she abandoned threatened to take his revenge and told her to go to the devil. A man in the village, who was supposed to be a sorcerer, offered her body up to the devil without her realising it.' Some years later, returning home one day from a long walk, she suddenly felt very tired, and then:

> she felt a movement and noises in her head, like the noise and movement of a spinning wheel; she took fright, yet nonetheless continued on her way, but, on the way, she was lifted up more than seven feet above the ground. Once home, she could neither eat nor drink; she remembered the threat made against her and was convinced she was under a spell. She took lots of remedies, she prayed, made novenas, pilgrimages, wore a stole which a priest had given her next her skin. All to no effect. The devil stuck with her.

Her attacks occurred every day, at the same time. She was brought to a sorcerer in a nearby village, who, before the girl's eyes, stuck nails into a sheep's heart. After this, she recovered until she met the sorcerer again, whereat she had a relapse. She was brought to the Salpêtrière three years later. The way the woman explained the onset of her illness was consistent with ideas that were commonly received in her environment: her behaviour had been resented, she had been threatened, and her sufferings were retrospectively attributed to the incident.

It was the kind of explanation which the family and neighbours of the mentally ill were often ready to accept – especially when their symptoms were theatrical. Maria C. came from a family of uneducated superstitious peasants, and worked as a farm servant near Coutances. She was courted by a young man, who was thought to be a sorcerer and whose advances she treated with bemused disdain. One day the sorcerer's eye lit upon a neighbour's apples and he clambered up the orchard wall, leaving his clogs at its foot, to help himself to the fruit. While he was thus employed, Maria came past, noticed his clogs and decided to hide them. When the sorcerer scaled the wall again with his booty, he found to his displeasure that he would have to walk the rocky road barefoot. He lay in wait for the girl that evening at nine, on the road she would have to take when she had finished milking the cows, to remonstrate with her. He met her as he had anticipated, began to plead his suit, and being no better received than usual, grew angry. He left her brusquely, upbraiding her for her 'bad joke' and promising that he would have his revenge by casting a spell on her. Maria was frightened by his threats because of his reputation and became terrified when, a few minutes after the sorcerer had left, a big black dog rapidly crossed the road near her. At this glimpse of the metamorphosized wizard, she abandoned her jug of milk and her aplomb and rushed back to the farm, where she instantly had an attack of convulsions. 'Ensuite elle fit des efforts pour "grimper le long des murs et se *grappiner* aux poutres, comme un chat", nous dit un témoin.' As her antics became more public, the entire village thought that the sorcerer had cast a spell on her.[25] As was often the case, witchcraft served to vindicate the person who had initially been in the wrong.

Spells were frequently evoked by hysterical girls to justify their deviant behaviour, a manoeuvre which was mostly tolerated by their background. In March 1899, a fourteen-year-old girl from Blanzac had an attack of convulsions on seeing an old neighbour, Madame F., whom she felt tempted to follow. This recurred a month later when the girl, standing at her window, was greeted by Madame F., who was passing. Thereafter, whenever the old woman came near the house, the girl had an attack, during which she could tell the audience when her attack would end and what Madame F. was doing. On account of this coincidence, local opinion agreed with the girl's family in judging Madame F. to be a witch, with the result that the old woman was obliged to move away from the district.[26] Similarly, at Caudebec (Seine-Inférieure) in June 1835, Victoire Choulange, a twenty-year-old girl, began to suffer from hysteria at Sunday mass, brought on by the presence of a boy with whom she was infatuated. She and her family, as well as the congregation in the church, believed that the young man had cast a spell on her. Her father even intended to bring in a legal charge against the boy for charming her.[27] This kind of case was not unprecedented. Trébucq recorded the account given by an old woman from the Vendée of an attack of hysteria which she had had as a young girl under similar circumstances. Her approved suitor was expected for supper on the evening of the village fête, when she suddenly began to scream violently. Her father was, understandably, annoyed, but her behaviour was attributed to a spell cast by a malicious old woman. The local healer was called in. He blocked up all the entrances to the house and then prepared a concoction of salt, holy water and blessed bread which the girl consumed to the accompaniment of appropriately dramatic creakings and shakings of the house. The intrepid healer was calm, however, which reassured the girl, who felt that 'it was the good God in combat with the devil'. Suddenly the counter-sorcerer held a mirror before her, asking her if she did not recognize her mortal enemy.

> Aussitôt, *bonnegent*! aussi vrai que je vous parle, j'aperçus ma voisine, qui, le matin, m'avait donné de *vrin* [spell]. J'etais *désenjominée* [The charm was broken]; je cessais de *bauler* [yelping] et le *vrin* dont je souffrais entra dans le sang de la sorcière.

The healer gave her a little sachet of herbs plucked on the morning of Saint John's feast day, to preserve her from other spells, and she thenceforth was protected from any ill-intentioned neighbours.[28] The convenience of this kind of ritual was that it legitimized the girl's feelings. The spell had given her an alibi which allowed her act out her anxiety and then, when she felt relieved, she was able to resume her normal life without losing face.

Collective Madness: Liberation and Revolt. The readiness with which family and neighbours collaborated in these imaginary combats and sustained the ill in their illusions was a striking feature of traditional attitudes to possession. And it was precisely the status of the possessed as victims and as activators of this traditional imagery of revolt and liberation which accounts for the ease with which people acted in concert with the mad and even succumbed to similar symptoms. The available evidence seems to bear out Bastide's contention that 'the delirium of mental illness is elaborated not exclusively by the ill, but collectively, and is derived from the surrounding environment at least as much as from the ill person himself'.[29] The ravings of the ill drew support, at times, to the point where local people joined in elaborate or primitive rituals organized around their delirium. In 1817, a girl from Saint-Rémy in the Bourbonnais claimed that she was tormented by a devil. Her neighbours were curious and many people came to see her:

> ... The evil spirit held sway over this girl only during the night, and, even then, there had to be neither light, nor fire in the house. The demon, once he had entered the girl's body, replied to the questions he was asked by knocking a certain number of times on the wood of the bed or partition. He was dumb in every other place and manner. It was even necessary to tell him the number of times he had to knock to be understood.

That possession might involve collective conventions, as much as individual aberration, is illustrated by the fact that between them, the visitors and the girl organized an almost theatrical production and means of communication – which, incidentally, resembled those of the séance. The reason why the prefect's attention was drawn to the proceedings was, however, that they began to develop into political demonstrations. 'It is also said that the demon, having been consulted about the fate and return of the person banished to Saint Helena, replied to the satisfaction of some supporters of that person. These common reports drew crowds which obliged the local authorities to defend themselves.' The girl and her father were arrested for disturbing the peace and for breaking the law forbidding prophesy.[30] People's readiness to participate in these extraordinary antics is less strange than it seems at first. For this mode of expression of anxiety and hope is indicative of the limitations placed on practical politics, both by the legal dispositions of the government and by the inaccessibility of informed contemporary debate to the rural poor.

The greater tolerance of and attention paid to madness in traditional society survived until well into the nineteenth century. An incident which happened in Doubs towards the start of the nineteenth century illustrated this. A poor servant was going through the forest of Chassagne, lamenting his fate and saying to himself that he would happily be damned in exchange for some temporal well-being in the present, when, at the foot of an oak-tree at a crossroads, he saw a man dressed all in black. The man gave him a purse filled with gold and told him to return to the spot at the same time the following year. On his arrival home, the servant became ill and melancholy, refusing to eat anything. He told his master what had happened to him and the master consulted the local priests. They decided that the boy was possessed and that the devil in person had appeared to him. The purse was thrown into a mountain stream and on the day marked by the pact, a solemn procession of clergymen, their flock and the boy went to the oak-tree in the forest, to confront the devil. When they arrived by the tree, the young man cried out: 'There he is! Deliver me from the evil that torments me!' No-one else could see anything, but the priest sprinkled him with holy water and he instantly fell asleep, although he had not slept for a year. Several old men from the area claimed to have been present at the cure.[31] Rather than challenging the boy's account of what he had seen in the forest, his master and other people around him accepted it. The clergy, invoking the traditions of the Church, explained his experiences and legitimized his statements, because they could be seen as confirming received ideas about reality. They even organized a healing ritual, through which everyone joined in a sort of imaginative battle between good and evil.

When the Church was not involved, these collective attempts to help the ill tended to degenerate into outbursts of collective hysteria and primitive violence. Thus on 12 February 1833, in the commune (appropriately named) of La Folie near Bayeux, a maniac was killed by members of her own family, while local villagers failed to prevent the murder. After the death of a clerical uncle to whom she had been devoted, twenty-three-year-old Marie Charles began to have fits and convulsions. She decided she was possessed – a judgement in which her family and neighbours concurred. The identity of the person guilty of casting the spell was openly discussed and Marie, in her attacks, claimed to be able to see the evil-doer who caused her so much pain. Exorcisms proved ineffective; but on 6 February, she suddenly recovered her strength and, rising from her bed, she

> is suddenly able to exercise absolute authority over her family and those around her, due to the *supernatural* deeds and the inspired speeches she makes. During the night of the 6th and 7th, she keeps her whole family and two or three of her neighbours prostrate on the ground for more than six hours; she makes them recite prayers and allows no-one make the least movement. . . .

Some hours later, she ordered her mother and a woman called Leredde to press and beat her so as to expel the demon. Her young brother and her sister Victoire, having witnessed this hysterical violence for several hours, developed similar symptoms which received the same brutal treatment, as a result of which Victoire was inadvertently killed. Meanwhile, the locals, who had been terrified by the extraordinary goings-on, finally summoned up the courage to force their way into the presbytery:

> Finally, the captain of the national guard breaks down the door to the appartment where the Chasles family and the Leredde girl were staying... A great many inhabitants of the commune come in on the heels of the captain of the national guard and it's at this point that Marie Chasles' influence over all who approach her becomes apparent. She orders the new arrivals to apply to her the same treatment that her unfortunate sister has just undergone, and she is obeyed; three big strong men crush her, at first in turn, then stand on her body simultaneously to make the pressure more effective... She makes them pinch her, bite the small of her back, she makes *the mayor of the commune kneel*, put bags of money in his hat, recite prayers, and all of this is done without provoking the least opposition. The schoolmaster doesn't dare enter because he's *afraid of compromising himself*...[32]

The scene was worthy of Flaubert, with everyone from the schoolmaster and the captain of the national guard to Marie's three stalwart assistants playing, within the extraordinary parameters of the occasion, a predictable role. The incident indicated how readily people collaborated in myth-making, how easily they exploited traditional images as a means of eschewing the restrictions and frustrations of everyday life. Marie Chasles' delirium was rooted in ideas which were common currency and the events surrounding her illness bear out Roger Bastide's argument that the 'symbolic activity' of the ill complemented that of the normal,[33] and contributed to the definition and reinforcement of the collective imaginative heritage.

This kind of incident was by no means unparalleled in the nineteenth century. In 1854, the *Gazette des Tribunaux* reported a case which bore some similarity to that of the Chasles family. In a commune in the area of Caen, in 1854, a girl was subject to frightening attacks of mania. She imagined that a spell had been cast on her and most of her neighbours agreed with her. At certain hours, various local men went to her home to help her fight the evil spirits which possessed her, although they were all terrified. Some were even afraid to go out at night after performing this neighbourly duty. She induced these worthies to carry out a number of ridiculous orders: one day, she imagined that demons had taken refuge in her bread. She had six twelve-pound loaves of bread bought and in the evening, having lit an enormous fire with the aid of her neighbours, put the bread on the fire and with twelve helpers stuck forks into it, presumably in order to kill the demons.[34]

What persuaded people to take part in such antics? It seems improbable to suppose that mental instability was so general that the inhabitants of entire villages or areas readily became mad. But if organic disorder does not explain such incidents, what does? It would seem that these baroque incidents were a form of escapism – a kind of macabre, morbid festival, not unlike a spontaneous, travestied carnival, in which people abused authority and convention and absolved themselves from their ordinary duties. In the latter part of the nineteenth century, psychiatrists identified and began to take note of the phenomenon of shared madness.[35] Misery was apt to provoke this kind of derangement – in six out of eight of Lasègue and Falret's cases, want and insecurity were determining factors in the development of the syndrome.[36] The significance of *folie à deux*, however, was that it established the importance of environment – both mental and physical – in provoking madness, even in those who would not have ordinarily succumbed to it. In Bastide's opinion, it justified studies of mental illness which were not confined to the psychopathology of the individuals concerned, but which also embraced their social world, and particularly relationships in the family.[37]

Other forms of mental illness testified to social tensions, and few as evidently as hysteria, especially in its collective form. Charcot, in his lessons in 1884 and 1885 on hysterical monoplegias, had shown that a great number of paralyses and contractions were due to shock or sudden emotional stress. Those most inclined to it, according to Dr Lhermitte, were the uneducated, and he noted that hysteria was common among country-folk and farmers. He felt that contemporary cerebral pathology provided no explanation for this behaviour, and he concluded that the disease needed to be considered in its immediate social context.

> ...Symptoms which we call hysterical correspond to a specific psychosomatic constitution, which can remain latent for a lifetime, but which can break out openly due to social disturbances. Hysterical reactions are of a social, familial, ideological nature; a particular moral and social climate is a necessary condition of their manifestation. Neurotic hysterical reactions are inconceivable in a person isolated like Robinson Crusoe on a desert island.

Hysteria, he felt, tended to reveal the unconscious or subconscious tendencies of the subject – a view akin to that of Janet. The trauma or shock which in the first instance provoked the attacks simply opened the dam which had contained the hysteric's frustration.[38] Hysteria seems to have been largely the result, as well as a reflection, of individuals' difficulties in dealing with the pressures and tensions of their physical and social environment.

A case observed by Buisson, in which two young girls from Apte-du-Puy (Haute-Loire) succumbed to hysteria simultaneously, illustrates this. Towards the end of the winter of 1803, the girls – thirteen-year-old Marie Sarda and twelve-year-old Anne Fournate – were brought to him, apparently suffering from mania. The girls were both pupils in a school directed in part by Maria Sarda's aunt. They shared the same sleeping accommodation and relied for their food on provisions their parents brought them once a week. One day, an old beggar woman asked Anne for charity, but the girl refused, fearing that the bad weather would prevent her parents from bringing her usual supply of food and that she would go hungry. The old woman threatened her angrily, but nonetheless subsequently gave the girl some potatoes, urging her to eat them, which Anne and Marie did. The next day, Anne again met the old woman, who, learning that the potatoes had been consumed, announced she would have her vengeance and that Anne would soon become ill. The girl was frightened and regretted having accepted the old woman's offering, fearing that some misfortune would ensue. She fell asleep feeling ill and awoke trying to vomit, and Marie followed suit. The aunt heard them and interrupted them, whereupon their delirium broke out. For a week, periods of hyperactivity alternated with bouts of drowsiness and they were stuck dumb – except in their delirium, during which they were very ill-tempered and violent towards all around them. They were separated, brought to a surgeon who was unable to help and to an old priest with a reputation for wisdom and sanctity, who pronounced their illness to be supernatural and prescribed pious remedies which proved futile. Those around them thought that the old woman had casts a spell on the girls, an opinion which the girls themselves shared. This belief in charms furnished them with a pretext for their behaviour.

Buisson was struck by the similarity of the girls' delirium, gestures and speeches, and concluded that they had reached some accord beforehand. Their outbursts of hysteria recurred at the same time each day and took the same form. After the first few days, however, their attacks became more violent and flamboyant: they enjoyed playing children's games, clambered up walls, ran about them, seemed insensible to the pain of fire or of pinching. They were very irritable: annoyance or opposition to their wishes sometimes provoked their attacks; and if interrupted during their fits, they struck the offender and their outbursts then lasted longer than the usual two hours. This hostility to discipline was extended to those around them, at whom they poked fun in their fits: after a blood-letting they imitated the operation, and they copied a dance they had witnessed:

> ... Our two patients were very much inclined to mimic people they had observed between their attacks and imitated everything down to their facial expressions, reproducing in their visionary pantomimes, their gait, habits and even their dress.

This tendency to mimesis points to a degree of tension between the girls and their community. For a while, their attacks became worse and more violent. The doctor's attentions began to have some effect, however: during a hysterical attack Marie gave Buisson a detailed account of her illness, its origins and her feelings during it – emphasizing how acute her sufferings were when she was interrupted during an attack – and predicted that she would have a violent fit before the end of her illness. The predictions – which were accurate – followed unpleasant medication administered by Buisson.[39] This dialogue with the doctor, held within the roughly pre-established patterns of the acknowledged illness, is reminiscent of that which characterized witchcraft trials and exorcisms; it shows too that the girls' antics were by no means involuntary and that they were both conscious of and capable of controlling them – that their illness was, to some extent, a form of theatre. The speech and acts of hysteria enabled them to express their feelings – of desire, rebellion and disorientation – without acknowledging either this normally hidden identity to be their own, or responsibility for their behaviour and instincts.

Their attacks took a relatively standard form – flamboyant escapades, the use of foul language, the expression of desires and feelings normally suppressed, the refusal to submit to social conventions or economic requirements – and this constituted a form of liberation and catharsis. But the very inevitability of the pattern, by endowing the attacks with an apparently objective complexion, tended to legitimize them: they seemed to be involuntary because their form was predictable. It also made them easier to imitate – even if the deception thus practised usually involved psychological processes more complex than those implied by crude fraud. The susceptibility of the rural poor to this disorder was probably related to the pressure and privations of their lives. Since it was widely thought that people could be bewitched or possessed, extraordinary behaviour which bespoke witchcraft was viewed sympathetically.[40] The restraints on hysterical antics were thus relatively weak, and it was acceptable then to act in ways which would not now be admitted. Given the role of suggestion and mimesis in the disease, it is not surprising that the combination of social attitudes and beliefs about hysteria with the pressures engendered by penury, hard labour and the demands of inbred, conventional communities, tended to engender frustrations and psychological problems that were sometimes expressed in hysteria – or even mass hysteria.

Thus, in the autumn of 1864, the two eldest of the five children of Joseph Burner, a pedlar of starch and matches from the village of Illfurt near Mulhouse, developed symptoms of hysteria. Thiébaut, who was nine, and his seven-year-old brother Joseph, had eaten an apple given to them by a poor old woman, who had been hounded out of her home village because of her bad reputation. The boys' disorder was subsequently ascribed to this incident and their parents believed that a spell had been cast on them. By September 1865, they were subject to convulsive attacks, during which they lay on their backs and flayed about, or hurled themselves and the furniture about the room. They shouted abuse about the Church; showed violent annoyance when confronted by blessed objects; apparently miraculously produced feathers and mosses from their clothes. During their attacks they spoke foreign languages, and Thiébaut described in vivid detail a monster which, he claimed, visited and ruled him. When the local priest decided that they were possessed, the monster was identified as the devil. The devils not only expressed their hostility to established authority as embodied in the Church, but also evinced sympathy for this society's pariahs – Protestants, Jews and freemasons. The children's symptoms grew more flamboyant as more attention was paid to them and crowds gathered to watch them. Thiébaut furnished his first description of the monster when observed by about a hundred astonished people. In February 1868, he suddenly became deaf – except during his attacks. By May, the children's violence was such that the mayor decided to have them exorcised – a wish to which the bishop reluctantly agreed the following spring. Joseph tried to avoid the exorcists, hid from them and when examined by them, made his anger plain. Finally, in September 1869, Thiébaut was sent to an orphanage at Schiltigheim, where, despite his deafness, he carried on conversations in French and Latin with visitors, refused to tolerate involvement with the Church and continued for a time to have fits. The exorcisms were continued, however, and after a particularly dramatic encounter, the boy was cured. Shortly afterwards, Joseph, who had remained at home, was also restored to health after a similarly flamboyant ceremony.[41] In cases like this, the Church became the focus-point for a reaction that was not properly religious but rather a protest against the pressures of society. The refusal to live normally was indicated, in Thiébaut's case, by his apparent deafness; he conversed only on his own terms; and being possessed, he could curse and argue against the authority represented by the priest and against the attitudes and conventions embodied in ecclesiastical morality. Through their illness, the boys escaped the duties and responsibilities that would have been placed on them as the eldest children of a poor man, while drawing attention and sympathy to themselves. The ritual of exorcism both enabled them to specify and enact their disorder or rebellion in a manner which inspired awe and admitted of little scepticism, and also permitted them to discard the role when it had ceased to be necessary or desirable.

Another case of collective hysteria in a family was furnished by the famous Morcet children, from the village of Grand-Hirel, near Plédran in the Côtes-du-Nord. In 1881, the family achieved notoriety in the provinces and even in Paris, when all seven children allegedly showed signs of diabolical possession. The three eldest children ran about the village, climbing up walls and onto roofs, dancing, hurling insults at the *curé* and stones at passers-by. They had hallucinations, seeing Satan and armies of devils. The local people were convinced that a spell had been cast on the children, and that the devil was responsible for their deeds and words. The clergy said masses and blessed the children's home in the hope of banishing the annoying demons, but to no avail. Finally, doctors were consulted and diagnosed classic hysteria.[42] The outburst made the elder children's hostility to their environment plain: they abused the local priest and people, while commanding their attention and concern; their antics absolved them from the work which, as members of a large and impoverished peasant family, would normally have been expected of them. It is hard to escape the conclusion that hysteria was an inarticulate form of protest, a symptom of the inadequacies not only of the individual but also of society itself.

Hysteria could also assume epidemic proportions.[43] Fenayroux, who interested himself in the forms of mental illness to be observed in the countryside, reported an epidemic of hysteria which had plagued the villages of Druhle, Peyrusse and neighbouring hamlets in Aveyron for a number of months around 1859 and 1860. He did not observe it himself, but was informed of it by a witness:

> According to the local people, the epidemic began because a peasant invoked evil spirits so that misfortune would befall another person, who had not paid money he owed him back. Sure enough, some time later, a daughter of this fellow began to have visions and developed a nervous illness which prevented her from behaving as she wished. Seized by convulsions, she thrashed about like a real mad-woman, and, exhausted, groaned and shouted incomprehensibly, without, according to some people who were present, her lips moving and proving that it was really she who cried out. (According to them, it was the devil speaking).

As soon as the girl regained consciousness and someone reached out to help her, she would seize his hand and mutter briefly, whereupon the second person would be taken with similar convulsions. Many people visited the girl, who was now held to be a witch; among them were several boys and girls, who developed her disorder. One day four of these girls were in the church at Peyrusse, just as the priest was about to start mass. Suddenly, they rushed up to the altar, where they began to gesticulate and dance. A man who tried to prevent their antics suffered for his trouble: one child predicted that misfortune would shortly overtake him, and not long afterwards he died. Several masses were said to cure the children, to no effect; the local priest blessed the homes and families of the possessed with no success. The children continued with their extravagant behaviour, even in the middle of the day. It took the clergy five months to stop the antics.[44] Possession enabled the children to do and say what they pleased, without incurring criticism or being held responsible for their behaviour. Actions which would ordinarily have been punished had to be tolerated and viewed with concern – even if this was mixed with impatience and amazement. The children were given an excuse for shirking the duties and restrictions usually placed on them. To this extent, possession was a kind of liberation as well as revolt. Demonstrations such as these were symptomatic of social disorder – as history and abundant anthropological evidence confirm. In the view of Philippe de Félice, periods of calamity, famine or economic crisis were a breeding ground for collective delirium and ecstasy. 'Physiological misery', he observed, 'and the mental disorders which result from it, by making their victims more vulnerable to the least external pressure, can turn some of those who are thus affected into sources of instability among their fellows.'[45] Roger Bastide, referring to the work of Norman Cohn and Michel de Certeau, largely agreed with this assessment, observing that 'the great epidemics of mysticism in the West appeared in times of crisis, whether political or social crisis (changes in structure) or crises of food supply . . .'[46] The stress and tension engendered by privation, together with social attitudes to possession and belief in witchcraft, pedisposed people to hysteria in undeveloped communities in pre-modern Europe.

A number of incidents of epidemic possession were recorded in the nineteenth century;[47] but the relation of mass hysteria to deprivation, and the scope afforded to imitation and the theatre of illness by rural culture were more clearly illustrated by the epidemic of possession which broke out in the village of Morzine (Haute-Savoie) in 1857. Morzine was a remote and poor mountain commune. While the physical environment generated hardship and undermined the health of those who lived in it, the ambient culture tended to encourage rather than repress demonstrations of nervous illness. The region had been incorporated into France only in 1860, and barely a tenth of the population could read and write. Emigrants were reported to bring back and read books of magic, such as the *Grand* and *Petit Albert*, works which encouraged them in their traditional beliefs. Fairy stories were loved:

> Everyone like folk-tales, unbelievable stories; although innately honest, some of them lie with imperturbable aplomb in maintaining what they have told in this line, so that they end up, I'm quite convinced, by lying in good faith, by believing their own lies and those others tell as well. In fairness, it should be said that the majority don't even lie, but just tell what they've seen inaccurately . . .[48]

This predilection for turning the world upside down, for making it conform to the realm of fantasy, may be seen as expressing a sense of the inadequacy of reality, as reflecting on the monotony, privation and inevitability of want. The temptation to celebrate the world of dream and imagination was not limited to proclamation; it extended to enactment too, as hysteria demonstrates, with its stereotyped visions and dialogues, protests and performances.

The stress of living in a small, conventional, patriarchal society, in which children and women were allowed little independence and most people suffered from deprivation, took its toll – and indeed was reflected in the general complexion of the epidemic. It started in March 1857, when two pious young girls, who were being prepared for their first holy communion, went hysterical. By September, thirteen girls, aged between ten and twenty-two, had developed similar symptoms; and by the end of 1861, when the episode reached its climax, a hundred and twenty people were affected. Their attacks were characterized by rebellions vociferation and assaults: children lost all affection for their families and all reserve.

The possessed occasionally delivered insults or refused to comply with orders and requests; they were very insolent; blasphemy and hatred of God predominated in their delirium, although even at the height of their fury they seemed to be able to control their words and deeds; they were also able to predict when their attacks would start. Conventional decorum and activity were replaced by acrobatics; the normally weak showed unusual strength; the ignorant revealed an astonishing command of foreign languages and knowledge of the future. Some seemed to receive supernatural messages – hopeful ones from paradise and gloomy ones from hell. The possessed became commanders and leaders, where previously they had been subject to the rule of patriarchal tradition and the dictates of poverty. Tall stories told about their exploits proclaimed that fantasy had for the moment become fact, that the normal limitations of the possible and permissible had been temporarily overcome.[49]

Not only did the epidemic turn the place upside-down, compensating the poorest and weakest for their ordinary submission and deprivation, but it also constituted a fairly deliberate protest against traditional authority. In April 1864, the symptoms of hysteria occurred among many of the women of Morzine when, after a retreat, the archbishop of Annecy, Mgr Rendu, arrived to administer confirmation to the younger parishioners. His arrival provoked scenes of mass hysteria, both outside and within the church, during the two days of his visit. Dozens of women and girls screamed insults at him, attempted to assault him – with some measure of success – and created uproar during the religious ceremonies. The archbishop's temperate sermon, in which he declined to become involved in mass exorcisms, provoked even more violent reactions from the women; and as the ceremonies proceeded, the relatives of the afflicted showed little more respect for the churchman than did the possessed. Throughout Mgr Rendu's visit, chaos reigned – it was, the under-prefect insisted, scarcely imaginable:

> One can, nonetheless, have some idea of the frightful disorder that reigned everywhere, when one learns that, almost at the same time, throughout the commune, in the cemetery, in the village square and on the roads, and inside the church, women were to be seen having dreadful attacks of convulsions.

The assault on authority, enshrined in the archbishop; the general rebellion against convention and disruption of the normal order characterized the paroxysm of epidemic. The scenes of 1864 had been rivalled earlier, in 1860, when the parish priest – under pressure from the secular and religious powers – renounced in a sermon his previous opinion that the phenomenon was supernatural in nature. The congregation reacted by standing up and 'hitting the chairs angrily, shouting insults to the *curé* and threatening him in a deplorable manner'. About twenty young women had an attack of hysteria in the church; one threw a book at the priest; women tried to climb onto the pulpit to hit him, and many left the church, criticizing him.

Throughout the epidemic, those who were not affected by the illness showed themselves to be sympathetic to the possessed, and supported them both in their beliefs and in their behaviour. Administrators commented with displeasure on the fact that the efforts of the police to curb the excesses met with passive – and indeed, sometimes active – resistance.[50] The readiness of the healthy to support the possessed in their extravagant behaviour was a notable feature of the epidemic. On one occasion, the deputy-mayor, Jean Berger, was chased by a furious band of thirty or forty men, women and children, only some of whom were hysterical. For three hours, armed with pitchforks, hatchets and sticks, they hunted Berger, whom they believed to be responsible for the illness, across the commune, and no-one made any attempt to stop them. Nor was Constans in any doubt that Berger would have been killed, had he been caught. On another occasion, a large group of people trooped out at night to a ruined chapel, where under the guidance of a suspended priest they practised a ritual bewitchment, in the hope that the sorcerer's sufferings would force him to lift the spell.[51]

The medical and administrative authorities had a different answer to the problem: intimidation. Constans felt that as the *cause première* of the epidemic had been belief in possession, the ecclesiastical and secular powers should denounce the idea and punish anyone who expressed such convictions – either in deed or in word. Having persuaded the bishop to support him in his combat, Constans had a brigade of policemen and a small detachment of soldiers dispatched to the commune, and spread rumours to the effect that arrest and imprisonment would follow any demonstrations of madness. Fits in church and on the streets ceased; 'fantastic stories were told only nervously and on the quiet; and there was no longer any question of killing or burning anyone'. The revolt ended. Everyone was afraid of being sent to hospital – where, indeed, many were dispatched and where the discipline and limitations on individual freedom were even stricter than in an ordinary prison. The techniques adopted by Constans were social and political rather than medical; what Constans intended to effect involved not only the remission of the hysterics' symptoms but also the repression of a revolt against a harsh social and economic order, and the extirpation, as far as possible, of the culture which allowed such behaviour and beliefs to be expressed.

Conclusion

These attacks of collective hysteria resembled a spontaneous, travestied carnival – insofar as people threw restraint to the winds and allowed their darkest fantasies to overwhelm their self-control and common-sense – parodying and rebelling against conventional authorities, adopting new, theatrical roles. Like many other forms of superstition, they celebrated not reality but a morbid world of fantasy, into which people escaped with an ardour that was all the more intense in that the daily business of living was difficult for them. The boundaries between celebration and revolt were blurred in these outbursts, which became more readily general because traditional society emphasized mimesis and furnished forms of collective myth-making in deed as well as in word. The symbolic, demonstrative nature of rural revolt is well known, and festivity too drew on a limited vocabulary of dress and gesture. This may well account for the ease with which people adopted their roles in these strange parodies of reality. Yet however peculiar these manifestations were, their emotional inspiration and theatrical character reappeared transformed in analogous exhibitions of hysteria in twentieth-century Europe and hence cannot be said to be typical of the 'archaic' mind.

VI

Prophets and Prophecy

Both the nature of popular visions and the manner in which they were interpreted illuminate the workings of the imagination of poor men and women. In France in the nineteenth century, many country people claimed to have seen and even to have conversed with supernatural beings, and the details of their visions were carefully recorded – often in an acrimonious atmosphere of mutual recrimination by the credulous and the sceptical. Most visionaries were peasants living in considerable poverty, and their visions normally recorded threatening predictions about the future course of public affairs and critical appraisals of the shortcomings of contemporary society.

Predictions had always been popular, and a long tradition of chapbook literature testified to this interest in prophecies. Serious curiosity about the future seems to have been peripheral to the appeal of some of these publications, which often contained a mixture of purportedly practical advice and exotic marginalia. One branch of this quasi-literary tradition was concerned less with casual commentary about the weather or the imminence of curious events than with the need for a revolution in mores, a radical change in the way men lived. This tradition served as a channel for the frustrated ambitions and desires of the poor and, at times, virtually as a form of dissent. At least since the Middle Ages, in times of stress, people appear to have listened to announcements about the imminent downfall of political régimes with an interest and satisfaction that testify to the existence of an archaic form of political consciousness.[1] What made the expression of these hopes or criticism possible, and even legitimate, was that they came not from man but from God: visionaries and prophets were merely conveying the divine message; those who listened to them were attending to God's word.

Celestial Letters

Celestial letters – supposedly written by God (or by almost as distinguished heavenly personages) to his erring flock – exemplify this tradition. The

Enchiridion Leonis Papae (Lille, 1813), which was closely modelled on the Ancona edition of 1649, gives an exchange of letters between Abagare, King of Odessa, and Jesus. The form of its greeting suggests that this version was of medieval origin: 'Abagare, son of Theoparee, King of Odessa, to Jesus, our Saviour, who manifested himself in Jerusalem, greetings.' Abagare goes on to invite Jesus to live in his small, but 'well-protected' town, where he will be safe from the Jews, and can cure Abagare from his chronic illness. Jesus replies politely, congratulating Abagare on his faith in terms borrowed from his sermon on the mount, promising – since he has to go through with things in Jerusalem – to send his disciple Thaddeus in his stead, and assuring the king that if he carries the letter, he will be safe in all circumstances and will eventually go to heaven.[2]

While letters of this kind were popularly viewed as talismans, they also furnished a conventional means of communication that lent weight to the views and recommendations hung upon them – much as an academic thesis is likely to carry more authority if published in a journal of the Royal Society than it would in a popular magazine devoted to spiritualism. An edifying legend illustrates the combination of picturesque naiveté and transparent calculation involved in this tradition. Saint Vincent Ferrier, called to the death-bed of an inveterate sinner, promised that if she confessed, her absolution would come from heaven. He wrote a brief note of supplication to the Trinity and a few minutes later, received a prompt reply, written in gold to this effect:

> We, the Very Holy Trinity, at the request of our servant, Vincent, grant the sinner . . . pardon for her sins . . . if she goes to confession, she will be transported to heaven in half-an-hour . . .[3]

The persuasive powers of such enticing promises (combined with equally compelling threats) were not lost upon bishops, struggling to evangelize and discipline recalcitrant populations. Although apocrypha of this order appear to have been popular in the ancient Near East – the Syrian tradition was rich in such letters, while they also existed in Ethiopian, Arabic and Greek religious culture[4] – the first mention of a letter purporting to come from Christ is thought to have been made by Lincinianus, bishop of Carthage, at the end of the sixth century. He reproaches a bishop for having taken a supposed letter from Christ seriously and having read it aloud to the common people. The letter, like most of those circulated in the nineteenth-century French countryside, had been sent from heaven to induce the faithful to be more attentive to their religious duties, specifically to the observance of Sundays. Sceptical censoriousness informed the reaction of the higher ecclesiastical authorities to the first divine epistles. In the first half of the eighth century, Adalbert circulated a letter from Christ which had, he asserted, fallen from heaven; it was read to the Lateran Council in 745, whereupon Pope Zacharias declared that Adalbert was mad. In 789, one of Charlemagne's capitularies condemned a similar piece to the fire.

A second spate of celestial missives appeared at the time of the Crusades. Eustace, Abbot of Flay, went through England in the early twelfth century, exhorting people to go to mass and using a divine letter to back himself up. Wulfstan, Archdeacon of York, had discussed in his sermons a similar letter written in gold and found in Saint Peter's in Rome. Peter the Hermit carried a letter which Christ had entrusted to him personally in Jerusalem and which enjoined people to go on the first crusade. In Easter 1251, three men began to preach a crusade in Picardy, Brabant, Flanders and Hainaut; among them was a renegade monk, Jacob, popularly known as the 'Master of Hungary', who claimed that the Virgin Mary, surrounded by a host of angels, had appeared to him and given him a letter. This epistle appealed to all shepherds, rather than to the proud ostentatious knights, with whom divine displeasure was expressed, to help King Louis free the Holy Sepulchre. Shepherds had been the first to learn of the birth of Christ and they were again to be the agents through whom the Lord was to manifest his power and glory. Young shepherds and cowherds flocked to Jacob's banner, which was soon the rallying-point for a variety of vagabonds, criminals, prostitutes and apostate monks. Observing a (presumably accommodating) law of their own, they rampaged through cities north of the Loire, where Jacob's violent anti-clericalism won considerable support, until royal disfavour and the crusaders' extravagant outrages turned opinion against them.

When the flagellant movement crossed the Alps and reappeared in the towns of South Germany and the Rhine in 1261–2, its leaders also possessed a heavenly letter, which affirmed that a marble tablet had recently descended upon the Church of the Holy Sepulchre at Jerusalem before an admiring multitude. An angel appeared and read out the divinely inscribed message: it gave the assembled faithful to understand that God was angry with men for their many shortcomings – including pride, usury, blasphemy, and the failure to fast on Fridays and go to church on Sundays. Mankind had already been punished by earthquakes, floods, famines and wars, and their persistence in vice invited God to obliterate his unsatisfactory creatures. However, thanks to the intervention of the Virgin and the angels, man was to be given one last chance to turn from sin, and an angel graciously indicated that flagellant processions would assuage the irritated Omnipotent. This letter inspired the populace, to whom it was read during the rites of the flagellants. It surfaced again in virtually identical form in Germany during the great flagellant movement of 1348–9. In the early sixteenth century, the 'Revolutionary of the Upper Rhine', an elderly fanatic from Upper Alsace or Breisgau, claimed similar sanction for his radical populist millenarian ideas (which envisaged the founding of an anti-clerical brotherhood and the thousand-year reign of an avenging emperor (who would assassinate the reigning Emperor Maximilian and distribute bread, barley and wine cheaply). The Archangel Michael, he affirmed, had given him a letter from the Almighty, which expressed divine ire with the waywardness and vice of man, on whom He intended to visit the most fearful punishments until He had the happy notion of enlisting the help of His servant from Upper Alsace/ Breisgau.[5]

In short, in the early and later Middle Ages, the heavenly letter was used by those who wanted to lend weight to their arguments or exhortations. Whereas initially it seems to have been a means of enforcing a religious discipline that was extraneous to the central Biblical message, a tool in the hands of unenlightened prelates, during the crises of the later Middle Ages, it became a means of expressing popular dismay, of legitimizing radical, even violent criticism of existing ecclesiastical and political authorities – criticism that might even verge on revolt. In the late eighteenth and nineteenth centuries, divine letters still fulfilled these purposes, sometimes serving as an archaic form of political criticism. They were carried by dissenters, who believed the contemporary order to be contrary to God's will. These apocrypha illustrate the way in which apparently religious vocabulary and behaviour might be used as a pretext for pursuing practical concerns and justifying political or economic claims.

Divine letters and similar talismans appear to have been particularly popular in times of individual and collective crisis. According to Black, Irish emigrants leaving Cobh for America a hundred years ago used to buy a printed version of a prayer found on Christ's tomb in 803 and sent by the Pope to Charlemagne. The prayer promised safety in battle and journey, protection against sudden death, drowning and poisoning, and safe delivery to pregnant women; it would cure fits, protect against thunder and lightning and even accord three days' warning of imminent death (presumably to allow for insurance against hell) to those who repeated it, heard it repeated or carried it with them.[6] This prayer would seem to be very similar to that much cherished by the Emperor Charlemagne – according to the *Enchiridion Leonis Papae*. This promised: '. . . If you believe firmly . . . whether at home, on the sea or wherever you may be, none of your enemies will get the better of you; you will be invincible and preserved from the worst infirmities and every adversity.' The man who devoutly recited and carried it with him would end his life happily. It went on to stress the safeguards it provided in war, sea-journeys and childbirth.[7] With a different attribution, this prayer was popular in Flanders. In the early twentieth century, it was known as the 'prayer said to be that of the Emperor Charles', which had been found on the tomb of Christ in 1503 and sent by the Pope to the Emperor Charles on his going to war, and thence 'sent to the town of St Michel, in France, where you will find it, printed with astonishing beauty in letters of gold'. Pregnant women bought the prayer in the hope of a safe delivery. It was printed in a little book, entitled *Le Trépassement de la Vierge Marie* which was sold very discreetly in some bookshops.[8] According to Hermant, many soldiers wore this talisman during the Great War and many also claimed to have owed their lives to it.[9] This popularity indicated the trust placed in the claims of these broadsheets by ordinary people, while reinforcing the contention that magic and religion were substantially undifferentiated in the popular mind, since the purposes of such charms were overwhelmingly practical (although orthodox concerns about the afterlife were assuaged by highly reassuring commitments on the forgiveness of sins and salvation) and as the means of their efficacy were apparently more dependent on physical proximity than on the idea of divine action or grace.

The use of talismans in individually appropriate cases cannot surprise us once we are at all familiar with popular culture. However, they also came to the fore in times of general social upheaval – and in this we can discern not only the avarice of printers with an eye to the propitious market, but also the credulity that comes from the temporary suspension of an habitual framework of thought and criteria of judgement, due to the irruption of the abnormal and unfamiliar into ordinary life. This sudden dislocation of reality – while provoking some of the anxieties which the talismans were meant to allay – could not easily be rendered in common speech, which was so deeply rooted in ordinary perception and activity.[10] The conceptual framework, the abstract vocabulary necessary for the understanding of profound and widespread political and economic change, were generally lacking. The sense of the familiar world becoming strange could be expressed most readily by adopting the language traditionally reserved for strange, meteoric or miraculous occurrences.

Divine letters seem to have been popular during the Revolution in Brittany and the Vendée. On 6 November 1789, a citizen Robinet of Rennes wrote to the local bishop to inform him of two letters which had arrived in the town from Saint Brieuc. Both had been printed that year: the first had supposedly been found in Rome, while the second had appeared at Meston. These were both divine missives, charging men with the errors of their ways and threatening to visit dire punishments on those who did not obey the law of the Church – and especially on those who ignored the obligation to hear Sunday Mass.[11] Another letter, allegedly found at Saint Peter's in Rome, discovered and dispatched by the pope on Saint John's Day (21 June) 1793, was carried by a *chouan* of the Vendée, who was prosecuted in Laval in 1794.[12] The text of this letter was the same as that left among the posthumous papers of an inhabitant of the commune of Fontaine-Milon (Arrondissement of Baugé). This ran:

> Miraculous letter, found in a place called Arrois, written in letters . . . of gold by the hand of Our Saviour and Redeemer Jesus-Christ:
> On Sundays you will do no servile work on pain of being cursed by me.
> You will go to church and pray God to pardon your sins.
> I have given you six days for work and the seventh for rest.
> After having heard divine service, you will give of your goods to the poor and

> your fields will be fertile and you will be filled with blessings. But, if on the contrary, you do not believe the present letter, the curse of God will fall on you and your children and your livestock will be accursed. I will send you war, pestilence and famine, sorrow, anguish of heart and to mark my just anger and cruel vengeance, you will see signs and prodigies.[13]

This was evidently the same letter that was printed in the *Médecin des Pauvres*, which continued to be popular throughout most of the nineteenth century. Its appeal seems likely to have been twofold. In the first place, it promised physical protection. Secondly it suggested that the distressing and confusing turbulence of the world was just a manifestation or affirmation of a higher, permanent order and justice.

If poor men were often preoccupied with justice in para-religious contexts, this was no accident, for it indicated the frustrated appreciation of temporal injustice, which occasionally surfaced – usually in transformed guises – in pre-modern society. In this perspective, divine justice was opposed to the secular order. Publication of God's promises of vengeance could thus express not just conventional piety but also political disaffection. During the Revolution, to carry one of these documents, which affirmed God's displeasure with man and His intention of disrupting life to express this, was analogous to possessing a document predicting revolution in the name of the public good, during the Restoration. The publications were viewed with hostility by the revolutionary authorities, because they indicated opponents of the régime and because the publications themselves represented and expressed an independent current of thought. Those who were found carrying celestial letters as talismans during the Revolution were usually harshly punished. On 14 *messidor* 1795, a poor wretch arrested at Carpentras was carrying a letter supposedly written by Christ and sent by God to Pius VI; and on 22 *messidor*, a group of fleeing nuns was found with a letter from the mother of God, which claimed to preserve those who carried it from the plague, sudden death and famine. 'Despite the holy letter,' commented a petty official, 'the nuns died.' The revolutionary representative, Brue, wrote to the Committee of Public Safety from Vannes on 27 January 1795, enclosing a heavenly letter. Berriat-Saint-Prix also found a similar missive in the Comtat Venaissin.[14] The authorities were quick, in this period, to see in these documents expressions of dissent and disapprobation – a deliberate dissociation from the values and aims of the new political society. On 31 December 1798, the Directorate at Mons banned as seditious a work which claimed to be a 'copy of a miraculous letter written in the blood of Jesus-Christ', in which 'he lets it be known that he will punish the world with an inexpressible punishment'. The commissioner noted: 'Forgiveness for the greatest crimes is promised and people are consequently encouraged to commit them'.[15] Crimes had replaced sins; morality had become not just secular but political, since the new law-givers defined virtue as that which helped the institution of the new political society. What might pass for

F

an innocuous or prudent administrative decree in the name of public order, in fact represented a considerable erosion of individual liberty. By implicitly identifying the broadsheet as a kind of propaganda which disseminated undesirable or erroneous ideas, the commissioner arrogated himself the right to define error and the undesirable and to impose his definition on society.

If divine letters enabled the anxious to seek reassurance, do they not also furnish ample evidence of naive receptivity to the prodigious and the incredible? A typical broadsheet published in Bourges in 1771 purported to give an account of the events surrounding the appearance of a divine letter in the church of Paimpol, near Tréguier in South Brittany, on the Feast of the Epiphany 1771. A rainbow descended on the church and for half an hour the people were able to contemplate Christ in his natural form; his footprints were visible on the tabernacle and many miracles occurred. The *curé* found the letter when the vision disappeared. The bishop then ordered forty hours of prayer in every church in the diocese, and the rustic populace trooped off to see the letter, which the *curé* had been unable to lift. The bishop and clergy, fasting, processed to the church, where they collected the letter without difficulty. The bishop read the epistle aloud and recommended that all those who knew how to read should peruse the document reverently on the first Friday of each month, while urging the illiterate to pray. The text of this letter, deploring the vices of the times, announced the punishments which God reserved for the evil, and added: '... If you do not mend your ways, I will send you extraordinary illnesses, through which all will perish...you will be reduced to such a state that you will not know each other.' Those who ignored the warning would be afflicted by an early death, followed by the everlasting flames of hell.[16]

The critical assessment of such anecdotes is inevitably hampered by the texts which recorded them. The written word was almost always an instrument in the hands of those who wanted to control the illiterate poor, to convert them to the morality and political persuasions of the relevant narrator. Objectivity is striking by its absence in popular narratives too: critical curiosity was rarely mobilized to discover precisely what was seen and heard and how this primitive experience was converted by rumour into a version of events that was subsequently recorded. However, rumours and popular accounts of marvellous events were frequently characterized by the uniformity of their style and content, and the structural analysis proposed by Vladimir Propp is indeed a useful instrument in demonstrating this. In the account of the miracle at Paimpol as given by Saintyves, the familiarity of the supposed prodigies is such as to transform them into commonplaces: the rainbow – the Biblical symbol of divine appeasement and of God's reconciliation with man; the visibility of Christ's footsteps (throughout France, folklore ascribed accidents of topography to traces of Christ and his saints); the miraculous heaviness of the letter, akin to the deeply embedded swords which only heroes can free.[17] The function of these elements in the text was not to furnish evidence of the astonishing unpredictability of the supernatural (as historians and folklorists once supposed), but to confirm the nature of the phenomenon being discussed by introducing all its characteristic attributes and all the circumstances usually attendant upon such an event. Traditional accounts of events sometimes surprise us as much by their failure to consider or even mention all the facts – even those which would seem most relevant – as by their emphasis on repetitive, ridiculous or even incredible circumstances. But such accounts were not so much annotations as interpretations of events, all the more authoritiative in that rather than being original, possibly aberrant inventions of individuals, they conformed to a standard, familiar pattern. The predictable, conventional elements in traditional texts indicated the significance of their contents and hence, predictability was an important literary value. Popular taste demanded not novelty but convention, and those who catered for popular literary taste – story-tellers and printers – responded appropriately. That heavenly letters should have adhered to a stereotype under the dual pressure of narrative tradition and ulterior motive is hardly surprising. Furthermore, they were derived from medieval literary models, preserved and popularized partly through the *Bibliothèque Bleue*, and reprinted because of their continued appeal. The way they were used and accepted evidently reflected the ambient culture, and the stories surrounding them demonstrate narrative conventions which had few illusions about the eloquence of apparently objective facts.

The popularity of these products may be ascribed, *inter alia*, to gullibility and simplicity of religious belief. A letter from heaven, if conceived of in naively familiar terms, was not absolutely astounding. Nonetheless, almost all apocryphal letters seemed to anticipate encountering some scepticism, to judge by the threats addressed to the disbelieving. Indeed, one should be careful to note the transparent lack of detachment which informed them. Some clerics had originally invoked divine wrath to shepherd the flock back into the fold of orthodox righteousness; their commercial successors had more immediate, worldly considerations in mind – failure to believe in and circulate the letter meant that the income of the printer and hawker alike dropped. Sceptics seem to have been alive to both the improbability of such letters having been written by God and the pecuniary needs and ambitions of travelling salesmen, and of half-destitute priests in search of congregations. But there were also those who accepted and trusted these miraculous documents, who felt them worth keeping or transcribing. During the Restoration, the vogue for letters from heaven re-emerged in popular broadsheets, and the theme of miraculous encounters with semi-mystical personalities (such as a Cordelier or a wandering soldier) who predicted the future was also revived.[18] This doubtless reflected the new government's tolerance of popular religiosity and mysticism. This vein of publication was continued into the second half of the century, when the government decided to extirpate what it considered to be superstitious and immoral popular literature.

An updated *Médecin des Pauvres*, published in Armentières probably during the Second Empire, printed one of the most popular of these letters – the 'Miraculous letter found in a place called Arrois, written in letters of gold by the hand of Our Lord and Redeemer Jesus Christ'. The letter seems to have been remarkably similar in theme and text to that of its early medieval forerunners, but it went on to promise salvation in the next world and safety in this one to those who believed in it and popularized it, as well as apocalyptic torment to the sceptical:

> If you do not believe firmly in this letter, I will send fierce and monstrous animals to consume your children. Fortunate is he who keeps a copy of this letter and carries it with him, reads it or has it read or kept in his house. No evil spirit, no fire, nor lightning will affect him.[19]

God was, as usual, showing himself to be indifferent to his own Church's teachings, punctuating excessive cruelty with excessive indulgence – and proving himself to be an unscrupulous businessman as well. Yet not everyone was struck with the incongruity of the missive, to judge by its popularity and the number of hand-written versions of this letter and similar ones which have been found. A Madame Menin, a miller's wife from Nemours, copied a virtually identical version of this letter into her notebook around 1850, while it was also preserved in similar copybooks from Coulommiers, Senlis and Paris.[20] A poor woman from Vieure in the Bourbonnais transcribed substantially the same letter, with the following foreword:

> Letter from the good God. Words of Jesus Christ at La Chapelaude, 23 June 1867. This letter was written by God, in letters of gold, found at *la fougeur des prés* . . . by Saint Amand, with a little cross. The said letter was explained by a child of seven years, who had never spoken, in these terms . . . [21]

In a sense, Lucien Febvre was right to observe that the miraculous was commonplace to the pre-modern sensibility. God deigned to send letters to man – letters which might be found nearby, in a place which could be visited or might even be known by the reader – despite the fact that the divinity signed off: 'J'écris cette lettre du Très-Haut des cieux. Bénédiction.'[22] Then, too, the letter might be accompanied by a purely terrestrial prodigy: a child suddenly speaks and explains the enigma. In fact, this does not testify to the fantasy so often attributed to the pre-scientific mind. On the contrary, such a circumstance was something of a cliché. A popular theme of the *Bibliothèque Bleue* was that of the *enfant sage à trois ans*, who suddenly amazes his elders with his wisdom and knowledge (an episode which occurs in the Biblical account of Christ's childhood). Mensignac found that a version of the letter, printed by Durand at Bordeaux, was popular in the Gironde during the early Third Republic. This broadsheet claimed that the original had been found in Languedoc, 'in a place called Darest'. It was explained by 'a child called Orphan, aged seven years, who had never spoken . . .'[23] The detail of the child, with its prophetic overtones, added an extra note of authority to the letter – it was just the sort of episode that frequently betokened marvellous events and, as it were, emphasized their importance. These promises of prosperity and eternal salvation, however implausible, nonetheless found a devout audience who bought and on occasion transcribed the publications (often in response to stress), being assured of their authenticity by the very predictability of their extraordinary contents.

The revolts and reactions of the war of 1870 provided printers with the opportunity of issuing more contemporary missives from heaven, which promised solace to the afflicted and punishment to the wayward. One such claimed to have been discovered on the feast of the Assumption in 1850, in the church of Notre Dame de Bon Secours at Nancy, at the foot of a miraculous crucifix. The miraculous crucifix of Strasbourg, not to be outdone, issued its heavenly prayer exactly a year later. Both these talismans were printed by Buffet at Charmes, probably around 1871. A letter, whose original was supposed to have been found in Rome under an altar by a priest who had just said mass, appeared at the time of the battle of Sedan, when MacMahon was wounded. It started:

> Praised and adored be Jesus in the Most Holy Sacrament of the host. Long live Jesus, long live Mary, long live Joseph! Letter sent by God, written in his own hand, in letters of gold. Sunday's battle was explained by a child of six years, who had been thought, until then, to be dumb. I am writing this brief note to you to warn you to sanctify Sunday by good works . . .

Having reviewed the Catholic's duties, it continued:

> I am sending you signs in the sun, earthquakes and other scourges; to protect yourselves you must pass this letter on with great reverence, and give it to others, and all those who have any doubts about this letter, verily, they shall feel the weight of my wrath . . .[24]

This association of contemporary events with the usual characteristics of the miraculous points both to the self-interest of printers, anxious to corroborate their claims, and to the way in which crisis might be viewed in mythical, rather than in overtly political or analytical terms.

The readiness in times of crisis to slip from a modern to an archaic vocabulary was again displayed during the Second World War. In August 1941, an old lady from Coulommiers showed a folklorist her version of the 'Saint Odile's prophecy', which was very common in devout circles throughout Brie. It started by evoking apocalyptic scenes:

> Listen, listen, my brother, for I have seen the terror of the forest and mountains. . . . The time has come when Germany shall be called the most bellicose nation on earth. The time has come when from its bosom a fearful warrior

> shall arise, who will make war on the world and whom the peoples at arms called 'the antechrist' ... He will be victorious on earth, at sea and even in the skies, for his warriors shall be winged ...

It predicted the outcome of the war and affirmed that the catastrophe would make men turn to God. The prophecy of Saint Cécile was also known in the area, while a number of manuscript versions of the miraculous letter written in gold by Christ and found in Artois were also discovered in the Ile-de-France.[25] Printing had familiarized people with allegorical religious and mythical language, and hence, this was sometimes used to express anxieties and aspirations with little overt relation to the concerns of orthodox spirituality. The fact that an event as recent as the Second World War – or indeed the Franco-Prussian War – could be seen in the perspective of and expressed in a form dating from the Middle Ages points to the tenacity and vitality in the modern period of what has been called a pre-modern outlook. In the mid-twentieth century, people could draw on two cultures to voice their concerns: political preoccupations could be expressed in the familiar language of contemporary journalism and with a quasi-religious medieval vocabulary. Alongside the modern was an older idiom, more deeply-rooted, it would seem, and largely irrational in its categories.

What one might tentatively see as an indication of interchangeability of vocabulary (between that of the broadsheet and that of the newspaper, for example) suggests that the differences between the modern and the pre-modern mentality may not be so great as was at one time thought, and points to the dangers of seeing one set of ideas as indicative of a scientific and the other as emblematic of a pre-logical mentality. Not only would this evidence suggest that irrationality had been less successfully banished from modern consciousness and culture than the organization, ideals and assumptions of contemporary society would lead one to believe, but it also points to the striking persistence of archaic forms of thought. One may object that these letters can in no way be taken as the authentic voice of often illiterate peasants, and that their similarity, deriving from literary plagiarism, simply reinforces the argument that these productions were neither spontaneous nor representative. This ignores both their continued popularity and their integration into predominantly oral tradition. Not only were such printed works kept, carried, noted down, but – and the independent borrowings within the literary tradition should not obscure this – their language also informed the popular idiom.

Visionaries

Visionaries often aroused curiosity, and sometimes even enthusiasm, among their poor neighbours, who would flock to see their extraordinary behaviour and listen to their pronouncements – indeed, even to receive their blessing and help. The long-term prosperity and popularity of visionaries was, however, largely determined by the attitude of the clerical authorities, who usually dismissed their claims as fraudulent, inflammatory or as the symptom of diseased minds. A summary catalogue indicates that even in the latter half of the century, several visionaries enjoyed temporary vogue. From 1849 on, in the Vosges, Rosine Horiot was subject to long comas, during which she saw the Virgin Mary, but her cult was short-lived due to the clergy's hostile attitude towards her. At Vorey in Haute-Saône, around 1850, Alexandrine Lanois imagined she saw paradise; at Frandrais in Loire-Inférieure, in 1873, Marie Julien saw the Virgin and Child. Pauline Périe, from Francoulès near Cahors, was subject to stigmata and visions, and at Javrier in Cher, Josephine Reverdy saw apparitions.[26]

These people were frequently regarded as possessing unusual powers and capacities, as healers or prophets, and their popularity reflected the dreams and needs – practical and emotional – of their poor contemporaries. In 1803, when an old woman known as the 'Sainte de Valence' passed through Gap on her way to visit the shrine of Notre Dame de Lans, vast numbers of devout people from the south of France went there to see her. Many people gave her alms, asked her for her protection and stole or accepted some of her rags as relics. Ladoucette, who was then prefect of the Department, questioned her and finding her to be mad and drunk, dispatched her to the asylum at Grenoble, thus, he claimed, diminishing the credit of magic in the Hautes-Alpes.[27] Similarly, Eugène Vintras, a factory foreman from Tilly-sur-Seulles, who was subject to visions, gradually acquired a large following throughout France. In August 1839, Vintras had his first vision: he saw an old ragged man, who seemed to follow him around. The apparition even accompanied him on the road to Paris, where he had business to do. After a remission, the visions recurred: but now the old man revealed that he had been sent to inform Vintras of a prophetic mission with which God had decided to entrust him. The prophet began to inscribe the words he received from God in a *Livre d'Or*. At first, these predictions were confined to 'the misfortunes which will befall man, punishments that are near at hand, divine wrath, the gathering of a great council, then divine mercy and the forgiveness of men's sins, the arrival of a great King on the throne of France . . . ' Like most prophets, Vintras drew on a religious vocabulary, which he shared with admonitory bishops and chapbook literature. The favour which Vintras initially enjoyed was gradually lost, however. The Church led the assault, denouncing him from the pulpit and forbidding him to receive communion. Eventually even Popes Gregory XVI and then Pius IX condemned him. The government had also turned its attention to him as, in 1841, Vintras persisted in announcing the imminent accesion to the throne of Louis XVII. Louis Philippe ordered his arrest and trial, following which he was condemned to five years in prison. At this time, Vintras had a large following; even after his death, his teachings inspired enthusiasm.[28] His popularity may be explained, to some extent, by the fact that his predictions appealed to a deeply-rooted popular taste for apocalyptic perspectives, a taste which had been confirmed and exploited by the Church and which sometimes assumed a political aura – a development which usually resulted in the punishment of those involved. While, in the Middle Ages, popular millenarianism was more evidently divorced from reality – in that the coming of Christ or of some legendary emperor like Frederick Barbarossa was expected – by the nineteenth century, similar longings for a radical transformation of the world through the return or advent of a redeeming hero lent themselves to exploitation by politicians (as the associates of Louis Bonaparte were quick to prove), since Napoleon or the Bourbons had replaced their archaic prototypes.

For all the eccentricity of Vintras and his disciples, however, the interest they aroused was by no means unprecedented. The poor, especially in the countryside, seem to have been avid for apparently miraculous events. A letter written on 13 May 1819 by the prefect of Ain to the Minister of the Interior illustrates this hunger for the curious and marvellous. For some days, the prefect explained, fairly large numbers of country people of all ages and both sexes had been gathering on the road from Châlons to Bourg, about two leagues away from Bourg. Interest was focussed on a place where:

> . . . Under a bush and in a ditch, which runs alongside the road, some individuals . . . children and women claim to see a small outline of the Virgin intermittently. This figure, as you may well imagine, is only seen by some people, and even those who say they have seen it do not appear to agree on the shape and dimensions of the object of their vision.
>
> What appears to have given birth to this tale is the circumstance that two young girls discovered in this place a bone and skull, which they buried several times and which, according to them, kept reappearing. The bones were finally removed, no one knows by whom, and immediately the young girls declared that they saw the bones transformed into a living figure. No matter how absurd the origin of this supposed prodigy and how great the efforts made by the priests and authorities of the local commune to discourage the country people from the virtual cult which they devote to this bush, their authority and indeed their fervour have only served to strengthen it and each day the crowd of worshippers grows.[29]

What seems to have started as an attempt by two initially shocked girls to draw attention to themselves, was adopted by the adults of the area as an escape from ordinary life and as an emblem of hope.

The interest in the marvellous,[30] which sometimes led people to invest ordinary events with extraordinary significance, was indicative both of man's insecurity and of his dissatisfaction with his surroundings. The attention paid to the claims and predictions of visionaries was not gratuitous nor unrelated to reality and men's appreciation of it. Prophets seem to have captured people's imagination. An eighteen-year-old girl from

Normandy, imprisoned in Rouen for arson, developed symptoms of mental derangement: she flung herself around the dormitory and appeared to be subject to terrifying hallucinations, and her delirium was soon manifest in both her speech and acts. The people about her believed her to be possessed, but confrontation with prayers and blessed objects only served to exacerbate her disorder. 'Her slightest acts, her slightest movements,' commented the doctor, 'even her delirious talk, were interpreted as being supernatural phenomena. She *predicted the future*, described illustrations hidden in closed books, read the intimate thoughts of her astonished audience.' Nonetheless, she was allowed to return with her mother to her home village, where her illness soon impressed the local people. In one of her attacks, she foretold that many priests would die within the year, if a chapel in honour of Notre Dame de la Salette were not established in the locality. Her predictions were ignored and, as luck would have it, many more priests in the district died that year than was normal. The commotion surrounding the girl became greater and finally the bishop was asked to accede to the girl's demands. At this, the prudent cleric asked Morel to examine the girl. The doctor found her at Le Havre, where she had been sent to stay with a relative, under the supervision of a 'most enlightened' priest. When Morel met her, she was unwilling to answer his questions:

> ...She was possessed by a *silent devil*. She wrote her replies, which were all concerned with commands, given by the Virgin, not to talk until such a time as she had herself decreed, when *the truth would be known*.[31]

The interest of her story lies not in her hysteria, but in the curiosity elicited by and attention paid to her pronouncements, the apparent readiness of many ordinary people to take her at her word and to tolerate her behaviour – no matter how outlandish it might be. This sort of reaction was not uncommon, however difficult it may be to understand.

The reputation and authority of visionaries' pronouncements was partly a matter of chance. Catherine Labouré, a twenty-four-year-old novice in a Parisian convent, had a vision of the Virgin Mary in 1830. The ninth of eleven children, Catherine came from a village near Dijon. She awoke one night in the convent and was guided by a child, whom she subsequently identified as her guardian angel, to the chapel, where she saw a woman whom the child affirmed to be Mary. Catherine gave a more detailed description of a later vision, which she saw during meditation: the Virgin was middle-aged, rather sad, and wearing a white dress 'taillée à la Vierge'; she held a small globe and her eyes were turned to heaven. Catherine imagined that the Virgin ordered her to have a miraculous medal struck and, despite the scepticism of her Lazarist confessor and the indifference of the bishop, she achieved her purpose. Indeed, following the Lazarist's unsympathetic attitude to her revelations, the novice had no further visions.[32] Both the conventional character of Catherine's visions and their abrupt cessation indicate how far the culture around her influenced her behaviour. Her environment furnished her with the vocabulary for expressing herself and encouraged her to behave as she did. The novice of humble background, who had experienced or subjected herself to frequent humiliations and self-denial, was suddenly transformed into a privileged, important person by her vision of the Virgin and by the mission with which she was entrusted. Her story – like that of many other prophets – reflects the reversal of fortune so often adumbrated in folk-tales.

Similarly, the renowned *Extatique du Fontet* was a poor woman, whose extraordinary experiences and claims briefly transformed her existence and redeemed her misery.[33] Marie Bergadieu, who was nicknamed Berguille, was born into a family of poor sharecroppers in 1829 at Loupiac (Gironde). She had a hard life as a farmer's wife and only two of her several children survived infancy. Although her physical health seemed good, doctors diagnosed her to be hysterical when she was fifteen. Later, between 1854 and 1865 when living in a lonely locality, she had terrifying nocturnal hallucinations, seeing the devil and hunting him across the woods at night, armed with a pitchfork. These visions vanished when she moved to a busier area. However, when her daughter, of whom she was very fond, died, Marie was deeply affected and again began to suffer from hallucinations at night, during which she imagined she saw her dead daughter. She became very devout and some time afterwards, in 1873, she consulted her doctor again. This time she claimed to have stomach pains and to be unable to eat anything. The doctor tentatively diagnosed cancer, but discovered, two months later, that the symptoms had disappeared when Marie had gone to Lourdes (about which she had read) and drunk some miraculous water. Soon, a rumour, to the effect that she had been cured of cancer diagnosed by a doctor, began to do the rounds. A miracle was proclaimed, and crowds flocked to see her. For a week after this, she consumed nothing but Lourdes water and then, on 27 April 1873, she had the first in a new series of visions: a beautiful lady clad in white in a bright cloud of light confirmed that Marie's illness had indeed been cured.

In the next year, she had forty visions and frequent bouts of ecstasy, although during the remissions she was able to work and eat normally. In the spring of 1874, her visions became more frequent and more regular – occurring every Friday afternoon and following a more or less standard pattern. Her illness had developed into a virtual performance, timed conveniently so that visitors could look on. She made political and religious predictions, all of which were wrong, but which were reprinted by Legitimist newspapers amid much fuss. On 11 September 1873, she announced that 'the great king Henry V will come, not by the vote of men, but by the all-powerful will of God, and because it must be so to save France, which is failing and dying.' On 23 August she affirmed that 'The three days of darkness are at hand; terrible events shall come to pass; Paris will be completely destroyed.' The subject and style of these predictions were indebted to chapbooks.[34] But why did Berguille repeat them? In the first place she was ill. Secondly, the prophecies ostensibly conferred on her an importance which she would not otherwise have enjoyed: the political pronouncements of poor peasant women were not usually the object of curiosity – their opinions were discounted, as politics were a matter for men and participation in high affairs of state was largely confined to the middle and upper classes.

If the reasons for Berguille's behaviour are obvious enough, the explanation for her popularity is less readily available. Berguille prophesied the destruction of the existing order and its replacement with a different régime. The myth of the return of the king – as exemplified in popular legends about King Arthur – was perennially popular and reflected a desire for change, for a new kingdom in which order and justice would be re-established. The pretensions of the Legitimists lent themselves readily to grafting upon this tradition – they furnished a new vocabulary for expressing old aspirations. Gloomy predictions about the destruction of the world were a feature of religious and, to some extent, of political predictions. The satisfaction which people appear to have derived from these apocalyptic pronouncements and the persistence with which they were reiterated were hardly gratuitous, but reflected an element of anger and dissatisfaction with the present.

Discontent traditionally found an outlet in the contemplation of horrors and destruction, as well as in the anticipation of a change in the order of things. The popularity of prophecies suggests that people occasionally rejoiced in the ephemeral nature of power and its works. To judge by the contents of chapbooks, people had long revelled in apocalyptic prophecies and seemed more interested in predictions of disaster than in agreeable tidings. Good fortune and happiness were evoked in the dream of the all-conquering hero, who would inaugurate a new age, rather than – as in the horoscopes of the late nineteenth century – as an element of the individual's destiny. Traditional predictions were general rather than personal, embracing the entire natural and political order. In the wake of the Revolution of 1789, a variety of old prophecies were republished and discussed. One, supposedly dating from 1731 and found in a Benedictine's lead coffin, was in fact a vernacular copy of an earlier prediction, popular in Italy in the sixteenth century. It ran:

1755 Great Earthquake.
1790 The wrath of God is felt on earth.
1800 Christ is little known on earth.
1840 There will be no pastors left.
1888 Advent of a great man.
1899 Conversion of the heathens.
1999 Extinction of the stars, one flock and one shepherd.[35]

This prognostication was fairly typical of one vein of popular prophecy.

Disaster, the effects of divine ire, the reign of godlessness, the advent of the hero, the ultimate triumph of the good, were all recurring features of popular eschatology. This homogeneity may be ascribed, in part, to the plagiarism of authors and publishers; but, on the other hand, it would not have been worthwhile to reproduce books filled with such prophecies had there been no interest in them.

Some of these sanguinary publications were interpreted in an overtly political way in the first half of the nineteenth century. During the Restoration, the pronouncements of a variety of fashionable seeresses and, in particular, those published by Mlle Lenormand, aroused the interest of those prone to dabble in the esoteric. In 1827 Mlle Lenormand printed in her *Mémoires sur l'Impératrice Joséphine* the *x*[e] *Prédiction de Philippe-Dieu-Donné-Noël Olivarius* which was, she claimed, an opuscule originally published in 1542. This proclaimed the birth in Gaul-Italy of a supernatural being:

> This man will emerge from the sea as a boy, will take his language and customs from the Celts of Gaul, will, when still young, and despite a thousand obstacles, open a path for himself among the soldiery and become their chief leader.

This was taken to be an allusion to Napoleon, as later remarks about 'les rois du vieil . . . sang de la Cap' were assumed to refer to the Bourbons. The *Prévisions certaines révélées par Dieu à un Solitaire*, known as the *Prédiction d'Orval*, were in a similar vein. In spurious sixteenth-century idiom, they announced that 'moults hauts et puissants rois seront en crainte vraie', and in nebulous terms that allegedly foretold Napoleon's triumphs and defeats, furnished a picturesque account of the activities of sybilline characters in the 'century of desolation'.[36] This prophecy, which initially surfaced in the 1820s and which was reprinted in a number of chapbooks in the 1840s, caused a considerable stir – on account of its supposed political import – despite its obviously derivative character.

The political debates inspired by such predictions accounted for the speed of the authorities' reaction to prophets and visionaries. This attitude was evident especially in the aftermath of Napoleon's defeat, when rumours and commotions were carefully noted and examined for seditious inspiration. This policy was perpetuated throughout the nineteenth century and it accounts for our knowledge of some minor rural visionaries who never attained notoriety, due to their prompt incarceration by the government. It also explains the attention paid to one Thomas-Ignace Martin, a labourer from the Chartres area, who claimed to have seen and conversed with the Archangel Gabriel and to have received important messages from God through this celestial intermediary. Martin had been working in the fields one day in January 1816, when he was approached by a character wearing a light frock-coat and a tall round hat, who, having made a speech, ascended into the skies. Much alarmed, Martin consulted his *curé*, who sensibly advised him to drink and sleep properly and continue his normal routine. But going about his work – in the cellar, or fetching fodder for the horses – he continued to see the strange person. The latter, having grown impatient with the visionary's obtuseness and lack of curiosity about the identity of his marvellous interlocutor, finally informed him: ' . . . I come from the one who sent me and He who sent me is above me [pointing to heaven].'

When Martin objected that it was not sensible to appear to a poor, ignorant peasant with complicated instructions, the messenger affirmed that it was intended to punish the proud. He went on to recommend – much as in a Sunday sermon – that Martin should avoid the inn, dances, and work on Sundays, and that he should attend to his Christian duties. The tenor of this conversation was indebted to eschatological tradition – in particular, that of celestial letters in which God fulminated against the shortcomings of his creatures and which children sometimes had the honour of finding and explaining. The apocalyptic theme – and political overtones – of Martin's visions became more pronounced as time wore on. In February, the Archangel revealed that the usurper had reappeared the previous year, because God wanted to punish the royal family for their ingratitude on receiving the throne. He pressed Martin to continue with his mission, adding: ' . . . Those who are dealing with the matter are intoxicated with pride; France is in a state of delirium; it will be prey to all kinds of misfortune!' Martin was to seek an audience with the King and tell him that, 'If they don't do as I say, the greater part of the people will die, France will be at the mercy of all other nations, which shall hold her in contempt.' Martin's agitated response brought him to the attention of the bishop, the prefect and finally, the Minister of Police, who interviewed him when he arrived in Paris to see the King. As a result, he was incarcerated in Charenton (where Pinel treated him). At this, the angel became even more sanguinary, informing him that:

> . . . The most terrible plague is about to fall on France and . . . it is very near at hand. Seeing these things coming to pass, the peoples will be overcome with astonishment and consumed by fear . . . France is lost in irreligion, pride, incredulity, impiety, impurity and is given over to every kind of vice. If the people make ready to repent, what has been predicted will be stopped. . . .[37]

This was the language traditionally used by visionaries, in their attempts to invest themselves with authority and to claim attention. It implied an oblique criticism of those who exercised political power and a rejection of the unreformed world. It appealed for change, a conversion to new standards of humility and obedience to God's rule.

This language was also to be a feature of one of the most famous visions in France in the nineteenth century – that of La Salette. On 19 September 1846, Maximin Giraud, an eleven-year-old child not distinguished for his piety, and Mélanie Calvat, a weak small girl of fifteen, claimed to have seen the Virgin Mary while minding sheep on a mountainside near the remote village of La Salette. Maximin spoke only a few words of French, while Mélanie's education extended only to a knowledge of the Pater, Ave and Credo. Both children came from very poor families and earned their livings as farm-servants: Mélanie, whose father was a pit-sawyer and mason, had started work at the age of eight, prior to which she had been obliged to beg for her food. It was a Saturday evening when, on their way down from the mountains, they saw a woman in a bright light. At first she spoke to them in French, until she realized (slowly for one so omniscient) that they could not understand, whereat she used the local dialect. She predicted imminent famine and disasters, with a gusto that was hardly in keeping with the benevolent nature of celestial beings. She expatiated on the moral shortcomings of the people of the area and warned that their failings would be punished.

This story existed only in outline at first and the reception initially accorded to it was far from enthusiastic. The children were beaten several times by their elders, at first because they were suspected of lying and then because their parents feared their antics might cause trouble. The *curé*, however, heard about it the next day, and preached an exalted sermon on the happy occurrence. The children achieved immediate notoriety and curious pilgrims soon began to arrive and to bathe in the spring which had sprung up again near the site of the Virgin's apparition. The bishop of the diocese was inclined to share his curate's enthusiasm – although some of his episcopal colleagues and diocesan clergy had reservations about the tale, as well as about the character of the children. The bishop ordered an inquiry into the episode, which, in 1851, found in favour of the children. Thereafter, the cult developed rapidly and miracles occurred at the shrine. Its popular renown was established, and the Church did nothing to discourage the devotion. Just as official disapproval had destroyed the appeal of some myths, this episode owed its fame and standing to the tolerant attitude of the bishop.[38]

The people at the centre of these astounding occurrences were unusually poor and insignificant. This was characteristic of popular visions, not only because their idiom was conceivable only in a society hardly touched by modern beliefs, but also because visions were a means of protest and of compensation: the humble were exalted, being selected by God as his agents and entrusted by him with important missions. Mélanie and Maximin were no exception to this rule: initially they were particularly unfortunate children, but their story transformed their lives. After their visions, they enjoyed respite from ordinary work and the cares of poor children. Indeed, it seems that they may first have told their tale in the hope of avoiding work the next day – which happened to be a Sunday. The children disguised their wishes with a story that reiterated God's explicit desire to see Sunday as a day devoted to His worship, rather than to secular concerns like work, and whose alleged origin was such that those who challenged it were impious. Through the story, the normal order and normal authority were reversed: instead of the children challenging their parents' authority, their elders were guilty of the infinitely more serious offence of challenging God's word and divine authority. Subsequently the children were plucked from their miserable homes and placed in religious institutions, where they distinguished themselves by their ignorance and in Maximin's case, taste for money and alcohol – much to the disedification of those clerics who had always disagreed with the bishop.

How, in view of the early inconsistencies in the children's story and of the boy's subsequent behaviour (which included boasts to the effect that the entire incident had been invented), on which contemporary critics had insisted, was credence lent to their tale? It would seem that the demands of clerical politics, as well as silliness, prevailed against the evidence. An authenticated appearance by the Virgin was a helpful development for a local church struggling against indifference, materialism and poverty, for it aroused ostensibly religious curiosity and enthusiasm and became a means of reconversion of the erring faithful. It drew attention and, in due course, influence and money to the diocese. While it seems improbable that such motives would have been consciously avowed by the clergy in the diocese, they no doubt informed the attitude of some influential churchmen and disposed them towards visionaries. And the implausibility of the story? The very familiarity, the lack of originality of the children's claims added to their authority and authenticity. Far from seeming plagiaristic, the tale – through its banality – seemed less extravagant and far-fetched. The Virgin (after some initial disagreement between the witnesses) looked as people expected her to look, as she appeared in holy pictures and as earlier visionaries had described her (being dressed in white, beribboned and covered in roses).

Then, her message was familiar and predictable (and honey to the hard-pressed clergy's ears). She complained about the fact that only the old went to mass in the summer while the young worked; and that in winter, the population attended mass only to deride the cult. God was displeased, and the shortages and crop-failures which the region had experienced the previous year were sent by him as a punishment. Further famine and sufferings would ensue if man did not repent.[39] Not only was this message modelled on themes long emphasized by the Church – and frequently reiterated in times of crisis – but the language used was also derivative. According to the children, the Virgin had started her discourse by saying: '. . . *I have given you six days for work and the seventh for myself, and it would be denied me.* That is what makes my son's arm so heavy. . . . ' This phrase was borrowed almost verbatim from the version of Christ's letter to his sinful followers that was sometimes reproduced in the *Médecin des Pauvres*.[40] This began by exhorting the reader not to work on Sundays, but to go to church instead and pray for the forgiveness of his sins, and it continued: '... I have given you six days for work and the seventh for rest, having heard divine service ...' The chapbook letter went on to promise war, plague, famine, pain and anguish to the sceptical; fertile fields and blessings to the obedient. The Virgin's speech (as given by the children) developed similar themes – applying them more precisely to contemporary local circumstances: hence, the blight on the potato the previous summer was a token of God's anger and further punishments were promised if men did not repent:

> I showed it to you last year in the potato-harvest but you paid no heed to it ... They [the potatoes] will go on rotting and by Christmas there will be none left ... Let he who has wheat not sow it ...; if some plants should come, they will turn into dust at threshing-time ... A great famine will come; before the famine, little children under seven years will be taken with shivering fits and will die in the arms of those that hold them and adults will do their penance by fasting. The grapes will rot and the nuts go bad. If [men] turn to God, the stones, rocks will turn into wheat, potatoes will be found sown in the ground.

The Virgin then reminded Maximin that he had seen rotten wheat, the previous year, when a man had said to his father:

> 'Come and see my rotten corn.' You went; he took two or three ears in his hand, then he rubbed them, and then it all turned into dust. And then going home ... your father gave you a piece of bread and said: 'Here, little one, eat this bread; I don't know who'll get any to eat next year.'[41]

Apart from this final episode, which is more sharply characterized than the rest of the speech and points to the incorporation into it of the memory of an actual incident, the Virgin's homily was but a modulation on a well-known text. It would seem that the children had – whether consciously or not – embroidered on the famous letter from Christ, drawing on local incidents to expand it and make it more apt.

This apocalyptic message was likely to have appealed to the children, given the general suffering of that time. Not only did visions enable the young, the poor, and women to arrogate to themselves an authority and importance normally denied to them, but their vogue sometimes coincided with and seems even to have been encouraged by the deprivation and stress caused by food shortages, disease or war. The desire to explain crises and the distress caused by them in terms of moral, rather than of physical, causality informed much of the folklore of disaster. Apocalyptic thought often amounted to an inverted form of protest, in that it implied a rejection of reality: its obsessive (if stereotyped) evocations of catastrophe and its celebration of the grotesque belonged to the realm of fantasy, where the longed-for redemption was also situated; nightmares and dreams alike were voiced in this tradition, which was closer to surrealism than to naturalism. However improbable the supposed prophecies, they drew on a familiar intellectual tradition[42] and expressed deeply-rooted anxieties and aspirations.

The famous visions of Bernadette Soubirous at Lourdes took place in a context similar to that of the apparitions at La Salette. In 1854–5, cholera had caused many deaths in Lourdes; while in the winter of 1856–7, famine affected the three departments of Landes, Hautes- and Basses-Pyrénées, following bad weather, poor harvests, the ruin of the potato and vegetable crops and the continuing plague of vine-mildew which reduced many vine-growers to beggary. Bernadette's family, which had formerly known some modest prosperity, suffered acutely in this period, being virtually destitute and living on the verge of starvation, crowded into a dark room known as the 'dungeon'. Bernadette herself, then the eldest of six children, suffered from asthma, was illiterate and, it would seem, backward. Early in February 1858, as it was snowing, Bernadette (who was fourteen), her sister and a friend were dispatched to collect firewood at Massabielle on the outskirts of the town. Massabielle was a cold, desolate rock-mass pierced by caves and grottoes, about which local legends abounded. When they arrived there, the children found they had to wade across an icy river to reach the firewood which was strewn on the opposite bank. At first Bernadette did not wish to follow her companions, but having done so, she saw a bright light, which – she later explained to her companions – gradually became more clearly recognizable as a young woman, dressed in white, draped in a veil and blue sash, with roses at her feet. On her return home, her mother scolded her for telling stories and admonished the child to keep away from Massabielle. Her playmates, however, spread the story, and the next Sunday joined her in another expedition to the grotto to see the vision (duly armed with holy water). Bernadette again went into a trance, much to the alarm of her companions and subsequent anger of her mother. By Wednesday, the commotion was sufficient to have attracted the attention of a pious lady, who thought (uncharitably) that Bernadette's vision might be none other than the late president of the local Children of Mary come to ask for prayers for the repose of her soul. The apparition was more communicative than hitherto: while declining to write her wishes down, the lady in white encouraged Bernadette to visit the grotto daily for a fortnight (and thereby to disobey her mother). The episode was daily becoming more elaborate, with Bernadette repairing to the grotto accompanied by processions of the curious and devout and furnishing those who questioned her with accounts of her conversations with the mysterious lady. The crowds grew and soon many people – in particular local servants, beggars, slate-quarrymen (of whom there were many in the district) and the ill – began to believe that Bernadette saw the Virgin Mary. They took her part when she was subjected to hostile questioning by the local police-commissioner, demonstrating noisily outside his office. The secular authorities attempted to restrain the child while the clergy remained reserved;[43] but popular enthusiasm was such that, less than a month after Bernadette's first vision, about twenty thousand people were estimated to have visited the grotto to see her.[44]

The entire community plunged into an atmosphere that bordered on hysteria, following the discovery of the spring. The first miracles occurred almost immediately after this. Following an explosion which had injured his right eye twenty years earlier, Louis Bouriette, a quarryman, lived in constant fear of going blind. In fact he was suffering from amaurosis, and when he applied water to his eye from the spring Bernadette had just discovered, he declared his eyesight to have been miraculously restored. This news spread rapidly through the town and inspired others to emulate him. Jeanne Crassus, whose hand had been paralyzed for ten years, was cured after she dipped her hand in the spring. As doctors were subsequently to note, nervous disorders were to predominate among the afflictions which yielded to the miraculous waters. Meanwhile, local people became increasingly carried away. A peasant swore he had heard voices on returning to his cottage. An innkeeper's servant began to have ecstasies. Several children of Bernadette's age began to have hysterics and visions at the grotto. There were cases of possession and a missionary exorcised the disturbed. Extraordinary events, were local people to be believed, became commonplace. A soldier who told a joke at the grotto was suddenly struck motionless. A man who had stolen forty centimes from the offerings-plate at the grotto was also frozen to the spot until he returned the money. A policeman who had treated Bernadette roughly caught cholera. A sceptical innkeeper was shaken and beaten during the night, while a voice cried: 'Will you believe now!' Another disbeliever, as he claimed to have seen nothing but stones at the grotto, was suddenly hit on the head by a stone falling from the tower of Baous. From April to July, a number of older girls – in particular, a very poor and hard-worked servant girl, Marie Lacadé – claimed to have visions similar to those of Bernadette.[45]

What accounts for this reaction, for the virtual hysteria which developed so quickly in response to Bernadette's vision? How did adult men and women, who were initially so sceptically censorious about the child's antics, feel able to tell and do such extraordinary things? The explanation would seem to be related to the poverty and difficulties recently experienced in the area. As was so often the case in times of crisis, fantasy (albeit, fantasy fashioned by folklore) revealed its great appeal when circumstances allowed – or indeed, encouraged – people to give rein to it. The tall stories told about the punishment of the sceptical were no more than exemplary legends adapted to fit the occasion: offended saints were commonly depicted as striking the irreverent with sickness, or rendering them motionless, or inflicting other punishments on disbelievers.[46]

Little in the stories told in Lourdes during the spring of 1858 appears to have been original. It seems that the poverty and distress of the area was such that curiosity was quickly transformed into hope – into the archaic fantasy, encouraged by the Church's eschatological teachings and by popular literature, of a radical transformation of reality. Affliction and misery would end, as was attested by the miracles and visions experienced by some. And as for these apparently privileged few – who showed classic symptoms of hysteria – the exceptional circumstances allowed them to indulge their impulses without restraint. Bernadette's visions furnished the pretext, at a time when most people in the area had experienced acute hardship, for what might be called a black carnival – an episode in which certain kinds of social inhibition and, in particular, the limitations placed on the intellect and imagination by daily necessity were eschewed in favour of the conventions of myth. Some might insist that their dreams were real rather than fantastic; others could adduce normally unnoticed incidents – suitably presented – as evidence of the advent of extraordinary times; for a few, reality was apparently transformed; while more gave way to enthusiasm and hope.

Episodes of this sort were more likely to occur in times of want or crisis than in periods of well-being and stability. After Lourdes, the next vision to create something of a rumpus took place at the little village of Pontmain in Mayenne. On 17 January 1871 between 5.45 and 8.45 in the evening, according to the local bishop's pastoral letter of the following year, a number of children claimed to see in the sky a beautiful tall lady, dressed in a blue star-studded dress and sporting a golden crown. The children's 'loud enthusiastic exclamations' soon drew to the spot a generally sceptical crowd, which before long was entertained to the gradual disclosure of a message slowly written, according to the children, by an invisible hand on a long white band that gradually unfurled at the lady's feet. The cumbersome communication urged the children to pray and informed the assembly that 'God will grant your request shortly'. The crowd now understood that the Mother of God had deigned to come to Pontmain with this consoling news – which could not have been better timed, for that day the advance guard of the Prussian army had reached nearby Laval. The next day, the village could hear the heavy gunfire of the ensuing battles; but three days later the Prussians began to pull back and eleven days after the vision, the armistice was signed – a coincidence which did not escape the bishop.[47] How did this ridiculous incident – which was, by the prelate's own admission, greeted with incredulity by two thirds of the villagers – attract any attention outside the locality, and how did the bishop come to involve himself with it? What seems to have weighed with the churchman and – if his account of the episode is to be trusted – what seems to have impressed part of the children's audience at the time, was the message, in the context of the war and of the military disaster, of which the village had just had first-hand experience. It is also worth noting that the villagers and children recognized the vision because of her conventional appearance and attitudes.

Conclusion

No concessions to modernity were made by celestial personages, nor were they expected of them. While conventional visions might be accepted at face value, more eccentric apparitions were apt to be taken as evidence of the visionary's insanity. Why did the culture of popular eschatology not adjust to the changing environment? Why did it remain wedded to an increasingly outmoded official ideology and so fall into discredit with it? Or is this disappearance of an outlook and disposition illusory? The association of these phenomena with orthodox religious dogma was more apparent than real. The vocabulary used to clothe and interpret these events did not so much describe a religious impulse as mask or simplify a complex social and psychological phenomenon. Belief in visionaries and their visions enabled people to express their hopes and anxieties – aspirations and fears that were to be differently channelled in a culture which encouraged the belief that politics could furnish solutions to all significant problems, and which rejected and confined manifestations of intellectual or cultural eccentricity. The enthusiasm which prophets and visionaries inspired was rooted in the desire to transcend the shortcomings of this world. The more difficult ordinary life became, the more ready people were to flock to shrines, to witness and even to participate in the miraculous transformation of reality, to believe promises in the imminence of new and better times. This enthusiasm and ill-considered hope did not disappear with the waning of overt religiosity but simply assumed new forms, resurfacing notably to transform the nature of politics.

5. Marine Monster (The British Library)

6. Invocation of a devil by a witch (Musée Historique et Archéologique de l'Orléannais)

WonderKruis te Migné bij Poitiers te zien geweest den 17 December 1826.

Croix miraculeuse, vue a Migné près de Poitiers le 17 décembre 1826.

DOOR DIT TEEKEN — IN HOC SIGNO VINCES — ZULT GIJ OVERWINNEN.

Par ce signe tu vaincras.

GOD ALLEEN

DOET WONDEREN.

Psalm 71. 18.

De wonderdadige verschyning van een Kruis in de beneden-lucht, gelyk het zelve hier is afgeteekend, heeft plaatsgehad te Migné in Frankrijk, tijdens het sluiten van 't Jubilé door Paus Leo XII. vergund, waartoe men een Kruis had opgerigt, en wel op 't oogenblik dat door de Predikant aan het Kruis, weleer aan keizer Constantijn verschenen, herinnerd werd. Naar het oog afgemeten had het kruis eene lengte van 140 voeten; was omtrent 200 voeten boven de aarde verheven, en van eene wit zilverachtige kleur. Het is gedurende een half uur gezien geweest door 3000 menschen.

Op last van den Hoogw. Heer Bisschop van Poitiers is deze gebeurtenis onderzocht door den Vicaris-generaal, den Burgemeester, den Pastor, een Professor (beroemd natuurkundige en protestant) en een Advocaat die van de echtheid schriftelyke getuigenis hebben gegeven

Paus Leo XII. van de waarheid overtuigd, vergunde een jaarlyksche Feestdag met aflaat.

Z. M. de Koning van Frankrijk Karel X. schonk ter dezer gelegenheid 40,000 francs, om die kerk te verbeteren, welke God door zoodanig wonder had vereerd.

Dat wy dan eindelyk roemen in het Kruis ons Heeren Jezus-Christus.

Dieu très-élevé a fait des signes étranges et des miracles; il lui a plu de les révéler. Dan. 3. 99.

Une apparition miraculeuse d'une Croix en l'air, comme elle est représentée ici, a eu lieu à Migné en France, commune de l'Evêché de Poitiers, le 17 décembre 1826, lors de l'élévation d'une Croix pour la clôture du Jubilé accordé par notre Saint Père Léon XII, et au moment que le prédicateur rappelait au peuple le miracle de la Croix, qui était jadis apparu à l'empereur Constantin et son armée lorsqu'il marchait contre Maxence.

Il était presque 5 heures du soir; la Croix paroissait avoir une longueur de 140 pieds, élevée d'environ 200 pieds de la terre; elle était d'une couleur argentée, elle a été contemplée, pendant une demie heure, dans la même position et la même splendeur, par environ 3000 personnes, et a disparu quand le peuple se rendait à l'Eglise pour recevoir la Bénédiction du Saint Sacrement.

Par ordre du très-révérend Seigneur Evêque de Poitiers cet événement a été examiné par un Vicaire Général, un Professeur de Theologie, le Maire qui fut témoin oculaire, un Professeur de Physique, étant protestant et un Avocat qui ont fait déclaration par écrit de la véracité.

Notre très-saint Père Léon XII, convaincu de la vérité a envoyé à Migné une Croix en or, contenant une partie de la Sainte-Croix à laquelle le Sauveur a repandu son sang pour le salut du genre humain. Il a en outre accordé une *Indulgence plénière*, à mériter annuellement à l'Eglise de Migné le troisième dimanche de l'Avent.

Glorifions-nous donc dans la Croix de notre Seigneur Jésus-Christ.

VRUCHTEN VAN HET HEILIG KRUIS.

De mensch die hier verduldig lydt,
Maakt dat zyn ziel in God verblydt.
Het lyden is het beste goed
Dat God zyn liefste kinders doet,
Het lyden is de regte baan,
Waar in God ons is voorgegaan.
Het lyden stelt den mensch in staat,
Om wel te zien waar dat hy gaat.
Het lyden maakt den mensch verstand,
Die door de weelde was verblind,
Het lyden heeft God ons geleerd,
Waar door hy wordt het meest vereerd.

Het lyden heeft God ons getoond,
En dat is 't dat hy 't meeste loond
Het lyden doet u 't meest profyt,
Daarom ziet dat gy gaarne lydt.
Het lyden maakt den mensch zoo zoet,
Gelyk een schaapje van gemoed.
Het lyden opent het verstand,
Daarom hebt 't kruis altyd ter hand,
O goede God, o klaar' Fontein,
Ach! maak weer onze harten rein,
Zoo zal het kruis, daar gy aan scheidt,
Ons breugen eens ter zaligheid.

O Jesus geef my moed,
Myn kruis met u te dragen
En leer my dat ik mag
Wat lyden zonder klagen,
Maar kom ik niet zoo verr'
Dat 't lyden my verheugt:
Verwerk my, dat ik maak
Ook van den nood een deugd.

AMEN

Turnhout, BREPOLS & DIERCKX Zoon — N.° 68.

7. Appearance of a cross in the sky to a crowd near Poitiers (Bibliothèque Nationale)

8 (*facing*). Mr Homebreaker and Mrs Scolder (Bibliothèque Nationale)

Te uoila donc uenu chien d iurogne de puis huict heur e s du matin que tu est parti d'icy
tu me demande de l'argent pour achever de te saouler tuauras la peste qui te creve le Diable
qui t'emporet en'es tu pas content depuis quatres Jours que tu fais la debauche voilatrois en=
fans qui meurent de faim vilain pillier de taverne bouchons de Cabaret

Ha vous raisonnez vous criez quand on vous bat et vous grondez quand on vous demande
de l'Argent par la morbleu Je vais casser tout

Casse Diable Je vais achever voyons qui fera pis de nous deux

A Paris Chez *Simon Duflos .*

9. Land of Cockaigne (Bibliothèque Nationale)

VII

Demonology and Inventive Magic

A popular and lucrative branch of magic exploited the perennial fantasies of the peasant – primarily the dream of possessing fabulous treasures, lovers or, more prosaically, good jobs, and of avoiding conscription. Many of these benefits – in particular, treasures – were supposed to be procured with the devil's help. This dimension of the proceedings has, not unnaturally, absorbed the attention of sceptical and amused commentators, so that their cosmological implications have tended to obscure the real motives and concerns of the naive people who looked to this kind of magic for the realization of their dreams. These practices were, of course, a form of fraud practised by usually unscrupulous thieves on the simple-minded, but they also cast light on archaic fantasy. Demonology should be seen as an old-fashioned kind of crime and a form of escapism which reflected the ambitions and dreams of people confined by poverty, and not merely as a naive cosmology.

Books of Spells

Many fraudulent activities were inspired by the demonology peddled in chapbooks. Inventive magic, which typically purported to procure happiness for those who had recourse to it, was inspired primarily by literature – unlike the witchcraft used in times of distress, which drew on folklore and reflected the exasperation of the suffering. One of the sorcerer's most redoubted weapons was his book of spells: this reputedly indicated how to summon the devil, make a pact with him, cause a neighbour's illness and so on. One of the reasons why the Avril family of Tours was so feared, in the middle of the July Monarchy, was because the father used to read. It was understood that he was studying or casting spells. When a judge asked one man how he thought spells were cast, the peasant replied: 'With bad books'. The fact that Madame Avril could not read constituted, for him, no objection – for she could have learnt the formulae by heart, or could have read in different kinds of books.[1] This remark corroborates, to some extent, Geneviève Bollème's suggestion that in the study of popular literature, one needs to extend the concept of 'reading' to include somewhat arbitrary interpretations of the indecipherable;[2] it also lends some weight to Michelet's contention that the book provided a *texte élastique* on which the imagination elaborated. Books like the *Dragon Rouge*, as well as many pages of the unrevised almanacs, were filled with hieroglyphs and symbols, the interpretation of which hardly depended upon the ability to read. For those who bought and consulted such books, the importance of the symbols perhaps lay more in their power to prompt the imagination than in the furnishing of any clear exposition of the ostensible subject-matter. To the sorcerer, at all events, the *Dragon Rouge* was probably a profitable investment, and it was commonly believed that such volumes conferred marvellous powers on their owners. That some sorcerers owned chapbooks devoted to magical techniques seems assured for a number of reasons. In the first place, it is reasonable to suppose that the books would not have been published had there been no market for them. Laisnel de la Salle, in his memoirs about Berry, asserted that sorcerers generally learnt their secrets from their fathers, or else used the *Grand* or *Petit Albert*. The villagers held that these books gave them great powers.[3] In Poitou, in the early twentieth century, the *Petit Albert* was supposed to be the sorcerer's book of spells and peasants spoke of it with terror.[4] One of Macario's patients, a gardener who had been born at the start of the century, suffered from the belief that he was possessed by devils, one of whom taught him the secrets of the *Grand Albert*[5] – an example of how popular beliefs might be reflected in the delirium of insanity. In the Tarn, this fear of the *Grand Albert* survived into the twentieth century: in 1935, the book was still supposed to confer extraordinary capacities on its owner.[6] According to some traditions, it was sufficient to read the book to be possessed by the devil or to make him appear. In the Bocage Normand, according to Boismoreau, it was believed that if one read such a work, one automatically made a pact with the devil.[7] In fact, a Breton spell-book found in the twentieth century by Kerbirou contained specific formulae for renouncing heaven and the Catholic Church.[8] This was not usually the case in the books of spells peddled in the countryside – although plenty of dubious enterprises were explained therein. At Saint Etienne de Tarn in the Tarn, it was supposed that the devil took possession of the soul of the reader daring enough to proceed beyond a certain page; the devil was also believed to appear to him.[9]

In fact, rumour was not as inaccurate as might be supposed in that dubious publications abounded in the countryside, even if they were less powerful than the credulous supposed. Several trials mention the fact that the sorcerer was wont to have reference to his book of spells,[10] while Bouteiller reports that a sorcerer offered to lend the uncle of her old informer 'bad books'.[11] Some of these volumes had impressively bizarre names – such as the *Abracadabra Monumentissima Diabolica*, with which Louis-Joseph Bernard of Saint Omer broke spells,[12] or the

Cyprien Mago ante Conversionem, dated Salamanca 1460 but printed in French and bad Latin and illustrated with versions of 'magic, cabbalistic and diabolical' images, which informed its owner, among other things, how to obtain a treasure of eighteen millions.[13] Most of the works mentioned belonged to the *Bibliothèque Bleue*. One sorcerer, who was unmasked by a young teacher and a doctor on proceeding to attempt to break a spell, referred to his books as 'Agrippa, . . . in which there is to be found a piece of the devil's skin'.[14] Doubtless, this prestigious possession won him much healthy respect. This book was probably the *Grand Grimoire d'Agrippa, ou l'art de commander les esprits celestes, aériens, terrestres, infernaux avec le vrai secret de faire parler les morts, de gagner toutes les fois qu'on met aux loteries, de découvrir les trésors cachés*, which was part of the *Bibliothèque Bleue* during the Ancien Régime[15] and was re-edited by Regnault in 1845. Near Niort in the late 1820s, an unscrupulous couple, who relieved an old widow of her savings by passing themselves off as sorcerers, possessed copies of the *Dragon Rouge*, the *Grand Grimoire* and the *Petit Albert*, as well as *Jean de Paris* and other books not named in the account of the trial.[16]

Another volume from the *Bibliothèque Bleue* which appears to have been used by sorcerers is the *Enchiridion Leonis Papae*. Gautier, from the commune of Izeure, used to apply remedies from this work to the illnesses of farm animals and possessed a modern copy of the work (although it was dated Rome 1660).[17] Letourneux, a sorcerer in the area of Pierre-Lise in Angers, treated people for illness and spells with dangerous drugs and his copy of the *Enchiridron*, before his arrest and trial in October 1840.[18] The most extensive diabolical library of which I have read a description was that of Père Roussel, a sorcerer from the commune of Blainville in lower Normandy. He possessed the *Oeuvres Magiques de Henri Corneille Agrippa par Pierre d'Alban, avec des secrets occultes* (1547) and the *Grimoire du Pape Honorius*, as well as the *Enchiridion*. When consulted by the farmer Renoult for his sick cows, around 1837, Roussel proceeded thrice around the stable, reading prayers from the spell-book – having first hung a talisman (written in bovine blood) about an animal's neck, scattered salt and holy water and used a holy candle. The *Dragon Noir* gave remarkably similar directions for lifting spells from animals: it advised that one should walk around the beasts three times, reciting a garbled Latin formula.[19] A more complicated *garde* for sheep and horses also involved the recital of a magical prayer, walking around the animals, throwing salt on them, repeating the formula, bleeding one of the animals and making a talisman with the help of an Easter candle[20] – quite a complicated (and doubtless expensive) rite. In any case, Roussel was careful to impress his client with his occult powers; for, at the trial, the witness was terrified when asked to indicate which black picture marked the point at which the book had been opened during Roussel's consultation: 'The witness advances his hand to take the spell book three times; and three times, he withdraws it, fearfully. On being again invited to do so, he takes the book, but immediately throws it down in terror. (Laughter). *President*. "Are you afraid?" *Witness* "Yes, sir." '[21] The spell-book might then have exercised some influence on the rites which sorcerers performed; in any case, even if they were not used as reference works, they inspired a tremulous confidence in the sorcerers' capacities. Thérèse Caly used to summon up the ghosts of enemies and cure illnesses of man and beast with the aid of the *Petit Albert* in the Aude during the July Monarchy.[22] J. L. Blandin (known as Gaucher), a day-labourer from Saint Fulgent, was, according to the trial, a middle-aged sorcerer, of bad reputation and worse morality. One of the witnesses at his trial affirmed: 'I was very afraid of Gaucher because he had told me he owned the *Petit Albert* and other books, which enabled him to do anything he liked.'[23] Gaucher, like others, was not slow to exploit popular credulity for his own profit.

Such books were not necessarily possessed only by those who intended to use them practically. J. Lemoine met an old man, near the end of the century, whose library consisted of the *Double Almanach du Pays de Liège*, the *Paroissien Romain* and the *Dragon Rouge* (which enabled him to inform Lemoine of the technique of meeting the devil at a cross-roads by sacrificing a black hen)[24] – an interesting mixture of the devout, the practical and the condemned. Even a volume which did not overtly sin against orthodoxy might, however, be put to unorthodox uses. Such was the *Miroir de l'Ame*, a popular manual of religious devotion, exhorting the erring faithful to repent and adorned with engravings of large hearts being assaulted by devils. According to Nisard, this book dates from the 1320s, while the engravings included in the *Bibliothèque Bleue*'s edition from the early seventeenth century were the work of the Breton missionary Nobletz.[25] Perdiguier notes that, as a child in Provence, he bought a copy of this work.[26] A seventeen-year-old labourer and mentally deficient sorcerer Goyou from the communes of Villiers-Charlemagne and Louverne (Mayenne) used the book in 1827 to lift a spell.[27] The frightening pictures sufficed to make it inspiring and useful, even if the sorcerers were illiterate. The defending lawyers alleged that the simplicity and illiteracy of the accused rendered them incapable of inventing such rites, which might more correctly be taken to reflect the beliefs of the community from which they came. This incident gives a slight indication of the uses of literature in an illiterate society. For Perdiguier, as for the aspiring sorcerers and the witness in Roussel's trial, the pictures were the point of departure. The exact contents of a book were not necessarily of the first importance: reading might amount to little more than directing one's mind into a certain channel, stimulating one's imagination; it was not necessarily a means of acquiring knowledge and expertise.

Of the diabolical books Nisard reviewed, that which excited his warmest indignation was the *Dragon Rouge*. 'Everything in this booklet,' he declared, 'has been devised so as to terrorize feeble imaginations, to horrify the mind as much as to shock the sight... one is almost obliged to reason with oneself, every second, not to become ... agitated.'[28] Among the indications furnished by the *Dragon* was that of how to summon up the devil. One had to repair to a cross-roads at midnight with a virginal black hen, which one killed in the middle of a circle drawn with a cypress stick, while reciting: 'Eloim, Eslaim, frugativi et appellavi'. A variety of invocations were followed by the appearance of the devil (wearing a scarlet suit with gold braid, a yellow jacket and green trousers: his feet and legs were to be those of a cow, his head that of a dog, with horns and donkey's ears), and he would be obliged to obey the invoker's orders. The book added prudent advice to the effect that before such proceedings, one should have accomplished certain religious devotions and be in a state of grace: 'This is all the more essential in that, were it not so, you would rather be at the disposal of the evil spirit, than he at yours'[29] – a consideration which doubtless provided some grounds for hesitation. The instructions were so impractical as to suggest that this kind of idea took the place now filled by science fiction and the thriller. However, the latter are considered to have no reality, whereas, at least in some areas of rural France, it was thought possible to evoke the devil in the manner described by the *Dragon Rouge*. In the mid-century, the Comte de Résie was told by an old man in the mountains of Bresse that a man who wanted to make a pact with the devil should go to a cross-roads where there was a wayside cross, where he should kill a black hen and invoke the devil, who would appear (but might sometimes remain invisible).[30] A famous sorcerer who lived in a ruined dungeon at Thil (near Semur, Côte d'Or), having been called in to lift a spell from a cow, advised the father and son, after the ceremony, to go at midnight to a certain road, where they would meet and kill the devil, thus ridding the country of him for ninety-nine years.[31] Marcelle Bouteiller cites a number of examples of the persistence of this tradition, culminating in the testimony of some old men from around Fougerolles (Indre) who maintained that to see the devil one had only to go at midnight to the cross-roads at Génitou, then offer up a black hen and invocations.[32] Thus, what might seem a literary extravagance had either passed into popular culture, or had at some earlier period drawn upon popular belief which had survived independently in the oral tradition. The latter hypothesis seems more likely, as the belief predated the apparition of the chapbooks of the *Bibliothèque Bleue*.

The sorcerer who evoked the devil might make a pact with him, to dire effect. In the Vendée, in the mid-thirties, a wandering healer claimed to be able to relieve illnesses by the power of the devil.[33] Paul Laserre, from the commune of Sainte Radegonde (near Libourne, Gironde), came from a labouring family; in 1840, he was tried for fraud. Laserre believed he could cure illness and preserve fields from devastation, and affirmed that he had concluded a pact with the devil, who had given him these powers in return for money. The locals (including the gamekeeper) took him seriously.[34] The counter-sorcerer, Laurent, from Villiers-sous-Praslin, agreed on trial that it was possible to 'make an agreement with the devil ... to give someone a fever'.[35] This belief that the sorcerer could act by the devil's power was reinforced by the notion that he might have sold his soul to the devil. In 1800, two sorcerers from the arrondissement of Baugé (Maine-et-Loire) were put on trial: they had been consulted by a man who wished to find a treasure and by another who wanted to be delivered from a spirit which haunted him at night in the shape of a cock. The sorcerers owned, among other books, a *Petit Albert* and the *Oeuvres Magiques d'Henri Corneille Agrippa* (published at Liège in 1788), as well as a variety of talismans and bones, including parts of a skull. The law officers also discovered a pact which ran: 'Je promets au Grand Lucifuge de l'indemniser dans vingt ans de tous les trésors qu'il me donnera en cas qu'il fasse en toutes choses ma volonté et tout ce que ma tête pourra porter, en foy de quoi je me suis signé, Joseph Jean Mignard.'[36] The business-like legalism, at once shrewd and naive, shows how the supernatural could serve quite immediate and terrestrial concerns, commonplace feelings and needs. It furnished the imagination with a common culture and language, which could be manipulated and exploited by those whom reality failed to satisfy. On the one hand, the pact expressed an archaic form of ambition;[37] on the other, the powers it supposedly conferred on Mignard enabled a person suffering from an obsession to consult him for relief. This suggests that the sorcerer, through magic, provided a vocabulary which enabled people to make sense of disquieting experiences, or to escape into fantasy – much as contemporary psychoanalysts do through their science today.

When a shepherd who passed for a sorcerer was found apparently murdered in his locked caravan, the locals concluded that Satan had killed him, as he had sold his soul to the devil. When his widow read his book of spells, the devil appeared to her and tried to force her sign a pact with him. However, she resisted heroically. During the three days for which her torment lasted, her neighbours heard her scream and wail, but were too frightened to approach. When finally her moaning ceased, she recounted her exploits and, while unable to produce the pact with the devil, could show them the spell-book open at the page of invocation. She was congratulated on her fidelity to the Church.[38] This woman resembled Leuret's debt-ridden 'demonomaniac', who, after childbirth and the perusal of the Apocalypse and various works on witchcraft, imagined that the devil, surrounded by the flames of hell, appeared to her and promised to pay off her debts if she would renounce God. Finally, she decided to sell her soul and sign the pact, after which – much to her neighbours' terror – her mania apparently worsened.[39] Tradition had elaborated a rich and detailed imaginative world to which people referred in times of trouble and strain. It helped them come to terms with their experiences – sometimes even to transform them; legitimized forbidden behaviour;[40] and enabled the expression and realization of frustrated ambitions, whether political, economic or private. And it was also exploited by the unscrupulous.

Magic and the Pursuit of Happiness

The Enlightenment had castigated superstitions which enabled charlatans to exploit the credulous and there was some justice in this condemnation. Criminals showed themselves to be astonishingly audacious in exploiting the naiveté of the poor in the nineteenth century. The antics of the perpetrators and victims of fraud are often hard to credit, and nowhere more than in the course of magical treasure-hunts. This was the magic that claimed to satisfy, in a material way, wishes that could not otherwise be gratified. The sorcerers who practised it were usually unscrupulous – if enterprising – spirits. However, they were not as bold or inventive as we might at first think, for most of them confined themselves to exploiting vague legends and beliefs with the aid of rituals derived principally, it would seem, from popular manuals on sorcery. The demand for these services – as apart from those of reassurance and retribution which formed the core of witchcraft practice – was not inconsiderable. Magicians did a flourishing business in procuring wives and husbands, recovering lost property and finding treasures, in helping those who wanted to avoid conscription, and in treating the ill and breaking charms. The imaginary world they exploited enabled people to allay their anxieties and to attempt to satisfy their dreams. For seven or eight years, a witch practised happily in the Fignereau district of Bordeaux: she provided a number of services, which included reading cards to predict the future, winning lotteries, procuring lovers and husbands by magical means, breaking spells and making husbands love their wives.[41] Another example of the range of activities covered by sorcery is provided by the trial of Julie Raquin and her husband, the carpenter Desormeaux, in Bourges in 1815. Madame Raquin promised, among other things, to cure livestock and to avert conscription – and in the declining years of the First Empire, plied a satisfactory trade in this. In 1813, Charles Gautier, who was about to be called up, bought an unguent from her which, when applied, was to make him unfit for service. She promsied the miller Guinard that she would effect his son's return from the army, and also treated his livestock for a spell with an expensive ritual. She sold a farm-servant a love potion (for one *louis*), to put under her master's pillow so that he would marry her – but this proved to be Raquin's undoing, for the girl was dismissed from her job and decided to report the couple for fraud. Sometimes women, like Madeleine Protat, the servant who brought about Raquin's downfall, consulted magicians in the hope of finding a husband or lover.[42] A twenty-seven-year-old dressmaker from Paris,

Amélie Merlin, was left by her lover for a wealthier party. She consulted a fortune-teller, who promised to find her a swain and took all the money she could give him for this purpose. Eventually, realizing that she had been duped, Amélie denounced the diviner, who was sentenced to one year for theft, another year for 'offending modesty' and five years of confinement, wearing an iron collar, for fraud.[44]

Conscription. Sorcerers were often consulted to get young men off military service, which was anathema to peasant families who could not afford to lose a healthy young man for seven years and who in any case viewed the hazards of distance and service with repugnance. Trials of magicians who had promised young men the right numbers (i.e. very high numbers) at the draw, were common.[45] In July 1828, a seventy-four-year-old man named Liérville was condemned to five years imprisonment and payment of costs, for having promised to get the right numbers by corresponding with the devil.[46] The women of Saint Symphorien-le-Château (Loire) had it that Pierre Philibert could avert the conscription of young men into the army. In 1824, Madame Péret consulted him with a view to sparing her son from military service and, when her progeny was not called up, was sure that it was thanks to Philibert. Her daughter extolled his powers to a person called Combe, who was due to be drafted into the army; Combe protested that he did not believe Philibert to be a sorcerer, but sought advice from him anyway, feeling that there was nothing to lose. It seems that Combe adopted an 'enlightened' position for the benefit of the court, as he had previously recommended the sorcerer to a man who wanted to get his son off military service – but his attitude was interestingly pragmatic: the source or essence of Philibert's power was unimportant, only the results counted. For people like Combe, it was easy to switch from having recourse to one technique, supposedly mystical, to another supposedly scientific. In 1836, another pragmatic young man, who was going to insure himself against military service, finally decided to consult Charles Caron, a sorcerer from Hornoy (Somme) instead. Caron had inherited a recipe from his forefathers, whereby the reluctant conscript made a novena to the Holy Spirit, reciting five Paters and Aves and reading the Veni Creator morning and night for seven days, offering mass, and burning a candle to Christ.[46] Madame Péret also advised the Fléchet brothers, in 1826, to see Philibert: they bargained with him at the inn on market day, paying six francs in advance and owing another 200 francs in the event of success! Unfortunately for Philibert, the young men were conscripted and, having invested in their freedom, they decided to recover at least their money by sueing him.[47] This, perhaps tells us less about their attitude towards sorcerers like Philibert than about the importance they attached to money. It also suggests, however, that they felt his failure to produce the desired result was due not so much to the essential inefficiency of his techniques, as to the fact that he omitted to do what was necessary, an omission which constituted a breach of contract. In this view, occult powers could be controlled and directed as easily as the familiar physical forces of the profane world, once one was initiated into their workings.

Wealth. Some people consulted sorcerers to become wealthy. Stories about hidden treasures – buried in mountains or under ancient monuments, guarded by fairies, serpents, dragons or other diabolical creatures – abounded in folklore, and almost every area had its own legend about the riches awaiting the intrepid. Caverns were supposed to open at midnight mass at Christmas, as the priest said the words of the consecration, when the nimble could slip in to the marvellous treasury and make their fortunes.[48] Extraordinarily, there were people naive and ambitious enough to attempt to unearth these funds. Sometimes they simply had recourse to magic to get the winning ticket in the national lottery. In 1832, at Auteuil, a couple named Gaillard persuaded a husband and wife called Thiébaud that they could win a law-case against their cousin and the national lottery, with their magical help. Proferring this prospect of life-long prosperity, the Gaillards relieved the Thiébauds of all their belongings.[49] A young workman gave all his money to a mounteback in order to draw the winning numbers in the national lottery: he was told to say three Paters and Aves before the statue of the Virgin Mary at the church of Saint Geneviève in Paris as well as five Paters and Aves to the saint herself, and to light a candle to her – in short, the prescription differed little from orthodox religious supplication.[50] At Nogent-sur-Seine, in February 1831, a fortune-teller and a sorcerer were tried for persuading a man from Bray that he could inherit a fortune.[51] Sorcerers were also supposed to be able to find stolen money. Those who undertook such exercises were often merely ingenious thieves – like Félicité Lebaube, who promised to find a widow Saussay's stolen money but made off with her remaining possessions instead.[52]

These cases were not as unusual as one might imagine, and some magicians deployed considerable imagination and audacity to attain their ends. Until the later 1840s, the sorcerer was frequently requested to procure treasures for his clients: in the 1820s and 1830s about 40 per cent of witchcraft trials reported in the *Gazette des Tribunaux* concerned treasures, love-potions and exemption from military service. Not infrequently, the devil appeared in the course of the ceremonies. Clients were not, apparently, startled into incredulity by this circumstance. Presumably, sorcerers felt that it would enhance their reputation, convincing the uninitiated rather than rendering them sceptical.

The difficulty of making any significant amounts of money, no less than the strength of the desire to acquire it, led to some very bizarre practices and to equally peculiar reactions to these rites, as is exemplified by the case of a farmer's family from Finistère at the end of the

Restoration. The farmer was well-to-do, but having an appetite for greater prosperity, decided, when he came upon a magic recipe for wealth amongst some old spell-books, to turn sorcerer and see if he could add to his fortune. He performed the rite and, as luck would have it, came into some money. His wife, however, was confirmed in her misgivings about the enterprise when she had a revelation to the effect that the family would be struck dumb and be rendered unable to use any of their wealth, as a punishment for having used the spell-books. She rushed off to confession, but on receiving absolution she was struck dumb. Before long, the whole family was in a similar predicament.[53] No record was made of how the situation was resolved. Guilt seems not infrequently to have prompted paralysis or other forms of motor disorder in hysterics, and suggestion occasionally induced people in the sufferer's circle of acquaintances – usually in his family – to imitate his behaviour, in what appeared to be a kind of magical contagion. The dispositions of father and mother in this family seem to have been such as to render reactions like these not unnatural. It is interesting to note, however, how the behaviour and fabulation of the disturbed tended to confirm, rather than to undermine, the imaginative world of traditional culture. What was seen in visions was usually, in general conformation, conventional: the warnings, threats, scenes evoked all tended to be predictable rather than original. Tradition gave people a specific, fantastic vocabulary with which to express and develop on their preoccupations. Equally well, it is easy to see how ravings like these could refurbish the language of legend.

One of the earliest nineteenth-century trials concerned with a diabolical treasure-hunt took place in Valognes at the beginning of *pluviôse* in the Year XII. Eight people from Saint Vaast-de-la-Houge were accused of fraud: Guillaume Allain, a fisherman, and his wife, who kept an inn; Saint-Amand, a guard in the convict prison, and his wife; Lecroisey, a customs officer, and his wife; Jean Lamache, an agricultural servant, in service with the Allain; and la Marquise, a fruit-vendor and washerwoman. A local soothsayer, *la femme* Chauvot, managed to escape accusation, although she too had extorted considerable sums for her services. These people, either individually or in collusion, exploited the cupidity and curiosity of a number of local people: the elderly Madame Joly, the draper's widow, who ran a shop; Madame Litais and her husband; Jacques Lefèvre, Madame Litais' brother-in-law; and two labourers, Guillaume Paille and Martin. Madame Litais came from the area of Gatteville. Her husband was a fisherman and she managed the family farm. Madame Litais, having noticed that her neighbour Madame Allain (who was also married to a fisherman) was doing well, asked her how she had attained that prosperity. Madame Allain replied that the soothsayer, Madame Chauvot, had uncovered a treasure for her. Madame Litais' curiosity was whetted, for she forthwith consulted the soothsayer on a point which might well have worried her: her husband's future (France being then at war with England). Chauvot predicted accurately that Litais' boat would be captured and freed shortly afterwards. This probably helped to establish her reputation, for, some time later, Chauvot entered into negotiations about a treasure of 750,000 francs which, she claimed, was hidden in the Litais' home. With apparent modesty of pretensions, she claimed only the costs of the proceedings neessary for the discovery of the fortune. As this amounted to a mere 180 francs, Madame Litais made what doubtless appeared to her a marvellous investment. Shortly afterwards, however, Chauvot announced that the treasure was in fact larger than she had originally anticipated and that it would be correspondingly more expensive to discover it. Madame Litais found an additional 600 francs. In fact, Chauvot contrived to relieve her of 8,000 francs, scraped together from borrowings and relatives' savings.

Not content with this, Madame Litais put Madame Allain in touch with her brother-in-law, Jacques Lefèvre, who became their most lucrative victim. In order to extort fabulous sums from this naive man, Madame Saint-Amand, M. Allain and their accomplices engaged in a grotesque farce. As we have seen, it was popularly believed that one could summon the devil and command his obedience. He was also supposed to be able to uncover treasures, and manuals like the *Dragon Rouge* gave detailed instructions about how to invoke him. Those who exploited these traditions counted upon the credulity of their clients. Madame Saint-Amand and her accomplices were no exception to this rule. She suggested to Lefèvre that she should summon up the devil and oblige him to deliver a treasure. The prospect of a huge fortune tempted the man into acquiescence. So one night in his house, Madame Saint-Amand began the appropriate rites; at midnight, a strange light appeared, followed by an explosion and then by the devil – dressed in black, sporting horns and a black mask adorned with strips of red material (much as he appeared in popular chapbooks). Madame Saint-Amand braved the ferocious demon and received a written communication, signed 'Cerberus' and demanding 3,200 francs from Levèvre, under pain of having his three children carried away and his house burned down. Suitably impressed, Lefèvre paid up. Shortly afterwards at night in Lefèvre's courtyard, in bright light, a number of possibly diabolical figures went on the rampage, beaking shutters, battering at the door (and leaving claw-marks thereon); they deposited another bill. These antics continued for some time. Lefèvre gave almost 40,000 francs, thereby ruining his family, to be rid of them. Nor were the Lefèvres the only family to suffer from such visitations: two labourers were also tormented by a visit from the devil in person.[54] The victims in question may well have been unrepresentative of the rest of the community; but similar incidents occurred frequently enough to suggest that traditional beliefs were still held by enough people to ensure an adequate quota of naive victims for extortioners. This form of fraud was obviously a proletarian crime, since to suceed, it supposed acceptance of traditional lore about the sorcerer's power of discovering hidden treasures. This form of crime was made easier by the close contacts between members of communities. Later in the century, soothsayers were obliged to advertize to draw clients, thus also attracting the unsympathetic attention of the authorities.

In Paris 1 August 1827, a woman called Riaux was prosecuted for promising to discover treasures, through her magical skills, for a wine-merchant's widow and a shoemaker.[55] In February 1828, the Bouchet family, husband and wife, were tried (in Niort, Deux Sèvres) for ruining a credulous old widow, Madame Martin. All the village knew she was being misled, but no-one intervened to save her – a reflection, perhaps, on the Bouchets' reputation and on the unwillingness, then as now, to interfere in the criminal pursuits of dangerous individuals. To make their claims for money effective, Madame Bouchet called up the devil, who appeared one night clad in goat-skin, greatly frightening Madame Martin; and on another occasion, a ghost terrorized the old woman. These various roles were played by the versatile M. Bouchet, who found that acting enabled him to live in unwonted ease.[56] This incident may be of minimal interest to those anxious to discover the magical beliefs of a typical peasant, insofar as the old woman was the only person to believe she had seen the devil. However, this form of fraud does not seem to have been extraordinary; and while it suggests that there were poor people ready to perpetrate the crime, there were also enough credulous people to make it worthwhile.

Considering the lengths to which this kind of criminal went to establish his or her credit, affirmations on the part of victims that they had seen devils or ghosts are hardly surprising. In June 1829, Anne-Marie Fehl of Dangolsheim was tried in Strasbourg: she had travelled around the countryside, promising to find hidden treasures and thus deceiving many people. In court, one woman affirmed that her arms and legs had been pulled by ghosts, while a man testified to having seen Lucifer or Beelzebub.[57] Résie recounts the story of a young man suddenly afflicted with paralysis, who consulted a sorcerer: the latter was attempting to cure him at midnight on Good Friday 1836, when the proceedings were interrupted by an aggressive little man, who terrified both magician and patient. Both they and the locals considered this to be an apparition of the devil – an interpretation which Résie attributed to traditional beliefs, and to the general climate of credulity.[58] In some cases, however, the victims' senses were not misleading them, even if the fraud could never have been perpetrated in a different cultural context. Around 1828, two peasants, Jalau and Bazouin, from the area around Barbézieux (Charente), having bought a field in which treasure was reputedly hidden, decided to employ a 'wise man' to unearth it. The sorcerer, a miller who also ran an inn when not engaged in conjuring up the devil, demanded 50,000 francs upon the discovery of the treasure, and a fee of 50 francs on account (which Bazouin raised by selling a field for 180 francs). The peasants had evidently no mean idea of the extent of the fortune which they were to find. Jalau and Bazouin remained convinced of their sorcerer's magical capacities, despite the fact that the treasure was never discovered. This belief might be ascribed to their apparent encounter with an irritable devil (after the sacrifice of a black hen and consultation of a spell-book), who, having informed them that the treasure amounted to 200,000 francs, did not disdain to make off with a purse and the fowl. Madame Jalau was especially terrified as the demon had initially demanded her daughter in return for the fortune. After this episode, Bazouin retired to his bed, where he stayed restoring his nerves for the following three weeks; while Madame Jalau did not let her six-year-old daughter out of her sight for three months, and firmly locked her door after dark, refusing to go out. The incident provoked much sceptical gossip in the village. Significantly, only the opinion of the village doctor finally convinced Jalau and Bazouin that they had been defrauded.[59]

Sometimes neighbours might enlighten victims of fraud. In Paris in 1840, Madame Leroy, a fruit-seller who supported three children, had been ill for six months. A neighbour, Eulalie Courtault, told her that the devil would make her rich, to which Madame Leroy replied: 'But I don't want to see the devil, I'd be too afraid.' Thereupon, her neighbour generously undertook the interviews in her stead, but required money to travel by coach to meet him: the devil was to give Madame Leroy and each of her children 30,000 francs, a house and much else besides. Madame Leroy's gullibility was not entirely exceptional: two other women had also been exploited by Eulalie. This kind of fraud, although rather more banal than the enterprises of some rural sorcerers, sheds light on the nature of dreams or unattainable ambitions. Clearly, little imagination is needed to understand why people entertained such hopes, given the misery which attended almost every aspect of their lives.[60] In circumstances in which the boundaries of the possible and the limits of expectation were so restricted by the material circumstances of life, hope easily became fantasy. Madame Leroy, explaining her apparent credulity, informed the court that, in that part of Normandy from which she came, the devil was firmly believed in[61] – thus indicating tht it may be misleading to overemphasize, in the early stages of urbanization at least, the difference between urban and rural mentalities.[62] Belief in the devil enabled her to regard her personal fantasies as having some objective reality. Just as dreams and hallucinations were no longer so disorientating and alienating when interpreted in the light of traditional beliefs, so passionate desires lost their hopeless character. Indeed, Malinowsky has considered magic to have resulted from 'those passionate experiences which assail [man] in the impasses of his instinctive life and of his practical pursuits'.[63]

While frustrated desires at odds with an intractable reality may account for part of the appeal of magic, and may even have helped people to believe in it once it had been elaborated into a tradition, there can be little doubt that at least some of the victims of fraud were not just simple-minded, but ill. In 1838, a clog-maker, Bernoin, from Clion (Indre), came under the influence of a vagabond, Louis Arnault, who pretended he was a former seminarist with occult powers. Arnault suggested to Bernoin that his neighbours would try to poison him and his family; when Bernoin found dust in his cabbages he identified it as poison, and the sorcerer's reputation for wisdom was confirmed. Arnault called up the devil one night in a cemetery to back up another prediction – namely that Bernoin would inherit 1800 francs – and the devil, having obligingly confirmed the truth of this assertion, demanded to be paid. He then tormented Bernoin's family, leaving notes smelling of sulphur, which Madame Bernoin, the only literate person in the house, read. One of these announced, much to everyone's terror, that Pluto had passed the death sentence on Bernoin. Thus, the family was frightened into giving all their money to the devil and signing various bills. Arnault's escapades ended with his repairing in Bernoin's company to a cross at a cross-roads at night, there to call up the devil and persuade him to carry off Bernoin's evil neighbours, who had tried to steal his money as well as poison him. Not only did the devil appear (dressed in black and equipped, according to the trial, with horns and forked feet), but the Virgin accompanied him. Beelzebub initially wished to make off with the terrified clog-maker, but the Virgin opposed this. Frustrated, the devil claimed a fee of 230 francs for obliging in the matter of the obnoxious neighbours. The Virgin, somewhat forgetful of her dignity and loving forgiveness (if not of the market-place) replied:

> A la bonne heure, . . . qu'il donne de l'argent pour son salut et la perte de ses voisins, ce sera bien; mais 230 francs c'est beaucoup trop cher, et il faut, cher maître Satan, que vous vous contentiez de la somme toute ronde de 200 francs.

> (Just hold on a minute . . . it's fine for him to give money to save his soul and for his neighbours' downfall and damnation; but 230 francs is far too dear, and, my dear Sir Satan, you'll have to content yourself with the round sum of 200 francs.)

The clog-maker, who had with difficulty been restrained from departing, agreed to the devil's demand before tearing away to the local inn – prior to spending the next day abed, reputedly ill with terror.[64]

The facility with which Bernoin believed the worst of his neighbours suggests that he suffered from paranoia – not that it was so unusual to wish one's neighbours to the devil (if not always with quite the literal emphasis favoured by Bernoin). We might be inclined to dismiss the representation of the Virgin as being without interest, since what appeared likely to the clog-maker might well seem improbable to everyone else; however, popular notions of the Virgin Mary, as implied by prayers and practices, were quite compatible with the picture presented here. Not only was she endowed with all too human qualities, but she even had difficulty in distinguishing right from wrong. Since masses might be offered for the death of enemies, it was consistent that the Virgin should countenance the devil's making off, on commission, with the erring faithful, and should see no contradiction between such revenge and the highly conventional virtue of concern with personal salvation. That good intentions should find material, indeed monetary, expression was normal – for most pilgrimages were accompanied by offerings – but that the devil and the Virgin should presumably divide the spoils of the interview might have puzzled a less impetuous and credulous nature than Bernoin's.

Spell-books were sometimes influential in determining the forms which such ceremonies took. For instance in 1832, the *Petit Albert*'s instructions about summoning up the devil were followed by a simple-minded individual called Segalié, aided by a number of people of bad reputation. They had frightened the locals from Foulay (Lot-et-Garonne) by frequenting a quarry at night. Spurred on by complaints, the intrepid local law-officer discovered Segalié on Friday 13 July, at midnight, standing in the middle of a circle, holding a magic wand, reading the *Petit Albert* by candlelight and surrounded by an intimidated audience. This group had, the previous March, disinterred a coffin to procure four nails required by the ceremony.[65] The scepticism with which one might be tempted to regard the spell-books of the *Bibliothèque Bleue* must therefore be mitigated by the realization that some people took their instructions seriously.

The coincidence between a rite conducted in 1841 in the commune of Bruges and the instructions given in the *Dragon Noir* for summoning up the devil is remarkable. Jean Grangé, a gunsmith, inherited in his father's coffers a tome entitled *Cyprien Mago ante Conversionem*, dated Salamanca 1400, which showed how to procure eighteen millions, with the devil's aid. Grangé consulted a local sorcerer, Lagrange, on how best to use the volume, which was written in Latin and French. The sorcerer insisted that the devil's signature was necessary and could be procured for 500 francs, if Grangé cared to come and dine with him. Accompanied by his workmen, Garié and Grassiès, Grangé repaired to the jovial sorcerer's dwelling-place on 3 September, where they indulged in a pleasant repast, post-prandial torpor being somewhat enlivened by Lagrange's playing (appropriately) the violin. The agreeable evening ended, however, when around midnight Lagrange made his preparations for the devil's visit: on the table were placed a white cloth and 500 francs; the guests were asked if they were in a state of grace, and warned that the exercise was dangerous otherwise. Thus forewarned, they were equipped with a twig of artemisia and, according to Grassiès, Lagrange 'drew a circle around us, which we were to be careful not to step outside, lest we be carried off by the devil. Then he began to gesticulate and strike big blows on the table with a laurel branch, shouting Haro, Habaro or Halof and calling on him to appear in human form.' There entered 'an individual in a really diabolical get-up. He was a big tall fellow, dressed in red trousers and a dragon's coat and wearing a black lambskin helmet.' The devil was in a temper, and threatened to carry off those who were present. 'Our circle was small, so we kept our arms tightly pressed against our sides . . . so as not to let the enemy get hold of us.' Thus preserved, they were able to await the issue of the discussions (during which the devil spoke French, not dialect), which ended with the devil signing a parchment and taking his fee. Subsequent diggings in a local hillside having proved fruitless, Grangè consulted two more sorcerers, one from Toulouse and the other from Montrejean. The latter told him Lagrange had cheated him and the trial for fraud was brought in. But belief in the existence of treasures and sorcerers was diminished neither in Grangé nor in the other witnesses.[66] This reaction, as we have seen, was not unusual, nor should it surprise us – as demonstrations of the weakness of human nature do not frequently lead us to revise our epistemological assumptions. The consciously theatrical nature of the crime (the devil's costume was quite inventive), while useful in that it was impressive, nonetheless testifies to the frequently figurative expressiveness of popular culture, whether in crime or in protest, which reinforced the tendency to make points or elaborate upon them through the visually dramatic.

The influence of the *Dragon Rouge* can also be discerned in the various activities during 1845, in the Oise, of the Abbé Louis Mouchet, *curé* of Bouttencourt, the two shepherds Naguet and Colas, and Bigny, a day-labourer from Flavacourt who had served a prison sentence of seven years. A Madame Constant from Jamméricourt, who had long been ill, decided she was suffering from a spell and consulted the shepherd Naguet for relief. Naguet applied a traditional remedy, prescribed in the *Dragon Noir* and the *Grand Albert*: he boiled an ox's heart with nails. Meanwhile the Abbé read prayers from his book, told her and her husband to do a novena, and promised to say a *messe du Saint Esprit* (a travestied mass). When the woman got no better, the family's reaction was not to doubt the efficacy of these rites or the assumptions on which they were grounded, but to consult another sorcerer, Colas, who diagnosed a spell cast by an enemy, whom he would kill by grilling a sheep's heart. These consultations cost the Constant family 200 francs. With their next victim, however, the four criminals were more inventive – if not entirely original. Appealing to the tradition whereby the devil accorded temporal wealth to those who promised him their eternal soul, the Abbé Mouchet convinced Naguet's employer, Luce, that the shepherd could indeed show him the devil. Despite an initial failure, the farmer persisted in his attempts to meet Satan. After making a novena, Luce signed a pact written by the *curé*, with the blood of a kid killed for the purpose, making over his soul to the devil – presumably seeing no incongruity between his devotions and his impiety. Bigny conducted the second summoning of the devil: this time he appeared at a cross-roads at midnight in a three-cornered hat and granted the farmer forty years of life and prosperity, in return for the pact and the pecuniary consideration of 1500 francs.[67] That the devil should not have disdained a trifling 1500 francs, given his ability to guarantee terrestrial wealth, does not seem to have struck Luce as disconcerting. The resemblance between this scene and that described in the *Dragon Rouge* is striking.

The attitude of making the most of the present at the expense of the future was understandable, at least in a worldly context, since many peasants could look forward only to indigent old age. Perhaps the habit of expecting nothing from the future was too deeply ingrained for the calculating morality of the Church to penetrate. Even where the dogmas of heaven and hell were preached, indifference and scepticism were apt to be present. This did not necessarily mean that the possibility of there being an afterlife was rejected, but it may have reflected a form of fatalism. Indeed, Catholicism as preached in the nineteenth century was, as we have seen, to some extent foreign to the outlook of the rural populations. The religion which did flourish, however, was that which wrought miracles, brought health and even wealth; a religion which could transform life, alleviate its suffering and monotony, and whose marvellous powers were not confined to the next world but counted in the present one also.

Sometimes fraud exploited other traditional notions, like the land of Cockaigne. In the 1830s, after a long career as a disreputable sorcerer, Jean Pagès Arbas, a seventy-year-old beggar, managed to make two farmers believe in a land of plenty beyond the infertile hills of Roquefixade (Ariège) where they lived. Gerard Lafont, a poor farmer, and his family were full of enthusiasm at the picture Arbas depicted of the property of M. Sibra of Lafialouse. According to Arbas, it was 'an immense region, eighty leagues away from here: Lafialouse is a rich, fertile, beautiful plain limited only by the horizon; there's no winter there, no frost; it's a land of green meadows, good harvests, fruit-filled orchards, forests stocked with game . . . '. M. Sibra was looking for a sharecropper for a farm worth 80,000 francs, and would be pleased to accept Lafont's son as a valet and his daughter as a ladies' maid. So attractive did this offer seem that the farmer, as part of the initial contract, signed a bill for 400 francs. Another farmer, while rather more chary about parting with his money, became involved enough with Arbas' story to enlist the *curé*'s aid to read M. Sibra's supposed letter of invitation to the plan and to draft a gracious reply.[68] Part of the interest of this incident lies in the very modesty of the extravagance. While Arbas' claims had to be reasonable to be plausible, they also had to promise the realization of probable ambitions which were unlikely to be satisfied by ordinary means. The nature of these hopes points to the narrow scope of life, in both geographic and economic terms: a landscape only two hundred miles away could be described in almost mythical terms; a little more prosperity could generate eager excitement. No presumptuous ambition was involved: no social revolution was envisaged, only a dramatic change in climate and physical environment. The plain – only a few days' journey away – was the antithesis of the mountain: fertile and abundant, it rewarded effort with well-being. Interesting too were the ambitions of the children – anxious to enter service in the master's household, rather than work the land. The change in circumstances for which they hoped was like an attenuated version of the dramatic reversals of fortune so often rehearsed in fairy-stories, where younger sons made good, married kings' daughters and assured the prosperity of elderly parents. It was the sort of fraud which could have been perpetrated only in communities where people had always been poor.

Are such anecdotes of any general interest, however? One might feel justified in dismissing evidence of these melodramatic antics as a trivial random collection of incidents, of only marginal interest to the historian, who must attempt to assess general trends and identify the typical. In answering this objection, there are two points to be borne in mind. First, devil-lore was not at the heart of these events. It was the desire for money – however naively framed – that made men embark on the enterprise, and the form taken by their ambitions not only indicates their intellectual limitations but, since the beliefs on which their ambition was based were shared by most people of comparable circumstances, reflects the limitations of their background. The accumulation of wealth – for all that Guizot might say – was so far beyond the scope of most people (in what was predominantly a subsistence level economy for most of the first half of the century) as to be all but impossible. It should, therefore, not surprise us to find that the imagination seized on precisely this point and took delight in presenting the impossible as possible, both in popular literature and in legends and beliefs. Secondly, the fraud which exploited this archaic ambition was too widespread geographically for the phenomenon to be dismissed as an isolated aberration. The internal consistency of these crimes implies a certain cultural background – common beliefs and ideas that reflected the economic and social restrictions on those who held them.

Exploitation of Magic for other Criminal Ends. The prevailing imaginative vocabulary not only lent itself to peculiar forms of fraud, but, more generally, bred archaic forms of crime. It provided criminals with a way of masking their intentions and activities, which sometimes enabled them to attain their goals more effectively than if they had been obliged to proceed in a more overt manner. It also furnished the discontented with a means of expression which, if it did nothing to effect a practical improvement in their position, at least provided them with the crude satisfaction of revenge through emotional terrorism. This was made possible because people sometimes looked for magical explanations for unusual events, or were driven to such explanations. One man in the town of Sézanne (Marne) perpetrated a variety of frightening events, in order to live off the family he tormented.[69] Belief in the devil was exploited in a more sinister way in the Department of Loiret towards the end of the Restoration. In November 1827, Joigneau and Rabourdin were accused of causing the death of an old farmer called Boucher, who had sold them his farm at Césarville in return for an annual pension of 800 francs. By playing on his superstitions, they were alleged to have made the old man die of fright. Boucher's inheritors insisted:

> 1 That during the night and on different occasions, Joigneau and Rabourdin had knocked violently on Boucher's windows, had broken the panes, and rolled empty barrels about his hayloft;
> 2 That at different times, they threatened him with their charms and spells, boasting to him about the power they had over demons;
> 3 That once, in a pub, they threatened him, saying they would make the demon come out of the stove, a threat which they pretended to drop at Boucher's request;
> 4 That by means of these threats they had driven Boucher mad, convincing him that he was bewitched to such an extent that he applied to a person from Malesherbes to be freed from the demon;
> 5 That following the advice he had given, he left Césarville and went to live in Orléans; that Joigneau and Rabourdin tormented him again at this new home and that on the day following their second visit to him, he was found in his well, into which he had doubtless flung himself as a consequence of the madness caused by their antics.[70]

The accusation was not proven to the satisfaction of the district court at Pithiviers, and the appeal court at Orléans ruled that death could not be proved as being attributable to these manoeuvres. However grotesque and difficult to believe such procedures may seem to us, analogous incidents happened elsewhere; while Joigneau and Rabourdin's motive – reluctance to pay the considerable pension – was not without precedent either.[71]

An example of such extravagances is furnished by the activities of a Madame Morisset, who was supposed to be a witch in her native Vendée. In 1829, she attempted to extort money from a family by threatening to send a horde of demons to pursue their herds. In lieu of the devils, she contented herself with sending her son dressed as Saint Angélique, to inform them of the future they might anticipate if they did not comply with her wishes. She deceived another family in the same manner, but was denounced by a young soldier on leave, who found it hard to believe that Angélique in person had visited peasants' cottages.[72] A similarly unscrupulous sorcerer exercised a flourishing trade around Château-Gontier (Mayenne). François Godin was apt to boast that he could 'summon the devil in all his various guises, and that, as he was invulnerable, more than ten bullets or pellets of lead shot had been fired at him without causing him the slightest injury' – evidence doubtless adduced to substantiate his claim of having a pact with the devil. In March 1821, he diagnosed (after reading his book) that a man called Heulin had been bewitched. He prescribed a number of remedies more akin to those of orthodox than to popular medicine (infusions, drugs, 136 leeches, copious blood-lettings and cold baths). He then announced that he would send the devil in the form of different animals – his therapy might well have induced delirium – and that the household would be frightened by the demon and spirits at night: this threat was followed by nocturnal batterings at the door.[73] Such events must have lent some weight to the sorcerer's demands for payment. Diabolical visitations were not infrequently enacted for the benefit of victims of fraud and extortion, as we have seen. They also accorded with the popular tradition of miming protest and revolt, and of expressing it allusively. This is illustrated by the reaction of two disgruntled women employees in Lyon in 1860. They pelted their employer with stones and sugared almonds every evening between five and nine o'clock, knowing they could not be seen, thus inducing in him the persuasion that he was possessed.

Conclusion

What was the reason for the appeal of this kind of behaviour? Were exploits of this sort necessarily the reaction of an inarticulate society, imprisoned in irrelevant modes of thought and expression? That there should have been enough credulous people to make such enterprises worthwhile is arresting. It should not lead us to assume, however, that there were more credulous fools then than there are now; it merely illustrates the fact that while crimes tend to reflect the society in which they have been committed, few illustrate frustrated ambitions and prevailing fashions in fantasy more graphically than does fraud.

VIII

Fantasy and Fiction: The Vocabulary of Discontent

Folktales

One of the hallmarks of popular culture, in the opinion of the contemporary positivistic observers, was its taste for the irrational and fantastic. The imagination, rather than ratiocination, was thought to play a disproportionate role in forming peasants' understanding of reality. The rejection of logic was nowhere more evident than in popular legends and stories, which delighted in evoking incongruous dilemmas and offering impossible solutions to them. The laws of nature were defied and the world was presented as an unpredictable place, where appearances were deceptive: fairies came to the rescue of the oppressed; dwarfs could spin gold, while witches and sorcerers were apt to set the world awry. Nostalgia for something better appears in many popular stories. An alternative order was frequently presented in fairy-stories, and this should restrain us from assuming this feature of popular literature to be insignificant. A whole series of tales, popular in Provence, the Bourbonnais, Brittany, the Agenais, Picardy and elsewhere, concerned God's somewhat summary justice, his mercy on the poor and his (albeit erratic) generosity in rewarding them with eternal riches.[1] Grimm's tales abound in heroes who are helped by magic patrons to vanquish the injustice of the world, and the theme appears too in French fairy-stories.

The story of Cinderella – 'Cendrillon' – was typical of this kind of tale. In the literary versions given by Basile and Perrault as well as by Grimm, Cinderella comes from a wealthy family; but in rural tradition – on which, incidentally, Perrault drew – she is a peasant girl.[2] In a version of the story recorded by Sébillot in 1884, the tale is set in a poor, rural milieu. As her father has remarried, Pondonette (who, Sébillot assures us, is the counterpart in oral literature of the more famous heroine) is obliged to hire herself out as a pig-herd. Unlike her sister, Pondonette helps a poor old woman whom she meets at the local fountain. The old woman turns out to be a fairy and rewards Pondonette by helping her magically, finally enabling her to marry the local marquess.[3] Delarue and Millien both noted the naturalistic setting of the version of the story they found in the Nivernais. In this, Cendrillon suffers from the tyranny of her step-mother, who forces her to do menial tasks like spinning and guarding the sheep. One day she meets some fairies, one of whom asks her to remove lice and vermin from her head. Cendrillon obliges. Soon afterwards, her half-sister is asked to help in the same way, but refuses. Her step-mother and half-sister dress up in their finery and go off to amuse themselves at church, leaving Cendrillon to prepare a dinner of lentils. But the fairy godmother comes to the rescue and sends Cendrillon after them in glamorous clothes, which catch the prince's eye and, of course, his heart and hand in marriage.[4] Perrault's story *Les Fées*, which seems to have been a transcription of a popular story, has a similar theme. There are two sisters: the older is spoilt and the younger overworked. At the fountain, they both meet a fairy, who asks for a drink. The older girl rudely declines to give her one and the fairy punishes her, making her spit vipers and toads whenever she speaks. But the young girl helps graciously, and flowers and diamonds fall from her lips – an attribute which proves irresistible to the prince whom she subsequently meets and marries.[5]

The same themes – the abuse of traditional authority, the ultimate vindication of the weak, the victory of generosity and humility over jealousy and arrogance – were perennially popular in the French folktale. In stories which Bladé heard in the Agenais, the virtues and merits of the humble were rewarded by wealth and high rank, while presumption and lack of charity were punished. *Les Deux Filles* concerns two step-sisters, one of whom is pretty and the other ugly. Three times, the pretty girl is brought deep into the woods in an attempt to get rid of her; twice, she manages to find her way home by means of a trail she has laid, but finally she is lost. In the course of her wanderings, she comes upon a castle, whose queen asks her to select jewels, dresses and horses for herself. Each time, she chooses the ugliest thing and consequently is rewarded with the most splendid gift. The queen sends her home, but on her way she meets the King of England's son, who marries her. The ugly sister, on learning of this, rushes off to the castle in the woods and is presented with the same choices as her step-sister. In her greed, however, she selects the loveliest garments and so is forced to wear the ugliest ones. She fails to thank the queen for her presents and disobeys her by looking back at the castle before she reaches the hill-top. So instead of being decked in stars, like her sister, she is covered with dung; in this array, she meets a dirty peasant who tells her: 'Je te trouve à ma fantaisie' and forces her to marry him. The heroine lives happily ever after while her step-sister has to contend with a violent old drunkard.[6]

If the vindication of the vulnerable was a theme that recurred in many folktales, so was that of the youth whose wit, courage and luck enable him to overcome apparently insuperable obstacles and so make his fortune. Heroes were often presented as conquerors. Chapbooks, which perpetuated medieval stories about the valiant exploits of knights, remained popular in the nineteenth century. Their heroes were larger than life – being bigger, stronger, braver than other men. Like *Robert le Diable*, they might start out as rebels, or, like *Richard sans Peur*, defy the world through their heroism. '. . . They are all . . . righters of wrongs', observed Robert Mandrou. 'Their prestige is rooted in their freedom of speech and action when confronted with the powerful of this world . . . They all behave . . . like rebels.' *Till Eulenspiegel* and *Scaramouche* steal from the rich; nobles and fat clergymen are objects of hostility.[7] *Puss in Boots*, which Perrault derived from oral tradition and popularized in literary form, furnished a characteristic example of this theme.[8] A miller has three sons: the two elder boys inherit the mill and the family donkey, but the youngest son is left virtually destitute, having received only a cat. The animal, however, comes to his aid and through a combination of cunning, presence of mind and fraud, provides the youth with wealth and a royal wife. Michel Butor remarked of this story that its 'revelation of a prince disguised as a miller's son constitutes a warning, an admonition. It exposes the lie of social appearances and hereby denounces injustice. It assigns a contingent character to what passes itself off as a permanent, definitive, unalterable reality.'[9] It can hardly be fortuitous that so many stories should concern revolutions in personal fortune.[10] The hero is a poor boy who triumphs over his surroundings and attains a social status and degree of luxury to which not even the most vaulting ambition could, realistically, have aspired. Should one then be surprised that the story of his success is neither naturalistic nor realistic by the standards of the Flaubertian novel? On the contrary, the 'marvellous' was freely exploited because it enabled the impossible to become possible. Those who listened to such stories did not, as far as our evidence enables us to ascertain, believe in them literally,[11] but their aspirations may have been reflected in them. The picture of the world presented in fairy-stories, however, was not utopian in the true sense, for while it affirmed a desire for wealth and plenty, it denied the possibility of its being satisfied in reality. The exact observation and delineation of character, attitudes and surroundings, which often distinguished popular stories, indicate that realism or naturalism were well within the scope of story-tellers; but magic was introduced to enable the realization of aspirations, precisely because they could not be achieved in any other manner. The prevailing order had to be shattered by magic before the hero's will and courage could prevail.

Trickery, as well as magic, enabled the hero to make his fortune in *Puss in Boots*, and according to Thompson, tales about clever deceptions and swindles were very much appreciated.[12] Such, for example, is the story of the poor boy who, by learning all the devil's tricks, accumulates a fortune and marries a princess.[13] Some of these stories, like the *Clever Peasant Girl*, show how the heroine marries a king through her aptitude for solving riddles. In others, a princess is won by a hero of humble extraction who has the wit (and the benefit of some magic aid) to make her laugh or talk, or otherwise outwit her family. Some heroes are unscrupulous – like that of *The Student from Paradise*. A wandering student tells a woman that he is back from Paris: she thinks he has said 'paradise' and gives him money and valuables to take to her dead husband. The student makes off, but is soon pursued by the woman's son, who realizes the deception that the student has practised. The son catches up with the thief, whom he fails to recognize. The student, however, sends the son off on a wild goose chase and takes the opportunity to appropriate his horse.

Something of this ambivalent admiration for native wit and the successes owed to it, and disenchantment with the unjust and dishonest world, is perceptible, too, in the stories about the *Bonhomme Misère*, or the *Smith and the Devil*, a tale familiar throughout Europe and whose theme was known in antiquity.[14] In a version of this story heard by Carnoy in Picardy, an impertinent, sprightly gardener, who combines laudable generosity with irascibility and a certain lack of compunction (which has led him into killing a man and keeping silent about it), climbs up his God-given beanstalk to heaven's marble castle and slips inside – despite Saint Peter's reluctance to admit him. God regretfully banishes him, whereupon the gardener asks God's permission to nip inside to pick up his hat and, once within the heavenly walls, establishes himself in a modest corner where the Almighty, much amused, leaves him. In another version of this story, entitled *Le Diable et Le Forgeron*, the hero slides into paradise in much the same way.[15] The motif of the beanstalk reappears in a Norman variant of the story, cited by Champfleury. Misère begs from God and from Saint Peter, who recommends that he should work. Misère, with the fluent ironic patter of the professional beggar, reports:

> On ne peut pas pêcher avec la main . . . Saint Pierre lui-même, qui était pourtant un si grand saint, avait des filets et encore ne trouvait-il pas que le métier fut bon, puisqu'il a mieux aimé être crucifié la tête en bas que de suer plus longtemps à la peine.

God gives Misère a bean – much to the displeasure of Misère's wife, who considers the gift impractical, and proof of the well-to-do's indifference to the needs of the poor. However, the bean, once planted in the earth, flourishes instantaneously, and Misère's wife soon dispatches him up it to collect beans for dinner. He climbs up and arrives at paradise, where he asks for 'a piece of bread . . . white bread if that's all the same to you'. Saint Peter generously promises to provide meat and wine too. Misère's wife is nonetheless irritated by her husband's modesty and he is soon sent back to paradise to obtain 'une maison bourgeoise, solide comme une prison . . . ', then to be made a king and finally, to be made God.

With this final request, Saint Peter deprives him of everything, but Misère is consoled by the demise from chagrin of his wife.[16]

In a story told by Albert Boulougne of Beaucourt-sur-l'Hallne (Somme), in March 1881, the hero – the Bonhomme Misère – is condemned to eternal life on earth. He makes a meagre living as a smith and lives with a devoted dog called Pauvreté: '... When Poverty went by, one could say to oneself: Misery isn't far behind.' One day God and Saint Peter arrive and are wined and dined by the poor smith, so God decides to grant him three wishes to reward him for his hospitality. Misère does not choose heaven, but simply devices which enable him to trap the devil and enjoy a good life, by promising him his soul, which he always manages to rescue in the end. He spends more time in the inn than at church, so when he dies, he is not allowed into heaven. Nor is he on the books of the angel in charge of purgatory (the chief angel is a real bureaucrat, who initially tries to refer Misère to another department, namely heaven). As for the devil, he has already suffered too much at the Misère's hands to be willing to accommodate him. So Misère 'is still alive. Many have met him, followed by his dog Poverty, and many will meet him yet.'[17] This rendering of the tale seems closest to the printed versions, which first appeared in chapbook form in 1719 and thereafter went through thousands of editions.[18] In this, Misère expresses the desire to partake of a last pear. Death, having refused to hand Misère his scythe to cut it down, obligingly clambers up the tree to pluck it for him. He is trapped and has to promise to spare Misère until the Last Judgement.[19] This clever story indicates the delight taken in the reversal of the ordinary course of events, whether with ironic – as in this case – or frivolous intent.

Many attempts have been made to establish the intellectual coherence of fairy-stories through the discovery of their common archaic origin. Some scholars have seen fantastic stories as a degenerate form of religious myth.[20] Saintyves devoted a large volume to proving the ancient liturgical origins of Perrault's fairy-stories, an interpretation which found a surprising amount of support[21] despite being dismissed by specialists.[22] However, less far-fetched approaches are at least as fruitful in explaining their popularity. In the first place, the fantastic of oral literature was generally less gratuitous and unpredictable than was once assumed. Boas remarked that popular tales often reflected many of the preoccupations and problems of the society which engendered them. Fantasy was as much a product of the values and beliefs of the ambient culture as anything else.

Nor did fantasy exclude an element of realism: most European fairy-stories 'give us an imaginative picture of rural life in semi-feudal societies.'[23] Realism was not always confined to accurate reflections of society, and indeed, sometimes seems to have been less evident in the formal overt content of stories than in the style in which they were told. Delarue thought the French were more realistic than the Germans or the Russians, as they tended to eliminate magical elements from stories, replacing these mainsprings with human motives and thereby rendering the stories more reasonable.[24] Yet the Siberian story-teller studied by Azadovsky minimized the supernatural in the stories she told, and concentrated on the psychologically and historically true and forceful.[24] Lo Nigro was struck by the same phenomenon when listening to Giorgina Vadalà, a Sicilian story-teller with a preference for long complicated tales, which were at once fantastic and realistic.[25] For want of adequate studies of the style in which stories were wont to be told, it is difficult to establish whether this tendency was exceptional or whether, as Delarue seemed to think, it was a relatively recent development due to the popularization of the ideas of the Enlightenment.[26]

But why, if men had a firm grasp on reality, did they delight in evoking the fantastic and extraordinary? One answer is suggested by Freud's observation that only unhappy people invent fantastic stories.[27] In this perspective, the fantastic compensates for the deficiencies of reality. However, this view – popular as it may once have been – hardly accounts for the conventional features of the folktale. Helvétius suggested that we like fairy-stories because they satisfy an inarticulate desire for boundless happiness.[28] The escapism of fairy-tales was not insignificant, nor was their form fortuitous. Helvétius advanced the idea that the inspiration of the stories was an unconscious utopian impulse, which took a literary rather than a social or political form, and that it was this deep-seated need for happiness that shaped the constant contours of the marvellous. Nodier predictably embraced a less radical view of the mainspring of the fantastic, but also saw in it a rejection of the prevailing order. He suggested that 'the taste for the marvellous . . . is innate in man'. It was 'an essential instrument of his imaginative life and perhaps the only really providential compensation for the miseries inseparable from his social life'.[29] Nodier thought that a disenchantment with reality – akin to his own pessimism – rather than the frustrated radicalism discerned by Helvétius, informed the urge to tell fantastic stories. He did not see in them the constant features observed by the materialist, which were to hold the attention of later generations of scholars.[30]

Increasingly, however, commentators have come to consider, like Helvétius, that the lack of realism of popular literature is deceptive. Paul Delarue noted that the folktale reflects the organization of society and its hierarchy and reveals the attitudes and feelings of the poor to the privileged.[31] Marc Soriano agreed substantially with this position in his study of Perrault's fairy-stories, observing that they depict the revenge of the poor.[32] Lo Nigro thought the characteristic component of the fairy-tale to be its preoccupation with morality:

> The fable presents a distinct contrast with what we actually see happening in the real world, a world which, in the light of naive spontaneous morality,

> is judged to be . . . immoral and unjust . . . This is the significance of the marvellous in the fairy-tale . . .[33]

With this assessment, Michel Butor is largely in agreement: 'A world invented, an exemplary world, fairy-land is a criticism of ossified reality . . . it suggests that we transform it, that we reinstate what is out of place.' The tales, by exaggerating the wealth and the poverty of the characters, 'make them into the very type . . . of the rich and the powerful', of the poor and weak. By the improbability of the victory over inequality which they present, the tales stress 'the weight and rigidity of real social inequalities, the difficulty there is in overcoming them'. The realm of the imaginary is not, he suggests, arbitrary, but 'appears to have covertly provided a deeper vision of that very reality to which at first it had been so contrary'.[34]

At another level, fantastic stories reflect an aspect of popular eschatology in that they announce a different order, antithetical in some respects to the present one. In this context, Todorov has pointed to the distinction between the strange and the marvellous: by implication, natural laws can account for strange phenomena – it is a question of defining the problem correctly; marvellous phenomena, on the other hand, are supposed to defy rational explanation. Hence Todorov comments: 'the marvellous corresponds to a phenomenon that is unknown, never as yet seen, still to come: hence to the future; with the strange, however, the inexplicable can be elucidated by reference to known facts, to previous experience, and, therefore, to the past.' Even if fairy-stories are set in the past, the possibilities for advancement which they depict can only be realized, and will only seem natural, in the future, when a different picture of human destiny has become generally accepted.[35] In the fairy-story, the extraordinary and impossible were presented as natural and possible, not because authors and audiences were ignorant and credulous, but because they were not satisfied with reality. They were interested in representing not what was, but what was not possible. In the fairy-story, the poor man is a hero, who manages to attain wealth and happiness – but this is only possible when he has been helped to break through the limitations of time, place and position which initially inhibit him. The invocation of magical rather than social or economic power as the means of liberation was a commentary on the means of advancement which, in reality, were open to the poor. The hero's ultimate success realized aspirations for well-being which were unattainable in reality.[36] Fantastic tales painted an inverted image of reality, satisfied dreams and desires by reversing the normal order of things. Inversion and reversal were characteristic of the popular idiom. Sometimes seen by educated contemporaries as indicative of gross materialism, this idiom afforded its devotees temporary liberation from the constraints of reality.

Broadsheets and Chapbooks

Pre-modern popular utopiae, as expressed in prints and stories, contrasted radically with the reality of contemporary society, depicting a world in which the order and logic of the normal were inverted. This tradition is well illustrated by the Land of Cockaigne, which presented a materialistic ideal in a humorous vein. One late eighteenth-century Flemish print adopted a comic-strip technique to describe it. First, a traveller is shown setting off for Cockaigne. He has to breach the sugar rampart, which acts as a kind of defensive town-wall, before he can enter and enjoy the marvels of the place: roofs of tarts, roads paved with larded veal, seas of wine on which marzipan and cinnamon boats float. It rains sugared almonds, wheat is made of almonds, flowers and reeds of sugar. When he opens his mouth, fruit falls and wine pours in; roast birds press themselves on him; pigs – with knives handily struck into their backs – run about the street; fried fish jump out of the river. The traveller eats so much that he becomes unable to walk and eventually too lazy to feed himself. He is finally banished from Cockaigne by the ruler, who has lost patience with the sybarite.

According to Van Heurck and Boeckenoogen, the theme was very popular in Flanders in the late eighteenth and early nineteenth centuries, although it knew its greatest success earlier, in the seventeenth and early eighteenth centuries. Of the fifteen written versions of the story studied by one of Jean Delumeau's students, all concerned gastronomic paradises, in which people never had to work or exert themselves. Festivity, peace, love, reigned in almost all of these utopiae. In about half, people enjoyed eternal youth; gold and silver were dispensed in some, clothes in others. Virtuous people were banished from three of the carnivalesque paradises, while another excluded lawyers and tax collectors.[37] The impossible and extravagant delighted because they were the antithesis of reality, an imaginative extension of the disorder and extravagance that reigned at carnival time, when people celebrated liberation from social and economic constraints, amid abundant eating, drinking and love-making.

The same taste for grotesque exaggeration and obsession with food were evident in the story of Gargantua, which was known in the oral tradition in much of France – but especially in the west and centre, north of the Loire. Gargantua was renowned for his gigantic stature, his capacity to cover immense distances quickly, and especially for his enormous appetite. He drank rivers dry, created mountains and rivers with his excrement and, although helpful, was apt to create havoc. His name was associated all over France with dolmens and outcrops of rock; and in almost every province, he had a dwelling. Both printed and oral stories of his exploits were popular in the nineteenth century, as they seem likely to have been even before Rabelais' time.[38] A chapbook version of the story, published by Deckherr at Montbéliard in 1848[39] emphasized all of these Rabelaisian features – notably Gargantua's enormous dimensions and appetite. He is sent into battle against the Dutch and Irish by King Arthur, who gives him:

> . . . Pour réveiller son apétit [sic] les jambons de 400 pourceaux, sans compter les andouilles et les boudins, qui faisaient l'accompagnement. La soupe fut faite dans 50 grandes chaudières. Il y avait encore 500 pains de 50 livres chacun. Il mangea plus de deux cents boeufs et pendant le dîner, il y avait quatre hommes forts et robustes qui, à chaque morceau qu'il mangeait, lui jetaient une pellée de moutarde en la gorge . . .

His uniform makes similar demands on the king's resources (his dressing gown requires 1450 ounces of frieze and 2500 fox skins). Later, during a truce in the fighting, Gargantua breakfasts off a boatload of fresh herring, 200 casks of salted sardines and a proportionate amount of mustard. To quench his thirst, he drinks a river dry, accidentally swallowing a ship carrying gunpowder for the relief of the town to which Gargantua is laying siege. This disagrees with him:

> . . . et pour y rémédier, Merlin et les médecins ordonnèrent à Gargantua de tourner le . . . vers la ville . . . Gargantua s'étant mis en disposition, on lui fit ouvrir la bouche, et ils y jetèrent une charrettée d'allumettes dans le corps qu'ils avaient allumées avec des torches. D'abord que le feu y fut, Gargantua ferma la bouche et ouvrit le . . . Alors on entendit un effroyable tonnerre car du bruit et du feu sortit de son corps, les faubourgs furent brûlés, et la ville fut endommagée.[40]

The text was characteristic of another facet of the popular imagination: it was marked not only by a taste for the marvellous – in the sense of impossible achievements and adventures – but also by delight in the grotesque. The physiological loomed large in this – abnormalities, deformities, the monstrous, exaggerated dimensions and capacities were all described with gusto and insistence. What lay at the heart of this fascination, and how can we attempt to understand it? Whereas the marvellous dislocated reality in order to transform it, the grotesque distorted it. Ribald humour was frequenly ambivalent, as Bakhtine observed: as manifested in carnival, it celebrated sensuality liberated from normal restrictions, and also rejected official norms, being both an oblique form of criticism and a source of amusement. The grotesque image, in its more expansive expressions, proposed a model world of plenty, informality and good cheer, while at the same time debunking normal authority and formality.

Indeed, a striking aspect of much popular humour was its tendency – shared with literature – not to re-present reality but rather to turn it upside down. An incidental theme of popular iconography was *Le Monde Renversé* or the topsy-turvy world, which commented on the order which people had come to see as natural. Van Heurck and Boekenoogen date the earliest known version of the theme to the late seventeenth century.[41] One of the broadsheets they reproduce, which dates from the eighteenth century, shows children punishing adults, animals ruling man, the king having to walk while the poor man rides, and the gentleman begging for bread.[42] Another depicted masters waiting on servants, while a contemporary French print showed a mule driving its owner to market and a village in the clouds with the sun and moon rather glumly on earth.[43] Another favourite theme of popular iconography, which bears some relation to the topsy-turvy world, was that of the domineering and arrogant woman who does not know her place in society.[44] Indeed, one sometimes appeared in *Le Monde Reverse* carrying a gun, or wearing trousers and smoking a pipe, while her husband was busy at the spinning wheel.[45] A late seventeenth-century print entitled *Who Should wear the Trousers?* commented on this reversal of roles and found in favour of husbands. Authoritarian women were unsympathetically depicted as scolds in the seventeenth and eighteenth centuries. Those who had inflated ideas about their abilities might have their heads brought to Lustucru, to have them remodelled in his forge.[46] Two perennially popular monsters illustrated man's gentle temper and female tyranny: Bigorne, who eats dutiful husbands, grows fat, while Chiche-Face, who lives off docile women, had his last meal two hundred years ago.[47] Women were sometimes treated more sympathetically, however: the counterpart to Mrs Scold was Mr Homebreaker. This use of humorous or grotesque personification was typical of the way points were made and values conveyed in the popular idiom before the advent of journalistic polemic.[48]

These broadsheets, insofar as they were intended to amuse by showing incongruous deviations from the established order of things, pointed to acceptance rather than rejection of an inevitable hierarchy. On the other hand, the tendency to invert and thereby parody the social and religious order was an important feature of popular festivities in the Middle Ages and Renaissance.[49] The theme of the topsy-turvy world appears to belong to this tradition, since it represents the kind of reversal of roles that was enacted in the antics of carnival and the feast of fools.[50] During periods of licence, people could express their instincts and feelings more freely than usual; they took advantage of this to escape constricting convention, as well as to mock the pretensions of the secular and religious authorities.[51] Behind the ritual revolutions lay irreverence and scepticism about the benefits of the prevailing order – even if the cumulative effect of the festivities was to reinforce it, by helping people tolerate normal cares and conventions.

Carnival

Nowhere was this reversal of roles and the normal order, this irreverent jollity and feasting, more evident than in the secular merrymaking of carnival. These pre-Lenten festivities varied in length – some were confined to Shrove Tuesday, others started as early as Christmas or the Epiphany, while sometimes they began around the Thursday before Shrove Tuesday. Carnival's rites varied from year to year and place to place. People dressed up: men wore women's clothes, and women men's; others preferred to appear as devils, priests or animals; some blackened their faces or wore masks; others scurried around on hobby-horses. This may have encouraged people to banish their inhibitions, for the celebrations witnessed a great outburst of spontaneous behaviour – insults and bawdy songs were bandied about, people ate and drank as copiously as possible and pelted each other with eggs or mud. Grenier noted that the celebrations from Christmas onwards were known as the *liberté de décembre*, and Van Gennep also stressed the dimension of liberation. Carnival-time was distinguished, he felt, by its licence, 'the temporary suspension of the rules governing normal life', and by the exuberant expression of sexuality.[52]

Liberty consisted not just in the suspension but in the reversal of the normal. Carnival enacted a formal revolution: people changed places – men with women; children with adults; the young assumed titles of authority and presided over the madness, permitting what was normally forbidden and imposing an independent burlesque law.[53] The way in which the young leader was designated was significant: he was the Lord of Misrule, the *Prince des Fols* or *des Sots*. In the little town of Ham, in Picardy, 'there was a company of fools called the *fools of Ham* ... The leader of this band had the title of *prince of fools*. His retainers accompanied him in the ceremonies of the *sottise*, mounted on donkeys, holding the tail instead of the bridle. No pranks could be played in the town without the prince's permission.' His followers wore fancy-dress and were divided into infantry and cavalry (the latter riding hobby-horses), while the prince himself 'wore as insignia of his dignity, a suit such as that Momus is often painted in and a similar cap, all set off with bells, and he had a fool's bauble as a sceptre'. His troops collected a 'tax' at the town gates. If a husband allowed himself to be browbeaten, they paraded him around the town in a rubbish-cart; and when old women married, 'the prince of fools and his band were sure to treat them to a *charivari*'.[54] This was the reign of folly – a time both of merrymaking and liberation from ordinary constraints, and of submission to an authority which, in its reflection of the attributes of kingship, derided both itself and all similar pretensions. But the alternative order thus installed did not attack all normal values: traditional attitudes to marriage were reaffirmed by an unofficial system of justice (which lends some confirmation to the theories that both carnival and traditional *charivaris* – noisy satires – reflected a preoccupation with fertility and renewal).

The election of alternative leaders, who by the nineteenth century enjoyed traditional – as opposed to official – authority, was a feature of popular culture. Each year, on 1 May or during carnival, young unmarried men elected a *chef des bacheliers* or King or 'Abbot of Youth', whose once extensive functions had originally included the pacification of rivalries and the punishment of certain offences. Principally, however, he directed young men's participation in the festivities and celebrations of the year, and sometimes their rowdy protests as well. The young collected a sort of tax from the newly-wed of their area, to finance feasts for themselves.[55] Describing the role of the young leader in the May-day festivities in the Hautes-Alpes, Ladoucette observed, 'I notice the abbot's power everywhere' – although he was little more than a master of ceremonies.[56] During the May-time celebrations, in many parts of France, a young girl was often designated 'Queen of the May' and in some regions they elected a king as well.[57] Similarly, in Berry until the mid-century, on the eve of the Epiphany at a festive meal, a large cake was shared out among all those present and the person who received the slice containing a bean was deemed 'King' for the rest of the evening. Grenier cites Pasquier's sixteenth-century account of the practice: a child, under the table, indicated who got which slice:

> ...Sans acception de la dignité des personnes, jusques à ce que la part est donnée à celui où est le febve, et par ce moyen, il est réputé Roy de la compagnie, encore qu'il fust réputé le moindre en autorité. Il n'y a respect de personnes, la festivité de la journée le veut ainsi.[58]

Some traditional festivities, like the medieval celebrations at Christmas-time, inaugurated a popular order which stood the world on its head – dignifying the humble and humbling the privileged; they celebrated brief utopiae of plenty, the possibility of a marvellous transformation of reality.

One of the most popular features of carnival was the mock trials and plays with which it sometimes ended. These parodied – albeit with jocular insouciance – lawyers and the law. In Auvergne, Caramantran, the personification of Carnival, was put on trial and executed. A strangely dressed mannequin was paraded about the town in a cart, accompanied by a troupe of people in grotesque outfits. At the head of the procession were people dressed up to look like lawyers and judges, and a tall, thin person who played the part of Lent. Then a number of young men in mourning followed, lamenting Caramantran's fate. In the main square, the procession halted and Caramantran was condemned to death by the judges and stoned.[59] The ceremony marked the end of festivities and the start of an ecclesiastically prescribed period of deprivation, Lent. Its significance for the people who took part in it has been variously interpreted as the execution of winter, or a catharsis of the community's shortcomings and sins of the previous year,[60] but it remains elusive, because of the essentially dramatic and metaphorical language in which it was couched. But ambiguity is characteristic of this and analogous customs: they lend themselves to various interpretations. It may be nearer to the truth to stress the elasticity of any given tradition, its adaptability, the multiplicity of purposes it could serve and meanings it could have.

The meaning of the trial and execution of Carnival is, however, at least partially illuminated by some popular plays which have survived. The trial could take place either as a sort of street festival or as a fully-fledged play. Many versions of the farce, *Lou proucès de Carmantran*, were supposed to have been known in the Comtat Venaissin, between 1600 and 1830. 'Bands of country actors', comments Cerquand, 'went here and there staging the trial and the sufferings of the hero, who was burnt in effigy as a heretic.'[61] Similar plays were known and performed among the Basques: they were organized by young men of the area and usually took place in the town square. The versions of the carnivalesque comedies found by Hérelle dated from no earlier than the eighteenth century and had not been performed since the middle of the nineteenth century, so it was impossible to know how they had been staged. Their themes and manner, however, encapsulated the mood of the carnival season. In the first play, entitled *Bacchus*, the hero Pansart (the Good Life) suggests to the people that Lent and Ashes should be destroyed. This proposal is greeted with enthusiasm, and the people promise to make Pansart king if he rids them of these enemies. 'La Justice, qui n'aime guère à faire maigre, donne son assentiment à cet enterprise, pourvu que Pansart s'engage à ne plus quitter le pays.' Pansart allies himself with Bacchus and Phintzirt ('le ventre de la bouteille'). The people insist that the allies marry so that their line will never die out, but discord instantly ensues as all the wives demonstrate their exclusive interest in Bacchus. Meanwhile, Lent has allied himself with Ashes and Phétiri Santz (poverty). As Pansart's camp is engaged in internecine legal strife (which affords the opportunity to satirize lawyers), Lent wins the battle, despite the assistance given to the bon-vivants by an obliging party of devils. The officers of justice now find it timely to recognize the authority of Lent, and they condemn Pansart to death with all the more alacrity when they learn that he has been consuming all the country's food supplies. Lent's victory is likely to be short-lived, however and the play ends with the assurance that: '. . . Another king will succeed him, our Lord the Spring: and after Spring, it will be our Majesty the Summer: and after Summer, the son of the late Bacchus will regain power.' The second play was in a similar vein and differed mainly in that Pansart escaped from Lent's justice and established himself in comfort in a nearby village.[62]

Pansart and Bacchus epitomized the enjoyment of the fruits of the earth once winter was over. The connection between simple hedonism and the earth's fertility was expressed quite explicitly in these plays. The reign of Lent was co-terminous with that of winter, and it would be replaced by the cornucopia of spring and summer. The theme of renewal and plenty recurs in the folklore of the period. In Spain, on the eve of Easter, a lay brother would try Lent, make an apology for food and draw from his tunic a bottle and a ham.[63] Utopia reasserted itself in the spring. But the spirit of carnival was more complex than this simple equation with a celebration of fertility and abundance would suggest. Its parodies, reversals, its liberations from ordinary constraints and mad antics sometimes struck a critical note. Medieval and Renaissance literature used the theme of folly to illuminate the shortcomings of contemporary society. Similarly, the folly of the medieval Christmas season and of carnival was not entirely innocuous. Its humour was double-edged, for it implied a rejection of actuality. Mikhail Bakhtine pointed to the significance of the timing of the festivities. The fact that they were held on the threshold of spring suggested that 'the popular and comic side of the celebrations showed what this better future would be like: instead of conservative immobility, instead of timelessness, of the immutability of the established order and established ideas, it emphasized *change* and *renewal*, including on the historical and social level'. The parodies of power, the abolition of normal hierarchies and privileges, the revolution played out in these festivities amounted to a declamatory – as opposed to an analytic – form of criticism. In this, the whimsicality of the popular imagination was neither as inconsequential nor as unreasonable as superficially it seemed to be. Instead, the fantastic and grotesque elements in popular amusements commented obliquely on reality and its shortcomings and reflected the utopian impulses and dreams of the poor.

Tall Stories

Country people characteristically expressed themselves obliquely, in an idiom which often seemed misleadingly strange and exotic to those unfamiliar with it. Early ethnologists proclaimed their astonishment at the numerous tales of incredible encounters and experiences recounted at *veillées* (gatherings for communal work and story-telling during winter evenings) and sometimes during crises – and they tended to regard them as evidence of the peasants' credulity and delight in the marvellous. In fact, these stories were often informed by anger and resentment – feelings which the legendary vocabulary they used both disguised and justified – and their purpose was to incriminate those about whom they were told, or to excuse the narrator's shortcomings. If one wanted to suggest that one's neighbour, or the local landowner or gamekeeper, was despicable and dangerous, one might tell a story about him, which appeared to be a statement of fact rather than of opinion and which cast him in the role of a legendary evil-doer – as a sorcerer or a werewolf. This switch from the particular to the general, from the anecdotal to the legendary, indicates not only how prejudice sustained itself in the absence of critical thought, but also suggests that man, in seeking to avenge himself on those whom he envied or feared, often preferred to hide behind collective judgements, rather than to state and to examine his attitudes openly. This reaction – which also explains the interest occasionally shown in eliciting false confessions to impossible crimes – was not peculiar to traditional man, but has also informed the processes and vocabulary of politics in modern totalitarian régimes.

Witchcraft. Tales about werewolves sometimes served as a form of allegation and a justification of the narrator's attitude. One man took advantage of the rumpus created by the famous *Bête de Gévaudan* and the spate of stories which suggested it was a werewolf, to spin a yarn of his own. His name was Bégou and he came from the village of Pontajou. One night, he saw a large hairy man bathing in the stream by moonlight. The hirsute bather, noticing his observer, changed himself into a wolf and flung himself on Bégou, who survived the onslaught and so was able to identify his assailant, the werewolf, as Antoine Chastel, the unpopular son of an unscrupulous local hunter.[64] The particular circumstance of a controversial animal meant that Bégou could adapt a stereotyped legend to compromise a person disliked in the locality. Stories about metamorphoses of sorcerers seem often to have served to accuse of magic criminality people whom the narrator and his audience knew. Yet amid the spate of fabulation engendered by the Bête de Gévaudan, one cannot but be struck by its lack of originality. The fantastic, both in its spontaneous and in its literary or printed forms, was highly conventional – and this, as far as individual invention is involved, may be due to the fact that one of its functions (that of discrediting someone) required a standard formulation of recognized misdeed – all the more because the crime could not be proved. Stories about werewolves and diabolical metamorphoses were frequently invoked to explain and vindicate one's behaviour. Thus, in the village of Boin near Beauvoir in the Vendée, a farm servant was visited every morning by a *cheval mallet* (a transmogrified sorcerer). The master advised shooting it with blessed bullets. When the servant did so, the animal collapsed and suddenly there appeared a young girl, whom the servant had courted but since abandoned.[65] Had the *cheval mallet* not plagued him, the servant would have stood in the wrong, having misled and then disappointed the girl; but, after the incident, his stance was fully justified, as she was cast in the role of both persecutor and criminal. Similarly, the story was told of a young man from Asasp who was courting a girl from Lurbe. One evening, accompanied by a friend, he went to visit her, but found no one at home. On their way back, they saw a little goat, which they pursued: when caught, it was transformed into his fiancée. 'They let her go free but any talk of marriage was abandoned.'[66]

Other stories accounted for broken friendships, as the following tale indicates:

> At Arthex, a young man, when out at night, often met with a dog on his way, which seemed to want to throw itself on him and which he had great difficulty in pushing aside. The animal always appeared at the same crossroads and never barked. One lonely evening, it wasn't a dog but a goat that accosted him

and, rearing up before him, placed its fore-hooves on his shoulders. Drawing his knife, the youth stabbed the animal, which was immediately transformed into a man. To his astonishment, he recognized his best friend, who said to him: 'I have been trying for a long time to be wounded thus. Don't speak of this to anyone and we'll go and have a drink together!' 'No,' replied the other, 'I'll speak of this to no-one, but I'll never drink with you again.'[67]

Some stories were told long after the alleged encounter, for it was dangerous to reveal the werewolf's identity. One Laburthe, who was assailed at night by a horse, shot the animal, which suddenly turned into an acquaintance who informed him that he had been under a spell. But he added 'if ever you let slip a word of this, you're a dead man'. So Laburthe told no one about what had happened until the former werewolf's death. Then, one evening when all sorts of extraordinary tales were being told, Laburthe thought it safe to recount his adventure. The next day, he was found dead in his bed.[68]

That the need for discretion should have been invoked in some stories is readily understood, for they often amounted to an accusation of magic criminality. The dangers involved in this accusation served as a plausible reason for not having recounted the adventure when it happened, and made it possible to present an invented tale as a true story and thus join in on an evening's fun. More importantly, however, the allegations contained in many fables of this kind were damaging and hence a grave matter. One of the ways of confirming the identity of a sorcerer was to see him with the wound that corresponded to an injury inflicted on him by the narrator hero. One woman, when she found an obstinate big sheep barring her way, scratched it under the eye with a needle; when, the following day, she met a woman whose eye was scratched, she concluded the woman was a witch who had transformed herself into an animal.[69] Some children from the area around Saint-Août noticed that they were followed every morning on their way to school by a strange animal. Their father shot it with salt and hit it on the thigh; the next day, the village sorcerer was to be seen hobbling around, clutching his thigh. The legend of the werewolf translated personal or collective animosity or fear into conventional terms, which, reversing the roles of victim and aggressor, tended to justify the narrator's hostility.

Some people claimed to have seen other proofs of magical criminality in their neighbours. One Pierre Lavielle believed that a woman who tried to fly up the chimney to escape his rough justice was a witch. In July 1826, in Saint Paulse (Landes), he had forced Marie Lasalle to admit that she had cast a spell on his cousin, by placing her on a pile of burning straw – torture which he renewed when the confused woman, confronted with the sick woman whom she had promised to cure, hesitated. In court, Lavielle declared 'in a convinced tone, that he had seen Marie Lasalle escaping up the chimney, when he had put her on the fire, and that he had been obliged to catch her by the hair to hold her down; during the hearing, he repeated his belief that Marie Lasalle had supernatural powers' – which did not stop the judge from sentencing him to five years' imprisonment, public exhibition and life surveillance.[70] The terms of his description of the way in which Lasalle had attempted to escape, rather than seeming outlandish to his peers, would have tended to corroborate his contention that she was a witch – for witches, according to legend, commonly transmogrified themselves, entered and left houses via the chimney and flew through the air. It was a conventional form of designation, to which literal veracity was largely irrelevant.

Similarly, people sometimes claimed to have witnessed sabbaths, and to have seen their neighbours there. In January 1811, four landowners of the commune of Joux indicted Claude Griffe, who, on 6 January and on following days, had publicly proclaimed:

> That he had seen them on the aforesaid day, towards five o'clock in the evening, at a sabbath, in the area of Boligny, parish of Joux, dancing around a fire and table, on which there was a quantity of bottles and glasses filled with wine, and in the centre of this dance there was placed a big golden throne, in which the devil sat presiding over the above-mentioned dance; that his talk was too injurious to their honour and reputation to be passed over in silence and not be punished severely in accordance with the law, all the more so because, at this moment their children dare no longer go to school, or even into the street, without being followed by the other children, who upbraid them on this account, which is the cause of much disturbance in the afore-mentioned commune of Joux.[71]

The tale was a classic form of slander.[72] The reaction it provoked was more complex than that implied by literal belief in the charges.However, Polyte Deshaies (nicknamed the Toad), a famous sorcerer from the Cotentin, was said to have organized meetings with other sorcerers in the forest of Varnavast, during the Restoration, where various sacriligious rites were supposedly performed.[73] In Picardy, a story was told about a peasant who went to a place where sabbaths were reported to be held; he saw one taking place and heard a neighbour from his village say that she had cast a spell on a local herd, which had recently died. When he returned to the village, however, he could no longer remember who she was. Dreams and hallucinations were probably at the root of some tales, like those told in the Hautes-Vosges about men returning from *veillées*, who thought they saw sabbaths in the forest of Châtillon.[74] Carnoy heard a more elaborate story of this kind from a villager from Thièvres in 1880. In it, a man saw a villager from Thièvres who was a werewolf turn back into human form by rolling in a muddy pond. He explained his behaviour thus: '. . . I'd like to stop myself doing it, but the devil is in me when it gets near the time for the witches to meet and I'm driven, against my will, to turn myself into a werewolf.' However, he could be delivered if the neighbour came to the next sabbath wielding his sword until he felt it hit something – this would be the invisible werewolf. The neighbour obliged, and saw fairies and witches dining, before disturbing the supernatural repast and rescuing the werewolf.[75] It is possible to understand the story in terms of obsession, delusion and suggestion, but its interest – both internally, in the relation between the characters, and externally in the relation it presupposed between narrator and audience – lay in the readiness it reflected to collaborate in myth-making.[76]

People sometimes appear to have been anxious to evade reality and enter an inherited imaginative world, to adapt and elaborate legend as seemed appropriate or useful. Foix told a story about an incident involving attendance at a sabbath, which was supposed to have taken place in Commensacq about twenty years earlier. A housewife had charitably taken in an eight-year-old girl who was gentle, obedient and healthy and whose only peculiarity was that, whenever she stopped running about and fidgeting, she fell into a deep sleep. The housewife began to think that the child was under a spell and was destined to become a witch. One Sunday morning, when the good woman returned home from early mass, expecting to find her charge looking after the swine in the field, she discovered her asleep under an oak-tree. The girl could not be roused and only awoke an hour later. The housewife, determined to solve the mystery, asked her, with a misleading appearance of commiseration, whether she was ill. The child, sobbing, replied that she was not, but could not help falling asleep during the day, because her godmother would not let her rest at night:

> 'As soon as I am in bed, she comes to get me up, dresses me, takes me and carries me off, where I don't know. She leaves me down in a big byre; but all the doors and windows are closed.'
>
> 'What way does she get in, then?'
>
> 'She leaves by the chimney and comes in the same way.'
>
> 'What's in this byre and what goes on there?'
>
> 'There's a big, brightly lit room, filled with girls and women. The girls are dressed in white and dance around a man dressed in red, who is seated in the middle of the room on a really beautiful throne. The women chat and gossip and look at the dancing and eat cakes.'
>
> 'And what about you, what do you do?'
>
> 'I eat cakes with my godmother and I watch the dancing.'
>
> 'How's that? The women don't dance?'
>
> 'A little, but not much.'
>
> 'Are girls and women from Commensacq present?'
>
> 'Yes, a few.'
>
> 'Name them.' . . . 'When do you leave?'
>
> 'I don't know, but when it's all over, she carries me away in the air and puts me back to bed.'

The housewife, having thus learnt why the child was sleepy during the day and why she never wanted to eat her breakfast, brought her to the local priest to have her rebaptized and to name a different godmother for her.[77] The story was reported to the bishop of Aire and Dax by the incumbent of the parish in 1887, and was presented not as a legend but as an actual incident.

If, rather than being a stylish story of primarily literary interest, the adventure happened more or less along the lines reported, we are confronted with the difficulty of explaining the behaviour of the woman and child. In the first place, their culture predisposed them to admit tales of witchcraft and strange encounters, but that this idiom should be applied to their own experience is, initially, surprising. The relationship between the foster-mother and the girl appears to have been somewhat strained on two counts: first, the child was adopted and secondly, her behaviour was sometimes so odd and strangely wayward that the housewife became concerned and began to wonder who the girl was and whether she had sinister antecedents. The child, on the other hand, while usually obedient, quiet and apparently happily enough employed with the usual menial tasks, dreamt about going to festive dances and eating cakes. The convenience of traditional myth for the child, in these circumstances, was that it both explained her behaviour and absolved her of responsibility for it. She could not be blamed for sleeping when she should be working, if in fact she was under a spell, if someone else was in charge of her. The story she told, however much it drew on the ambient culture, was not a spontaneous tale. The woman who sheltered her helped to suggest it by the questions she posed:

> 'How is it that you're such a miserable little thing that you can't keep awake?'
> 'Because I'm prevented from sleeping at night.'
> 'And who stops you?'
> 'My godmother.'

Significantly, the housewife wants to know not what, but who, is preventing the girl from sleeping. Thenceforward, the story becomes more fantastic – although conforming in general outline to simple ideas about the sabbath. The housewife elicits some assertions, which, although they seem particularly outlandish, were among the clichés of the folklore of witchcraft: thus, the witch uses the fire-place as the means of entrance and egress, neighbours attend the proceedings, and the girl and her godmother fly home on the return journey. The housewife also prompts the descriptions of the scene of her charge's nocturnal exploits and the nature of the activities that take place there. The question then ceases to be: why did the housewife believe the little girl's story? and becomes instead: why did she help the child to spin this yarn? The answer would seem to be related to the fact that it confirmed her own suspicions about the girl. Perhaps the most interesting thing about the use of folklore in this case, however, is that it enabled the woman and child to resolve the relationship: the woman's feelings are justified; the girl's behaviour is revealed to be a kind of magical illness; the responsibility for the past does not lie with them but with the godmother. The girl can be cured by being rebaptized and excluding the godmother from her life, then they can start again with a clean slate.

While people rarely seem to have lent any great significance to their dreams, Seignolle discovered a woman from the Cévennes who explained her problems through her dreams. She owned a machine for drying chestnuts and used it every year to dry her own nuts as well as those neighbours brought to her. One year she agreed to dry two hundred kilos of nuts for a person for whom she normally did not work. She put her machine into operation, carefully kept the fire alight, but found to her consternation that when the nuts should have been ready, they were as green as when they had first been put on the apparatus. She began to dream about the machine and have nightmares about the owner of the two hundred kilos of chestnuts, so that she came to believe he had cast a spell on her. As a result, she asked him to remove the nuts and the remainder dried normally. Why did the woman – rather than ascribing her dreams to her worries, and her difficulties with the nuts to the fact that the machine was overloaded – prefer to believe her dream and ascribe her problems to a spell? The explanation would seem to be that the dream confirmed and justified her feelings, providing evidence which corroborated her persuasion that she was charmed, that her difficulties had been caused by someone else.[78]

Fantasy rarely revealed its whimsicality or originality in these often repetitive stories – principally because their interest lay not in the picturesque details which they ostensibly presented but in the accusations they made, exonerations they afforded through the manipulation of myth. This use of myth is particularly evident in some 'primitive' trials, where the accusations were more formal and where a usually vulnerable person was induced to present traditional fables as an account of actuality – as Claude Lévi-Strauss has shown in an analysis of a Zuni Indian witchcraft trial. Bernheim recounts an analogous case from the Hungarian village of Tisza-Eslar, where a fourteen-year-old Protestant girl was murdered. Local opinion believed the Jewish community had killed the girl for her blood, to mix with unleavened bread for the Passover, and thirteen Jews were arrested. The thirteen-year-old son of the synagogue's sacristan was questioned by the local magistrate, an anti-semite, and by the police chief, who finally got him to confess. The child maintained that his father had lured the girl to the synagogue, where her throat had been slit and her blood collected in two plates. He affirmed that he had seen these events through the keyhole of the synagogue's door. He was kept away from everyone for three months and kept to his story at the trial – despite his family's pleas. Bernheim affirms that justice was finally done, however.[79]

Public crises provoked similar reactions among poor French peasants. Behind the extraordinary notions and stories which surrounded freak storms, famines and epidemics, lay quite prosaic preoccupations. Many of the tall stories and rumours which surfaced on these occasions resembled each other both in framework and in perspective, and expressed latently 'modern' feelings and ideas. A critical impulse informed many of these beliefs and stories, so that one must question whether to switch from inculpating magical or mythical animals to blaming the rich or the secular authorities for catastrophes, from a traditional to a modern idiom, implied as radical a change in outlook and sensibility as some historians have assumed.

Storms. Legends moulded spontaneous accounts of experience in a variety of ways, furnishing people with a vocabulary with which to express their criticism or otherwise inarticulate feelings, as the folklore of bad weather illustrates. When hail seemed likely to fall, the peasants of Isère rang the church bells, lit candles blessed during the feast of the Purification or used branches blessed on Palm Sunday to ward off the danger. At Saint-Laurent and at Saint Michel-en-Beaumont, while the bells rang, they recited: 'Forgive your people, O Lord, and do not show us your anger eternally.'[80] Brief prayers asking God to banish storms were also said in the Confolentais, where bells were rung to preserve parishes from storms in the belief that they frightened the devil away. The idea of assigning responsibility for storms to God, or other beings, was expressed more elaborately in the folklore of the celestial hunt. It was known by different names in the various provinces: in Lorraine, it was called the *Haute-Chasse*; in Vendée, the *Chasse Galléry*; in the Bourbonnais, the *Chasse Gayère*; near Blois it was known as the *Chasse Macabre*; and in Lower Normandy and the Pyrenees, as the *Chasse du Roi Artus*; while the Bretons referred to it as the hunt of the Red Man.[81] The fantastic hunt was usually evoked *à propos* of exceptionally severe or frightening storms – for example, one man affirmed that his father had heard the *Chasse Alequin* one night when crossing a forest; while a farmer of about fifty from Mauprévoir claimed to have been sceptical about the hunt as a young man, until one evening on the way to a *veillée* three kilometres away, he and some friends had heard the hunt and were frightened; in the village no one had heard anything unusual.[82] Usually, God was held to have condemned a sacriligious rebel to be buffeted around the skies for eternity. Thus, in the Landes and Gascony, over the din of the storm one was supposed to be able to hear the horns and barking dogs of King Arthur, who had been sentenced to hunt eternally in the sky as a punishment for having hunted on a holy day.[83] In Poitou, the *Chasse Galléry* was a favourite topic of conversation during the *veillée*. A number of people claimed to have seen it – but in their accounts of it they agreed only on its noisiness and frightful character. According to one legend it was caused by the nobleman, Galléry, who, anxious to go hunting, had left mass with his suite at the consecration. The hunt had started, but as a punishment, it was to continue until the last Judgement.

H

In other accounts, the din was made by dead men unable to escape the ceaseless torment of damnation, or by devils chasing the souls of the dying, or the souls of children who had died without baptism.[84] The explanation offered in legends tended to consider causality not so much from a physical as from a moral perspective.

These legends – with their exclusive emphasis on the danges of impiety – sound like *exempla* which passed into folk culture, rather than independent popular creations.[85] Other legends were deceptively exotic, being informed by more secular preoccupations. Like exemplary legends, they were concerned with the problem of responsibility and with the need to identify a palpable culprit. Storms were frequently attributed to the criminal practices of sorcerers and even of priests (which, given the ambivalent attitude to clerics, is not entirely surprising). Belief in the *meneur de nuage* (a person who was able to stir up a storm and who rode along on the storm clouds, directing them) was widespread in Normandy, the Ardennes and the Sologne Bourbonnaise.[86] One of the legends of the village of Thévet (Indre) concerned a sorcerer and his son, whom the villagers had heard quarrelling in the gathering storm-clouds about which parishes they should ruin.[87] For some, bad storms were linked to the black mass or sabbath: sorcerers and other magical criminals were obliged to hunt, metamorphosized, with devils. If one shot at the storm-clouds, an arm or leg would fall out of the heavens, and the neighbour who appeared the next day without the relevant limb was an associate of the devil. One legend in the Bourbonnais had it that a man, who had heard the storm, said: 'Apporte-moi de ta chasse' and received through his chimney a human arm, while a voice said 'Voici ta part'. Satan had given him his share of the hunt.[88]

Cauzons heard a similar story from a peasant from the village of Cutting in Lorraine. One evening, in the autumn of 1859, the narrator and his family were disturbed by a monotonous song: the man went outside to see what was happening and heard voices, which seemed to come from high in the sky and which rapidly became more distinct as the clouds drew nearer. 'I was very frightened and my mother's words weren't calculated to reassure me: "Look out, me boy... It's the Great Hunt" (as the flight of witches and sorcerers on their way to the sabbath is called in these parts). I braced myself against my fear and began to mock the monsters and hurl insults at them; the song suddenly stopped.' As he was about to go back inside the house, 'a bone of a human corpse' hit him, almost knocking him out. Yet it was so rotten that it could not be picked up. 'I found my mother as terrified as I was: indescribable carrion had fallen down the chimney into the hearth. You won't catch me railing at the Great Hunt any more.'[89] A more arresting instance of what Marc Bloch called 'an astonishing receptivity to supposedly supernatural occurrences' could hardly be adduced.[90]

However, the story was conventional rather than original or individual, and borrowed from a tradition composed of legends and stories about carrion falling from the sky on the irreverent and sceptical. The story was amusing and interesting, and it would have been embarrassing to challenge it. Even its apparently odd elements were not, in contemporary terms, extraordinary. The theme of objects falling from the sky, which emphasized or made manifest a message, was an ancient device, occasionally exploited in less enlightened medieval religious texts. Among the relics and talismans alleged to be of divine provenance were magical weapons, ritual objects (like the bell of the monastery founded by Saint Fursey), parts of saints' bodies and of course divine letters.[91] On the other hand, Satan too had his atmospheric armoury, with which to make mischief in the world. Flocks of birds were sometimes interpreted as cohorts of demons. Saint Edmund Rich, as a young man, seeing a flight of crows at sunset, took them to be a swarm of devils on their way to fetch the soul of an usurer at Abingdon (a supposition he was gratified to find corroborated by the coincidental death of the money-lender).[92] If one wanted to justify an opinion or order, it was helpful to appear to enjoy explicit divine sanction; similarly, accusations and condemnations might be lent added weight if the culprit could be shown to be a creature of the devil. The purely human and personal judgement of the nefarious character of the usurer was confirmed once it was seen that the devil had carried off his soul. In the story of the peasant from Cutting, as in most legends on this theme, the storm is the work of those who have rejected God's laws. The preoccupation in most extraordinary tales about storms was as much – or indeed, even, more – with the ethical as with the physical dimension of the practical problem. The assumption that quasi-scientific curiosity prompted legends of aetiology is undermined by the fact that legends offered explanations that were more moral than mechanical and appear to have had a social and emotional, rather than intellectual, inspiration. Relatively mundane preoccupations – such as hostility to usury, or anger about the loss of the harvest, fear of supposedly powerful criminals, resentment of envious neighbours or grasping clergymen – were reflected in and sometimes even legitimized by the exotic language of a figurative or exemplified morality.

The naturalism which inhabited extraordinary legends and tales emerges more clearly in cases where specific accusations were made. It appears to have been quite common to assert that local priests were responsible for storms. In many parts of France, they were believed to be able to control the weather,[93] or, through negligence or conspiracy, actually cause bad weather. During the July Monarchy, attempts to hold ecclesiastical conferences in the canton of Thiron in the diocese of Chartres had to be abandoned, since the locals thought that the gathering of priests had precipitated all kinds of disasters.[94] The belief that priests could cause hailstorms and might be seen riding the storm-clouds was held in some parts of the Indre, Maine-et-Loire and the Nivernais in the nineteenth and early twentieth centuries.[95] In the diocese of Orléans, during the reign of Louis-Philippe, priests were supposed to be able to find lost money, to make hail and to ride on storm-clouds. In 1864, missionaries were still held responsible for any storms which followed their retreats – so much so that one old cynic suggested that the Parisian insurance companies (then beginning to extend their operations and exploit a more popular market) dressed their agents up as preachers to frighten the peasants into buying their policies.[96]

According to Nogués, priests were thought in the Saintonge to be endowed with all these powers. To cause a hail-storm, they had only to beat water. Some peasants affirmed that they had seen priests directing the winds. Unlikely as this may seem, when one learns how priests' activities might be interpreted it becomes less astounding. The Abbé Meschinet was interested in photography, which was then in its early days. He departed to the countryside to take a picturesque shot, set up his tripod and dived under the black cape of the machine. Meanwhile, a number of peasants had been watching him doubtfully. As the abbé fiddled with his camera, a hail-storm broke out. The peasants descended on him, armed with pitchforks and sticks, shouting that he was a sorcerer and that he had just caused the tempest. The abbé was only just in time to make off with his camera.[97] This kind of accusation and incident was by no means unique.[98] The replies of the curates in the Allier, in 1840, to a questionnaire on religious practice and superstition yielded similar stories. At Arfeuilles, the venerable informant explained that

> ...Only last year, a good old priest was accused of driving the storm. If one were to believe them, a benign priest of the locality had glimpsed him in the heavens casting both lightning and torrential hail about him and had shouted to him with all the strength his almost octogenarian lungs could muster: 'There you are, rascal, I recognise you, if you make it hail on my parish, I'll denounce you to the bishop', and his parish was spared...Endless other stories were told; one could never record them all: in one place, a peasant claimed to have seen him during the storm, on top of a cherry-tree, preparing in this manner to ascend to the realms of thunder; elsewhere, it's another adventure of the same kind; and the poor people were so convinced of this that they would have stoned him twenty times over if he had appeared in the village.[99]

In the largely dechristianized, politically radical Allier, where priests were commonly thought to be sorcerers, it was not surprising that they might be the targets of popular ill-feeling. But such stories were told almost everywhere.[100]

In the diocese of Chartres in the area of Nogent-le-Rotrou in June 1839, a violent storm which destroyed much of the harvest was imputed, by some peasants, to the local parish priests. They were endangered by the popular fury, and the *curé* of Gironville was publicly accused of having directed the storm-clouds and decided their route: he had been seen reciting his office and making the sign of the cross in the plain, as well as being heard making noises in the church – supposedly preparing the storm. Some people insisted they had seen the priests sitting on storm-clouds. When Miron attempted to disabuse his informants,

> a farmer assured me that one of his neighbours had seen, with his own two eyes, a priest perched on the storm-clouds, pouring down hail. The irate rustic shot at the cloud and instantly a dead crow was seen to fall to the ground, hit by a bullet. What happened was that the priest, realising that he was mortally wounded, suddenly metamorphosised himself into a crow to save the honour of the corporation.[101]

In the south too, the same sort of story was told. Between 7 and 22 July 1838, the harvest of the parish of Champagne-Mouton was ruined by hailstorms. The peasants were convinced that sorcery lay behind this. They gathered to hold a council and one declared: 'It's the priest, I saw him going by in the clouds and I recognized him very well, he was waving the storm-cloud on with his square hat and he was directing it towards our fields.' Incensed, the locals armed themselves with forks and scythes and repaired through the village to the *curé*'s house. Luckily, the mayor, having been warned of the proceedings, carried the curate off to his house and sent for the police at Confolens. Some of the peasants were imprisoned for two days as a punishment for their antics.[102]

Behind the hysteria of this incident and its unfamiliar cultural form was an instinctive, violent revolt – misdirected as much on account of an inadequate understanding of society and of the nature of political power as on account of an erroneous grasp of physics. For concern with a satisfactory theoretical explanation of the natural phenomenon, or a taste for metaphysical speculation, were at best peripheral to this event: its focus was moral and social. A familiar antagonist was held responsible for the troubles of the poor, an antagonist who usually represented an alien authority. Magic was simply the well-known, if underhand, means whereby his malice might take effect, and which enabled the accusation to be made and recognized as just. And because violent revolt with a specific target was at the heart of this incident, it was punished and repressed by the secular authorities – who were always quick to recognize the political dangers of superstition. This story is typical of the disconcerting affirmations that have led historians and anthropologists to suppose that the sensibility and intellect of those who accepted them were radically different from our own. However, it may be also seen as suggesting simply that men in expressing themselves use the available idiom and observe the conventions which facilitate communication. Under the circumstances we should not be surprised to discover that devastating storms were not described naturalistically or scientifically, but fantastically – although the fantastic element hid natural antagonisms and jealousies.

Explanations which ascribed disasters to the malevolent machinations of clerics reflected not only the petty squabbling between *curés* and parishioners over money, dues and religious conformity, but also the sometimes hysterical anger of the ruined peasants. Bladé, in the late nineteenth century, was told a popular story entitled *Les Mauvaises Oeuvres du Curé* by his uncle, the curate of Pergain-Taillac; he said it was widely known before 1789 in Armagnac, Lomagne and the surrounding countryside, before being revived after 1830 by liberal bourgeois anxious to stimulate anticlericalism. It should be remembered that this region of France was in general characterized by its precocious detachment from orthodox piety and by its early political radicalism – phenomena which have been ascribed to the careless but financially exigent ecclesiastical government of the area in the *Ancien Régime*.[103] The tale may be seen, perhaps, as reflecting this background and as expressing quite natural reactions in an idiom which was both familiar and entertaining. In this perhaps more modern version of the story, three priests meet on a roadside. In the best traditional fashion, they repair to the local pond, where they mix the water with mud and make a 'dough of hail' with it, which they throw into the sky. The storm breaks out and hail destroys 'the people's bread and wine'. Delighted with this success, the delinquents proceeded to ruin harvests for the next three years.[104] The appeal of this story would be hard to explain without an understanding of its social and economic context, and without knowledge of the tradition of linking natural catastrophes which afflicted the poor to the evil intentions of the poorer and jealous, or of the more wealthy and powerful, by means of stylized, stereotyped narrative – a narrative which was but a variation on a theme, the *Chasse Gayère*, or the *Chasse Artus*. The picturesque folklore of storms sounds as though it were derived from medieval *exempla*, but its apparent adaptation to a secular, latently radical world-view indicates that the minds and feelings of poor men were not as strange as their flamboyant mode of expression would suggest.

Epidemics. The ease with which traditional beliefs could be replaced by less outlandish ideas – indeed, the interchangeability of the traditional with the comparatively modern – which again points to the universality and consistency rather than the diversity of man's constitution, also emerges in the folklore of epidemic disease. The *semeur de peste* ('sower of plague'), who was initially akin to a magician or sorcerer, was gradually eclipsed by the doctor, who was believed to give vent to the violent animosity of the rich towards the poor. The transition to a modern outlook and the mythical roots of apparently rational contemporary attitudes can be glimpsed in this process. Just as severe storms were attributed in the abstract to legendary criminals and in practice to *meneurs de nuage*, who were frequently identified with targets of local animosity, so too a misleadingly exotic mythology surrounded epidemic illness. The stories and rumours which gained currency during the outbreaks of cholera in the nineteenth century drew on traditional beliefs. According to some, the illness had been sent by God to punish men for their apostasy and vice – a view that was popularized by broadsheets.[105] In Saint-Cast in 1832, cholera was supposed to have caused a great many deaths because unbaptized children had died that year in the area.[106] In Le Havre in the same year, the disease, coinciding with storms and the appearance of dead fish in the bay, was taken to be a manifestation of God's anger, a presage of his punishment and of the end of the world.[107] In one contemporary report, God appeared as an omnipotent personage, who acted ruthlessly according to his private unpredictable plans. On 16 June 1832, the ditches separating Ingouville from Le Havre were filled with fish which leapt convulsively out of the water in an attempt to reach the bank, where they died, 'au grand ébahissement de la foule'. Everyone was upset by the spectacle:

> ...For some, it was a warning from heaven, for others the beginning of the end of the world. Those who were creating a great commotion at that time, regretting and invoking with all their hearts the fallen dynasty, were convinced that it was the hand of God, punishing us for our iniquities.[108]

In crises, the poor were intellectually and emotionally ready to accommodate the horrific story and the apocalyptic image into reality – particularly if it enabled them to express exuberantly or exorcise their grief.

However, the mode of thought discernible in the folklore of storms – the preoccupation with responsibility, with the moral and, more explicitly, the social order at the expense of mechanistic or physical explanations – was also evident in the folkore of epidemics. It was most clearly reflected in the beliefs about the *semeur de peste*, a character analogous to the *meneur de nuages* or the *meneur de loups*. The *semeur de peste* was essentially a kind of poisoner, who spread the contagion through magic. During the epidemic in Brittany in 1853, people near Brest maintained that they had seen the traditional source of disease – the Red Woman – 'sowing the plague in the valleys'. One beggar-woman, brought before the courts, maintained that she had seen and talked to them.[109] In part of the Nivernais, the culprits were less mysterious – being more akin to sorcerers. Here, criminal characters, known as *metteux de choléra* were said to have little pills, distilling the disease, which melted in the dew; they were thought to scatter their tablets at night, principally in wells and fountains and on roads. The pills worked only before sunrise, which explained why the poor suffered more than the rich, who rose later.[110] Belief in the *semeur de peste* persisted until the end of the century: it was noted in Toulon in 1884; and in Brittany, during the cholera epidemic of 1893, excursionists were attacked by peasants who accused them of poisoning the air and water and sowing cholera in the fields.[111] These ideas – which superficially point to a mentality which accommodated the bizarre without difficulty – were in keeping with the popular notion of illness, especially acute or strange illness. All sorts of ailments – from warts to alleged spells – were thought to be contagious disorders picked up from an infected object,[112] a mode of thought which was essentially naturalistic and materialistic, rather than extraordinary.[113] The *semeur de peste* was not unlike the sorcerer in his malevolence and *modus operandi*. In the Hautes-Alpes, sorcerers were believed to murder by means of poison: one tale, noted by Van Gennep, concerned Antoinette de Vif, who killed her neighbour by poisoning the fountain from which he drew his drinking-water. This was a technique employed – in popular myth – by the *semeur de peste*. The distinction between sorcerers and *semeurs de peste* was not always drawn. Hence, priests were sometimes identified as being responsible for epidemics: in 1854, in the Gâtinais, when cholera broke out, clerics reported that 'almost everywhere, priests have been accused of giving the cholera'.[114] In 1836, in Méry, a woman was tortured when a doctor announced that he thought that the epidemic in the area could be due only to a spell.[115]

In the eighteenth and nineteenth centuries, however, these traditional, magical scapegoats were gradually eclipsed by modern, secular culprits. Accusations of guilt were levelled against doctors. This was in keeping with the popular mistrust of academic medicine, which fostered a number of strange beliefs about doctors' activities. One of these was the persuasion that people who caught rabies were smothered between mattresses in hospitals, while in Brittany, peasants were unwilling to go to hospital, as they were sure that patients became the objects of peculiar experiments.[116] Rumours based on these beliefs sometimes spread during crises. Writing towards the end of the *Ancien Régime*, a bourgeois from Moulins noted that disturbances had broken out in Lyon 'on the question of some children who had allegedly been carried off by doctors and surgeons of the aforementioned town for experiments'. In May 1760, police in Paris arrested a number of beggars and young children: the mothers of the latter gathered in a number of squares, lamenting the occurrence and alleging that the authorities wanted gold in exchange for children. Rumour had it that Louis XV wanted to kill them to recover his health, as doctors recommended bathing in human blood as a restorative. This led to violence, in which one policeman was killed and others were beaten.[117] Analogous behaviour and beliefs can be traced back to the Middle Ages, where similar allegations were levelled against Jews.[118]

The poor seem, not infrequently, to have suspected the educated rich of trying to kill them. Repeatedly during the epidemics of cholera, it was rumoured that, through their agents, doctors, the wealthy and the government were poisoning the poor – a feeling which was not entirely unjustified in the view of one doctor from Toulon, given the living conditions of the poor and their inevitable vulnerability to disease.[119] Fear of doctors as people who caused rather than cured disease is recorded in Lyon as early as the sixteenth century. During an outbreak of plague there, doctors and surgeons were pursued by angry crowds who imagined that they were responsible for the epidemic.[120] Analogous incidents occurred in the seventeenth and eighteenth centuries, as for example in Arles, where doctors sent from Paris were treated with hostility.[121] These attitudes persisted in the nineteenth century.[122] Dr Vingtrinier, who conducted medical relief during the cholera epidemic in Rouen and the surrounding communes in 1832, found that the local peasants feared both him and his prescriptions.[123] In Bordeaux, the poor were unwilling to accept help and showed 'downright fury' when it was offered.[124] In Paris, the popular belief that the disease had been 'sown' and that doctors were in some way guilty of causing the disease, is well known.[125] In April 1832, at Douai, popular feeling, both in the town and in the neighbouring area, was directed against doctors: there were gatherings in the local villages which helped to spread extravagant rumours about the fate of those sent to hospital. The poor assembled outside the building and stopped a convoy of coffins, declaring as they opened one of them: 'You'll see how poor folk are tortured. They're skinned for experiments'.[126] In Lille, it was rumoured that the government had poisoned the water-supply to destroy the poor, and that the ill were poisoned and burnt in the hospitals.[127] In Provence, when cholera made its first appearance in 1835, Drs Dubreuil and Rech, who carried out the official survey of the extent and consequences of the epidemic, frequently found themselves in danger of being attacked by the angry and frightened populace. In Beaucaire, '... the masses ... believed it to be a poison ordered by the government and the rich and spread, in particular, by foreign doctors'. They forced medical students to abandon their attempts to minister to the ill and attacked a number of individuals thought to be doctors. They had also shown themselves to be hostile to the administration's edicts concerning public hygiene – in particular refusing to allow the streets to be hosed down, as this would 'add to the effect of the little grains of poison spread during the night at the orders of the authorities'.[128]

The poor suffered far more than the wealthy from the effects of the repeated epidemics of cholera in the nineteenth century – especially on its first appearance.[129] The victims were not slow to observe this: in Doubs, in 1854, they were reported to have complained that 'the cholera pursues us pitilessly, but it spares the rich'.[130] To pass from this realization to the inculpation of the wealthy, from customary passivity to sudden aggression was, under the circumstances, understandable.[131] This order of reaction – in disease or famine – cannot be explained simply by being labelled 'class hatred', as Réné Baehrel did in his study of the plague in Provence during the *Ancien Régime*.[132] Fear of the *semeur de peste* was more complex than he suggests. In the popular aversion to doctors, who were thought to be 'sowing' disease, were concentrated both fear and hatred of the rich (who were traditionally seen as oppressors) and fear of death and of modern medicine; and above all, traditional misgivings about the consequences of individual and collective malevolence.[133] Whether confronted by epidemic, isolated illness or famine, the instinctive popular reaction seems to have been to try to identify the malevolent individual or power resonsible for the crisis. Where this responsibility was attributed to the government or the rich, the remedy was seen in pragmatic, profane terms and the rebellious riot was never far off.

Conclusion

However strange the forms taken by the insecurity and consequent anger and fear of the poor, it should be observed that its peculiarity was more superficial than fundamental, for the accuracy of anecdotes and rumours recounted under such circumstances was of secondary importance. They expressed fear and indignation at the horrors of suffering. People unfamiliar with the vocabulary of contemporary political and social debate naturally tended to express their thoughts and feelings through legends and images consecrated by tradition. Hence the conflict between the real and the ideal was sometimes expressed by distortion – exaggeration, reversal, caricature, grotesque or burlesque images – which revealed the incongruity of reality; sometimes, as in fairy-stories, the impossible was presented as possible, making the shortcomings and limitations of reality, by contrast, all the more evident. The escapism of popular fantasy reflected not only the shortcomings of actuality but also people's difficulty in accepting things as they were – especially in times of crisis – a reluctance which seems to have fuelled the tendency to blame others for one's misfortunes. The imaginative world of tradition, with its stories and legends – which were so easily manipulated and which the art of traditional narrative accustomed people to repeat and adapt – helped men not only to escape briefly into happy dreams but also, more dangerously, to evade truth, to confirm their suspicions and prejudices. This impulse was not unique to pre-modern culture. The tales of fantastic depravity sometimes told during crises were inspired partly by the unwillingness or inability to accept the misery of famine or disease; and their burden was moral and latently political, insofar as analogous or even the same culprits would be held responsible for the plight of the poor or deserving citizen in modern political debate. The similarities in the structure of stories explaining catastrophes, the ease with which the legendary *meneur de nuage* and *semeur de peste* became the priest or doctor, with which a recognizably modern idiom replaced an archaic one, suggests that the rise of modernism has more to do with evangelism and the spread of new vocabulary than with any profound change in man's sensibility and outlook.

Conclusion

Contrary to the opinion of many early ethnologists and subsequent historians, superstition appears to have been naturalistic, if not rationalist, in inspiration. Superstitious beliefs and practices were often less strange and unreasonable than they seem at first sight. Much of the folklore of religion, medicine, amusement and protest reflected natural, often perennial concerns and aspirations, which such traditions expressed and attempted to assuage in imaginative terms. They were, therefore, not so much practical as psychological techniques – even if this was not how they were usually seen – which were not devoid of sophistication in the appreciation of the workings of the emotions which they implied. On the other hand, this culture was profoundly marked by the impulse of escapism. This lack of realism was, in many ways, insidious, for not only did it involve an inability to accept actuality, but it also betrayed a tendency towards self-deception on a large scale. The profusion of fantastic beliefs afforded a rich heritage of imagery, which was habitually manipulated to justify personal resentments and animosities, to exculpate the guilty and inculpate their victims, to reinforce prejudice. In times of personal and public crisis, tradition encouraged men to hold someone responsible for their misfortunes – however unfounded this urge might be – and it furnished them with a legendary vocabulary which enabled them to do so. Myth and legend, therefore, were not only exploited to afford people relief in illness or amusement and compensation in leisure: they allowed men to deceive themselves and others, to distort their experience, to take refuge in fantasy and prejudice; they confirmed and legitimized accusation, revolt and escape. In this, the archaic may be said to have held the seeds of the modern. Many of the aspirations once expressed in diverse aspects of traditional culture – such as religion, demonology, prophecy, folktales and carnival – were channelled into politics in the twentieth century, and the characteristic idiom of traditional superstition significantly informed the methods of twentieth-century politics, particularly of totalitarian politics. The importance in modern political life of demonstration and rally, slogan and symbol; the exploitation of the notion of class hatred, conspiracy theories, anti-semitism and show trials: all betray the influence of traditional popular culture – with its taste for re-allocating responsibility for difficulty and disaster, its old hostility to wealth and power, its tendency towards self-deception and self-justification, its delight in collective celebration and evasion through myth. Early commentators were therefore justified in characterizing superstition as irrational, but not in thinking it to be incomprehensible and divorced from modern culture and outlook.

How then should we answer the question asked at the start of this essay? Can the historian affirm that the mode of thought and feeling of pre-modern man was essentially different from that of twentieth-century man? How can he explain the revolution in common attitudes, beliefs and emotional range witnessed in the past hundred or hundred and fifty years? The answer would seem to be that the revolution was more apparent than real. It was long assumed that history chronicled the progress of man and society, the gradual triumph of rationality and its concomitant benefits – tolerance, peace and prosperity – over obscurantism and oppression. According to this thesis, the irrational (fear, fanaticism and superstition) was held to have lost its sway over men's minds during the Enlightenment. In reality, the influence of reason on, and even its appeal to twentieth-century man seems tenuous: interest in bizarre marginalia[1] persists in phenomena as varied as the contemporary fashion for obscure religious cults, the popularity of horoscopes and fortune-tellers,[2] and the widespread receptivity to spurious medical theories. The interchangeability of techniques based on rational method with others which are entirely irrational in conception – which is to be observed in people's readiness to consult both doctors and faith-healers or charlatans – points not only to human inconsistency but also to the superficiality of modern man's conversion to rationality. Psychology, too, abounds with a multiplicity of mutually contradictory and sometimes irrational beliefs and systems, the most prestigious and popular of which is psychoanalysis. The status of psychoanalysis is another indication of the place accorded (albeit unadmittedly) to irrationality in modern culture.[3] In contemporary politics, the importance of fantasy and the aversion to consistent rationality is also evident. Many twentieth-century political leaders, in getting and keeping power, have exploited the appeal of myth, of feeling rather than of critical thought, and have attempted to curtail the influence of rational analysis, which they have seen as a threat to their pretensions. Contemporary politicians have increasingly abandoned argument for image, as the vast sums expended on advertisement indicate, in deference to the electorate's apparent preference for this form of politics. Even journalists, during elections, seem to devote more time to analysing opinion polls and campaign management than to the issues and policies which voters are supposed to be assessing. It would sometimes seem that the advent of mass democracy has led not so much to the extension of debate and consultation as to the generalization of pretence, to the substitution of manipulation on a grand scale for closeted intrigue.

The persistence of irrational and inconsistent attitudes in the late twentieth century suggests that one of the terms of the problem as initially stated – that which assumes that modern man has eschewed irrationality and embraced a Voltairean outlook – is misleading. The survival of some superstitions, the adaptation of others, and the integration into modern political debate of traditional prejudices and mental operations suggest that it is reasonable to conclude that man's vocabulary rather than his nature has changed, and that his feelings and patterns of thought have remained substantially unaltered.

The problem of explaining the change from a traditional to a modern outlook is largely an artificial one, generated by the radical revision, in the eighteenth century, of man's view of his nature and his destiny. The new vision of man was proclaimed by writers as various as Voltaire, Rousseau and La Mettrie. Rousseau described this revolution in his *Rêveries du Promeneur Solitaire*. At forty, he decided to eschew the constraints of society's conventions and expectations:

> Je quittai le monde et ses pompes, je renonçai à toute parure; . . . et mieux que tout cela, je déracinai de mon coeur les cupidités et les convoitises qui donnent du prix à tout ce que je quittais . . . Une grand révolution qui venait de se faire en moi, un autre monde moral qui se dévoilait à mes regards, les insensés jugements des hommes dont . . . je commençais à sentir l'absurdité . . . tout m'obligeait à cette grand revue dont je sentais depuis longtemps le besoin.

The new man discerned by Rousseau was a creature of instinctive feeling and spontaneous virtue.[4] Rousseau, if an eccentric among his great literary contemporaries, shared their enthusiasm for rediscovered nature and their conviction that the principles of ethics and action should be founded on knowledge of nature rather than on spiritual or metaphysical ideals. The reorientation of political life, the redefinition of social order and of the purpose of history, which found expression in the Revolution, was indebted to the reassessment of human nature in the late seventeenth and early eighteenth centuries – a reassessment that was experienced as a liberation from fear and from the constraints on mind and body imposed by ignorant and ambitious authority.

The idea that the natural world should hold no terrors for man, whose physical and moral well-being depended on his heroic rationalism, was first elaborated in the early dawn of Enlightenment. Both Corneille and Racine isolated the conflict between private, instinctive feeling and reason – which dictates submission to public virtue and to the needs of the state – as the source of tragic tension. Descartes, in one of the first modern attempts to provide a naturalistic classification and account of the passions in their relation to man's physical constitution, wrote of fear, in 1869, that 'pour exciter en soi la hardiesse, et oster la peur, il ne suffit pas d'en avoir la volonté, mais il faut s'appliquer à considerer [sic] les raisons, les objets et les exemples qui persuadent que le peril [sic] n'est pas grand . . . '.[5] He sought to liberate man from instinct and to create a reassuring, predictable world through the application of reason to man's perceptions. Descartes identified the evil effects of the passions not in theological terms – that is, as irrevocable steps in man's destiny, insofar as they affected his relation to God – but in secular terms, as generating obsessions which obfuscated clear thought.[6] He defined virtue, then, not so much as an impulse towards God, whether affective or effective, but in terms of secular utility: it no longer implied a movement away from the world, but celebrated integration – intellectual and emotional normality. The attack on superstition and the marvellous was mounted in this spirit.

Throughout the eighteenth century, rationalists saw superstition as a form of emotional tyranny and, by extension, as a means of political oppression.[7] As a result, they regarded attempts to inculcate rational principles in men's minds as a battle for liberation, which would enable man to recognize his own nature and destiny and, in doing so, to possess the key to public and private happiness. Initially, the *philosophes* tended to identify superstition with religious customs and beliefs – other than those associated with vague deism. Typical of this outlook was Voltaire, when he declared that 'nearly all is superstition that goes beyond the worship of a supreme being and the submission of the heart to his eternal commands'.[8] Jaucourt, in the *Encyclopédie*, defined superstition as 'that kind of enchantment or magical power which fear exercises over our souls; the unfortunate daughter of imagination, she employs to stimulate it spectres, dreams and visions; it is she, says Bacon, who has forged these idols of the common people, the invisible genies, propitious and unpropitious days . . . Superstition is a despotic tyrant.' It was, he insisted, perpetuated by interest and calculation.[9] Voltaire, too, saw superstition primarily as a means through which men's minds were manipulated by an élite avid for power and wealth. Addressing himself (at least rhetorically) to peasants and artisans, he wrote:

> Men fed by your labours in a comfortable idleness, enriched by your sweat and your misery, struggled for partisans and slaves; they inspired you with a destructive fanaticism, that they might be your masters; they made you superstitious, not that you might fear God the more, but that you might fear them.[10]

In this perspective, government had too often been founded on perversion and degradation, on an insidious attempt to diminish man – both in his nature and in his rights. Hence, the *philosophes*' campaign against fear and ignorance, their appeal for the intellectual and moral liberation of man, was self-consciously political. Voltaire exhorted:

> Appeal to the people, and, brutalised as they are, they listen and half open their eyes. They partly throw off the most humiliating yoke that has ever been borne. They rid themselves of some of their errors and win a part of their freedom, that appanage or essence of man of which they have been robbed. We cannot cure the powerful ambition, but we can cure the people of superstition. We can, by speech and pen, make men more enlightened.[11]

Perspicaciously, however, Voltaire counselled caution in this crusade. 'How far does public policy permit the destruction of superstition? It is a very thorny question. It is like asking how far one should go on tapping a dropsical man, who may die during the operation.'[12] This caution may have been informed by Voltaire's rather sceptical conservatism, which made him go to mass on Sunday for the benefit of his servants and labourers, but he had identified a significant question. How far may the state go in eradicating an outlook which its leaders find erroneous and objectionable? How far is such an intrusion justifiable? Few people after Voltaire paused to consider this difficulty and the majority pressed forward with messianic fervour on their radical mission.

It was in Holbach that Descartes' ideal of banishing fear through the application of reason's standards to social and personal problems found one of its most dedicated exponents.[13] In destroying hell, Holbach was bent on obliterating a source of unhappiness – which was not even an effective guarantee of morality.[14] Holbach wanted to liberate men from this noxious spiritual and physical terror:

> No, mortals, blinded by terror! . . . This destroyer of your phantoms is not the destroyer of your happiness . . . if it shatters these idols incensed by fear,it is to put in their place the consoling truth made to reassure you. . . . Return then, child . . . to Nature! She will console you, she will drive from your heart the fears which overwhelm you, the anxieties which beset you . . . Be happy then![15]

From this idealistic materialism, or optimism about human nature – which asserted that man was adequate unto himself and that his feelings and his passions were the principal means of knowledge and happiness[16] – sprang the frenetic cultivation of the individual sensibility which was to characterize the French Romantics.

The new man, liberated from artificial prejudices and fears, could rely on his natural constitution and on the observation of nature to guide him to virtue and happiness. Man, according to La Mettrie, was a machine with an innate sense of right and wrong; he had only to turn to nature to resolve problems that had long seemed intractable. 'Break the chain of your prejudices; arm yourself with the torch of experience and you will do Nature the honour which she deserves . . . ', he exhorted. 'Only open your eyes and leave aside that which you cannot understand . . . He who thinks thus will be wise, just, tranquil about his fate and therefore happy.'[17] Diderot also subscribed to this heroic empiricism. His definition of man in the *Encyclopédie* was aggressively reductive and materialistic: pride, superstition and fear had engendered systems which had prevented man from understanding his own nature and had distorted it. Philosophers, he maintained, needed to study the natural mainsprings of human behaviour in order to improve man and make him happier.[18]

This new-found delight in human independence and self-confidence were fully shared by Condorcet. In his *Esquisse d'un Tableau Historique des Progrès de l'Esprit Humain*, which he finished in October 1793 while in hiding from the Convention, he reiterated his belief that crime and misery were engendered by despotism, which had a vested interest in ignorance. 'Every time that tyranny strives to subject the mass of the people to the will of one of its parts, it counts among its means the prejudices and ignorance of its victims.' For centuries, people had been oppressed and misled by a tiny élite of kings and priests. Consequently, Condorcet emphasized the importance of education, which alone enabled man to enjoy freedom and saved him from exploitation and deception. Able to act for himself, or to cast a critical eye on his agents, the educated citizen alone could ensure the survival of the republic. Finishing his work in contemplation of the fruits of good government, Condorcet rejoiced in 'this picture of mankind, freed from all these chains ... walking with a firm and sure step in the ways of truth, virtue and happiness ...'.[19] It was this vision of the heroic individual, of independent and fearless man forging his own destiny, that inspired the assault on superstition and the drive to impose positivistic norms in the nineteenth century.

The war waged on superstition by heroic rationality was overtly a battle for men's minds – a self-proclaimed revolution of consciousness, promising liberation from the constraints on man's vision, creativity and happiness. The danger of these assumptions was scarcely appreciated in the early nineteenth century, save by a handful of conservative apologists and romantic writers like Nodier, who were dismissed as sentimentalists and dreamers. But this was no mere academic debate, for political power was at issue. In the eighteenth century, ideas and their expression in law, politics and the natural sciences were redefined by a rigorous logic, based on observation, which sought to rediscover the inherent order of the universe that man would then make explicit. Rationalism tended to organize the disparate elements it considered into systems, and it is not surprising that the political theories most indebted to it emphasized the right of the state to extensive powers of inquiry and execution. This evolution in political thought had been prepared by developments in the seventeenth century. When the claims of the Church to total authority in France were eroded through effective implementation of the theory of the divine right of kings, some of the most gifted and influential churchmen of the period – among them Richelieu and Bousset – lent their administrative skills and eloquence to the cause of the omnipotent state and its right to command the subservient obedience of its subjects. The Church made itself an effective weapon in the hands of the state, which, thus bolstered, was soon to shuffle off its dependence on theology and to elaborate a secular theory of the origins of moral authority, while arrogating to itself many of the Church's methods of governing the individual – not just in his public, but also in his private life – which had formerly been regarded as the province of man's relation to God. Modern political theory learned much from ecclesiastical government about the manipulation of popular opinion, about the eradication of dissent and the imposition of moral norms. Politics ceased to be about the administration of the king's temporal estate, once theoreticians adopted, for the secular state, the Church's ultimate aim of effecting the individual's perfection and salvation. These goals justified the state's intrusion into the realm of the individual's private persuasions, and its attempts to shape and control them through its administration of the law, medicine and education. Superstition, that independent popular idiom and collection of beliefs, became a heresy in the eyes of the governing élites of the nineteenth century, to be extirpated and replaced with an orthodox outlook and conformity of expression. For tradition embodied a mode of thinking and feeling which was peculiarly popular and which had been outside the sphere of secular government; and in its many latent and explicit expressions of hostility towards the assumptions and demands of the authorities, in its very independence of vision, superstition challenged the norms and objectives of the political order born of eighteenth-century radicalism. Pursuing the aim of the general good, the nineteenth century effectively developed ways of governing the individual, to a degree and in a manner not previously realized. The formation and expression of man's private thoughts and feelings now became legitimate territory for the government, as it sought to found the ideal state and the ideal citizen. This led to anxieties and aspirations being expressed in new ways, with politics and psychology tending to replace religion and magic.

The proponents of radical rationalism, in their campaign against superstition, held a view of human nature and of the state which in practice undermined the individual's right to dissent and differ. It was assumed that men – when ignorance and prejudice, knavery and despotism had been destroyed – would naturally tend to agree about the conduct of public affairs and to conform in their private behaviour to society's ethical norms. A dissenter himself, Condorcet nonetheless asked:

> Does the perfection of law and public institutions . . . not have the effect of reconciling and identifying the common interest of each man with the common interest of all? Is the goal of government not the destruction of this apparent opposition? And is the country whose constitution and laws most nearly reflect the wishes of reason and nature not the one where virtue is easier and the temptation to stray from it rarer and weaker?[20]

Dissent might therefore become the pretext for vigorous campaigns against superstition and fraud – campaigns which were seen as the prelude to the foundation of a new and better order, as identified by the enlightened. Behaviour and ideas which did not fit these categories were dismissed as aberrant, lacking utility and, hence, legitimacy. The integrity of popular culture was thus threatened in the nineteenth century, as it had been in the seventeenth, by apparently progressive forces. But whereas classical ecclesiastical assaults on superstition had involved a frankly authoritarian assumption of power by an élite, later secular attacks were waged in the name of the people and their interests, in the name of greater freedom and new-found individual integrity. While promising to withdraw power from government and to give it to the individual, radicals of the left and right set out to destroy existing forms of popular thought and expression. They not only attempted to reform the structures of government, but also led an assault on man's freedom by attempting to prescribe his thoughts and feelings.

But was Condorcet's vision realistic rather than idealistic? Did the liberated, confident man whom he celebrated at the end of the *Esquisse* – modern man, as he would have been understood in the nineteenth century – actually exist? Historians have tended to assume that he did – and have therefore been confronted with the problem of explaining the rise of modernism. But even if one discounts the indications that irrationality flourishes in modern culture, the history of psychology suggests that positivistic assumptions about human nature need to be revised. Psychologists, throughout most of the nineteenth century, adopted the assumptions of the philosophers of the Enlightenment about man's nature and ends – namely, that man was instinctively good, as morality was a function of the biological urge to seek pleasure and avoid pain rather than a matter of individual choice; and that education and laws founded on reason, on the correct appreciation of man and his social vocation, would eradicate crime and other aberrations like illness. One of the most categorical statements of this philosophy was made by Cabanis – a friend of Condorcet, of Helvétius' widow, and later of Richerand, Pinel, Antoine Petit and Desgenettes. He influenced pioneers like Bichat and ensured, both through his person and his writings, that the intellectual heritage of the sensationalists left its mark on the premises of nineteenth-century French medicine.[21] Cabanis made the implications of sensationalism clear for the new school of clinical medicine in his *Révolutions et Réformes de la Médecine*, when he wrote:

> . . . Medicine and morality are two branches of the same science, which united form the *science of man*. Each rests on a common basis; the physical knowledge of human nature. They have to find the solution of all their problems in physiology . . . The real source of morality is in the human organisation . . . There, written in indelible characters, by the very hand of nature, are these eternal principles, the sole, solid foundation of our laws and our duties. Equality, liberty, virtue, happiness . . . are mingled in a way with our existence: oppression, iniquitous prejudices, vice, misfortune . . . are the invariable consequence of direct and open blows struck at our nature; of the erosion of the connection established by their common organisation between man and his fellow-men.

The doctor, by defining the order and laws of the individual constitution, furnished the moralist with a factual basis for his ethical and pedagogical prescriptions and the legislator with the knowledge that enabled him to frame laws which were necessarily conducive to public virtue, private happiness and social progress.[22] In this scheme of things, the doctor became, if not the arbiter, then the prophet of public morality and social order; the scope of medicine was extended beyond the pragmatic aim of relieving individual illness to embrace that of establishing allegedly incontestable ethical and political norms. These pretensions were, both in their assumed epistemological status and in their scope, implicitly totalitarian. Yet Cabanis' confidence in human nature was shared by most French psychologists and psychiatrists until the latter part of the century.

The impact of sensationalism on the psychiatric theories of the early nineteenth century was evident in the rejection by Pinel and Esquirol of the nosologies that had hitherto obtained, and in their attempts to attribute mental illnesses to emotional perversion and intellectual vagaries. Pinel, who had studied the English and French philosophers of the eighteenth century as a prelude to his own work, had adopted both their psychological theories and their vocabulary. Accepting the contention that man's behaviour was governed by his fear of pain and desire for pleasure, he believed that madness was caused principally by misdirected and ill-governed feelings and by environment. He saw madness as 'a lesion of some kind in the intellectual and emotional faculties', and the new classification of mental illness, which he established and which was to provide the framework for psychiatry in France for the next fifty years, ascribed characteristic groups of symptoms to isolated intellectual or emotional disorders. Pinel's approach inspired that of his pupil Esquirol, who in turn taught most of the eminent French psychiatrists of the first half of the nineteenth century. '... With mad men,' he wrote, 'feeling is exalted or perverted, their sensations are no longer related either to outward or inward impressions; the ill appear to be playthings of the errors of their senses, of their illusions.'[23] This view was adopted to a greater or lesser extent by many of Esquirol's disciples.[24]

Until the later nineteenth century, emotional life tended to be treated by psychiatrists in a fragmented manner. Under Esquirol and his disciples, as passions were identified as the cause of many mental illnesses, doctors attempted to extirpate feelings and ideas that distorted the individual's behaviour. The definitions of illness thus offered reflected an attitude to the emotions not dissimilar to that of the contemporary Church. The need for moderation, restraint and self-discipline was stressed; the evil effects of over-indulgence and intemperance were exposed. Esquirol deplored the effects of libertinage, excesses and *écarts de régime*.[25] Writer after writer stressed the importance of education. Falret affirmed that 'individuals whose characters have not been formed, who have been left without moral or religious principles, are certainly more exposed to madness than those who enjoy these precious advantages'.[26] In the closing years of the century, some psychiatrists condemned the contemporary aesthetic and intellectual fashion for pessimism and decadence, which they compared to madness, and accounted for it by blaming deficiency of education.

In their preoccupation with the role of passion in generating madness, psychiatrists criticized not only education but social mores too. In trying to explain the greater number of mad women in France and England than in Mediterranean countries, Falret suggested that

> the state of public morals, debauchery, co-habitation without marriage, followed by desertion, poverty, shame, jealousy, in short the condition, at once depraved and unfortunate, of a great number of women in London and Paris explain the predominance of their sex among the mental patients of these two great cities.

The extent of civilization, of well-being, of cultivation as opposed to *abrutissement*, of *bonnes moeurs* rather than immorality, accounted for the variations in the incidence of madness in different societies.[27] In this, Falret was entirely at one with Esquirol who, although he shared many of the intellectual premises of the *idéologues*, was nonetheless socially and politically conservative. Esquirol, to whom the Revolution and its disorders were anathema, had insisted on the deleterious influence of environment on the individual constitution and, through this theory of dependency, his ostensibly medical analyses became a means of social and even political criticism. Madness, according to Esquirol, was of all illnesses that whose dependence on public and private morality was the most evident. In France, political radicalism had undermined the nation's health: 'the ideas of liberty and reform have led minds in France astray, and it is remarkable that the epidemics of madness which have broken out for the last thirty years have taken their character from the different storms which have troubled our country'. Even worse, however, than political extremism in its impact upon public well-being, was the growing irreligion and rapacious individualism of contemporary society:

> For more than thirty years, the changes which have taken place in our morals in France have produced more madness than our political upheavals. We have exchanged our ancient customs, our old opinions for speculative ideas and dangerous innovations. Religious customs are only observed in the most solemn acts of life; no longer does religion bring its consolation and its hope to the unfortunate; religious morals no longer guide reason along the straight and narrow path of life; cold selfishness has dried up all sources of sentiment; there is no longer any familial affection, nor respect, nor love, nor authority, nor any mutual dependence; each man lives for himself alone . . . [28]

In deploring the effects of an unpropitious environment – whether cultural or physical – upon the well-being both of the individual and of society, psychiatrists reinforced the demands of those reformers and politicians who wanted to extend the scope and the nature of political activity to cover such matters as customary belief and behaviour. Education was but one element in this campaign. Building on the precedent set in the

Ancien Régime by their predecessors, who had exercised considerable social authority in time of plague, doctors devoted increasing attention to public hygiene. Their attempts to extirpate contagious illness by introducing public health regulations, however, frequently met with opposition – both from the illiterate poor and from the devotees of liberalism.[29] One of the earliest treatises written on the subject by a member of the clinical school of medicine was unabashed in ascribing to the doctor-legislator a primarily moral purpose – that of converting the unenlightened from their deplorable customs to mores founded on reason and therefore conducive to health and happiness.[30] Fodéré adumbrated themes that were to become popular with psychologists, biologists and subsequently with politicians in the latter half of the century. He discerned in his contemporaries a distressing 'decadence in physical strength'. What was the reason for it? With all the gusto of a seventeenth-century divine, he declared: 'This cause is in us, in our effeminate education, in our passions, in our morals and in our present way of life.' Like conventional psychologists and their clerical predecessors, he laid claim to an authority (in this case, that of scientific fact) which could not be challenged, in his criticism of social customs and private behaviour and his recommendation of changes. 'It is for public authorities to give the impetus', he affirmed; 'they are the soul of the social body, and from its good or bad institutions more or less vigorous generations will issue, generations more or less capable of resisting the destructive action of physical factors and more or less endowed with those magnanimous and generous virtues which are rarely met with in weak and worn-out bodies.'[31] In this scheme, the state had a cardinal role to play in instituting the reign of morality. Furthermore, he stated explicitly the ideas implicit in Cabanis' view of man's nature and behaviour. The equation of health with virtue was the logical consequence of the emphasis laid upon the biological origins of morality; while the individual was inevitably seen as the tributary of the state, when this was understood to be the chief means of realizing the good.

The deprecation of the weak and ill and the criticism of societies whose members tended, really or apparently, to be unhealthy, was taken up later in the century. While Fodéré's assumptions and arguments were implicit in the campaign to change the mores of the country people of France, they were – once they had been developed into more systematic scientific theories after the 1850s[32] – to furnish a pretext for colonialism. The tendency to see the ill as beings whose degradation entailed their rejection by society and deprivation of their ordinary rights was most obvious in psychiatry. Ball exemplified this school of thought when he wrote that the madman, whatever the nature of his affliction,

> has nonetheless fallen from the high dignity of our species; he has lost the essential attributes of humanity: and from the moment he has been marked with the official seal of his fall, he no longer belongs to our common life, he is

> cut off from society, he is beyond the law . . . Beyond the law in everything relating to his individual rights, to his civil capacity and above all to his personal liberty.[33]

This rejection, enacted in the legislation of 1838 governing asylums, was indebted to the materialist tradition which regarded health not only as an ideal but also as a moral norm – a tradition which was strengthened by Morel's studies, in the 1850s and 1860s, into the contribution of heredity and environment to pathological changes in man's constitution.

In 1857, Morel, in his *Traité des Dégénérescences* and again in 1864 in the *Formation du Type dans les Variétés Dégénérées*, introduced the concept of the 'degenerate being', that is, 'a morbid individuality in which are accumulated and distilled the elements which have altered the constitution of his ancestors, interfered with the evolution of their faculties, distorted their tendencies and corrupted their instincts'. Degenerates could be recognized by 'the evil tendencies of some and the depraved instincts of others, the intellectual level on which they can never improve, the impossibility of inventing anything, perfecting anything'.[34] This being was ultimately destined to become extinct. As described by Morel, the degenerate was an updated version, a scientific account, of the medieval monster – the creature whose distorted physique announced his moral depravation and degradation, a being to be feared and rejected. Morel's interest in pathological types had first been excited by the moral decline of contemporary society: madness had become more common and neurosis had spread to the countryside; the suicide and crime rates had increased and the 'monstrous precociousness' of young criminals was alarming; the army often had difficulty in finding healthy conscripts – further evidence of the 'degeneration of the race'. All of these phenomena indicated the development in the human species of a number of 'morbid varieties'.[35] Morel introduced a note of pessimism into medical philosophy by challenging the ideas that man was naturally healthy and that illness could be cured by observing the symptoms and applying the laws governing the healthy constitution, and could be ultimately eradicated by good government. Instead, he postulated the existence of degenerates, people whose illnesses were attributable not to incidental, but to congenital modifications in their organization.

The optimistic premises of classical psychology, which had insisted on the perfection of the norm, were thus gradually undermined in the latter half of the nineteenth century.[36] So, too, its belief in the natural rationality of man, in his level-headed equanimity and self-confidence were lost. In Esquirol's school, isolated sensations, isolated passions and their consequences were observed; but they were not integrated into a complete picture of man's soul, as the assumptions of empirical and utilitarian philosophy about human nature were not questioned. As a result, the nature and formation of the individual personality tended to be overlooked until the 1880s and 1890s, when psychiatrists began to broaden the scope of their investigations. In the 1860s, following the work of Braid on hypnotism, interest in the abnormal states of mind and body that could be induced in healthy people grew and doctors began to investigate the sources of irrationality with the aid of hypnosis. The pioneering work in this field was written by one Dr Liébeault, from Nancy, who was prompted to examine the relation between physical and mental illness by his study of Braid. His conclusions, first published in 1866, laid the foundations of modern psychotherapy.[37] Liébeault decided to hypnotize his patients and, in the course of his experiments, hit upon the phenomenon of selective memory. He was the first psychiatrist to enunciate the theory that unconscious mind held the key to many forms of illness, and that it was possible to communicate with it through suggestion and thereby discover the cause and determine the cure of the disorder. Sleepwalkers could be asked to describe their previous dreams and 'they will remember things forgotten since their awakening and which in fact took place during their earlier trances'. The hypnotized person could always remember episodes of dreams from his previous 'sleep', when the suggestion to do so was made to him. What the conscious mind forgot or had not even seemed to be aware of, the unconscious mind remembered:

> . . . Even if we cannot become fully aware of our memories while awake, there is no reason for affirming that traces of them no longer exist . . . If astonishing feats of memory exist, they are precisely those which refer to what we have perceived almost without realising it and of which we become consciously aware long afterwards . . .[38]

Alfred Maury, in his work on sleep, had already maintained that the unconscious mind revealed in dreams what the conscious mind hid.[39]

Liébeault's originality and historical importance, however, were also evident in his belief that aberrations in conscious behaviour could be explained by unconscious psychic activity.

> There is a singular property of profound sleep, it is that which 'sleepers' have of being obsessed, by means of a suggestion emanating from themselves or from another, with hallucinations, after they awaken, of doing certain things, experiencing organic modifications, etc., without their suspecting the cause of these phenomena. When they want to act, they believe themselves to be free agents, although they are inevitably the playthings of an earlier mental impression.

While many of the illnesses he treated were physical, others were nervous disorders, and, before Charcot, he held that certain paralyses, contractions and spasmodic affections yielded to suggestion. In the place he ascribed to the unconscious mind – in seeing dreams and neuroses as products of its activity and as sources of inspiration, as well as of possible relief of illness – Liébeault anticipated Freud, who studied with and was influenced by Liébeault's disciple, Bernheim, in Nancy. 'Doctors can draw from dreams invaluable clues, from which they can learn not only about developing illnesses, but also about their remedies', Liébeault wrote. He had obeyed the eccentric instructions which his patients had issued to him, with successful results.[40] That many of the patients on whom Liébeault first tried his new therapy were poor country people, at least as familiar with traditional psychological as with conventional clinical medicine, was perhaps not without consequence for some of the forms taken by modern psychiatric treatment.

The study of the role of the unconscious in irrational behaviour only assumed a central place in the history of psychiatry, however, when Charcot turned his attention to the study of hysteria. French medical thought on hysteria had long been dominated by Louyer-Villermay, according to whom hysteria was a disease affecting only women (the corresponding disease in men being held to be hypochondria) and was attributable to inflammation of the womb. Despite the dissent of a number of doctors, from Georget to Briquet, it was only when Charcot examined the problem that Louyer-Villermay's theories were finally discarded.[41] Charcot argued that hysteria was a hereditary disease to be observed both in men and women. From 1878 on, he studied the syndrome through hypnosis – a state which, he believed, could be induced only in hysterics – and he described in detail the attacks of hysteria which he witnessed in the course of his investigations. The *grand attaque hystérique* – the grand model from which other forms of hysterical attack were derived – was, by Charcot's own admission, theatrical: after two preliminary stages, the attack proper started with the *période épileptoïde*, which was characterized by muscular spasms; this was followed by the *période de clownisme*, during which the hysteric adopted peculiar or obsessive poses, gave displays of acrobatics, struggled with imaginary beings and shouted; after this, came the *période d'attitudes passionnelles*, in which the patient had hallucinations and then acted out a scene, which was usually morbid and violent; finally, the last phase was characterized by delirium, cramps and distorting grimaces.[42]

Charcot's theories were developed by his pupil Paul Richer, in his monumental *Etudes Cliniques sur l'Hystéro-Epilepsie ou Grande Hystérie*, published in 1881. In this study, Richer elaborated on the importance of traumatic experiences and anxiety in the disease, suggesting that these both determined and were revealed by hysteria. In the initial stages of the disorder, the hysteric was unable to concentrate on his work, as he was overwhelmed by unhappy memories and greatly upset by minor difficulties in his daily life. In the third phase of the *grande attaque*, according to Richer,

> passionate attacks, besides scenes of pure imagination, most often reproduced the events which, by the vivid impression stamped on the mind of the patient, had caused the first attacks. These scenes . . . reappear at each attack, without ever losing their intensity and are expressed by gestures attitudes and words which never vary.

This re-enactment of a painful memory was followed, in the fourth phase, by the delirium which 'draws its theme from the patient's everyday impressions and from the preoccupations of his heart and mind'. In this phase, when the hysteric had lost all self-control, 'the patient reveals . . . sometimes his most secret thoughts and . . . communicates his best hidden plans'. Richer described the theatrical element of the illness and the cure, emphasizing the doctor's ability to provoke in his hypnotized patients certain symptoms, similar to those triggered off by touching the 'hysterogeneous zones' in other patients.[43]

The performances described by Charcot and Richer bear striking resemblances to the institutionalized, ritual hysteria associated with popular medicine in parts of Africa and South America and observed by anthropologists. Nonetheless, in stressing the importance of gaining access to the unconscious mind, where traumatic memories continued to fester, in emphasizing the importance of self-revelation, Charcot and Richer anticipated some of the main themes of psychoanalysis. Their method of communicating with the disturbed person also recalled – as they to some extent realized – earlier techniques, as revealed in the provoked dreams in classical antiquity or the witchcraft trials of the sixteenth and seventeenth centuries. The fact these attacks were shown by Charcot's pupil Babinski to have been stimulated by suggestion, thereby discrediting theories based on them, does not diminish Charcot's importance. For not only did his studies awaken interest in the field of neuro-psychiatry, but they also reinforced the link between traditional and modern psychiatric therapies. Hypnosis or suggestion, which Charcot first had the idea of introducing to the investigation of hysteria, was supposed to enable the doctor to impose his will on his patient, whereas in fact it was a device which allowed the patient to disclaim responsibility for what he did or said. The analogy with seventeenth-century witchcraft cases did not escape Richer and other psychiatrists, although at first they did not realize the implications of their discovery. Suggestions legitimized the patient's behaviour, as did the allegation of sorcery or diabolical possession, permitting him to act out his revolt, fatigue or resentment. Similarly, exorcism, a visit to a miraculous fountain or to a doctor like Bernheim gave the neurotic a pretext for recovery, relieved him, at least apparently, of some of the pressures of life and of the impulses provoked by this illness.

On the other hand, there was a significant difference between attending a psychiatrist and being cured by a miracle or exorcism. The latter vindicated the victim, reintegrated him into society, having absolved him of guilt and demonstrated the sympathetic favour of God for him. The psychiatrist of the old school, however, pointed to the deficiencies of the patient's physical and moral constitution, and frankly attempted to impose his will and society's norms upon his recalcitrant victim. Not surprisingly, psychiatry failed to meet with popular enthusiasm until it had concocted theories which denied the individual's responsibility for his neurosis and blamed his maladjustment on his family and society. In the first place, Charcot had unwittingly hit upon the importance of providing the patient with an opportunity of acting out his complaint (almost theatrical performances were characteristic of some traditional therapies). Charcot, Liébeault and their disciples, Richer and Bernheim realized that the patient's feelings were of great importance in ensuring his recovery and that precisely the same mechanism (namely suggestion) which had raised the curtain on the performance could also mark the end of the act. 'To provoke through hypnotism this special psychic state and exploit the suggestibility thus artificially inflamed for the purposes of curing or healing, such is the role of psycho-therapeutic hypnosis', wrote Bernheim.[44] Subsequently, Gilles de la Tourette and Janet were to explore this avenue of research, the latter with some notable successes. Developing on this work, Janet saw dreams, delirium and the somnambulism of hysteria as manifestations of the subconscious, involving memory of traumatic past events, which the ill person had consciously forgotten. He used hypnosis as a therapeutic method, believing that if the patient became conscious of the initial cause of his disorder, he could be cured – and in this, Janet anticipated Freud.[45]

By the end of the nineteenth century, then, the Enlightenment's confidence in the essential rationality and natural virtue of man had been shaken, and psychiatry was ready to present man to the world, with great success, as an irrational creature who could only with difficulty know himself. Psychology revealed man not so much as the conquerer of nature but as being beset by anxiety and uncertainty, sometimes overwhelmed by the strangeness of the world. Seconded by art and literature, it proposed a picture of man different from that espoused by the Enlightenment.[46] In this view, arguably more contemporary than the positivistic one usually adopted by historians, man is indeed a creature of instinct, governed not by reason but by his primitive urges and feelings. The history of the twentieth century has tended both to confirm the contention that man is more irrational, that instinct is more central to his behaviour and fantasy more important to him than the heroic rationalists realized, and to lend weight to their belief that it would be better for him if rationality and tolerance played a greater role in human affairs. While the philosophers of the Enlightenment, particularly its earlier representatives like Voltaire and Montesquieu, were right to stress the importance of rational analysis, of scepticism, doubt and independent criticism – right to emphasize their role in intellectual and social progress and their contribution to individual liberty and dignity – it is far from clear that the later elaborations of these essentially pragmatic attitudes into a form of systematic utopianism, which idealized both man and the state, represented an equally beneficial addition to the sum of human knowledge.

Notes

Notes to Chapter I

1. Lecky, *Rationalism in Europe* (London, 1893), I, pp.141–2.
2. F. Boulard, *Premiers Itinéraires en Sociologie Religieuse* (Paris, 1966), p.48.
3. Le Bras, 'Les Transformations Religieuses', *Année Sociologique* (1937), pp.41–3.
4. J. Ferté, *La Vie Religieuse . . . 1622–1645* (Paris, 1962), pp.274, 372.
5. L. Pérouas, *Le Diocèse de la Rochelle de 1648 à 1724* (Paris, 1964), pp.176–7.
6. M. Vovelle, *Piété Baroque et Déchristianisation en Provence au XVIIIe siècle* (Paris, 1973), pp.610–14.
7. Cf. Boulard, *op. cit.*, p.50.
8. Y. H. Hilaire, 'La Pratique Religieuse en France de 1815 à 1878', *Info. Hist.* (March–April 1963), pp.57b–65b. Cf. also Boulard, *op. cit.*, pp. 44–7. Pataut, *Sociologie Electorale de la Nièvre* (Paris, 1956), pp.61–9. *Le Bourbonnais. Terre Chrétienne?* (Moulins, 1965), pp.12aff. Huot-Pleuroux, *La Vie Chrétienne dans le Doubs* (Besançon, 1966), pp.43–85. F. L. Charpin, *Pratique Religieuse . . . Marseille, 1806–1958* (Paris, 1962), pp.60–154. *Charente, 1966. Terre de Chrétienté* (n.p.d.), pp.7, 14–27.
9. Boulard, *op. cit.*, p.44 n.2, and map of ordinations per diocese, 1830–1950, p.46.
10. Cf. Boulard, *La Pratique Religieuse Urbaine* (Paris, 1968), map. G. Le Bras, 'Pratique Religieuse' in *Villes et Campagnes*, ed. G. Friedmann (Paris, 1953), p.290.
11. Boulard, *Pratique . . . Urbaine*, p.110.
12. *Ibid.*, pp.35–72. Verscheure, *Aspects Sociologiques* (Lille, 1961), pp.173–5, 282.
13. Pin, 'Religion et Passage d'une Civilisation Pré-industrielle', in *Essais de Sociologie Religieuse* (Paris, 1966), p.237. *Charente, Terre de Chrétienté?* pp.22–30. *Bourbonnais. Terre Chrétienne* (1965), pp.15–16; Pataut, *op. cit.*, p.68. Marcilhacy, *Diocèse d'Orléans* (Paris, 1964), pp. 214–16.
14. Cf. Cholvy, *Géographie Religieuse et l'Hérault* (1968), p.17. Sevrin, 'Sacrements', *RHEF* (1939), p.327. Marcilhacy, *Diocèse d'Orléans* (1964), pp.214–16. Boulard, 'La pratique religieuse en France, 1802–1939: les Pays de Loire', *Annales* (July–August 1976), pp.774, 779, 785.
15. Boulard, *Pratique . . . Urbaine*, p.107. Boulard, *Premiers Itinéraires*, p.49. Le Bras, 'Transformations', *Année Sociologique* (1937), pp.41–2.
16. Charpin, *op. cit.*, p.61. Pataut, *op. cit.*, pp.64–5.
17. Boulard, 'La pratique religieuse', pp.797–9.
18. Boulard, *Pratique . . . Urbaine*, pp.74–6. Pin, *op. cit.*, pp.242, 245–52.
19. Huot-Pleuroux, *op. cit.*, pp.62–3. *Bourbonnais, Terre Chrétienne* (1965), p.14a, for similar observation.
20. Le Bras, *L'Eglise et le Village* (Paris, 1976), p.186.
21. J. Delumeau, *Le Catholicisme entre Luther et Voltaire* (Paris, 1971), pp.192–330. Le Nobletz found Léon to all intents and purposes pagan in the seventeenth century.

The Lazarists in the area of Montauban in the later seventeenth century were hardly less disedified by the local people. Cf. Boulard, *Premiers Itinéraires*, p.54 n.17.
22. Le Bras, *L'Eglise et le Village* (Paris, 1976), pp.191–2.
23. Monnier and Vingtrinier, *Croyances et Traditions Populaires* (1874), pp.117–21. That 'advanced' (or socialist) political doctrines and religious indifference in no way attenuated superstitious beliefs and practices is demonstrated in the case of the Allier in both the nineteenth and the twentieth centuries.
24. Cf. Pierrard, *La Vie Ouvrière à Lille sous le Second Empire* (Paris, 1965), pp.114–15, 363–6. Lack of time and poverty (not having enough money for masses and ceremonies of 'rites of passage', for decent clothes for Sunday mass), fear of public opinion were among the factors which accounted for the very low rates of attendance at formal religious ceremonies.
25. Cavalier, *Croyance aux Sortilèges* (Montpellier, 1868), pp.220, 189, 207, 210. Cholvy, *op. cit.*, p.17.
26. Graulle, *Traditions et Médecine Populaire en Bourbonnais* (Montpellier University, PhD Thesis, 1963), pp.237, 234ff. Cf. Leproux, *Médicine, Magie et Sorcellerie* (Paris, 1954). Leproux, *Dévotions et Saints Guérisseurs* (Paris, 1957).
27. Ganachaud, *Mémoires d'un Paysan Charentais* (Angoulême, 1946), p.87.
28. Miron, *Le Prêtre et le Sorcier* (Paris, 1872), p.40.
29. E. Sevrin, 'Croyances Populaires et Médecine Supranaturelle', RHEF (1946), p.272.
30. Le Braz, 'Les Saints Bretons', *Annales de Bretagne* (1897), p.89; 'Les Saints Bretons', *Annales de Bretagne* (1893), pp.38–9. Sébillot, *Petite Légende Dorée*, (Nantes, 1897), pp.83–4.
31. Le Braz, 'Les Saints Bretons', *Annales de Bretagne* (1893), pp.49–50.
32. E. Sevrin, 'Croyances Populaires et Médecine Supranaturelle', RHEF (1946), pp.273–4.
33. E. Souvestre, *Les Derniers Bretons* (Paris, 1971, facs. of the 1854 edn), p.94.
34. J. Cambry, *Voyage dans le Finistère* (Paris, 1838), p.18A. Cf. also Quénot, *Statistique du Département de la Charente* (Paris, Angoulême, 1818), p.327.
35. *Dragon Rouge* (1896), pp.100ff. Self-styled sorcerers used it, cf. below, pp.165–71, 179–81.
36. A. Van Gennep, *Le Folklore de la Flandre et Du Hainaut* (Paris, 1934), II, pp.634–5.
37. Gagnon, *Folklore Bourbonnais* (Moulins, 1968), III, pp.21–2.
38. C. Nisard, *Histoire des Livres Populaires* (Paris, 1864), I, pp.312–14. Nisard included a prayer to Cupid for the same purpose.
39. C. Mensignac, 'Notice sur les superstitions...', *Bull. Soc. Anthrop. Bordeaux et Sud-Ouest* (1887), pp.250–51. He also cotes an analogous litany, which girls in a village in the centre of France said for husbands. Cf. also R. Lecotté, *Cultes Populaires* (Paris, 1953), pp.271–2. This version has been copied down in Meaux in 1944, and also figured, according to Lecotté, in Raban's *Catholicisme à l'usage des Grandes Filles* (Paris, 1848).
40. Sauvé, *Folklore des Hautes-Vosges* (Paris, 1889), pp.287–8.
41. Lecoeur, *Esquisses du Bocage Normand* (Condé-sur-Noireau, 1887), II, pp.111, 116. R. Kaufmann, *Pratiques et Superstitions Médicales en Poitou* (Paris, University, medical thesis, 1906), pp.43–4. Westphalen, *Petit Dictionnaire... Traditions Messines* (Metz, 1934), p.8. Cf. Leproux, *Dévotions et Saints Guérisseurs* (Paris, 1957), pp.222–53. Lecotté, *Cultes Populaires* (Paris, 1953), p.201.
42. L. F. Sauvé, *Lavarou Koz* (Paris, 1878), p.139.
43. P. Parfait, *Dossier des Pèlerinages* (Paris, 1877), pp.146–8. Miron, *Le Prêtre et le Sorcier* (Paris, 1872), p.285. Moret, *Histoire de Saint Menoux* (Moulins, 1907), p.58. Morin and Maison, 'Pèlerinages', RTP (1901), p.209. Bouteiller, *Chamanisme* (Paris, 1950), p.222. Ristelhuber, 'S. Antoine en Alsace', *La Tradition* (Paris, 1892), p.92. Laisnel de la Salle, *Croyances et Légendes* (Paris, 1875), I, 326–30.

44. Huyttens, *Etudes sur les moeurs... de la Flandre Orientale* (Gand, 1861), pp.78–9. Cambry, *Finistère*, p.98a. Habasque, *Notions Historiques... des Côtes-du-Nord* (Saint-Brieuc, 1832), I, p.307, n.1.
45. Sauvé, 'Charmes, oraisons et conjurations magiques de la Basse Bretagne', *Revue Celtique* (1883–5), p.77.
46. Some examples of such prayers are given in Michel, 'Un Petit Formulaire', *Connaître* (1948), p.22b. They were taken down from a person 'who knew how', around the turn of the century. Cf. Graulle, 'Médecine Populaire et Guérison Magico-Religieuse', *Arts et Traditions Populaires* (1963), p.107, for prayers heard in the canton of Huriel (Allier), some derived from the *Médecin des Pauvres*.
47. Pris, 'Carnet de Prières Magiques', *Bull. Folk. Ile-de-France* (1953), pp.488a–9a.
48. Laisnel de la Salle, *Croyances et Légendes* (Paris, 1895), p.I, p.327. Cf. also Janvrais, 'Offrandes aux Saints', RTP (1895), pp.178.
49. L. Sauvé, 'Charmes, oraisons et conjurations magiques', *Revue Celtique* (1883–5), p.76. Cf. also for other examples of practicality, Luce, *Bull. Soc. Archéo. Gers.* (1955), p.329. *Médecin des Pauvres*, p.4, n.1. Drouillet, *Folklore du Nivernais* (1964), IV, p.146.
50. Sauvé, 'Charmes, oraisons', *Revue Celtique* (1883–5), p.76.
51. Steib, 'Copie d'un Livret... ', *Revue de Folklore Français et Colonial* (1939), p.26.
52. Sauvé, *Folklore des Hautes Vosges* (1889), p.209.
53. Sevrin, 'Croyances Populaires et Médecine Supranaturelle en Eure-et-Loire au XIXe siècle', RHEF (1946), p.272. Cf., too, Andree, *Über Votiv- und Weihegaben...* (1904), p.8. Gabriel Le Bras largely agreed. The primacy of these material considerations, he contended, was illustrated by the fact that during the Terror, when they married and died without the help of the Church, peasants would ask priests in hiding to bless their fields and their animals at night. Cf. Le Bras, *L'Eglise et le Village* (Paris, 1976), pp.182–3.
54. Miron, *Le Prêtre et le Sorcier*, pp.54–5.
55. Srowski, 'Le Caractère Breton dans le culte des morts... ', *Revue Psychol. des Peuples* (1948), p.377.
56. Stany-Gautier, 'Les Saints Bretons', *Arts et Traditions Populaires* (1953), pp.311 n.3, 314, 317–19.
57. Ristelhuber, 'S. Antoine en Alsace', *Tradition* (1892), p.92. Du Broc de Segange, *Les Saints Patrons des Corporations* (Paris, 1887), pp.53–4.
58. M. Hahnloser, 'Du Culte de l'Image au Moyen Age', in *Cristanesimo e Ragione de Stato*, ed. E. Castelli (Rome, 1952), pp.225–6. P. Sébillot, 'Superstitions Iconographiques', RTP (1886), pp.18, 21. Droüart, *Les Saints Guérisseurs...* (Rennes, 1939), n.p., for a woman who used to converse with a statue. R. Lecotté, *Les Cultes Populaires* (Paris, 1953), p.199.
59. P. Sébillot, *Le Folklore de France* (Paris, 1907), IV, pp.161, 165.
60. Droüart, *Les Saints Guérisseurs* (Rennes, 1939), n.p..
61. P. Saintyves, *En Marge de la Légende Dorée* (Paris, 1930), p.514.
62. Miron, *op. cit.*, pp. 142–5 (faulty pagination in original).
63. Sébillot, *Petite Légende Dorée* (1897), pp.65–6.
64. Sébillot, 'Superstitions Iconographiques', RTP (1887), p.23.
65. Lecotté, *Cultes Populaires* (Paris, 1953), p.199.
66. Lecotté, *Cultes Populaires*, p.199. Sébillot, *Petite Légende Dorée*, p.180. Cauvin, 'La Médecine Populaire en Provence' (Lyons University, medical thesis, 1930), pp.71–2. Droüart, *Les Saints Guérisseurs* (Rennes, 1939), n.p.
67. M. Bouteiller, *Sorciers et Jeteurs de Sorts* (Paris, 1958), pp.204–5. Popular saints in North Africa were no better – causing tempests, turning their enemies into stone, indulging in vindictive mutual rivalry. Cf. E. Dermenghem, *Le Culte des Saints dans l'Islam Maghrébin* (5th edn, Paris, 1954), pp.11–17.
68. Leproux, *Dévotions et Saints Guérisseurs* (1957), p.81. R. Kaufman, 'Pratiques

et Superstitions Médicales en Poitou' (Paris University, medical thesis, 1906), p.46. L. Morin, 'La bonne femme qui tire les saints', RTP (1895), p.599.

69. *Gazette des Tribunaux* (21 March 1828), p.530b.
70. A. S. Miron, *Le Prêtre et le Sorcier* (Paris, 1872), pp.171–3.
71. Dr A. Sallet, 'Une rancune de saint dans le diocèse de Toulouse', *Revue de Folklore Français et Colonial* (1935), V, p.42.
72. Sébillot, *Le Folklore de France* (Paris, 1907), IV, pp.166–8. Sébillot, *Le Paganisme Contemporain* (Paris, 1908), pp.247, 280, 285. S. Trébucq, *La Chanson Populaire* (Bordeaux, 1912), I, pp.300–1. F. Pérot, *Folklore du Bourbonnais* (Paris, 1908), p.104. Cambry, *Finistère* (Paris, 1838), p.150a. Collin de Plancy, *Dictionnaire Critique des Reliques* (Paris, 1821), I, p.430.
73. Lecotté, *Cultes Populaires* (Paris, 1953), pp.199–200.
74. J. Michelet, *Histoire de France* (Paris, 1881), II, p.90. Le Bras, *L'Eglise et le Village* (Paris, 1976), p.267.
75. Colson, 'Saints et Idoles Châtiés', *La Tradition* (1892), p.115.
76. Laisnel de la Salle, *Souvenirs du Vieux Temps* (Paris, 1900), I, p.408. E. Souvestre, *Les Derniers Bretons* (Paris, 1971), p.92. Jobbé-Duval, *Les Idées Primitives dans la Bretagne Contemporaine* (Paris, 1910), part I, p.81.
77. Sébillot, *Le Paganisme Contemporain* (Paris, 1908), pp.150–51. Foix, *Sorcières et Loups-Gaous* (Auch, 1904), p.62. Mensignac, *Notice sur les superstitions* (Bordeaux, 1888), pp.84–5. Cf. also Westphalen, *Petit Dictionnaire des Traditions Populaires Messines* (Metz, 1934), p.14, for same belief.
78. Rocal, *Le Vieux Périgord* (Toulouse, 1927), p.54.
79. Laborde, 'Les Brouches (sorcières) en Béarn, Gascogne et le pays basque', *Revue Historique et Archéologique du Béarn et du Pays Basque* (1935), p.287. Mensignac, *Notice sur les superstitions* (1888), pp.84–5. Rocal, *Le Vieux Périgord* (1927), p.57.
80. G. Cauvin, *Médecine Populaire en Provence* (Lyons University, medical thesis, 1930), p.70. Foix, *Sorcières et Loups-Garous dans les Landes*, p.63. E. Genab, 'Messes Singulières', RTP (1895), p.231.
81. P. Sébillot, *Le Paganisme Contemporain* (Paris, 1908), p.150, n.4. Cf. RTP (1907), p.245. Usually, however, peasants tried to hide their intentions from the priest, Sébillot affirms.
82. Sébillot, *Le Paganisme Contemporain* (Paris, 1908), pp.149–50. Jobbé-Duval, *Les Idées Primitives* (1910), Part I, p.65. Habasque, *Notions Historiques... des Côtes du Nord* (Saint-Brieuc, 1832), I, p.88, n.1.
83. Jobbé-Duval, *Les Idées Primitives* (1910), part I, pp.8–9. According to legend, the rector who evicted the statue was killed by the saint. Cf. Le Braz, *Au Pays des Pardons* (Paris, 1901), pp.22–3.
84. Jobbé-Duval, *Les Idées Primitives* (1910), part I, pp.52 n.2, 53–5. Le Braz, *La Légende de la Mort en Basse-Bretagne* (Paris, 1893), p.222 n.2. Cf. also Le Braz, *Au Pays des Pardons* (Paris, 1901), pp.18–20. E. Harmonic, 'Adjurations et Conjurations: I. A Saint Yves', RTP (1888), pp. 139–41.
85. Cf. below, pp.207–10.
86. Sevrin, 'Croyances Populaires', RHEF (1946), p.303.
87. Marcilhacy, *Diocèse d'Orléans au Milieu du XIXe Siècle* (Paris, 1964), pp.372–3.
88. Sevrin, 'Croyances Populaires', RHEF (1946), pp.299–300.
89. Lemoine, 'La Sorcellerie Contemporaine', *La Tradition* (1892), pp.108–9.
90. Séguin, *Nouvelles à Sensation* (Paris, 1959), p.132. S. Thompson, ed., *Motif-Index of Folk Literature* (Bloomington, Indiana, 1935), V, pp.140, 144, 152–4, 356.
91. Bernoni, *Preghiere Popolari Veneziane* (Venice, 1873), p.18, n.1.
92. Cf. Dambielle, *La Socellerie en Gascogne* (Auch, 1907), p.28. Dubois, *Anciens Livres de Colportage en Sologne* (Romarantin, 1936), p.19. R. Romain, *Souvenirs d'une Enfant Pauvre* (Paris, 1866).
93. *Histoire du Juif Errant* (Clermont-Ferand, 1850), pp.2–3.

94. Ladoucette, *Hist. Topo.... des H. Alpes* (3rd edn, Paris, 1848), p.595.
95. Van Haudenard, 'Le Juif Errant', *Folklore Brabançon* (1929), p.319.
96. U. Rouchon, *La Vie Paysanne dans la Haute-Loire* (rpr. Paris, 1977), III, pp.117–20.
97. *Ibid*, p.114.
98. Told in 1878 in Picardy. Carnoy, *Litt. Orale Picardie* (Paris, 1883), pp.138–9.
99. Thompson affirms that numerous stories concerning the wandering of Christ and Saint Peter were originally medieval *exempla*. Cf. S. Thompson, *The Folktale* (Berkeley, London, 1977), pp.149–50.
100. Vinson, *Folklore du Pays Basque* (Paris, 1883), p.4.
101. F.-M. Luzel, *Légendes Chrétiennes de la Basse Bretagne* (Paris, 1881), I, pp.14–16.
102. *Ibid*, I, pp.17–19.
103. Gagnon, *Folklore Bourbonnais* (Moulins, 1968), III, 92.
104. Luzel, *Légendes Chrétiennes* (1881), I, pp.9–13.
105. Harou, 'Le Bon Dieu et S. Pierre', *La Tradition* (1892), pp.316–18.
106. Bladé, *Contes Populaires recueillis en Agenais* (Agen, 1874), pp.59–60.
107. Bladé, 'Le Voyage de Notre Seigneur écrit sous la dictée de Mme Lacroix', in *Contes Populaires* (Paris, 1874), pp.63–4.
108. Dardy, *Anthologie Pop. d'Albret* (Agen, 1891), I, pp.9–11.
109. Leproux, *Dévotions et Saints Guérisseurs* (Paris, 1957), pp.iii, xvi, n.1.
110. Carols seem to have developed in the fifteenth century, when mystery plays were forbidden. They spread from Maine, Poitou and Anjou to become popular throughout France. Cf. J. Delumeau, *La Mort des Pays de Cocagne* (Paris, 1976), pp.57–8. Cerquand, *L'Imagerie et la Littérature Populaire...* (Avignon, 1883), pp.30–31.
111. Mandrou, *La Culture Populaire* (2nd edn, Paris, 1975), pp.89–90.
112. Gagnon, *Folklore Bourbonnais* (Moulins, 1968), III, p.137. Carols were popular from the early eighteenth century on; children went around the town of Moulins singing them and collecting clothes and logs: the custom was prohibited in 1866 by a municipal decree, pp.134–5. Cf. also C. Richelet, ed., *Noëls Nouveaux* (n.d.p), p.14. Trébucq, *La Chanson Populaire* (Bordeaux, 1912), I, p.160.
113. Gagnon, *Folklore Bourbonnais*, III, p.139.
114. In carols from the Haute-Loire, the angel also talks in French and the shepherds in dialect. The latter, in a version heard at Saint-Jean-de-Nay, are sceptical about the angel's news. Cf. Rouchon, *La Vie Paysanne dans la Haute-Loire* (Paris, 1977), III, p.198.
115. J. Cénac-Moncaut, *Littérature Populaire de la Gascogne* (Paris, 1868), pp.255–66. Cf. also Cusacq, *Le Folklore des Landes* (Bayonne 1949), pp.134, 137–8, who maintains that medieval plays were still given in the early nineteenth century, in this area. The Christmas scene was acted in church for one of the last times at Rosampère, at Christmas in 1882.
116. S. Trébucq, *La Chanson Populaire et la Vie Rurale* (Bordeaux, 1912), I, p.163.
117. Pérot, 'Contributions au Folklore Bourbonnais', *Les Cahiers du Centre* (April-May 1912), pp.109–10.
118. Gagnon, *Folklore Bourbonnais* (Moulins, 1968), III, 139–41.
119. In nineteenth century limousin dialect, 'sau' meant salt; the *gabelle* may therefore be intended here.
120. S. Trébucq, *La Chanson Populaire et la Vie Rurale*, I, p.166.
121. J. Lecoeur, *Esquisses du Bocage Normand* (Condé-sur-Noireau, 1887), II, pp.126–5 (pages reversed). Cf. also L. Desaivre, *Les Chants Populaires des Rois, ou l'Epiphanie en Poitou au XIXe siècle* (Saint Maixent, 1888), pp.23–6. Cf. an account of the Passion sung by the *crécelleurs* of the *pays messin*, which adopted a similarly sanguinary tone. Westphalen, *Petit Dictionnaire des traditions populaires messines* (Metz, 1934), p.150.
122. Lecoeur, *Esquisses du Bocage Normand*, II, pp. 173–5. Westphalen, *Petit Dictionnaire des Traditions Populaires*, p.150.

123. Cf. Souvestre, *Les Derniers Bretons* (Paris, 1971), pp.165–9, who gives good examples. Also Caméliat, 'Deux Prières Populaires', *Mélusine* (1900–1), pp.79–81.
124. Luzel, *Légendes Chrétiennes de la Basse-Bretagne* (Paris, 1881), I, pp.80, 82.
125. Carnoy, *Littérature Orale de la Picardie* (Paris, 1883), p.47. Laisnel de la Salle, *Souvenirs*, I, pp.147–54. Luzel, 'L'Enfant qui fut à l'école', *Annales de Bretagne* (1894), pp.271–6, 409–415.
126. Cf. A. Maury, *op. cit.*, pp.168–9; E. Mâle, *The Gothic Image* (London, 1961), pp.355–83; J.-M. Charcot and P. Richer, *Les Démoniaques dans l'Art* (Paris, 1887), p.x; P. Saintyves, *En Marge de la L0egende Dorée* (Paris, 1931), p.160.
127. Nisard, *Histoire des Livres Populaires* (Paris, 1864), I, pp.90–97, for a reproduction.
128. Cf. also L'Abbé Lenglet Dufresnoy, *Receuil de Dissertations Anciennes et Nouvelles* (Avignon, 1752), I, pp.xxv–xxxiv; Collin de Plancy, *Le Diable Peint par lui-même* (Paris, 1825), pp.161–2.
129. F. Villon, 'Ballade que Villon Feist à la Resqueste de sa mère pour prier Nostre Dame', in *Oeuvres*, ed. A. Longon (Paris, 1968), pp.40–41.
130. Cambry, *Finistère* (Paris, 1838), p.48a.
131. A.N. F19 5555. 102. Report of 28 May 1819.
132. Baderot, *L'Influence du Milieu sur le Délire Religieux* (Paris University, medical thesis, 1897), pp.20–21.
133. Le Bras, *L'Eglise et le Village* (Paris, 1977), p.260.
134. Cf. Souvestre, *Les Derniers Bretons*, pp.25, 27–30. Buron, *La Bretagne Catholique* (1856), p.211, affirms that the *curé* and his flock went to the cemetery on 1 Nov., where the priest engaged skulls in dialogue. A. Bouët, *Breiz Izel* (1918), pp.110–11.
135. Guyard, *Analyse des Sermons du Père Guyon* (Le Mans, 1829), pp.69–70.
136. Anon, *Mission à Romans* (Valence, 1821), pp.6–7.
137. Germain, *Parler du Salut* (Paris, 1968), p.527. Cf. also for typical themes, Marcilhacy, *Diocèse d'Orléans au Milieu du XIXe Siècle* (Paris, 1964), p.248. Germain, *op. cit.*, pp.66–71, 104.
138. Anon. *Passeport pour l'Eternité* (1821), n.p.
139. Daniel, *Mission à Coutances* (1821), p.29.
140. Guyard, *Analyse des Sermons du Père Guyon* (Le Mans, 1829), p.173.
141. Guyard, *op. cit.*, p.177.
142. Cf. Daniel, *op. cit.*, pp.66–7.
143. *Ibid*, p.16.
144. E. Sevrin, *Missions Religieuses en France* (Paris, 1959), III, p.274.
145. A.N. F19 5555. 40.
146. A.N. F19 5556.
147. Germain, *op. cit.*, p.71.
148. Leuret, *Fragmens Psychologiques* (Paris, 1834), pp.398–9.
149. Ball, 'Folie Religieuse', *Revue Scientifique* (1882), p.339b. Nagaty, *Contribution à la Folie Religieuse* (Paris University, medical thesis, 1885), p.65.
150. Sevrin, *Missions* (Paris, 1948), I, p.187.
151. Sevrin, *Missions* (Paris, 1948), I, pp.283–4.
152. A.N. F19 5555. 62. Ice was another form of punishment in hell.
153. Marcilhacy, *Diocèse d'Orléans au Milieu du XIXe Siècle*, pp.213–14.
154. Dardy, *Anthologie d'Albret*, I, p.341.
155. C. Gagnon, *Le Folklore Boubonnais*, iii, p.9.
156. Cf. Pérot, 'Incantations', RTP (1903), p.302. Dardy, *Anthologie d'Albret*, I, p.339. Leproux, *Dévotions et Saints Guérisseurs* (Paris, 1957), p.24, says it was very common in the Confolentais and surrounding provinces, and existed in the Limousin and the Vendée also.
157. Caméliat, 'Prières Populaires', *Mélusine* (1899–1900), p.50. Cf. also Dardy,

Anthologie d'Albret, I, p.341. In 1885, a version of Dardy's prayer was also known in the Ruffecoix, cf. Leproux, *Dévotions*, p.23.

158. Gagnon, *Le Folklore Boubonnais*, III, pp.14–16. Cf. also Berriat-Saint Prix, *Vieilles Prières*, pp.15–17.

159. J. Berriat-Saint-Prix, *Vieilles Prières* (1906), pp.15–17. He traces it to the *Clef du Paradis* published in Clermont-Ferrand shortly after 1763. The *Clef du Paradis* also figures in Baudot's catalogue. Cf. also A. Assier, *La Bibliothèque Bleue depuis Jean Oudot* (Paris, 1874), p.28. The version Berriat-Saint-Prix found had changed the French of the original into local dialect, which suggests that the *Bibliothèque Bleue* influenced the imaginative world of the rural poor.

160. Abbé J.-B. Thiers, *Traité de Superstitions* (1733–6), pp.218ff.

161. Cf. Foix, *Poésie Populaire Landaise* (1902), p.7b. Favraud, 'Prières Populaires du Poitou', *Mélusine* (1884), pp.286–7.

162. Leproux, *Dévotions et Saint Guérisseurs*, pp.12–13, 21, 32. Cf. also Jalby, *Sorcellerie* (1974), p.107. A number of short colloquial versions of the prayer – known as the *Pigeon Blanc* – were said throughout France for the repose of the souls of the dead. Cf. J. Berriat-Saint-Prix, *Vieilles Prières*, p.11. M. Bouteiller, *Médecine Populaire* (1966), p.93, gives a version of it, which a ninety-four-year-old man recited at bedtime.

163. Gagnon, *Folklore Bourbonnais*, III, pp.16–17, affirms that many sorcerers knew it but notes that some variations were derived from manuals of popular devotion.

164. Lancelin, *La Sorcellerie des Campagnes* (1911), p.67.

165. Leproux, *Dévotions et Saint Guérisseurs*, p.15.

166. Cf. Rocal, *Le Vieux Périgord* (1927), p.224. According to Rocal, a sorcerer from Premilhec, called to the death-bed of an old man, recited the *patenôtre blanche*.

167. Juge, *Changemens* (1817), p.129. Both he and Leproux date this prayer to the eighth century. Cf. Leproux, *op. cit.*, p.15.

> Que Dieu fit, que Dieu dit, que Dieu mit en paradis. Au soir m'allant coucher, je trouvis trois anges en mon lit couchis, un aux pieds, deux au chevet, la bonne Vierge Marie au milieu, qui me dit, que je m'y couchis, que rien ne doutis. Le bon Dieu est mon père, la bonne Vierge ma mère, les trois Apôtres sont mes frères, les trois Vierges sont mes soeurs. La chemise où Dieu est né, mon corps en est enveloppé. La croix de Sainte Marguerite, en ma poitrine est ecrite. Madame s'en va sur le champ à Dieu pleurant, recontrit monsieur Saint Jean, d'où venez? je viens de loin. Vous n'avez pas vu le bon Dieu? Si est, il est en l'arbre de la croix, les pieds pendans, les mains clouées; un petit chapeau d'épine blanche sur la tête. Qui le *Verbe à Dieu* saura, sur la planche passera, au bout de la planche s'assoira. Qui le dira trois fois au soir, trois fois au matin gagnera le Paradis à la fin'.

168. Leproux, *Dévotions et Saints Guérisseurs*, p.16. Lancelin, *La Sorcellerie de Campagnes*, p.67. Gagnon, *Folklore Bourbonnais*, III, pp.16–17. Cf. Caméliat, 'Prières Populaires', *Mélusine* (1899–1900), pp.52–3. Variants were also given by Dardy, *Anthologie Populaire d'Albret*, I, p.337; Rocal, *Le Vieux Périgord* (1927), p.225; Lépinay, 'Prières Populaires... Corrèze', *Melusine* (1884), pp.220–24.

169. Bouteiller, *Médecine Populaire*, pp.92–5. Cf. note in *Mélusine* (1884), p.405. An old woman was heard by the Abbé Nyd reciting the *quarantaine* and a prayer like *pigeons blancs* in front of Our Lady's altar at Pont-de-Vaux, around 1846. Berriat-Saint-Prix, *Vieilles Prières*, p.6, asserted that these prayers were known in almost every village in his area. Cf. Leproux, *Dévotions et Saints Guérisseurs*, pp.5, 12, n.9–10, 31 n.44, n.46.

170. R. Jalby, *Sorcellerie* (Nyons 1974), p.108.

171. Berriat-Saint-Prix, *Vieilles Prières*, p.7.

172. R. Otto, *Le Sacré* (18th edn, Paris, 1968), pp.27ff.

173. Favraud, 'Prières Populaires du Poitou', *Mélusine* (1889), p.286a.

174. C. Rouleau, *Essai de Folklore* (Moulins, 1935), p.118. Cf. Leproux, *Dévotions et Saints Guérisseurs*, III 29, for a version from the Charente.

J

175. Berriat-Saint-Prix, *op. cit.*, pp.27–8.
176. Strikingly similar prayers were observed in the Tarn. Cf. Jalby, *Sorcellerie, Médecine*, p.108. Cf. also Carnoy, *Littérature Orale de la Picardie* (1883), p.375, for version of this prayer recited by seventy-two-year-old Eugénie Darras. Black, *Folk Medicine* (London, 1883), p.128, for version from Ulster, and Bernoni, *Preghiere Popolari Veneziane* (Venice, 1873), pp. 8–9 *passim*, for version from Venice.
177. Pérot, 'Incantations', RTP (1903), p.302. Cf., too, a longer version given by Gagnon, *Folklore Bourbonnais*, III, pp.16–17.
178. M. Bouteiller, *Médecine Populaire* (Paris, 1966), pp.94–5. Dardy, *Anthologie Populaire d'Albret*, I, p.343. A. Vernière, 'Prière Populaire Haute-Loire', *Mélusine* (1884), pp.220–24.
179. Caméliat, 'Prières Populaires', *Mélusine* (1899–1900), p.52.
180. Lépinay, 'Prières Populaires Corrèze', *Mélusine* (1884), p.224. Cf. also Vernière, 'Prière Populaire Haute-Loire', *Mélusine* (1884), p.499.
181. Dardy, *Anthologie d'Albret*, I, p.343.
182. Juge, *Changemens Survenus* (Limoges, 1817), p.128.
183. Leproux, *Dévotions et Saint Guérisseurs* p.5.

Notes to Chapter II

1. Cf. Tixier, 'De l'Exercice Illégale de la Médecine', *Congrès Scientifique de France.* (1871), p.338. Mathieu, *Médecine Populaire... en Haut-Albigeois* (Toulouse University, medical thesis, 1946), pp.47–52. Tourdes, *Exercice Illégale de la Médecine* (Strasbourg, 1844), pp.4–5, 9.
2. Graulle, *Traditions et Médecine Populaire en Bourbonnais* (Montpellier University, PhD thesis, 1963), p.7, n.1.
3. Cf. M. Bouteiller, *La Médecine Populaire* (Paris, 1966), pp.47–9, 61–2.
4. Dubalen, *Pratiques Médicales Populaires dans les Landes* (Lyon University, medical thesis, 1907), pp.33–50. Cf. Graulle, *op. cit.*, pp.134 *passim*, for healers' backgrounds and beliefs and those of their clientèle.
5. Remize, *Contribution à l'Etude de la Médecine Psychosomatique* (Aurillac, 1949), p.43.
6. Graulle, *op. cit.*, p.93.
7. C. Gagnon, *Folklore Bourbonnais* (Moulins, 1949), II, p.231.
8. Remize, *op. cit.*, pp.37–57. Cf. also the story told to Kérambrun about a popular bone-setter in Médoc. He was the son-in-law of a man who a century earlier had repaired a statue of Christ found on a beach after a storm, and whose gesture had been rewarded with the gift of healing. Kérambrun, *Les Rebouteurs et les Guérisseurs en Bretagne* (Bordeaux University, medical thesis, 1898), p.22.
9. Kérambun, *op. cit.*, p.20.
10. F. Durand, *Les Guérisseurs* (Paris, 1884), pp.71–3. This tale would seem to lend weight to Genieviève Bollème's theory about what reading and possessing books meant in largely illiterate socities. Cf. Bollème, *Les Almanachs Populaires* (Paris, 1969), p.16.
11. Debäcker, 'Lecture en Bas', *Mém. Soc. Dunkerque* (1907), pp.216, 218 Cantaloube, *L'Exercice Illégale de la Médecine* (Montpellier University, medical thesis, 1904), pp.20, 25. Bonnemère, 'Superstitions du Canton de Gennes et Maine-et-Loire', RTP (1890), p.675. Leproux, *Dévotions et Saint Guérisseurs* (Paris, 1957), p.91.
12. Remize, *op. cit.*, pp.52–4.
13. Dubalen, *op. cit.*, p.34. Cf. also Gagnon, *Folklore Bourbonnais*, II, p.229.
14. *Gazette des Tribunaux*, (22 October 1827), 1483b–1484a. Miron, *Le Prêtre et le Sorcier* (Paris, 1872), p.171. Cf., too, *Gazette des Tribunaux* (21 March 1828), 530B, for another prosecution along the same lines.
15. Kérambrun, *op. cit.*, pp.20–21. Gagnon, *op. cit.*, II, pp.232–3.
16. Cantaloube, *op. cit.*, p.29.

17. Cf. M. Eliade, *Le Sacré et le Profane* (Paris, 1965), pp.70–3.
18. H. Graulle, *op. cit.*, pp.153–62.
19. Dr R. Blanchard, 'Traditions et Superstitions', RTP (1890), p.747. Cf. Debäcker, 'Lecture en Bas', *Mém. Soc. Dunkerque* (1907), pp.216–17.
20. Cf. J. M. Charcot, *La Foi qui Guérit* (Paris, 1897), pp.16–38.
21. Cantaloube, *op. cit.*, p.42.
22. Dr J. P. Odenthal, *Etude sur la Sorcellerie Médicale en Dordogne* (Bordeaux University, medical thesis, 1924), pp.29–30.
23. Rocal, *Le Vieux Périgord* (Toulouse, 1927), pp.124–5. Cf. Gandrille-Ourcel, *Médecine Populaire en Bourgogne* (Paris University, medical thesis, 1957), pp.55–6.
24. Cf. Vinchon, 'Du Rôle de la Suggestion', *Revue Anthopologique* (1928), 38, pp.51–2.
25. Appolonia was a martyr whose tormentors took out all her teeth – hence she was invoked for toothaches: she was usually represented holding a forceps which grasped an immense molar. Thiers, *Traité des Superstitions* (Amsterdam, 1733–6), p.87.
26. *Médecin des Campagnes* (n.p., 1832), p.2. The Baudot edition of Troyes (1858), and the Armentières edition (c.1868), are almost identical with this.
27. Bouteiller, *Sorciers et Jeteurs de Sorts* (Paris, 1958), p.200. Cf. also mss. discovered by Wickersheimer.
28. Cf. Borianne, *Essai sur les Erreurs en Médecine* (Paris University, medical thesis, 1831), p.26, who notes the universal fear of blood-letting. Foucart, *Des Erreurs et Préjugés Populaires* (Paris University, medical thesis, 1893), p.34, notes the enduring fear of hospitals and operations.
29. Bidault, 'Superstitions Médicales du Morvan' (Paris University, medical thesis, 1889), p.57. Tiffaud, 'L'Exercice Illégale de la Médecine' (Paris University, medical thesis, 1899), p.50 gives the same version, as does the eccentric Abbé Julio (a disciple of a faith-healer late nineteenth-century psychiatrists discussed), in *Prières Miraculeuses* (1896), p.69. Cf. Lazarque, 'Médecine Superstitieuse du Pays Messin', RTP (1914), p.62, who noted a version around 1874.
30. Thiers, *op. cit.*, p.97.
31. *Enchiridion Leonis Papae* (Lille, 1813), p.144.
32. Thiers, *op. cit.*, p.86. *Médecin des Pauvres* (c.1832), p.5. *Médecin des Pauvres*, (Armentières, c.1868).
33. Moret, *Devins et Sorciers* (Moulins, 1909), p.8.
34. *Ibid*, pp.52–3.
35. Describing the village of Savignies in the Oise, Cambry wrote that its only tradition was that Jesus and Saint Peter came to visit it. Cambry, *Description de l'Oise* (Paris, 1803), p.200.
36. For rheumatism, a prayer featuring 'Mme Ste Anne': *Médecin des Pauvres* (1868); Thiers, *op. cit.*, p.97; Bouteiller, *Chamanisme et Guérison Magique* (Paris, 1950), p.263. Ulcers: Bouteiller, *Chamanisme*, p.235; *Enchiridion*, p.143. Epilepsy: *Enchiridion*, p.145; Thiers, *op. cit.*, p.85b, gives the formula: 'Gaspar fert myrrham' which Chéruel ascribes to Bernard de Gordon, author of the *Lilium Medicinae*, *Dict. Historique* (1855), p.759b. Wier also cites this as a remedy for epilepsy, *Histoires, Disputes et Discours…* (Paris, 1885), ii, p.46. Cf. also Boguet, *Discours des Sorciers avec six Advis en Faicts de Sorcellerie* (Lyon, 1610, 3rd edn), p.253. Thiers found a child wearing a talisman thus inscribed in 1679, *op. cit.*, p.86a. Ringworm: *Médecin des Pauvres* (1832). Thiers gives an almost identical prayer for fever, *op. cit.*, p.101. Bidault, Durandeau, Clément-Janin and Guillon all collected popular prayers resembling these literary models.
37. Cf. G. Vuillier, 'Chez les Magiciens et les Sorciers', *Tour du Monde* (1899), pp.315–17.
38. Rocal, *op. cit.*, pp.224–5.
39. *Ibid*, p.135.

40. Odenthal, *Etude sur la Sorcellerie Médicale en Dordogne* (Bordeaux, 1923), p.27.
41. Lecotté, *Les Cultes Populaires* (1953), pp.254–60.
42. Sevrin, 'Croyances', RHEF (1946), p.280.
43. Leproux, *op. cit.*, pp.22–53. Miron, *Le Prêtre et le Sorcier* (1872), pp.262, 280.
44. Gagnon, *Folklore du Bourbonnais* (1949) II, pp.103–7.
45. Cambry, *op. cit.*, pp.19b–20a.
46. Miron, *Le Prêtre et le Sorcier* (1872), pp.17–21.
47. Mazaret, 'Pèlerins et Pèlerinages', RTP (1911), pp.242–3. The saint was supposed to dispatch the illness to withering thistles in a nearby wood, rather less vengefully than the request suggests.
48. Droüart, *Les Saint Guérisseurs* (1939), n.p.
49. Sébillot, *Folklore de France* (1901) II, pp.284–5.
50. Sébillot, *Paganisme* (Paris, 1908), pp.142–3.
51. Dubalen, *Pratiques Médicales* (Lyon University, medical thesis, 1907), p.24 n.83.
52. Miron, *op. cit.*, pp.153–4.
53. P. Sébillot, *Folklore de France* (1901) II, pp.291–2.
54. Cambry, *op. cit.*, p.68b.
55. Souvestre, *Finistère* (1838), p.96b. Cf. Berthoumieu, *Fêtes et Dévotions* (Paris, 1873), p.11, for the cult of Saint Genevieve among the poor of Paris. Lecoeur, *Esquisses du Bocage Normand* (1887), II, p.208.
56. Rocal, *op. cit.*, p.143.
57. Miron, *Le Prêtre et le Sorcier*, p.152.
58. Chervin, *Traditions Populaires Relatives à la Parole* (Paris, n.d.), pp.33–4.
59. Miron, *Le Prêtre et le Sorcier*, p.151. Sébillot, *Le Folklore des Pécheurs* (1901), 91. Souvestre, *Finistère*, p.98b. Cambry and Sébillot refer to the offerings (bits of wreckage, sculpted boats) of grateful sailors who had escaped drowning.
60. Gagnon, *Folklore Bourbonnais* (1949), II, p.101.
61. Belbèze, *La Neurasthénie Rurale* (Paris, 1911), pp.35–6.
62. Leproux, *Dévotions et Saints Guérisseurs* (1957), pp.91–2. Cf. Lecoeur, *Esquisses du Bocage Normand*, II, p.191, for similar practices in Normandy.
63. Laisnel de la Salle, *Croyances et Légendes* (Paris, 1875), I, pp.58–9. Cf. also Bidault, *op. cit.*, p.58.
64. Monnier, *Traditions Populaires Comparées* (Paris, 1854), pp.390–1.
65. Bidault, *op. cit.*, p.69. Cf. Mensignac, *Notice sur les Superstitions* (1888), p.100, for the Gironde, where the hawthorn was supposed to protect against lightning.
66. Nozot, 'Usages et superstitions', *Revue des Sociétés Savantes* (July-Dec. 1872), p.131. Westphalen gives the same formula in his *Petit Dictonnaire... Traditions Messines* (1934), p.28.
67. Sauvé, *Folklore des Hautes-Vosges* (1885), p.189.
68. Delcambre, *Le Concept de Sorcellerie* (1951), III, Appendix 1, p.229.
69. Fagot, 'Formules... Langue d'oc', *Rev. Pyrénées* (1891), p.177.
70. Sauvé, 'Charmes', *Revue Celtique* (1883–5), pp.81–2.
71. Guillaumin, *Tableaux Champêtres* (1901), p.80. Cf. *Voyage à Bordeaux et dans les Landes* (Year VI), pp.17–18, for similar observation.
72. Sébillot, *Paganisme* (1908), p.126. Cf. Sauvé, *Lavarou Koza* (1878), p.140, who gives the following invocation to the moon: 'Salut pleine lune/Emporte celles-ci [warts]/ Avec toi, loin d'ici.'
73. Sébillot, *Paganisme*, p.128.
74. Bouteiller, *Médecine Populaire*, pp.300–1, 318.
75. Cf. Dussaud, 'La Matérialisation de la Prière en Orient', *Extrait des Bulletins et Mémoires de la Société d'Anthopologie* (Paris, 1906).
76. P. Sébillot, *Paganisme*, pp.127–8, 140.
77. Cf. Calhiat, 'Pèlerinages Thérapeutiques', *Bull. Cath. Diocèse Montauban* (10 June 1899), p.383, for the importance of water in popular healing.

78. Dubalen, *Pratiques Médicales* (1907), p.23. Cf. *Le Grand Albert* for a similar recipe.
79. Rocal, *Le Vieux Périgord* (Toulouse, 1927), p.80. Cf. also Charcot, *La Foi qui guérit* (Paris, 1879), p.11, who observed that 'les conditions du miracle sont restées identiques, ses lois d'évolution étant immuables.'.
80. Cf. Platelle, *Les Chrétiens devant le Miracle* (1968), pp.49–55, for popularity in the seventeenth century.
81. Ladoucette, *Histoire Topographique... des Hautes Alpes* (1848), p.593. *Chronique de Mme Bonnard* (b.1690), ed. Bouiller (1976), p.14, an account of one such miracle which took place in 1738. The child was brought to the church after having been buried for nine days, at the instigation of its mother and grandparents, although the father worried that 'il s'exposait à se faire moquer de lui'.
82. Saintyves, *En Marge de la Légende Dorée* (1930), pp.171–2, 191.
83. Cf. Quénot, *Stat. Dép. Charente* (1818), p.322, n.1. He affirms that people were sometimes buried before their death was established with certainty, and that Fodéré and others had cited cases of people who had regained consciousness during the funeral service or procession. Such incidents, however rare, may have fostered the persuasion that it was possible to rise from the dead.
84. Saintyves, *op. cit.*, pp.180–81.
85. Belbèze, *La Neurasthénie Rurale* (1911), p.106.
86. Terrien, *L'Hystérie et la Neurasthénie chez le Paysan* (Angers, 1906), pp.27, 29.
87. Boismoreau, *Coutumes Médicales et Superstitions Populaires* (1911), pp.35–7.
88. Cf. below, pp.124–8.
89. J. M. Charcot, *Leçons sur les Maladies du Système Nerveux*, I (Paris, 1875), pp.287–8, 341–5, 355–9; III (Paris, 1887), pp.226, 335–45.
90. Bernheim, *De la Suggestion et des ses applications à la Thérapeutique* (Paris, 1886), pp.228, 324–5.
91. Sigal, 'Maladie, Pèlerinage...', AESC (1969), pp.1526–7.
92. Diday, *Examen Médical des Miracles de Lourdes* (1873), pp.49–59.
93. Laurentin, *Lourdes* (Paris, 1959), v, pp.119–120.
94. J. Deery, *Our Lady of Lourdes* (Dublin, 1958), pp.165–6.
95. Terrien, *L'Hystérie et la Neurasthénie chez le Paysan* (Anvers, 1906), pp.58–9, 66–7. Cf. also Bernheim, *De la Suggestion* (Paris, 1886), pp.214–17, where he records cases of sudden recovery from blindness and paralysis in Lourdes.
96. Deery, *op. cit.*, p.157.
97. Du Broc de Segange, *Saints Patrons* (1887), I, pp.207–8, 374–5. Boué de Villiers, *Normandie Superstitieuse* (1870). Tabonnier *Dévotions Populaires* (1923), pp.5–6. Dubois, *Atrophies Musculaires* (1898), pp.9–10.
98. Donnadieu, *Salette-Fallavaux* (Grenoble, 1853), II, p.145. Deery, *op. cit.*, pp.168–9. M. de Saint-Pierre, *Bernadette and Lourdes* (London, 1954), p71. for other cases of recovery from blindness.
99. Kselman, *Miracles and Prophecies in Nineteenth-Century France* (New Brunswick, 1983), pp.195–6, 200.

Notes to Chapter III

1. Faure, *Hallucinations et Réalité Perceptive* (Paris, 1969), p.10.
2. N. Belmont, *Mythes et Croyances dans l'Ancienne France* (Paris, 1973), p.32.
3. Dambielle, *La Sorcellerie en Gascogne* (Auch, 1907), pp.14–15.
4. Laborde, 'Les brouches en Béarn...', *Revue Historique et Archéologique du Béarn* (1935), pp.113–14.
5. Cf. below, pp.199–202.
6. Sentoux, *De la Surexcitation des Facultés Mentales* (Paris, 1867), p.92.
7. Calmeil, Art. 'Lycanthropie', in *Dictionnaire Encyclopédique des Sciences Médicales* (Paris, 1870), pp.361–5.

7a. Year XII was 1804 according to the Republic calendar adopted in 1793 – the Year I started on 22 September 1792.
8. Brierre de Boismont, *Des Hallucinations* (Paris, 1852), p.384.
9. Tissié, *Les Aliénés Voyageurs* (Bordeaux University, medical thesis, 1887), p.31.
10. Itard, *De L'Education de l'Homme Sauvage* (Paris, 1801), pp.4, 7–8, and *passim* for unsuccessful efforts to integrate him into society.
11. Coignet, *Mémoires du Capitaine Coignet* (Paris, 1932), pp.7, 15.
12. Cf. Delarue, *Recueil de Chants Populaires* (Nevers, Paris, 1947), Facs. III, pp.15–16, for wolves in the Nivernais at the start of the nineteenth century.
13. Lecocq, *Les Loups dans la Beauce* (Chartres, 1860), pp.26–31, 48. Cambry, *Voyage dans le Finistère* (Brest, 1836), p.240b. Cambry, *Description de l'Oise* (Paris, Year XI, 1803), I, p.399. Grégoire, *Promenade dans les Vosges* (Epinal, 1895), p.40. Guillaumin, *La Vie d'un Simple* (Paris, 1977), p.27. Ganachaud, *Souvenirs et Espoirs d'un Paysan Charentais* (Angoulême, 1946), p.45. Bouteiller, *Sorciers et Jeteurs de Sort* (Paris, 1958), pp.171–2. E. Weber, *Peasants into Frenchmen* (London, 1977), p.15.
14. Cf. Lecotté, *Au Village de France* (Paris, 1945), p.171. He reproduces a print of the Beast which is identical with that depicting a 'Monstre Marin', given in Garnier. Cf. below, p.79.
15. Cf. Garnier, *Histoire de l'Imagerie Populaire* (Chartres, 1869), pp.358–65. Séguin, *Nouvelles à Sensation* (Paris, 1959), p.156.
16. Pic, *La Bête qui Mangeait le Monde en Pays de Gévaudan* (Paris, 1962), pp.16–25, 256–60.
17. Ellensberger, 'Le Monde Fantastique', *Nouvelle Revue des Traditions Populaires* (1949), pp.419–34.
18. Belmont, *Mythes et Croyances* (Paris, 1973), pp.36–8, 45. Bladé, 'Superstitions Populaires de la Gascogne', *Revue de l'Agenais* (Jan.-Feb. 1883), pp.25–7.
19. Lecotté, *Au Village de France* (Paris, 1945), p.173.
20. G. Sand, *Légendes Rustiques* (Verviers, 1975), pp.58–63. The resemblance between this scene, described in 1858, and that evoked in Maupassant's *La Peur*, which was written a generation later, is striking.
21. Garnier, *Histoire de l'Imagerie Populaire* (Chartres, 1869), pp.368–9.
22. P. L. Duchartre and R. Saulnier, *L'Imagerie Populaire* (Paris, 1925), p.69. Hélot, *Canards et Canardiers* (Paris, n.d.), pp.8–9. Séguin, *Nouvelles à Sensation* (Paris, 1959), p.182.
23. Hélot, *Canards et Canardiers* (Paris, n.d.), pp.29–30.
24. Garnier, *Histoire de L'Imagerie Populaire* (Chartres, 1869), pp.370–1.
25. R. Bouiller, ed., *Chronique de Madame Bonnard* (Cahiers du Musée Forézien, 1976), pp.24–5.
26. Séguin, *Nouvelles à Sensation* (Paris, 1959), pp.133–4. Luzel, 'L'Imagerie Populaire', *RTP* (1890), pp.629–30.
27. Garnier, *Histoire de l'Imagerie Populaire* (Chartres, 1869), pp.377–82. Séguin, *Nouvelles à Sensation* (Paris, 1959), p.135.
28. Séguin, *Nouvelles à Sensation* (1959), pp.135, 139–40.
29. E. Coulon, 'Les Apparitions en Franche-Comté', *Revue de Folklore Français* (1935), p.318. Sorcerers in the Bourbonnais had a *garde* 'pour écarter la poursuite du follet', which consisted of throwing a little change over one's shoulder and running away, while the will-o'-the-wisp paused to collect this pecuniary tribute, cf. Gagnon, *Le Folklore Bourbonnais* (Moulins, 1949), II, p.176.
30. Carnoy, *Littérature Orale de la Picardie* (Paris, 1883), p.40.
31. Ellensberger, 'Le Monde Fantastique dans le folklore de la Vienne', *Nouvelle Revue des Traditions Populaires* (1949), pp.408, 428. A. Le Braz, *La Légende de la Mort* (Paris, 1893), pp.65–70.
32. A. Van Gennep, *Folklore de la Flandre et du Hainaut* (Paris, 1936), II, p.573.
33. *Gazette des Tribunaux*, (13 February 1843), p.436c–d.

34. Evans-Wentz, *Fairy Faith* (Oxford, 1911/Gerrard's Cross, 1977), pp.188–9.
35. Moret, *Devins et Sorciers* (Moulins, 1909), pp.15–6.
36. Meyrac, *Traditions* (Charleville, 1890), pp.157–8.
37. Résie, *Histoire et Traité des Sciences Occultes* (Paris, 1857), I, pp.330–33. Maury, *Les Fées au Moyen Age* (Paris, 1843), pp.23–4, 27–9, 45. Cf. Evans-Wentz, *The Fairy Faith* (Oxford, 1911, 1977), p.205.
38. Résie, *Histoire et Traité* (Paris, 1857), I, pp. 334–5. Chéruel, *Dictionaire Historique* (Paris, 1855), II, p.1180a–b.
39. Moret, *Devins et Sorciers* (Moulins, 1909), p.15.
40. G. Sand, *Légendes Rustiques* (Verviers, 1975), pp.89–90.
41. Cf. below, pp.122–3 for descriptions of the devil.
42. P. Sébillot, *Folklore de France* (Paris, 1905), II, p.231.
43. N. Belmont, *Mythes et Croyances* (Paris, 1973), p.35.
44. A. Maury, *Les Fées au Moyen Age* (Paris, 1843), pp.46, 50, 52–3, 89.
45. N. Belmont, *Mythes et Croyances* (Paris, 1973), p.35.
46. Evans-Wentz, *Fairy Faith* (Oxford, 1911, 1977), p.197.
47. Evans-Wentz, *op. cit.*, pp.198–9, 210–12.
48. Evans-Wentz, *op. cit.*, p.207.
49. Evans-Wentz, *op. cit.*, pp.211–12.
50. Cf. also below, pp.124–8, 227–30.
51. Résie, *Histoire et Traité* (Paris, 1857), I, pp.141–2. Evans-Wentz, *op. cit.*, p.206, citing P. Sébillot, *Traditions et Superstitions de la Haute Bretagne* (Paris, 1882), pp.74–5.
52. Sand, *Légendes Rustiques*, pp.88–9.
53. Evans-Wentz, *op. cit.*, p.206–7.
54. Sand, *Légendes Rustiques*, pp.90–91.
55. J. Delumeau, *La Peur en Occident* (Paris, 1978), p.75, and his *Catholicisme* (1971), p239–41.
56. Cf. the remarks of Philippe Ariès: '...Ce merveilleux legs d'époques où la frontière était incertaine entre le naturel et le surnaturel...', *L'Homme devant la Mort* (Paris, 1977), p.16.
57. F. Lebrun, *Les Hommes et la Mort en Anjou* (Paris, 1975), p.361.
58. Sand, *Légendes Rustiques*, pp.35–44.
59. S. Thompson, *The Folktale* (Berkeley, London, 1977), pp.256–7.
60. J. Delumeau, *La Peur en Occident* (Paris, 1978), p.77.
61. Sébillot, *Paganisme* (Paris, 1908), pp.180–81.
62. A. Le Braz, *La Légende de la Mort* (Paris, 1902), cf. intro. pp.xi, xxxviii–xlii.
63. Moret, *Devins et Sorciers* (Moulins, 1909), p.15.
64. Evans-Wentz, *Fairy Faith*, p.215. Note the mesmeric technique.
65. Evans-Wentz, *op. cit.*, pp.214–15. Cf. also J. Delumeau, *La Peur en Occident*, pp.81–2, for other comments on the Breton belief in ghosts.
66. Thiers, *Traité des Superstitions* (Amsterdam, 1733–6), p56b.
67. Cf. N. Belmont, *Mythes et Croyances*, pp.64–5.
68. C. Gagnon, *Le Folklore Bourbonnais*, II, 176.
69. Cambry, *Voyage dans le Finistère* (Paris, 1838), p.154a. A. Le Braz, *Légende de la Mort* (Paris, 1902), pp.112–19, 123.
70. Lamiaud, 'Le Souper des Anciens Morts', *Etudes Locales* (1922), pp.26–9.
71. Résie, *Histoire et Traité* (Paris, 1857), II, p.624.
72. P. Ariès, *L'Homme devant la Mort*, p.437.
73. Cf. Dr Boismoreau, *Coutumes Médicales* (Paris, 1911), pp.75–6. M. Massol, *Description du Département du Tarn* (Albi, 1818), p.177.
74. Lévy-Bruhl, *La Mentalité Primitive* (Paris, 1976), p.143.
75. Thiers, *Traité des Superstitions* (Amsterdam, 1733–6), pp.43a–44b.
76. Abbé Goudret, *Moeurs et Coutumes des Habitants du Quéras au* XIXe *Siècle*,

(Nyons, 1974; mss. written in 1858), p.36. Nozot, 'Usages et Superstitions Populaires des Ardennes', *Revue des Sociétés Savantes* (July-December 1872), p.127.

77. *Almanach du Bon Laboueureur* (Rouen, n.d., *c*.1832–3), pp.20, 53, 56.

78. Cf. G. Bollème, *Les Almanachs Populaires* (Paris, The Hague, 1969), pp.11–17, who thinks – partly because of the substitution of signs for letters – that they were addressed to the substantially illiterate. For origins, cf. F. Pouy, *Recherches sur les Almanachs* (Amiens, 1874), pp.6–8. A. Denis, *Recherches Bibliographiques* (Châlons-sur-Marne, 1880), pp.1–16. Also H. Brugsch, *Matériaux* (Leipzig, 1864), pp.9–10. A. Court de Gébelin, *Le Monde Primitif* (Paris, 1776), IV, pp.1–2, 16–41, 461 *passim*. Grenier, *Introduction* (Amiens, 1856), pp.342–3, who was surprised to find similar calendars (indicating when it was safe to take a bath, eat hot food, be bled etc.) in medieval ecclesiastical books, such as the calendar of the Missal of Soissons cathedral, published in 1555.

79. C. Nisard, *Histoire des Livres Populaires* (Paris, 1864), I, pp.74–8. Some of these hieroglyphs were also adapted for use in manuals of sorcery, cf. *Le Véritable Dragon Rouge* (Nismes, 1823, in fact published in 1849), pp.102–3.

80. Some almanachs are alleged to have had print-runs of up to 150,000 and 200,000, cf. Bollème, *Les Almanachs Populaires*, p.14.

81. With the famous *Grand Calendrier et Compost des Bergers* (Oudot, Troyes, 1618).

82. Cf. also *Almanach des Campagnes pour 1860* (Hervé, 1860); *Grand Almanach de Jacques Bonhomme* (Paris, 1861), which attacks the old Laensberg almanac; the *Almanach du Cultivateur* (Niort, n.d.), p.67, which affirms that the only means of making money, 'c'est le travail et l'ordre'.

83. J. Michelet, *Pages Choisies* (Paris, 1935), pp.183–4. Luzel's researches on Breton popular literature confirmed this assertion, as did Anatole Le Braz' work. Farmers and artisans who transcribed and owned books were usually reluctant to part with them. A sailor, Jean Marie Lesquelen, who copied out a play, noted that it was 'fait par moi . . . après beaucoup d'embarras'. And when he went away to sea, he carefully indicated in his will who was to inherit the book and who was to have authority to lend it. A. Le Braz, *Le Théâtre Celtique* (Paris, 1905), pp.190–202, 211–19.

84. Thiers, *Traité des Superstitions* (Amsterdam, 1733–6), pp.63a–64b.

85. Cambry, *Voyage dans le Finistère* (Brest, 1836), pp.68b, 154a. Nore, *Coutumes, Mythes et Traditions* (Paris, 1846), pp.81, 140, 174. Résie, *Histoire et Traité des Sciences Occultes* (Paris, 1857), II, pp.556–8. Thiers, *Traité des Superstitions* (Amsterdam, 1733–6), p.44a.

86. Thiers, *loc. cit*.

87. E. Guillaumin, *La Vie d'un Simple* (Paris, 1977), pp.152–3.

88. Juge, *Changements Survenus* (Limoges, 1817), p.117. A. Vingtrinier and D. Monnier, *Croyances et Traditions Populaires* (1854), pp.172–3. E. Souvestre, *Les Derniers Bretons* (Paris, 1971), pp.16. J. Lecoeur, *Esquisses du Bocage Normand* (Condé-sur-Noireau, 1887), II, p.14. M. Nozot, 'Usages et Superstitions Populaires des Ardennes', *Revue des Sociétes Savantes* (July-December 1872), p.128.

89. E. Guillaumin, *La Vie d'Un Simple* (Paris, 1977), p.226.

90. Cf. also Résie, *Histoire et Traité des Sciences Occultes* (Paris, 1857), II, pp.548–9.

91. Cf. Dodds, *The Greeks and the Irrational* (Berkeley, 1973), pp.102–34.

92. Cf. M. Nadaud, *Mémoires de Léonard* (Paris, 1976), pp.64–5. Juge, *Changemens Survenus* (Limoges, 1817), p.131. A. Perdiguier, *Mémoires d'un Compagnon* (Paris, 1977), pp.66–7.

93. Cf. L. Ganachaud, *Souvenirs et Espoirs d'un Paysan Charentais* (Angoulême, 1946), pp.35–6, 87.

94. Cf. Charlotte Brontë, *Villette*, for ambivalent treatment of the storm as a portent of disaster.

95. Cf. Lévy-Bruhl, *La Mentalité Primitive* (Paris, 1976), pp.131–2, 141, for complexity of primitive beliefs about presages and of their application to actuality.

Notes to Chapter IV

1. Cf. K. Thomas, *Religion and the Decline of Magic* (London, 1971, 1973 rpr.), pp.769ff., esp. pp.786–7, where he discusses these difficulties.
2. Cf. Favret-Saada, *Les Mots, La Mort et les Sorts* (Paris, 1977), pp.18, 162, 175.
3. Foix, *Sorcières et Loups-Garous dans les Landes* (Auch, 1904), p.33. Lacouture 'La Sorcellerie dans le Béarn', *Réclams de Biarn et Gascounhe* (1913), no. 8, p.45, agrees with Foix: anxiety was followed by questioning and naming the culprit.
4. Cf. Favret-Saada, *Les Mots, La Mort et les Sorts* (Paris, 1977), pp.61, 72, 75. P. Saintyves, 'Foi à l'Envoutement', *Revue du Folklore Français et Colonial* (1935), v, p.35, for a change of attitude following on initial scepticism.
5. J. Lecoeur, *Esquisses du Bocage Normand* (Condé-sur-Noireau, 1887), II, p.38.
6. Cf. Favret-Saada, *op. cit.*, p.20. A. D. Allier, Series U, Trib. Correctionnel Cusset, 18 July 1842 – wife's relatives suspected. A. D. Allier Series U, Trib. Correctionnel Montluçon, 17 July 1875 (neighbour); *ibid*, 25 July 1875 (neighbour); *ibid*, July 1875 (relatives). Lecoeur, *op. cit.*, II, p.52 (enemy).
7. Mensignac, *Recherches Ethnographiques* (1892), p.58. Leproux, *Médecine, Magie et Sorcellerie* (Paris, 1954), pp.229–30: illegitimate children and the physically handicapped were held to have the evil eye. This belief was found also in the Saintonge. Cf. Noguès, *Moeurs d'Autrefois en Saintonge* (Saintes, 1891), p.140; in parts of Auvergne: Van Gennep, *Folklore de l'Auvergne et du Velay* (Paris, 1942), p.296; in the Vosges: Sauvé, *Folklore des Hautes Vosges* (Paris, 1889), p.169; in Haute Vienne: Juge, *Changemens* (Limoges, 1817), pp.184–5; Van Gennep, *Le Folklore du Dauphiné* (Paris, 1932), II, p.471; in the Bourbonnais: Delaigne, 'Dans la Montagne bourbonnaise' *Le Pays Gannatais* (July 1978), p.9a–b; Gagnon, *Le Folklore Bourbonnais* (Moulins, 1949), II, p.162; in the north-east: Westphalen, *Petite Dictionnaire des Traditions Populaires Messines* (Metz, 1934), p.685; Tavarne, *Médecine Populaire* (Ambierle, 1976), p.37; in Provence: Seignolle, *Le Folklore de Provence* (Paris, 1967), pp.356–9; Seignolle, *Le Folklore du Languedoc* (Paris, 1960), pp.213–14; on the sea-coast of Brittany: P. Sébillot *Le Folklore des Pêcheurs* (Paris, 1901), p.21.
8. Mahé, *Essai sur les Antiquités du Morbihan* (Vannes, 1825), p.480.
9. Mensignac, *Recherches Ethnographiques* (1892), pp.44–5.
10. Gagnon, *Le Folklore Bourbonnais* (Moulins, 1949), II, p.162. Leproux, *Médecine, Magie et Sorcellerie* (Paris, 1954), p.236, reports on similar practices in the Confolentais, in which cursing and spitting were associated. Foix, *Sorcières et Loups-Garous* (Auch, 1904), p.17. Here, the *maléfice* was accompanied by curses which caused the victim's illness or death.
11. Huyttens, *Etudes sur les Moeurs, les Superstitions... dans la Flandre Orientale* (Gand, 1861), p.95.
12. Van Gennep, *Folklore de l'Auvergne et du Velay* (Paris, 1942), pp.254, 296.
13. Schély, 'L'Envoûtement en Alsace', RTP (1935), p.35.
14. Cauzons, *La Sorcellerie en France* (Paris, 1912), IV, p.658. Cf. also R. Kaufmann, *Pratiques Superstitieuses* (Paris University, medical thesis, 1906), p.236. Saintyves, *Guérison des Verrues* (Paris, 1913), pp.9–10 for popular theory of contagion. M. Bouteiller, *Chamanisme et Guérison Magique* (Paris, 1950), p.236.
15. Le Carguet, 'Le Mauvais Oeil', RTP (1889), p.466. Van Gennep, *Le Folklore du Dauphiné* (Paris, 1933), II, p.471. Cf. L. Mazaret, 'Notes sur la Sorcellerie en Gascogne', RTP (1909), pp.267–8.
16. Lacouture, 'La Sorcellerie dans le Béarn', *Réclams* (1913), p.45. Laborde, 'Les Brouches (Sorcières) en Béarn', *Revue Historique et Archéologique du Pays Basque* (1935). Foix, *Sorcières et Loups-Garous* (Auch, 1904), p.33.
17. Leproux, *Médecine, Magie et Sorcellerie* (Paris, 1954), pp.227–8.
18. Laurand, Note in *Bull. Soc. Archéo. Gers* (1955), p.325. Dr C. Hélot, *Névroses et*

Possessions Diaboliques (Paris, 1897), pp.36–7, 54, 63–9, 71–2. Cf. also Van Gennep, *Folklore des Hautes-Alpes* (Paris, 1948), II, p.90.

19. Laurand, *op. cit.*, p.327.
20. Hélot, *Névroses*, pp.38–9. Cf. also below, pp.(165ff.), for further information on these spell-books.
21. Van Gennep, *Le Folklore du Dauphiné* (Paris, 1933), II, p.474. Van Gennep, *Le Folklore des Hautes-Alpes* (Paris, 1948), II, p.87 n.1.
22. Van Gennep, *Le Folklore des Hautes-Alpes* (Paris, 1948), II, p.88.
23. Cf. Le Carguet, 'Le Mauvais Oeil', RTP (1889), p.466.
24. Mahé, *Essai sur les Antiquités du Morbihan* (Vannes, 1825), p.480. Le Carguet, 'Le Mauvais Oeil', RTP (1889), p.466. Géniaux, *La Bretagne Vivante* (Paris, 1912), p.108. Leproux, *Médecine, Magie et Sorcellerie*, p.249. Van Gennep, *Folklore des Hautes-Alpes*, II, pp.88, 90.
25. Pérot, *Folklore du Bourbonnais* (Paris, 1908), p.220.
26. Van Gennep, *Le Folklore du Dauphiné* (Paris, 1933), II, p.472.
27. Van Gennep, *Le Folklore de la Flandre* (Paris, 1936), II, p.573.
28. Laborde, 'Les Brouches (Sorcières) en Béarn', *Rev. Hist. et Archéo. du Pays Basque* (1935), pp.16–17.
29. Van Gennep, *Le Folklore des Hautes-Alpes* (Paris, 1948), II, p.80.
30. Le Carguet, 'Le Mauvais Oeil', RTP (1889), pp.465–7.
31. Cf. Van Gennep, *Manuel de Folklore Française Contemporaine* (Paris, 1938), IV, p.557.
32. Noguès, *Moeurs d'Autrefois en Saintonge* (Saintes, 1891), p.140. Lecoeur, *Esquisses du Bocage Normand* (Condé-sur-Noireau, 1887), II, p.42. Lacouture, 'La Sorcellerie dans le Béarn', *Réclams* (1913), p.45. Similar formula is given by Bouteiller, *Sorciers et Jeteurs de Sorts* (Paris, 1958), pp.88–9. Trébucq, *La Chanson Populaire* (Bordeaux, 1912), I, p.276.
33. *Gazette des Tribunaux* (30 September 1835), p1250c.
34. *Gazette des Tribunaux* (28 February 1840), p.416b.
35. Lecoeur, *Esquisses du Bocage Normand* (Condé-sur-Noireau, 1887), II, pp.38–9.
36. Cf. Jobbé-Duval, *Les Idées Primitives dans la Bretagne Contemporaine* (Paris, 1911–14), on role played by divination and trial by ordeal in medieval Breton law.
37. Van Gennep, *Dauphiné* (Paris, 1933), II, p.471. Gilbert, *Les Sorciers en Bourbonnais* (Moulins, 1877), p.65. Rouleau, *Folklore de la Sologne Bourbonnaise* (Moulins, 1935), p.116. Vuillier, 'Chez les Magiciens et les Sorciers', *Tour du Monde* (1899), pp.522–4. Vézian, 'Les Contre-Envoûtements dans l'Ariège, *Revue de Folklore Français et Colonial* (1935), p.32. Rocal, *Le Vieux Périgord* (Toulouse, 1927), p.116.
38. Leproux, *Médecine, Magie et Sorcellerie* (Paris, 1954), p.225.
39. *Gazette des Tribunaux* (19 November 1829), p.55c.
40. Ladoucette, *Histoire, Topographie ... des Hautes Alpes* (Paris, 1848), p.592.
41. '''Ben vrai que j'étais confuse! Mon galant était à la maison et devait souper avec nous; mon père était furieux!''' S. Trébucq, *La Chanson Populaire* (Bordeaux, 1912), I, pp.276–7. Cf. Hélias, *Le Cheval d'Orgueil* (Paris, 1977), pp.442–4, for the formal behaviour expected on these occasions in Brittany in the early twentieth century. Fabre and Lacroix, *La Vie Quotidienne en Languedoc* (Paris, 1973), pp.127–33, for etiquette in the Languedoc in the nineteenth century. Cf. below, p.127 for details.
42. Meyrac, *Traditions, Coutumes* (Charleville, 1890), p.151, n.1. He hung a calf's heart in his chimney and stuck specially made nails into it each time his sick son had an attack; thereby imagining that the person he suspected suffered the same torments as her victim.
43. *Ibid*, p.153.
44. Schély, 'L'Envoûtement en ... Lorraine', *Revue de Folklore Français et Colonial* (1935), pp.32–3, and 'L'Envoûtement en Alsace', *ibid*, p.35. Sallet, 'Contre-Envoûtement en Haute Garonne', *loc. cit.*, p.35. Noguès, *Moeurs d'Autrefois en*

Saintonge (Saintes, 1891), p.31. Mensignac, *Notice sur les Superstitions* (Bordeaux, 1888), p.83.

45. Mensignac, *Notice*, p.90.
46. Ladoucette, *Histoire, Topographie... des Hautes Alpes* (Paris, 1848), p.590. Vézian, 'Les Contre-Envoûtements dans l'Ariège', *Revue de Folklore Français et Colonial* (1935) p.31. Favret-Saada, *op. cit.*, for similar beliefs in modern Vendée.
47. Ladoucette, *op. cit.*, p.591.
48. Piérart, *Guide Complet* (Paris, 1862), pp.363–5.
49. Drouillet, *Folklore du Nivernais* (Paris, 1964), p.148.
50. Meyrac, *Traditions, Coutumes... des Ardennes* (Charleville, 1890), p.158. Drouillet, *op. cit.*, pp.147–8. Van Gennep, citing Dieudonné's opinion, in *Folklore de la Flandre* (Paris, 1934), II, p.564.
51. Lecoeur, *Esquisses* (Condé-sur-Noireau, 1887), II, p.52. Some farmers saw misfortune as 'l'oeuvre d'un ennemi'. Cf. also Foix, *Sorcières et Loups-Garous dans les Landes* (Auch, 1904), p.11.
52. Rouleau, *Folklore de la Sologne Bourbonnaise* (Moulins, 1935), pp.115–16. Cf., for other examples, Nimal, 'Histoires contemporaines', *RTP* (1889), p.295. Sadoul, 'Les guérisseurs ... en Lorraine', *Pays Lorrain* (1934), p.75. Bouteiller, *Devins et Sorciers* (Paris, 1958), pp.70–71. Seignolle, *Folklore de Provence* (Paris, 1967), p.400. Ladoucette, *op. cit.*, p.592. Lecoeur, *op. cit.*, II, p.53 n.2.
53. A. D. Allier, Series U. Trib. Correctionnel Montluçon, July-August 1875.
54. *Gaz. Trib.* (15 May 1846), pp.800d–801a.
55. Van Gennep, *Le Folklore de l'Auvergne et du Velay* (Paris, 1942), p.296.
56. Meyrac, *op. cit.*, p.151.
57. Cabanès and Nass, *Poisons et Sortilèges* (Paris, 1913), I, pp.224–5.
58. Cf. also C. Rabaud, *Phénomènes Psychiques et Superstitions Populaires* (Castres, Paris, 1908), p.61.
59. *Gaz. Trib.* (3 December 1832), p.110b–c.
60. Cf. Hobsbawn and Rudé, *Captain Swing* (London, 1973), pp.165–6, 168, 173–4. 244. Cf. Duché, *Le Crime d'Incendie* (Paris University, law thesis, 1913), pp.33–5. Guerry de Champneuf, *Essai sur la Statistique Morale de la France* (Paris, , London, 1833), agrees with Duché in describing it as the poor's way of wreaking vengeance.
61. Mensignac, *Notice sur les Superstitions* (Bordeaux, 1888), p.89. Cf. also, for similar cases, Hermant, *Médecine Populaire* (Brussels, 1928), p.54a. Van Gennep, *Folklore des Hautes-Alpes* (Paris, 1948), II, p.80, Costedoat, 'La Criminalité Mystique', *Annales de Médecine Légale* (1930), pp.152–3, for case in Brabant.
62. *Gazette des Tribunaux* (3 December 1826), p.127b. *Gazette des Tribunaux* (22 November 1826), pp.82a–b. Cf. also Résie, *Histoire et Traité des Sciences Occultes* (Paris, 1857), II, pp.367–8. At Bournol (Lot-et-Garonne) in 1824, four women tried to burn alive an elderly neighbour whom they suspected of having caused their illness. In autumn 1876, the Gazette mentions the case of a family that burned a supposed witch to death. *Gaz. Trib.* (4 October 1826), pp.3–4.
63. In the country near Châtellerault, in 1831, Pichon, a day labourer who was locally thought to be a sorcerer was seized by three peasants who believed he had given a young girl an attack of convulsions by looking at her oddly. He was brought to the house of one of the men, where he was confronted with a fire and accused with casting a spell on the girl. As all his disclaimers were ignored, Pichon decided to admit the guilt: he improvized some rather tentative gestures, after which the girl declared she felt better. Early in August 1757, the body of the labourer Ménard was found near the village of Petit-Assil, in Cossé-le-Vivien. He had been killed and a woman called Gendry had been badly burned by a farmer, Mathurin Guéret, and his friends. Guéret's daughter suffered from some unknown disease, which was diagnosed as a spell cast by Ménard, Guéret's employee, and Gendry, the wife of another labourer to whom he occasionally gave work: Guéret assembled a band of men (composed of a weaver, a

sharecropper and his son, three farm servants and a tenant's son), and brought the victims back to his farm, where they were tortured but continued to insist on their innocence (imprudently refusing to cast a spell on a black hen, which had been procured for the purpose). Cf. *Gaz. Trib.* (8 September 1831), pp.1064c–1065a. Laurain, *Querelles et Procès* (1921), pp.53–63. Other instances of torture on the suspicion of magical crime are given by Béchon, *La Divination et sa Répression dans l'Histoire* (Riom, 1896), pp.47–8. Résie, *op. cit.*, II, p.368. In the same year (1836) at Méry-ès-Bois (Cher), a woman was tortured for having, in the general opinion, including that of the *officier de santé* of Aubigny, cast a spell on a family and its animals. *Ibid*, p.369. Cf. Costedoat, 'La criminalité mystique', *Annales de Médecine Légale* (1930), p.152, for another example.

64. Cf., for example, *Gazette des Tribunaux*, (6 October 1841), p.1324b–c.
65. Costedoat, *op. cit.*, p.150.
66. In Ariège, a sorcerer from Sentrailles, having revealed to his client the culprit in a basin of water, marked the reflection with a knife – being careful not to do this too vigorously lest the guilty man die. In Périgord, the prestigious sorcerer of Berbiguières, consulted about a theft, showed the image of the culprit in a basin of water and, with the consent of his client, thrust a dagger into the reflected head, whereat, far off, the sorcerer screamed and breathed his last, according to the old people of Bézénac. In the early 1920s, one man from Maine-Moulin announced that he intended to require of the sorcerer of Périgueux that the thief be paralysed, whereat, to avoid this fate, the intimidated house-breaker gave himself up to the police. Vézian, 'Les Contre-Envoûtements dans l'Ariège', *Revue de Folklore Français et Colonial* (1935), p.32. Vuillier, 'Chez les Magiciens et les Sorciers', *Tour du Monde* (1899), pp.522–4. Van Gennep, *Le Folklore du Dauphiné* (Paris, 1933), II, p.471. Rocal, *Le Vieux Périgord* (Toulouse, 1927), p.116.
67. Cf. the brilliant work of L. Chevalier, *Classes Laborieuses, Classes Dangereuses* (Paris, 1978), pp.117–225.
68. *Gaz. Trib.* (16 June 1839), p.831.
69. *Gaz. Trib.* (21 August 1834), p.979a–b.
70. Passivity could be more ambiguous, however, cf. Foix, *Sorcières et Loups-Garous dans les Landes* (1904), pp.33–4. Cf. also *Gazette des Tribunaux* (12 April 1838), p.586b. For a trial, during which local people expressed sympathy for a sorcerer, cf. *Gazette des Tribunaux* (30 April 1880), p.439a–d.
71. *Gaz. Trib.* (10 October 1836), p.1106a–b.
72. *Gaz. Trib.* (19 November 1837), p68c.
73. Ladoucette, *Histoire, Topographie... des Hautes Alpes* (Paris, 1848), pp.591–2.
74. Piérart, *Guide Complet du Touriste* (Paris, 1862), p.363.
75. Le Carguet, 'Le Mauvais Oeil', RTP (1889), p.465.

Notes to Chapter V

1. R. Benedict, *Patterns of Culture* (London 1971), pp.195, 198–9. Cf. also J. R. Fox, 'Witchcraft and Clanship in Cochiti Therapy', in A. Kiev, ed., *Magic, Faith and Healing* (New York, London, 1964), p.174. R. Bastide, *Sociologie des Maladies Mentales* (Paris, 1965), p.77.
2. R. Lowie, *Primitive Religion* (New York, 1970), pp.3–14. S. Fuchs, 'Magic Healing Techniques Among the Balahis in Central India', in A. Kiev, ed., *Magic, Faith and Healing* (New York, London, 1964), pp.127–37.
3. M. Leiris, *La Possession et ses Aspects Théâtraux* (Paris, 1958), pp.13–28, 33–4, 43–57, 67–70, 89–91, 95. Cf. also T. K. Oesterreich, *Possession Demoniacal and Other* (London, 1930), p.241.
4. Dodds, *The Greeks and the Irrational* (Berkeley, London, 1973), pp.75–7.
5. Bastide, *Le Rêve, La Transe et la Folie* (Paris, 1972), pp.84–5, 96–7. Cf. also

N. Rodrigues, 'La folie des foules. Nouvelle Contribution à l'étude des folies épidémiques au Brésil', *Annales Médico-psychologiques* (1901), XIII, pp.379–80.

6. For confirmation in observations of contemporary psychiatrists, cf. Dr E. Esquirol, *Des Maladies Mentales* (Paris, 1838), I, pp.401–2. Calmeil, *De la Folie* (Paris, 1845), II, pp.122, 124. Dr Baderot, *Délire Religieux en Bretagne* (Paris University, medical thesis, 1897), pp.16–17. Dr A. Frièse, and Dr A. Marie, *Asile de la Roche-Gandon* (Mayenne, 1891), pp.9, 20–22. Hyvert, *Délires Religieux* (Paris University, medical thesis, 1899), p.57. Cf. also Dagonet, *Traité des Maladies Mentales* (Paris, 1894), p.348, quoting Ball.
7. Gabriel Le Bras, 'Religion Légale et Religion Vécue', *Annales de Sociologie Religieuse* (Jan.-June 1970), p.19.
8. Boismoreau, *Coutumes Médicales* (Paris, 1911), p.117.
9. Villeneuve, *Le Diable dans l'Art* (Paris, 1957), pp.39–73, 111–55. R. Miquel, *Métamorphoses du Diable* (Paris, 1968) *passim*. J. Levron, *Le Diable dans l'Art* (Paris, 1935), pp.18–24, 51–68. E. Mâle, *The Gothic Image* (London, 1961), p.378. P. Francastel, 'Mise-en-Scène et Conscience: le Diable dans la Rue à la Fin du Moyen Age', in E. Castelli, ed., *Cristanesimo e Ragion di Stato* (Rome, 1952), pp.195–204. The tradition was perpetuated in works like the *Grand Calendrier et Compost des Bergers*, dances of death and *ars moriendi* and persisted, after the Revolution, in the *Dragon Rouge*, which showed him as a monstrous goat, standing on its hindlegs and dapperly dressed like a gentleman, appearing to a timorous magician. Nisard, *Histoire des Livres Populaires* (Paris, 1864), I, pp.92–5; II, p.298. For similarity of the work of some engravers of the Restoration with that of their late medieval and early modern predecessors, cf. Sébillot, *La Littérature Orale* (Paris, 1894), P. G. A. Bouët, *Breiz Izel* (Paris, 1844), p.133. Ducourtieux, *Les Almanachs Populaires* (Limoges, 1921), p.38. Bladé, 'Seize Superstitions Populaires de la Gascogne', *Revue de L'Agenais* (1881), p.156.
10. A. Wormser, 'Des Hallucinations Unilatérales' (Paris University, medical thesis, 1895), p.43.
11. Oesterreich, *Possession Demoniacal* (London, 1930), p.99.
12. Baderot, *De l'Influence du Milieu sur le Développement du Délire Religieux en Bretagne* (Paris University, medical thesis, 1897), pp.33–4.
13. Gayral, *Les Délires de Possession* (Paris, 1944), pp.69, 96.
14. *Ibid*, pp.33–4. They affirm that actual hallucinations are less important than the patient's intimate convictions, however, p.97.
15. Van Gennep, *Folklore des Hautes-Alpes* (Paris, 1948), II, pp.75–6.
16. Dr Boismoreau, *Coutumes Médicales* (Paris, 1911), pp.35–7.
17. Dr Marie and Violet, 'L'Envoûtement Moderne', *Journal de Psychologie* (1906), p.211. Hyvert, *op. cit.*, pp.57–8, 69.
18. Fanjoux, *Aperçu Médico-Légal sur la Magie et la Sorcellerie* (Lyon University, medical thesis, 1909), pp.60–61. For other cases, cf. *ibid*, pp.78–9. V. Magnan, *Leçons Cliniques sur les Maladies Mentales* (Paris, 1890), II, pp.272–3. *Ibid* (Paris, 1897), III, pp.113–16. Richer, *Etudes Cliniques sur l'Hystérie* (Paris, 1889), p.316. Dupain, *Etude Clinique sur le Délire Religieux* (Paris University, medical thesis, 1888), p.209. F. Leuret, *Fragmens Psychologiques sur la Folie* (Paris, 1834), p.411–22. M. A. Macario, *Etudes Cliniques sur la Démonomanie* (Paris, 1843), pp.10–11. Pézet, *Contribution à l'Etude de la Démonomanie* (Montpellier, 1909), pp.85–90. Dr C. Cavalier, *Etude Médico-Psychologique* (Montpellier, 1868), pp.61, 67–8.
19. One of the characteristics of hysteria is that it is partially voluntary; that it can be to some extent induced or controlled by the patient. Cf. Demangeon, *Du Pouvoir de l'Imagination sur le Physique et le Moral de l'Homme* (Paris, 1834), pp.52, 57–8, for the case of a premature and plebian psychiatrist.
20. Bataille, *Le Diable au XIXe Siècle* (Paris, 1894), II, p.325. Cf. Lancelin, *La Sorcellerie des Campagnes* (Paris, 1911), pp.90–96, for a dubious beggar who had hypnotic powers, in 1865. Also the case of a woman called Catherine Pfefferkorn from Villers

in Lorraine who was exorcised in Luxembourg in May 1842. She had been possessed at the age of sixteen, when she turned away some beggars who had come asking for charity. They had been angry and had responded by saying: 'The devil take you!' She began to feel ill and her symptoms worsened over the years. Cf. Dr Witry, 'Les Grands Exorcismes du XIXe Siècle', *Revue de l'Hypnotisme et de Psychologie Physiologique* (1905–6), XX, pp.163–4. Cf. also Regnault, *La Sorcellerie* (Bordeaux, 1896), pp.326–7.

21. Fanjoux, *Aperçu Médico-Légal sur la Magie* (Lyon University, medical thesis, 1909), pp.63–6.
22. J. B. Demangeon, *Du Pouvoir de L'Imagination* (Paris, 1834), p.45.
23. *Gazette des Tribunaux* (7 June 1837), p.769b.
24. Westermarck, *Magic and Social Relations* (London, 1905), p.174. Cf. also Regnault, *La Sorcellerie* (Bordeaux, 1896), pp.325–6. The information provided by Regnault's case is scant, but his details differ sufficiently from those given by Westermarck to impose the assumption that the two cases are in fact separate.
25. Regnault, *La Sorcellerie* (Bordeaux, 1896), pp.323–4.
26. Leproux, *Médecine, Magie et Sorcellerie* (Paris, 1954), p.223.
27. *Gazette des Tribunaux* (6 July 1835), pp.863c–4a.
28. This syndrome was a well-known form of mental illness in the area, according to Trébucq; cf. Trébucq, *La Chanson Populaire* (Bordeaux, 1912), I, pp.276 note 3, 276–7.
29. R. Bastide, *Sociologie des Maladies Mentales* (Paris, 1965), p.261.
30. C. Gagnon, *Le Folklore Bourbonnais* (Moulins, 1949), II, pp.182–3. Lhermitte reported a case involving a similar game, in which the rules of communication were changed by the ill. In 1853, a sixty-three-year-old carpenter from the Lyonnais, Antoine Gay, who thought he was possessed, met a thirty-six-year-old woman whom Satan had struck dumb when she had been in her twentieth year. Their respective devils conversed. Lhermitte, *Vrais et Faux Possédés* (Paris, 1956), pp.140–42.
31. Sébillot, *Le Folklore de France* (Paris, 1904), I, pp.287–8.
32. *Gazette des Tribunaux* (24 April 1833), pp.627b–c.
33. Cf. Bastide, *Sociologie des Maladies Mentales* (Paris, 1965), p.233.
34. *Gazette des Tribunaux* (26 October 1854), p.1032c. Cf. also Dupain, *Etude Clinique sur le Délire Religieux* (Paris University, medical thesis, 1888), pp.244–5, for a Breton family in which a mother, two boys and a girl murdered their sister, who thought she was possessed, in a fit of manic religious exaltation and under the direction of one of the sons.
35. In 1871, Legrand du Saulle introduced the notion of the communicated persecution complex into psychiatry and the first clinical descriptions of *folie à deux* were furnished at the end of the decade. In 1877, Lasègue and Falret established the importance of collective suggestion in what they called mental contagion. Lasègue and Falret, 'De la folie à deux ou folie communiquée', *Annales Médico-Psychologiques* (July-Dec. 1877), 18, pp.321–55. Régis, *La Folie à Deux ou Folie Simultanée* (Paris, 1880), pp.8–11, 22. Dr Maradon de Montyel, 'Des Conditions de la Contagion Mentale Morbide', *Annales Médico-Psychologiques* (Jan.-June 1894), 19, pp.267–9, 467–72, 483–6. Dr N. Rodrigues, 'La Folie des Foules', *Annales Médico-Psychologiques* (Jan.-March 1901), pp.21, 195. Dr G. Garrier, *Contribution à l'Etude des Folies par Contagion* (Evreux, 1903), p.10. Cf. R. Bsatide, *Sociologie des Maladies Mentales* (Paris, 1965), pp.94–103.
36. Lasègue and Falret, 'De la Folie à Deux ou Folie communiquée', rpr. in Dr J. Falret, *Des Maladies Mentales* (Paris, 1890), pp.551–3, 559–67, 571–4. Brierre de Boismont, *Des Hallucinations* (Paris, 1852), p.131. F. Leuret, *Fragmens psychologiques* (Paris, 1834), pp.264–8, for a particularly poignant case.
37. Bastide, *Sociologie des Maladies Mentales* (Paris, 1965), pp.96–7.
38. Dr. J. Lhermitte, *Vrais et Faux Possédés* (Paris, 1956), pp.37–48, 70, 83–101,

118–24. Cf. also Dr P. Janet, *L'Etat Mental des Hystériques* (Paris, 1911), pp.39, 45–7, 71, 91, 163, 197. P. Janet, *Névroses et Idées Fixes* (Paris, 1909), pp.94–5, 107–9, 112–19, 178–9, 234, 256, 279–302. P. Janet, 'Croyances et Hallucinations', *Revue Philosophique* (1932), pp.281–4, 288–9. Dr F. Desjars, *Les Récits Imaginaires chez les Hystériques* (Paris University, medical thesis, 1899), p.19. Dr. V. Stefani, *Les Délires Hystériques* (Bordeaux, 1912), pp.15–18.

39. Buisson, *Considérations Médicales sur deux Cas de Médecine Pratique* (Montpellier University, medical thesis, 1810), pp.5–19.

40. But cf. Friése and Marie, *Asile de la Roche Gandon* (Mayenne, 1891), pp.27–9, for physical abuse of the mentally ill. Also A.N. BB^{18} 985–4433.

41. Sutter, *Le Diable, ses Paroles, son Action dans les Possédés d'Illfurt* (Arras, 1934), pp.15–21, 30, 76–87, 107–18.

42. T. de Cauzons, *La Magie et la Sorcellerie en France* (Paris, 1912), IV, pp.585–8. Regnault, *La Sorcellerie* (Bordeaux, 1896), pp.124–5.

43. Cf. for examples, Lamouroux, *Essai Critique* (Paris University, medical thesis, 1865), pp.26–7. Bouchet, *Relation sur l'Epidémie de Morzine* (Lyon University, medical thesis, 1899), p.69. Dr Armangaud, 'Recherches Cliniques', *Mémoires et Bulletins* (1879), pp.551–2. Cf. also for an epidemic of hysteria which affected young factory workers (mostly girls under the age of fourteen) from the Marcols area of Ardèche in 1882: Bouzol, 'Relation d'une Epidémie à Phénomènes Hystéro-Choréïques', *Lyon Médical* (1884), 47, pp.142–8, 174–80.

44. A. Fenayroux, *Contribution à l'Etude des Folies Rurales* (Toulouse University, medical thesis, 1894), pp.133–4.

45. Félice, *Foules en Délire* (Paris, 1947), pp.326–9.

46. Bastide, *Le Rêve, la Transe et la Folie* (Paris, 1972), p.68.

47. In Sweden in 1841, the convulsions and prophecies of a sixteen-year-old girl were quickly imitated and reached epidemic proportions. A similar episode occurred in Italy, in the Friulian village of Verzegnis in 1878. L. Petit, 'Une Epidémie d'Hystéro-Démonopathie, en 1878, à Verzegnis, province de Frioul, Italie', *Revue Scientifique* (10 April 1880), No. 41, pp.974A–5A. Prouvost, *Le Délire Prophétique* (Bordeaux University, medical thesis, 1896), pp.76, 80. Richer, *Etudes Cliniques sur l'Hystérie* (Paris, 1889), pp.676–7.

48. Dr Constans, *Relation sur une Epidémie d'Hystéro-Démonopathie* (Paris, 1862), pp.7, 13–14.

49. Constans, *op. cit.*, pp.16–19, 21, 35.

50. A. Baleydier, *A Propos d'un Mal Mystérieux à Morzine, sous le Second Empire* (Chambéry, 1949), pp.14, 19–22. Dr A. Giraud, *Fragments d'Histoire de la Folie* (Bar-le-Duc, 1883), pp.20–21. M. J. Tissot, *Les Possédés de Morzine ou le Diable qui n'y voit goutte* (Paris, 1865), pp.30–31.

51. Constans, *op. cit.*, pp.31–7.

Notes to Chapter VI

1. The prophecies of the Camisards and of the 'prophets of the Dauphiné' in the late seventeenth and early eighteenth centuries showed how secular purposes could adopt ostensibly religious guises. Children were taught to have convulsions and to predict the triumph of Protestantism. The episode showed not only how artificial convulsions and prophecies could be, but also how they were exploited by prophets to establish both their authority and the importance of their opinions. Cf. Migne, *Nouvelle Encyclopédie Théologique*, ser. 2, 25 (1854), Art. 'Prophètes du Dauphiné', cols 680–82. *Ibid*, ser. 2, 24 (1852), Art. 'Fanatiques', cols 731–5.
2. *Loc cit.*, pp.75–8. This is presumably 'Abagare's letter' mentioned by Delehaye, copies of which were still venerated in eighteenth-century England, he affirms. He cites Cureton as remembering having seen copies in Shropshire peasants' cottages in 1864.

Delehaye, 'Note sur la légende de la lettre du Christ', *Acad. Royale de Belgique* (1899), pp.196–212.

3. Saintyves, *Reliques et Images Légendaires* (Paris, 1912), p.312.
4. Delehaye, 'Note sur la légende de la lettre du Christ', *Acad. Royale de Belgique* (1899), pp.196–212.
5. N. Cohn, *The Pursuit of the Millennium* (London, 1970), pp.62, 94–5, 119–20, 129–34. Saintyves, *Reliques et Images*, pp.311–17, who bases himself mainly on Delehaye.
6. Black, *Folk Medicine* (London, 1883), pp.83–5.
7. *Enchiridion Leonis Papae* (Lille, 1813).
8. Coulon, 'Erreurs, Superstitions', *Mémoires de la Société d'Emulation de Cambrai* (1911), p.27. This prayer was also discovered in the notebook of a faith-healer from the *pays d'Ajoie*, who had inherited her recipes from her father. Cf. Schindelholz, *Grimoires et Secrets* (Portentruy, 1973), pp.161–2.
9. Hermant, *Médecine Populaire* (Brussels, 1928), pp.161–2. Capré also found an apocryphal letter to Charlemagne in a late fourteenth or early fifteenth-century breviary. Cf. J. Capré, *Histoire du Véritable Messager Boîteux* (Vevay, 1884), p.164.
10. The abundance of proverbs, riddles, currency of metaphor were notable features of popular speech.
11. Saintyves, *Reliques et Images*, pp.323–4.
12. Perraudière, 'La Lettre de Dieu', *Mém. Soc. Nat. d'Angers* (1905), pp.134–5.
13. C. Fraysse, 'Les Lettres d'Origine Céleste au pays de Baugé', *Revue de Folklore Français et Colonial* (1935), p.119. He found a similar letter in the *pays de Baugé*, whose supposed origins coincided with those of the letter carried by Perraudière's *chouan* in 1793. Cf. *ibid*, p.120.
14. Perraudière, *loc. cit.*, pp.133–4.
15. Delehaye, *loc. cit.*, pp.192–3.
16. Saintyves, *Reliques et Images*, pp.318–22.
17. Cf. Delehaye, 'Note sur la Légende', *Acad. Royale de Belgique* (1899), p.194. Another example is furnished by a copy of a letter of Christ, written into the end of the death register for 1599 by the *curé* of Beaufort-en-Vallée. The missive was placed under a stone by the angel Gabriel: 'les villagiers circonvoisins de ce lieu ung chascun se tranceporta [sic] pour veoirs se beau miracle et pour veoirs lever ceste pierre; et se forsirrez tous les gens ne seures onques lever sans procession et prière à l'entour, afin de lever ceste pierre; enfin se trouve ung petit enfant azé de six ans lequel la leva tout seul...' Fraysse, in *Revue de Folklore Français* (1933), p.121. The last motif is familiar from Arthurian legend.
18. Séguin, *Nouvelles à Sensation* (Paris, 1959), pp.124ff.
19. *Le Médecin des Pauvres* (Armentières, Imp. Cadot-Petit, c.1868), pp.7–8.
20. Lecotté, *Les Cultes Populaires* (1953), p.275a–b.
21. Gagnon, *Le Folklore Bourbonnais* (1968), III, pp.20–21, and n.18.
22. Cf. letter cited by Mensignac, *Notice sur les Superstitions* (1888), p.29.
23. Cf. Nisard, *Histoire des Livres Populaires* (Paris, 1864), II, pp.15–17. Mensignac, *Notice sur les Superstitions* (1888), p.27.
24. Mensignac, *Notice sur les Superstitions* (1888), pp.28–9.
25. Lecotté, *Les Cultes Populaires* (1953), pp.274a–5a.
26. Cauzons, *La Magie et la Sorcellerie* (Paris, 1912), IV, pp.604–13.
27. Ladoucette, *Histoire, Topographie... des Hautes Alpes* (Paris, 1848), pp.595–6.
28. Prouvost, *Délire Prophétique* (1896), pp.73–5. Cf. also A. Kselman, *Miracles and Prophecies in Nineteenth-Century France* (New Brunswick, 1983), pp.79, 60–83 for interesting discussion of prophecies in the nineteenth century.
29. A. N. F.19 5555–22.
30. Interest in spiritualism was not confined to the well-to-do or to townsfolk, as the case of Jean Hillaire, a clog-maker from Sonnac (Charente Inf.) illustrates. Hillaire

claimed that his dead father, with whom he maintained a supernatural correspondence, effected miracles for him. Cf. Bez, *Les Miracles de Nos Jours* (Paris, Bordeaux, 1864), pp.20–22.

31. Prouvost, *Délire Prophétique* (1896), pp.88–90.
32. Goubert and Cristiani, *Messages et Apparitions* (Paris, 1952), pp.14–25.
33. Cf. also the case of Mlle Couëdon in the 1890s. Prouvost, *Délire Prophétique* (1896), pp.95–111.
34. Mauriac and Verdalle, *Etude Médicale sur l'Extatique du Fontet* (Paris, 1875), pp.5–21, 26–7, 35–40.
35. Migne, *Nouvelle Encyclopédie Théologique*, ser. 2. 25 (1854), Art. 'Prophéties', col. 215.
36. *Ibid*, cols 724–30.
37. *Les Vingt-Cinq Apparitions de l'Archange Raphaël* (1886), pp.3–11. Silvy, *Relation Concernant les Evénements* (Paris, 1817), pp.5–16, 62. Cf. also *La Vérité sur la Mort de T. Martin* (Paris, 1834).
38. Sabbatier, *Affaire de la Salette* (Paris, 1857), pp.1–8. Goubert and Cristiani, *Messages et Apparitions* (1952), pp.33–49. Donnadieu, *Salette-Fallavaux* (1851), I, pp.22–47, 151.
39. *Gazette des Tribunaux* (13 June 1847), pp.810c–d.
40. Cf. also Kselman, *Miracles and Prophecies* (1983), who makes the same point.
41. Sabbatier, *Affaire de La Salette* (1857), pp.2b–4b. *Le Médecin des Pauvres* (Armentières, c.1868), pp.7–8. Cf. Séguin, *Nouvelles à Sensation* (1959), pp.129–30, for reciprocal exploitation of the vision by broadsheets.
42. Cf. J. Hellé, *Miracles* (London, 1953), pp.114–15. In 1917 the visions at Fatima (a poor Portuguese village) promised that if man did not cease offending God, the world be punished by war and famine and (in a contemporary adaptation) Russia would spread error and devastation across the world.
43. The episcopal commission set up to investigate the case reported in January 1862 and confirmed the veracity of Bernadette's assertions.
44. J. Deery, *Our Lady of Lourdes* (Dublin, 1958), pp.11–14. Laurentin, *Lourdes* (Paris, 1957), I, pp.128–9. M. de S. Pierre, *Bernadette and Lourdes* (London, 1954), pp.21–68.
45. Michel de Saint-Pierre, *Bernadette and Lourdes* (London, 1954), pp.69–72. Laurentin, *Lourdes* (1958), II, pp.17, 23. Diday, *Examen Medical des Miracles de Lourdes* (Paris, 1873), pp.53–4, 61.
46. See above, pp.15–17.
47. J. Hellé, *Miracles* (London, 1953), pp.97–100.

Notes to Chapter VII

1. *Gazette des Tribunaux* (13 February 1843), p.436d.
2. G. Bollème, *Les Almanachs Populaires* (Paris, 1969), p.16.
3. Laisnel de la Salle, *Croyances et Légendes* (Paris, 1875), I, pp.313–15.
4. Kaufmann, 'Pratiques et Superstitions' (Paris University, medical thesis, 1906), p.19.
5. Macario, *Etudes Cliniques* (Paris, 1843), pp.42–3.
6. Jalby, *Sorcellerie* (Nyons, 1974), p.34.
7. Boismoreau, *Coutumes Médicales* (Paris, 1911), p.112.
8. L. Kerbirou, 'Sorcellerie et Diableries en Bretagne', *Nouvelle Revue de Bretagne* (1947), III, pp.164–5. He implies that the book dated from the eighteenth century.
9. Jalby, *op. cit.*, p.35.
10. Cf. *Gazette des Tribunaux* (22 November 1826), p.82a; *Gazette des Tribunaux* (19 April 1844), p.594d.
11. Bouteiller, *Sorciers et Jeteurs de Sort* (Paris, 1958), pp.152–3.

12. *Gazette des Tribunaux* (3 Oct. 1866), p.494b.
13. *Gazette des Tribunaux* (2 Feb. 1841), p.407b.
14. *Gazette des Tribunaux* (29 Oct. 1829), p.1227b.
15. Cf. R. Mandrou, *De la Culture Populaire* (Paris, 1975), p.84.
16. *Gazette des Tribunaux* (2 March 1828), pp.463b–4a.
17. *Gazette des Tribunaux* (14 Oct 1835), p.1303a. I consulted two copies of this work: one dated Ancona 1660, and the other Lille 1810. They were identical.
18. *Gazette des Tribunaux* (8 Oct. 1840), p1216a.
19. *Le Dragon Noir ou les Forces Infernales Soumises â l'Homme* (Paris, 1896), p.72.
20. *Ibid*, pp.87–90.
21. *Gazette des Tribunaux* (28 April 1837), p.628c.
22. *Gazette des Tribunaux* (29 July 1843), p.1009b.
23. *Gazette des Tribunaux* (18 July 1880), p.748a.
24. J. Lemoine, 'La Sorcellerie contemporaine', *La Tradition* (1892), p.110.
25. Nisard, *op. cit.*, II, 23–33.
26. Perdiguier, *Mémoires d'un Compagnon* (Paris, 1914), p.35.
27. *Gazette des Tribunaux* (16 Oct. 1827), p1458b–1460a, and *ibid*, (25 Nov. 1827), 75a.
28. Nisard, *Histoire des Livres Populaires* (Paris, 1864), I, pp.141–2.
29. Nisard, *op. cit.*, I, p.146. Cf. *Le Véritable Dragon Rouge* (Nismes, Garde, 1823), pp.64ff, which includes a prayer to God and the saints to protect the invoker from the devil.
30. Résie, *Sciences Occultes* (Paris, 1857), II, pp.361–2.
31. *Gazette des Tribunaux* (27 February 1835).
32. Bouteiller, *Sorciers et Jeteurs de Sort* (Paris, 1958), p.150.
33. *Gazette des Tribunaux* (20 Feb. 1835), p.390a–b.
34. *Gazette des Tribunaux* (31 Dec. 1840), p.215b.
35. *Gazette des Tribunaux* (18 May 1837), p699b.
36. C. Fraysse, 'Au pays de Baugé. Deux sorciers en justice', RTP (1906), XXI, pp.253–7.
37. Cf. Michelet, *La Sorcière* (Paris, 1964), p.74, n.1.
38. Miron, *Le Prêtre et Le Sorcier* (Paris, 1872), pp.196–8.
39. F. Leuret, *Fragmens Psychologiques sur la Folie* (Paris, 1834), p.405.
40. Cf. above, pp. 124–8.
41. *Gazette des Tribunaux* (12 April 1835), p.572c.
42. Bouteiller, *Sorciers et Jeteurs de Sort*, pp.48–56.
43. *Gazette des Tribunaux* (9 March 1828), p.488.
44. Cf. *Gazette des Tribunaux* (25 Dec. 1826), p.223b for the trial of a popular man for this offence, at Alençon. *Ibid* (12 June 1827), p.946b, for the trial of several fraudulent individuals at Villefranche (Haute-Garonne). *Ibid* (3 Nov. 1834), p.9b, for the trial of a weaver.
45. *Gazette des Tribunaux* (6 August 1828), p.1012a.
46. *Gazette des Tribunaux* (1836), p.108a.
47. *Gazette des Tribunaux* (27 June 1826), pp.3–4.
48. Cf. S. Thompson, *The Folktale* (Berkeley, 1977), pp.262–3. A. Hugo, *La France Pittoresque* (Paris, 1835), II, pp.214b–15a. Belmont, *Mythes et Croyances* (Paris, 1973), p.39. Résie, *Histoire et Traité des Sciences Occultes* (Paris, 1857), I, pp.145–207.
49. *Gazette des Tribunaux* (4 January 1833), p.217c.
50. *Gazette des Tribunaux* (3 October 1828), p.1208c. Cf. also *ibid*, 21 January 1846, for a woman who consulted a fortune-teller to reassure herself about her husband's fidelity to her and to win a fortune.
51. *Gazette des Tribunaux* (7 May 1837), p.657b.
52. *Gazette des Tribunaux* (1 and 2 Feb. 1830), p.310c.

53. Cauzons, *La Magie et La Sorcellerie* (Paris, 1912), IV, pp.195–6.
54. E. L'Homméde, 'Un procès de sorcellerie au village', *Revue des Etudes Historiques* (July-Sep. 1931), pp.261–77.
55. *Gazette des Tribunaux* (5 August 1827), p.1168b.
56. *Gazette des Tribunaux* (2 March 1828), p463b–4a.
57. *Gazette des Tribunaux* (11 June 1827), p.747a.
58. Résie, *Sciences Occultes* (Paris, 1857), II, pp.359–60.
59. *Gazette des Tribunaux* (29 July 1829), p.910.
60. The bibliography on urban poverty in this period is enormous. Cf. Haussonville, 'La Misère à Paris', RDM (15 June 1881), pp.14–49. *Ibid* (1 Oct. 1881), pp.611–51. Cère, *Les Populations Dangereuses* (Paris, 1872), pp.220–21, 279. Gasparin, *Rapport au Roi* (Paris, 1837). Watteville, *Statistique des Etablissements de Bienfaisance* (Paris, 1854), pp.55–1179, gives statistical material on poverty in France in the mid-century. F. Le Play, *Les Ouvriers Européens* (Paris, 1855). Villermé, 'Mémoire sur la Mortalité en France', *Mémoires de l'Academie Royale de Médecine* (1828), I, pp.51–98. For modern statistical surveys, cf. O. Voillard *et al.*, *Statistique d'Histoire Economique* (Strasbourg, Paris, 1964); Goulène, *Evolution des Pouvoirs d'Achat* (Paris, 1974).
61. *Gazette des Tribunaux* (25 May 1844), p.718d.
62. In Strasbourg in 1842, a workman had called a gipsy in to cure his sick wife, and she had concocted a story about Satan, ghosts and treasures before being reported by a neighbour. *Gazette des Tribunaux* (9 October 1842), p.1354a–b.
63. Malinowsky, *Magic, Science and Religion* (London, 1974), p.81.
64. *Gazette des Tribunaux* (4 October 1840), p1204a–c.
65. *Gazette des Tribunaux* (19 December 1832), pp.164c–5a.
66. *Gazette des Tribunaux* (24 February 1841), p.407b–c.
67. *Gazette des Tribunaux* (31 August 1845), p.1049a.
68. *Gazette des Tribunaux* (26 May 1833), pp.242c–3c.
69. *Gazette des Tribunaux* (29 August 1843), pp.1108–9b.
70. *Gazette des Tribunaux* (25 November 1827), p.97b.
71. Cf. above, p.248 n.70. According to Rabaud, a young man, who wished to hasten his uncle's death in order to inherit his wealth rapidly, consulted a Breton witch. She arranged for the uncle to be visited by a mysterious nocturnal apparition, which announced that he would die on Palm Sunday, at the third stroke of the bell for high mass. The man was terrified, fell ill and died at the appointed hour. Rabaud, *Phénomènes Psychologiques et Superstitions Populaires* (Paris, Castres, 1908), p.63. Cf. also Lévi-Strauss, *Anthropologie Structurale* (Paris, 1974 rpr.), pp.183–4 for similar phenomenon.
72. *Gazette des Tribunaux* (4 and 5 May 1829), p623b.
73. *Gazette des Tribunaux* (6 June 1841), p794c.

Notes to Chapter VIII

1. Cf. above, pp.24–7.
2. P. Delarue, *Le Conte Populaire Français* (1957), I, p.43. M. Belmont, *Mythes et Croyances dans L'Ancienne France* (Paris, 1973), p.19. Perrault, *Contes*, ed. Collin de Plancy (pseud. Baron C. A. de Walckenauer) (Paris, 1826), p.78. Delarue, 'Les Contes Merveilleux de Perrault et la Tradition Populaire', *Bull. Folk. Île de France* (1951), p.197. Bladé, *Contes Populaires recueillis en Agenais* (1874), p.93, n.1. He heard two versions of Peau d'Âne. M. Soriano, *Les Contes de Perrault* (Paris, 1977), pp.141–6.
3. P. Sébillot, *Contes de la Haute Bretagne qui Présentent quelques Ressemblances avec des Contes Imprimés* (Paris, 1894), pp.8–10.
4. P. Delarue and A. Millien, *Contes du Nivernais* (Paris, 1953), pp.50–58.
5. Perrault, 'Les Fées', in *Oeuvres* (1826), pp.27–30. M. Soriano, *Les Contes de Perrault*, pp.136–40.

6. Bladé, *Contes Populaires recueillis en Agenais* (1874), pp.15–21.
7. *Histoire de... Robert le Diable* (n.d.), *Histoire de Richard sans Peur* (n.d.). R. Mandrou, *De le Culture Populaire aux 17e et 18e siècles* (2nd edn, Paris 1975), p.58. Cf. *Histoire de Cartouche* (Paris, 1843). *Histoire du Célèbre Mandrin, Chef de Bandits* (Paris, n.d.) for popular chapbooks celebrating rebels.
8. Cf. S. Thompson, *The Folktale* (Berkeley, London, 1977), pp.106–7 for other examples.
9. Michel Butor, 'On Fairy Tales', in V. W. Gras, ed., *European Literary Theory* (New York, 1973), p.354.
10. Cf. Funk and Wagnall, *Standard Dictionary of Folklore, Mythology and Legend*, ed. M. Leach (New York, 1950), II, p.935, col. 1, for the universal popularity of this theme. S. Thompson, *Motif-Index of Folk Literature* (Bloomington, 1935), V, pp.3–23.
11. R. H. Codrington, *The Melanesians* (1st edn 1891, New York, 1972), pp.336–7. He suggested that the Melanesians' attitude to stories was no less complex than our own and that it implied a similar distinction between truth and interest in commonplace reality.
12. Thompson, *The Folktale*, p.152.
13. Laisnel de la Salle, *Croyances et Légendes* (1873), I, pp.139–53. Luzel, 'L'Enfant qui fut à l'école', *Annales de Bretagne* (1894), pp.271–6, 409–15, for a Breton version.
14. Thompson, *The Folktale*, pp.45–7.
15. Carnoy, *Littérature Orale de la Picardie* (Paris, 1883), pp.139–46, 67–78.
16. H. de Champfleury, *Recherches sur les Origines et les Variations de Bonhomme Misère* (Paris, 1861), pp.22–6.
17. Carnoy, *Littérature Orale de la Picardie*, pp.78–89.
18. P. Brochon, *Le Livre de Colportage en France depuis le XVI*e *siècle* (1954), pp.34–6. He seems to think that the theme passed into folklore by means of the *Bibliothèque Bleue*. However, the story's origins are older than he or Champfleury knew, cf. Champfleury, *Bonhomme Misère*, pp.5–6, 18–19. Nisard, *Histoire des Livres Populaires*, I, pp.413–14. Thompson, *The Folktale*, pp.45–7.
19. Champfleury, *op. cit.*, pp.8–19. Nisard, *Histoire des Livres Populaires*, I, pp.410–15.
20. P. Saintyves, *Les Contes de Perrault et les Récits Parallèles* (1923), pp.xviii–xix *passim*. He believed some stories to be commentaries on a ritual about seasonal renewal; others, like *Puss in Boots*, were related to initiation ceremonies, in his view.
21. Cf. M. Eliade, 'Les Mythes et les Contes de Fées' (1956), rpr. in *Aspects du Mythe* (Paris, 1963), pp.234–5, for his comments on Saintyves. Cf. also *ibid*, pp.243–4, and V. Propp, 'Les Transformations du Conte Merveilleux', (1928), rpr. in *Morphologie du Conte* (12th edn, Paris, 1973), pp.176, 180–81.
22. S. Thompson, *The Folktale*, p.386. M. Soriano, *Les Contes de Perrault* (2nd edn, Paris, 1977), p.45. N. Belmont, *Mythes et Croyances dans l'Ancienne France* (Paris, 1973), pp.130–33.
23. F. Boas, 'Stylistic Aspects of Primitive Literature' (1925), in *Race, Language and Culture* (rpr. New York and London, 1966), pp.497–8.
24. Tenèze, 'Du Conte Merveilleux', *Arts et Traditions Populaires* (1970), p.52. Thompson, *The Folktale*, p.453, citing M. Azadovsky, *Eine Sibirische Märchenerzählerin*, FF Communications No. 68. (Helsinki, 1926).
25. Lo Nigro, *Tradizione e Inventione nel Racconto Popolare* (Florence, 1964), p.34.
26. P. Delarue, *Le Conte Populaire Français* (Paris, 1957), I, pp.36–41, 43. Cf. G. Bollème, 'Littérature Populaire et Littérature de Colportage', in F. Furet, ed., *Livre et Société dans la France du XVIII*e *Siècle* (Paris, 1965), pp.88–9.
27. Cited in E. Zolla, *Storia del Fantasticare* (Milan, 1964), p.222.
28. Helvétius, *De l'Homme* (sect. II, ch. xx), in R. Desné, ed., *Les Matérialistes Français* (Paris, 1965), pp.100–1.

29. Nodier, *Du Fantastique* (Paris, 1852), p.xxix.
30. While pioneering studies of oral literature emphasized its whimsical unpredictability, modern studies have been dominated by the attempt to establish its characteristic forms, style and content. Cf. A. Van Gennep, *La Formation des Légendes* (Paris, 1910), pp.14ff. S. Thompson, *Motif-Index of Folk Literature* (Helsinki, 1932–6). A. Arne, *Verzeichnis der Märchen-typen* (Helsinki, 1910). V. Propp, *Morphologie du Conte* (1927/1973). M.-L. Tenèze, 'Introduction à l'étude de la littérature orale: le conte', AESC (1969), p.118. M.-L. Tenèze, 'Du Conte Merveilleux', *Arts et Traditions Populaires* (1970), pp.46–7, for the enterprise of Jan de Vries. R. Jakobson, 'Folklore', *Questions de Poétique* (Paris, 1973), pp.63–4, 69. E. S. Hartland, *The Science of Fairy Tales* (London, 1891). L. Dégh, *Folktales and Society* (Bloomington, 1969), pp.172–6, 179, 181, who stresses the importance of improvization within fixed forms.
31. Delarue, *Le Conte Populaire Français*, I, p.44. In 1926, Bartlett had already pointed to the importance of social relationships in forming the story. Cf. C. Bartlett, 'Psychology in Relation to the Popular Story', *Folklore* (December 1920), pp.266–7.
32. M. Soriano, *Les Contes de Perrault* (2nd edn, Paris, 1977), p.470.
33. Lo Nigro, *Tradizione e Invenzione nel Racconto Popolare* (1964), pp.13–14.
34. M. Butor, 'On Fairy Tales', in V. Gras, ed., *European Literary Theory and Practice* (New York, 1973), pp.353–4. Cf. J. Zipes, *Breaking The Magic Spell* (London, 1979), for a dogmatic and simplistic affirmation of the same point.
35. T. Todorov, *Introduction à la Littérature Fantastique* (Paris, 1970), pp.46–7.
36. R. Barthes, 'Introduction à l'analyse structurale des récits' (1966), in R. Barthes *et al.*, *Poétique de Récit* (1977), p.52.
37. Van Heurck and Bockenoogen, *L'Imagerie Populaire Flamande* (1910), pp.127–8. J. Delumeau, *La Mort des Pays de Cocagne. Comportements Collectifs de la Renaissance à l'âge classique* (Paris, 1976), pp.11–14. It seems to have been less well known in France than in Flanders or Italy.
38. Sébillot, *Gargantua dans les Traditions Populaires* (1883), pp.xii–iv, xxvii, i, 118 *passim*. Cf. Dambielle, *La Sorcellerie en Gascogne* (1907), p.28: he liked Gargantua, Artus and the Juif Errant best among his grandparents' collection of stories. Gargantua, the Wandering Jew, Geneviève de Brabant, Lustucru and Le Monde Renversé were among some of the most popular prints among artisans and peasants in the nineteenth century, according to Garnier. Cf. Garnier, *Histoire de l'Imagerie Populaire* (Chartres, 1869), pp.70–72, 85–8.
39. In the Hautes-Alpes, in the opinion of Joisten, traditional story-tellers were influenced by the Deckherr chapbook (which was printed at Montbéliard four times between 1823 and 1828). C. Joisten, 'De quelques sources d'influence dans la formation des récits légendaires alpestres', *Arts et Traditions Populaires* (1970), pp.152–3. The oral and printed traditions seem to have reinforced and influenced each other, although Sébillot thinks that the oral tradition was largely independent of the written one, and drew mainly on popular iconography. Sébillot, *Gargantua*, p.xxiv. This opinion does not seem to hold true of reciprocal influences in general.
40. *Histoire de Fameux Gargantua* (Deckherr, Montbéliard, 1848), pp.15–18, 24–6.
41. P. L. Duchartre and R. Saulnier, *L'Imagerie Populaire* (Paris, 1925), date it later and Peter Burke assigns it to the sixteenth century. Cf. P. Burke, *Popular Culture in Early Modern Europe* (London, 1979), p.188.
42. Van Heurck and Boekenoogen, *Imagerie Populaire Flamande* (1910), p.115. Cf. also *French Popular Imagery* (London, 1974), pp.99a for brief notes on prints from Orléans and Epinal, late eighteenth- and early nineteenth-century versions of the theme.
43. Van Heurck and Boeckenoogen, *Imagerie Populaire Flamande* (1910), p.348. J. J. Cuisenier, *French Folk Art* (New York, Tokyo, 1977), pp.166a–b, 261.
44. Jean Adhémar, 'Introduction', *French Popular Imagery* (London, 1974), pp.17–18. Garnier, *Histoire de L'Imagerie Populaire* (1869), pp.222–4.

45. Van Heurck and Boekenoogen, *Imagerie Populaire Flamande*, p.384. Garnier, *Histoire de L'Imagerie Populaire*, pp.75–6.
46. This theme was originally inspired by the artistic pretensions of the 'Précieuses', and quickly became popular.
47. *French Popular Imagery*, pp.62, 74b, 75b. Cf. the notion of the miraculous mill which husbands and wives were put through to improve their tempers, and which was popular from the sixteenth century to the nineteenth century.
48. The same predilection for grotesque personification is seen in the lore of childhood. Cf. Adhémar, 'Introduction', *French Popular Imagery*, pp.18, 59b. Children were encouraged to be obedient by being threatened with being carried off and punished by a variety of monsters, like *L'Ome Nègre* (in the Languedoc), the *Male Bête* or *Croquemitaine*. Cf. Fabre and Lacroix, *La Vie Quotidienne en Languedoc* (Paris, 1973), pp.111–13; R. Lecotté, *Village de France* (Paris, 1945), p.173. Good children were rewarded by characters like *Saint Nicolas*, *L'Enfant Jésus* and *Tante Arie*. Cf. D. Monnier and A. Vingtrinier, *Croyances et Traditions Populaires* (1874), p.23.
49. For the Feast of Fools, cf. Peter Burke, *Popular Culture in Early Modern Europe* (London, 1979), p.192. Grenier, *Introduction à l'Histoire Générale* (Amiens, 1856), pp.353–62, 370. Chéreul, *Dictionnaire Historique* (Paris, 1885), I, p.418a. A. De Nore, *Coutumes, Mythes et Traditions des Provinces de France* (Paris, 1846), p.36. Cf. also F. Bourquelot, *L'Office de la Fête des Fous* (Sens, 1856). H. Cox, *The Feast of Fools* (New York, 1970), p.23ff.
50. M. Bakhtine, *L'Oeuvre de François Rabelais* (Paris, 1970), pp.17–21 *passim*. P. Burke, *Popular Culture in Early Modern Europe* (1979), pp.181–95.
51. Cf. *Rapprezentazione e Festa di Carnesciale et della Quaresima*, in L. Manzoni, *Libro di Carnevale dei Secoli XVe e XVIe* (Bologna, 1881), pp.80–119. It is notable for its satire on the state.
52. Grenier, *Introduction à L'Histoire Générale*, pp.366–7. H. Cox, *The Feast of Fools*, p.3. Burke, *Popular Culture*, p.184. Van Gennep, *Manuel de Folklore Français Contemporain* (Paris, 1947), I, part III, p.881.
53. The phenomenon was also present in the burlesque festivities arranged by the lower clergy at Christmas during the Middle Ages, notably the *Fête des Innocents*.
54. Grenier, *Introduction à L'Histoire Générale*, pp.367–8. Their activities were initially suppressed in 1648 by a new magistrate.
55. N. Belmont, *Mythes et Croyances dans l'Ancienne France* (Paris, 1973), pp.68–78. A. Van Gennep, *Manuel de Folklore Français Contemporain* (Paris, 1947), I, part III, pp.868–995, 1049–88. P. Burke, *Popular Culture in Early Modern Europe*, pp.182–5. Grenier, *Introduction à l'Histoire Générale*, pp.366. Y. M. Bercé, *Fête et Révolte* (Paris, 1976), pp.16–18.
56. J. C. F. Ladoucette, *Histoire, Topographie... Hautes Alpes* (Paris, 1848), p.575.
57. Clément-Héméry, *Fêtes Civiles et Religieuses* (Cambrai, 1836), p.355 (bis), n.1. E. Cortet, *Essai sur les Fêtes Religieuses* (Paris, 1857), pp.160–62. Van Gennep, *Manuel de Folklore Français Contemporain* (Paris, 1949), I, part IV, pp.1452–87.
58. Cortet, *Fêtes Religieuses* (Paris, 1857), pp.33–4. Grenier, *Introduction à l'Histoire Générale*, pp.372–3. The practice was still current in Picardy in Grenier's time.
59. A. de Nore, *Coutumes, Mythes et Traditions des Provinces de France* (Paris, 1846), p.37. Cf. also Hérelle, *Canico et Beltchitine* (Paris, 1908), p.xxi, n.1.
60. Cf. N. Belmont, *Mythes et Croyances dans l'Ancienne France*, pp.71–3. A. Van Gennep, *Manuel de Folklore Français Contemporain*, I, part III, pp.992–5, 1148–9. J. Frazer, *Le Rameau d'Or*, III. *Le Dieu qui Meurt*, trans. P. Sayer (Paris, 1931), pp.188–200, 230–35. Cf. also J. Caro Baroja, *Le Carnaval* (Paris, 1979), pp.126–36.
61. J. Cerquand, *L'Imagerie et la Littérature Populaire dans le Comtat Venaissin, 1600–1850* (Avignon, 1883), p.33.
62. Hérelle, *Canico et Beltchtine* (Paris, 1908), pp.xix–xxiv. The second play was performed three times between 1787 and 1852.

63. S. Reinach, 'Le rire rituel', in *Cultes, Mythes et Religions* (Paris, 1912), IV, p.129, citing Desdevizes du Désert, *L'Espagne de L'Ancien Régime*.
64. Abbé M. X. Pic, *La Bête Mangeait le Monde en Pays de Gévaudan* (Paris, 1962), p.261.
65. S. Trébucq, *La Chanson Populaire et la Vie Rurale* (Bordeaux, 1912), II p.287.
66. Laborde, 'Les brouches en Béarn', *Revue Historique et Archéologique du Béarn et du Pays Basque* (1935), p.116.
67. *Ibid*, p.115.
68. Foix, *Sorciéres et Loups-Garous dans les Landes* (Auch, 1904), pp.15–16. Cf. Laborde 'Les brouches en Béarn', *Revue Historique et Archéologique du Béarn* (1935), p.115.
69. Regnault, *La Sorcellerie* (Bordeaux, 1896), p.125.
70. *Gazette des Tribunaux* (22 November 1828), p.82a–b.
71. Béchon, *La Divination et sa Répression dans l'Histoire* (Riom, 1896), p.49.
72. In Montpellier in 1837, a midwife who was accused of being a witch found that her trade declined to such an extent that she was obliged to bring an action against her slanderers. A man, who was called *meneur de loups* at the market in Riom, considered this remark so likely to have dangerous consequences that he brought a case for slander and defamation. Cf. *Gazette des Tribunaux* (10 June 1837), p.780a–b. Résie, *Histoire et Traité des Sciences Occultes* (Paris, 1857), II, p.514. Cf. *Gazette des Tribunaux* (13 Feb. 1843), p.436b; *ibid* (25 July 1842), p.1099a for other slander cases – the latter involving a colourful exorcism.
73. J. F. Détrée, *Sorciers et Possédés en Cotentin* (Coutances, 1975), p.116.
74. L. F. Sauvé, *Folklore des Hautes-Vosges* (Paris, 1889), p.172–4.
75. E. H. Carnoy, *Littérature Orale de la Picardie* (Paris, 1883), pp.103–4, 106–8.
76. Cf. above, pp.128–38, for collaboration in the deliria of people who were thought to be possessed.
77. Foix, *Sorcières et Loups-Garous dans les Landes* (Auch, 1904), pp.4–5.
78. C. Seignolle, *Le Folklore du Languedoc* (Paris, 1960), pp.218–19.
79. Bernheim, *De la Suggestion* (Paris, 1886), pp.186–7. Cf. also Lévi-Strauss, *Anthropologie Structurale* (Paris, 1974), pp.189–92.
80. A. Van Gennep, *Folklore du Dauphiné* (Paris, 1933), p.429.
81. Cauzons, *Sorcellerie* (1912), IV, pp.619–21. P. Sébillot, *Le Folklore de France* (1904), I, pp.165–74. D. Monnier, *Traditions Populaires* (1854), p.80. Leproux, *Dévotions et Saints Guérisseurs* (1957), p.36–7. Cf. M. Bloch, *La Société Féodale* (Paris, 1968 rpr.), p.129, and G. L. Coulton, *Medieval Panorama* (Cambridge, 1945), pp.105–9, for similar beliefs in medieval France and Britain.
82. A. J. Verrier and R. Onillou, *Glossaire Etymologique et Historique des Patois et des Parlers de l'Anjou* (Angers, 1908), II, pp.351a. Ellensberger, 'Le Monde Fantastique', *Nouvelle Revue des Traditions Populaires* (1949), p.434.
83. A. de Nore, *Coutumes Mythes et Traditions des Provinces de France* (Paris, 1846), pp.138–9. Foix, *Sorcières et Loups-Garous dans les Landes* (1904), p.6. J. F. Bladé, 'Quatre Superstitions Populaires de la Gascogne', *Revue de l'Agenais* (Nov.-Dec. 1884), pp.460–61. Sébillot, *Folklore de France* (1904), I, p.168.
84. Monnier and Vingtrinier, *Croyances et Traditions Populaires* (1874), pp.73–9. Ellensberger, 'Le Monde Fantstique', NRTP (1949), p.432.
85. Cf. J. A. Burrow, *Medieval Writers and their Works* (Oxford, 1982), pp.82–3, 107–18.
86. Meyrac, *Traditions et Coutumes* (1890), p.166. Rouleau, *Essai de Folklore de La Sologne Bourbonnaise* (1935), p.120. For devil's role and that of other spirits, cf. D. Monnier and A. Vingtrinier, *Croyances et Traditions Populaires* (1874), pp.28–9. Résie, *Histoire et Traité des Sciences Occultes* (Paris, 1857), II, pp.358, 364–5. Nore, *Coutumes, Mythes* (1846), p.70–80.
87. Bouteiller, *Sorciers* (1958), p.129.

88. Pérot, *Folklore Bourbonnais* (1908), pp.32–3. Achille Allier, *L'Ancien Bourbonnais* (1833), II, p.12 n.2. Ellensberger, 'Le Monde Fantastique', NRTP (1949), p.433.
89. Cauzons, *La Magie et la Sorcellerie en France* (Paris, 1912), IV, pp.525–6.
90. M. Bloch, *La Société Féodale* (1939/1968), p.116.
91. Saintyves, *Reliques et Images Légendaires* (Paris, 1912), pp.240–41, 250, 274.
92. G. L. Coulton, *Medieval Panorama* (1945), p.106.
93. Résie, *Histoire et Traité des Sciences Occultes* (Paris, 1857), III, pp.364–5. A. Maury, *La Magie, L'Astrologie dans L'Antiquité et au Moyen Âge* (Paris, 1896), p.155 n.3. Rocal, *Le Vieux Périgord* (Toulouse, 1937), pp.174–5. Monnier and Vingtrinier, *Traditions Populaires* (1874), p.31 n.i. pp.32–4. Bérenger-Féraud, *Superstitions et Survivances* (Paris, 1896), pp.222–4.
94. Sevrin, 'Croyances Populaires et Médecine Supranaturelle', RHEF (1946), p.302. Miron, *Le Prêtre et le Sorcier* (Paris, 1872), p.188.
95. Bonnemère, 'Superstitions du Département de l'Indre', RTP (1890), p.440. A. Millien, 'Messe de Tourmentation', RTP (1913), p.84.
96. C. Marcilhacy, *Le Diocèse d'Orléans au Milieu du XIXe Siècle* (Paris, 1964), p.314.
97. Abbé J. L. M. Noguès, *Moeurs d'Autrefois en Saintonge et Aunis* (Saintes, 1891), pp.128–30, 129 n.i. In 1791, the national guard at Montmoreau had to arrest four priests from Barbézieux to protect them from the fury of a crowd which thought they had caused a hail-storm. Bouteiller, *Sorciers* (1958), p.188.
98. At Réallon, in the Hautes-Alpes, at an unspecified date, the *curé* was obliged to run away, because the common people claimed to have seen him on storm-clouds, 'coiffé d'un chapeau de gendarme' (indicatively perhaps), and throwing hail onto fields. Not believing his denials, the people threatened him with guns. In 1900, the Abbé Chauvin died at Bar-le-Duc. He had been accused in his previous parish of flying on a storm-cloud directing the tempest. The folklorist Labourasse was told by an old gentleman that he himself had seenthe *curés* of Woinville and Buxières thus employed. Cf. Van Gennep, *Folklore des Hautes-Alpes* (Paris, 1948), II, p.89. Vartier, *Sabbat, Juges* (Paris, 1968), p.248.
99. Moret, *Devins et Sorciers* (Moulins, 1909), p10, 38.
100. In 1883, at Saint-Sulpice-en-Exedeuil, in Périgord, the local people allegedly shot at the gathering crows, which were thought to be the transmogrified priests getting together for the storm. Rocal, *Le Vieux Périgord* (1927), p.175.
101. Miron, *Le Prêtre et le Sorcier* (1872), pp.187–8. Sevrin, 'Croyances Populaires et Médecine Supranaturelle', RHEF (1946), pp.299–300, for amplified version.
102. Lardant, 'Un Curé de Champagne-Mouton', *Etudes Locales. Bull. Soc. Charentaise* (1922), no. 19, pp.23–4.
103. Cf. L. Pérouas, *Le Diocèse de la Rochelle de 1684 à 1724* (Paris, 1964), pp.176, 220n.4, 221.
104. Bladé, 'Superstitions', *Revue de l'Agenais* (1884), pp.458–9.
105. Souvestre, *Les Derniers Bretons* (1971 facs. of 1854 edn), pp.15–16. Séguin, *Nouvelles à Sensation* (Paris, 1954), pp.142, 152, 155.
106. Lucie de V. H., 'Les Enfants Morts sans Baptême', RTP (1901), pp.526–7.
107. Chevalier, 'Médecine Superstitieuse', RTP (1905), p.106.
108. Lecadre, *Une Panique, Souvenir du Choléra en 1832* (Le Havre, 1875), pp.7–8. A violent storm in the area of Bordeaux in May 1808 provoked similar reactions in the local people, several of whom according to the prefect 's'imaginèrent que c'était le moment du Jugement dernier'. A. N. F^{15} 2700, letter of 27 May 1808.
109. Souvestre, *Les Derniers Bretons* (1971 facs. of 1854), pp.15–16.
110. Drouillet, *Folklore Nivernais* (1964), p.135.
111. J. Palou, *La Peur* (Paris, 1958), p.105 n.13. C. Guyot, *Variations de l'Etat Mental et la Responsabilité* (Bordeaux, 1896), p.103.
112. Cf. J. Marucchi, *Psychologie Paysanne* (1950), p.25. He cites the case of a farmer, who when his vet's diagnosis was proved right, thought he had cast a spell on his herd.

113. Cf. Van Gennep, *Folklore Dauphiné* (1933), II, p.473, who says that in S. Maximin, magic was called 'physique'.
114. A. Van Gennep, *Folklore des Hautes-Alpes* (1948), II, p.80. Marcilhacy, *Le Diocèse d'Orléans sous l'Episcopat de Mgr Dupanloup, 1849–1878* (Paris, 1962), p.328.
115. Garçon and Vinson, *Le Diable* (1926), p.142.
116. Bessières, 'Etude sur les Erreurs' (Paris University, medical thesis), p.31. F. M. Kérambrun, *Les Rebouteurs et les Guérisseurs* (Bordeaux University, medical thesis, 1898), pp.35–6. Workers in Lille also feared doctors and hospitals, preferring traditional medicine. Cf. Piérrard, *La Vie Ouvrière* (Paris, 1965), pp.142, 144.
117. F. Claudon, ed., *Journal d'un Bourgeois de Moulins* (Moulins, 1898), p.29. Sighele, *La Foule Criminelle* (Paris, 1900), pp.106–7.
118. In England in the twelfth and thirteenth centuries, there was a spate of legends about martyrs, who were supposedly victims of ritual murders by Jews who needed the blood in order to return to Palestine (a theme that was common in the medieval folklore of the Continent). Jews were also charged – as were the rich, clergy and lepers – with having poisoned the water-supply, thus provoking the outbreak of bubonic plague which ravaged Western Europe in 1348. N. Cohn, *The Pursuit of the Millennium* (London, 1970), pp.86–7. R. W. Southern, *Western Society and the Church in the Middle Ages* (Penguin, 1970), p.308. D. O'Brien, 'The Origins of Anti-Semitism in Medieval England', *Retrospect* (1972), p.23–9. Cf. Chaucer, 'The Prioress' Tale', *Canterbury Tales*.
119. Dr L. Martinecq, *Le Choléra à Toulon* (Paris, 1848), pp.39–40.
120. Dr A. Cabanès, *La Peste dans L'Imagination Populaire* (Paris, 1901), p.116.
121. R. Baehrel, 'Epidémies et Terreur', *Annales Historiques de la Révolution Française* (April-June 1951), p.120.
122. In Egypt, Russia and Portugal, in the first half of the nineteenth century, doctors were held responsible for epidemics and were attacked and abused. Bienvenu, 'Les Semeurs de Peste', *La Médecine Internationale* (March 1911), pp.76b–7b.
123. D. A. Vingtrinier, *Des Epidémies* (Rouen, 1850), p.24.
124. Dr J. Mabit, *Rapport sur le Choléra-Morbus* (Bordeaux, 1832), p.8.
125. Lucas Dubreton, *La Grande Peur de 1832* (Paris, 1932), p.77–9, 120.
126. Anon., *Souvenirs à l'Usage des Habitans de Douai* (1843), pp.87–8.
127. L. Chevalier, *Le Choléra: La Première Epidémie du XIXe Siècle* (La Roche-sur-Yon, 1958), p. 94.
128. Dubreuil and Rech, *Rapport sur le Choléra-Morbus* (Montpellier, 1836), pp.19–20.
129. Cf. Paillard, *Histoire Statistique du Choléra* (Paris, 1832), pp.8–11. Lauvergne, *Le Choléra-Morbus... à Narbonne en 1854* (Narbonne, 1854), p.18. His patients were liable to be treated with strychnine. Billot, *Rapport sur les Epidémies de Choléra...* (Poligny, 1854), p.8–12. Fraisse *et al.*, *Rapport à l'Assemblée... sur l'état Actuel du XIIe Arrondissement* (Paris, 1851), pp.7–8. Anon., *Notice sur le Choléra* (1832), pp.8–11. Barth, *Rapport sur les Epidémies du Choléra* (Paris, 1874), pp.42–4.
130. Tueffard, *Mémoire sur l'Epidémie de Choléra* (Montbéliard, n.d., *c.* 1854), p.15.
131. Cf. Delpech de Fraysinnet, *Mémoire sur le Choléra-Morbus* (Lyon, 1833), pp.180, 182, for the panic caused by the sudden arrival, swift course and mysterious dissemination of the disease. All commentators remarked on the fear it engendered.
132. Baehrel, *op. cit.*, p.121.
133. Barthéty, *La Sorcellerie en Béarn* (Pau, 1879), p.70. Borianne, *Essai sur le Erreurs en Médecine* (Paris University, medical thesis, 1831), p.26. Foucart, *Des Erreurs et des Préjugés Populaires en Médecine* (Paris University, medical thesis, 1893), p.34. *Double Almanach de Liège* (1858), for humorous evidence of this distrust.

Notes to Conclusion

1. The taste for miracles has not diminished in modern Ireland, cf. *Sunday Tribune* (17 February 85) and *Irish Times* (18 February 85): hundreds of people visited the church at Asdee, Co. Kerry, when children claimed to have seen the statues of the Sacred Heart and Virgin Mary move. *Woman's Way* (1 March 85), pp.6–8, reports on a recent miracle at the Marian shrine of Knock. In the summer of 1985, the moving statue of the Virgin at Ballinspittle drew thousands of pilgrims, while in 1986 in England, a much publicized trial revealed that wealthy Christians (including a number of peers) gave a man over £200,000 to secure his release from the devil.
2. Instances of this are the fortune-telling service provided in West End branches of Selfridges; the comfortable living made by fortune-tellers in some areas of Dublin, who charge fees similar to those of doctors. Random conversation with post-graduate students in Oxford revealed that some believed personality to be to some extent determined by the planets. Civil servants appear to be no more consistent than their academic counterparts – some believing that fortune-tellers can predict the future and others even consulting them. There are more seers (*voyants*) than doctors or priests in France (50,000 as opposed to 49,000 and 38,000 respectively), and their earnings, which average five or six milliard francs p.a., yielded more to the taxman in 1983 than did those of doctors, lawyers and architects. A programme about exorcism which was broadcast in January 1985 resulted in the chief church exorcist being contacted by hundreds of people seeking magical cures and relief from spells. Cf. *Le Nouvel Observateur* (22 February 1985), p.47c–48a, 49b, 52b–c, 53a and *passim*.
3. Cf. P. Medawar, *Pluto's Republic* (Oxford, 1984), pp.56–8, 62–72, for controversy on this point.
4. Rousseau, *Rêveries du Promeneur Solitaire* (1st edn 1782, Paris, 1960), pp.17, 29–30, 86.
5. Descartes, *Les Passions de l'Ame* (Paris, 1649), in *Oeuvres de Descartes*, eds. Adam and Tannéry (Paris, 1909), p.363.
6. *Ibid*, p.363.
7. Cf. Cocchiara, *Storia del Folklore in Europa* (Turin, 1952), pp.81–95, for early Enlightenment writers' attitudes to superstition.
8. Voltaire, Art. 'Superstition', in *Philosophical Dictionary*, ed. and trans. T. Besterman (London, 1971), p.382.
9. Art. 'Superstition', in *L'Encyclopédie: Textes Choisis*, ed. A. Soboul (Paris, 1976), pp.245–7.
10. Voltaire, 'Homily on Superstition', in *Selected Works of Voltaire* (London, 1941), p.120.
11. *Ibid*, p.118.
12. Voltaire, Art. 'Superstition', in *Philosophical Dictionary*, ed. T. Besterman (London, 1971), p.385.
13. Holbach, *La Morale Universelle* (Paris, Year IV), p.8.
14. Holbach, *Essai sur les Préjugés* (London, 1770), p.42. Cf. also Diderot, *Supplément au Voyage de Bougainville* (Paris, 1957), p.223.
15. Sade agreed with Holbach's contention that political tyranny exploited men's religious fears to keep men subject. Holbach, *Système de la Nature* (London, 1775), pp.433–8. Sade, *Idée sur les Romans* (Paris, 1878), p.43. Holbach, *Préjugés*, pp.125–6.
16. Cf. Helvétius, *De l'Homme* (1772). Diderot affirmed that 'il n'y a que les passions, et les grandes passions, qui puissent élever l'âme aux grandes choses. Sans elles, plus de sublime . . . '. *Pensées*, (Paris, Year VI), pp.219–20.
17. La Mettrie, *L'Homme Machine* (Utrecht, 1966), pp.149, 157, 159.
18. 'Homme, c'est un être sentant, réfléchissant, pensant, qui se promène librement sur la surface de la terre, qui paraît être à la tête de tous les autres animaux sur lesquels il domine,

qui vit en société, qui a inventé des sciences et des arts, qui a une bonté et une méchanceté qui lui est propre, qui s'est donné des maîtres, qui s'est fait des lois, etc'. Diderot, Art. 'Homme', in *L'Encyclopédie: Textes Choisis*, ed. A. Soboul (Paris, 1976), p.126–8.

19. Condorcet, *Esquisse d'un Tableau Historique*, eds. M. and F. Hincker (Paris, 1971), pp.158–9, 263–4, 283–4.
20. Condorcet, *op. cit.*, p.274.
21. Cf. Labrousse, 'Quelques Notes sur un Médecin Philosophe' (Paris University, medical thesis, 1903), pp.18ff.
22. Cabanis, *Les Révolutions et les Réformes de la Médecine* (Paris, 1824), pp.274–5, 20–23.
23. E. Esquirol, *Des Maladies Mentales* (Paris, 1838), I, pp.5–6, 21–3.
24. Baillarger, *Maladies Mentales* (Paris, 1890), pp.152–3. Calmeil, *De la Folie* (Paris, 1845), I, pp.1–2, 66–7, 80. Lélut, *Le Démon de Socrate* (Paris, 1836), pp.259, 325. Falret, *Maladies Mentales* (Paris, 1864), pp.62–3, cf. also Leuret, *Fragmens Psychologiques* (Paris, 1834), pp.41–2: he considered madness to be a purely intellectual aberration, a view contested by Falret, *op. cit.*, pp.432–4. Macario, *Traité Pratique de la Folie Névropathique (Vulgo-Hystérique)* (Paris, 1869), pp.vii–ix.
25. Esquirol, *Maladies Mentales*, I, pp.43, 47.
26. Falret, *op. cit.*, p.63. Cf. also Esquirol, *op. cit.*, I, p.35. Duprat, *L'Instabilitè Mentale* (Paris, 1898), pp.136–7, 141. Régis, *Pessimisme Contemporain* (Paris, 1898), pp.21–6.
27. Falret, *op. cit.*, p.63.
28. Esquirol, *Maladies Mentales* (Paris, 1838), I, pp.24, 43, 48–50.
29. Cf. Fodéré, *Essai Médico-Légal sur les diverses Espèces de Folie etc.* (Strasbourg, 1832), p.277, on political debates on public hygiene during the cholera epidemics of 1832.
30. 'L'hygiène', declared Fodéré, 'ou l'art de conserver la santé et de prévenir les maladies, est encore une science étroitement liée à l'étude de la nature et à la philosophie morale; elle nous apprend à diriger nos passions vers le but qu'elles doivent avoir... Elle est l'égide de la Raison, la mère du bonheur.' Fodéré, *Traité de Médecine Légale et d'Hygiène Publique* (Paris, 1813), I, pp. lvii, lxix–lxx.
31. Fodéré, *op. cit.*, V, pp.15–16, 22–3.
32. Morel retained the censorious preoccupation of earlier writers with the influence of habit and environment on the individual, and their contribution to the genesis of illness. Despite the place he assigned to heredity, Morel also cited 'infractions à la loi morale et l'absence de culture intellectuelle' as important factors in causing degeneracy. Hence, profession, family background and medical history, climate and social traditions were all thought to influence the health or degradation of the individual and society. But whereas the study and treatment of degeneration caused exclusively by physical environment was straightforward, 'il n'est plus de même lorsque les influences exercées sur l'espèce dépendent du genre de vie des habitants, de leurs moeurs, de leurs habitudes, de leurs mariages, de leur plus ou moins d'instruction, de la manière de se vêtir, de se loger, de se nourrir etc.' It then took a more experienced eye to note the deleterious changes wrought by culture. In presenting medicine as a form of anthropology and of scientific social criticism, Morel systematized and made explicit the assumptions that had underlain much medical writing in the earlier nineteenth century, and claimed for it the authority in social and cultural matters which politicians soon exploited and which inspired later psychologists and sociologists.
33. B. Ball, *L'Aliéné devant la Société* (Paris, 1882), pp.6–7.
34. Morel, *De la Formation du Type* (Paris, 1864), pp.3, 17–18.
35. Morel, *Traité des Dégénérescences* (Paris, 1857), pp.vii–ix, 8–9, 47–8.
36. Cf. Moreau de Tours, *Psychologie Morbide* (Paris, 1859), pp.99–116, for a contemporary work which pointed to the importance of heredity and which emphasized etiology rather than symptomatology. V. Magnan, *Dégénérés* (Paris, 1895),

pp.10–12, 79, 90–113. According to Magnan, the degenerate tended to rebel against society's laws yet demand liberty, while also being credulous and superstitious; *ibid*, p.128. G. Le Bon, *The Crowd* (London, 1896). Sighele, *La Foule Criminelle* (Paris, 1900). Lombroso, *L'Anthropologie Criminelle* (Paris, 1891), for influential works indebted to Morel's thesis.

37. Cf. Ackerknecht, *The History of Psychiatry* (2nd edn, New York and London, 1968), pp.85–6. H. Baruk, *L'Hypnose* (Paris, 1981), pp.9–37.

38. Liébeault, *Du Sommeil et des Etats Analogues* (2nd edn, Paris, 1889), pp.89–90, 93.

39. A. Maury, *Le Sommeil* (Paris, 1866), p.88: 'En rêve, l'homme se révèle donc tout entier à soi-même dans sa nudité et sa misère natives. Dès qu'il suspend l'exercice de sa volonté, il devient le jouet de toutes les passions contre lesquelles, à l'état de veille, la conscience, le sentiment d'honneur, la crainte nous défendent.'.

40. Liébeault, *op. cit.*, pp.160–61, 163, 387–8.

41. Gilles de la Tourette, *Traité Clinique... de l'Hystérie* (Paris, 1891), I, pp.23–7. P. Bercherie, 'Le concept de la folie hystérique avant Charcot', *Revue Internationale d'Histoire de la Psychiatrie* (1983), I, pp.47–58.

42. Charcot, *Les Démoniaques dans l'Art* (Paris, 1887), pp.92–105. Charcot, *Leçons sur les Maladies du Système Nerveux* (Paris, 1875), I, pp.331–88. Cf. also Ackerknecht, *History of Psychiatry* (London, 1968), pp.83–4.

43. P. Richer, *Etudes Cliniques* (Paris, 1881), pp.3, 32, 92–7, 125–34, 364–94.

44. Bernheim, *De la Suggestion et des ses Applications à la Thérapeutique* (Paris, 1886), p.218. Cf. also Hartenberger, *L'Elément Psychique* (1895), pp.33–9.

45. Cf. Gilles de la Tourette, *L'Hypnotisme et les Etats Analogues* (Paris, 1887), pp.280–83. P. Janet, *L'Etat Mentale des Hystériques* (Paris, 1911), pp.241–5. Escandre de Messières, 'Les Rêves Chez les Hystériques' (Bordeaux University, medical thesis, 1895), p.37, for resumé of Janet's early ideas on hysteria.

46. C. Schorske, *Fin de Siècle Vienna* (Cambridge, 1981, rpr. of 1961 edn), for one exposition.

Select Bibliography

Manuscript Sources

Archival sources were of very limited use. None of the series consulted in the National Archives or in Departmental Archives (Allier and Gironde) yielded information about popular superstitions in significant volume or on a consistent, predictable basis. The response of directors of provincial archives in France to my inquiries and my own sample explorations led me to rely on printed sources for the bulk of my information. Some references will be found, however, to the following archival material:

A.N. F^{15} Poor relief.
A.N. BB^{18} Ministry of Justice. Criminal Division.
A.N. F^{19} Religion.
A.D. Allier, Series U. Justice.
A.D. Gironde, Series U. Justice.
A.D. Gironde, 5. m. 29. Illegal Practice of Medicine.
5. M. 44. Secret Remedies.
5. M. 112. Reports of Doctors on Epidemics

Printed Sources

The following abbreviations have been used:

AESC – *Annales: Economie, Société, Culture*
Gaz. Trib. – *Gazette des Tribunaux*
RTP – *Revue des Traditions Populaires*
RDM – *Revue des Deux Mondes*
RHEF – *Revue Historique de l'Eglise de France*

The following periodicals were consulted exhaustively:

La Gazette de France, 1826–40
La Gazette des Tribunaux, 1825–84
Revue des Traditions Populaires
Mémoires de l'Académie Celtique, 1807–12, vols. 1–6

Primary Sources

Dr H. Aguilhon and V. Nivet, *Notice sur l'Epidémie de Choléra-Morbus qui a ravagé le Puy-de-Dôme en 1849* (Paris, 1851).

J. and A. L. Aikin, 'On the pleasure derived from objects of Terror', in *Miscellaneous Pieces in Prose* (London, 1773).
— 'Enquiry into those kinds of Distress which excite agreeable sensations', in *Miscellaneous Pieces in Prose* (London, 1773).
Albert le Grand Translaté de Latin en François, lequel traicte de la vertu de Herbes, et Pierres Précieuses, et pareillement des Bestes et Oyseaux (Oudot, Troyes, n.d.).
Allier: Population Légale des Communes: 1806–1954 (Clermont-Ferrand, 1954).
A. Allier, *L'Ancien Bourbonnais* (Moulins, 1833).
Almanach des Campagnes pour 1860 (Josse, Paris, 1859).
Almanach Diabolique, dédié au Beau Sexe, ou Manuel du Jeu du Diable... suivi d'un Calendrier pour l'an 1813 (Garnier, Paris, n.d.).
Almanach du Bon Laboureur, ou Prognostications Perpétuelles des Laboureurs (Mégard, Rouen, n.d., *c.* 1832–3).
Almanach du Bonhomme Misère (Paris, n.d.).
Almanach du Cultivateur Dauphinois pour l'année 1850 (Paris, Lyon, 1850).
Almanach du Cultivateur de la Haute-Loire (Riom, 1869).
Almanach du Cultivateur des Départements du Midi, pour l'année 1834 (Toulouse, n.d.).
Almanach du Cultivateur Charentais, pour l'année 1842 (Lefraise, Angoulême, n.d.).
Almanach Stéréotype, Le Véritable Messager Boîteux de Bâle en Suisse, 1851 (Deckherr, Montbéliard, 1850. Has same iconography as 1788 version.)
T. Andreu, 'De l'Irresponsabilité des Hystériques en Matière Criminelle' (Toulouse University, medical thesis, 1905).
Aperçu Historique sur l'invasion, la marche et les effets du Choléra à Toulon. Résumé de la correspondance d'un ex-administrateur au bureau central de secours (Toulon, 1835).
Les 25 apparitions de l'Archange Raphaël au laboureur Thomas-Ignace Martin de Gallendon en Beauce, dans les premiers mois de 1816, suivies de l'entretien de Martin avec le Roi. écrits sous sa dictée en 1828 (5th edn, Nîmes, 1886).
J. Arago, *Promenades Historiques, Philosophiques et Pittoresques du Département de le Gironde* (Bordeaux, 1829).
Dr Armangaud, 'Recherches cliniques sur les causes de l'Hystérié. Relation d'une petite Epidémie d'hystérie observée à Bordeaux dans une école de jeunes filles', *Mémoires et Bulletins de la Société de Médecine et de Chirugie de Bordeaux* (1879), pp.551–79.
J. B. E. Arnaud, *Mémoires d'un Compagnon du Tour de France* (Rochefort, 1859).
Dr Arthaud, 'Relation d'une Hystéro-Démonopathie épidémique observée à Morzine', *Annales de la Société Impériale de Médecine de Lyon* (1861), 2nd series, No. 9, pp.292–344).
R. Artigues, 'Essai sur la Valeur Séméiologique du Rêve' (Paris University, medical thesis, 1884).
A. Assier, *La Bibliothèque Bleue depuis Jean Oudot 1er jusqu'à M. Baudot (1600–1863)* (Paris, 1874).
— *Légendes, curiosités et traditions de la Champagne et de la Brie* (Paris, 1860).

— *Livres Liturgiques du Diocèse de Troyes* (Paris, 1863).
— *Livres Populaires Imprimés à Troyes de 1600 à 1800* (Paris, 1864).
L'Astrologue de France (Paris, 1859).
Dr M. Aubanel, *Compte-rendu du service médical de l'asile des aliénés à Marseille, 1850–61* (Marseille, 1861).
A. Audiganne, *Les Ouvriers en Famille: Manuel élémentaire des sociétés de secours mutuels et de la caisse de retraite à l'usage des ouvriers des villes et des campagnes* (5th edn, Paris, 1858).
— *La Morale des Campagnes* (Paris, 1869).
— *Les Populations Ouvrières et les Industries de la France dans le mouvement social du* XIXe *siècle* (Paris, 1854), 2 vols.
Mme D'Aulnoy, *Les Contes de Fées* (Paris, 1881).
E. Auricoste de Lazarque, 'Médecine Superstitieuse, Pays Messin', RTP (1914), pp.61–4.
A. Aymar, 'Notes de Folklore Cantalien: recettes de médecine populaire', *Revue de la Haute-Auvergne* (1902), pp.428–34.
Victorine, B., *Souvenirs d'une Morte Vivante* (Lausanne, 1909).
Dr J. Babinski, *Recherches servant à établir que certaines manifestations hystériques peuvent être transférée d'un sujet à un autre sous l'influence de l'aimant* (Paris, 1886).
— *Grand et Petit Hypnotisme* (Paris, 1889).
H. Babou, *Les Païens Innocents* (2nd edn, Pris, 1878).
L. de Bäcker, *La Religion du Nord de France avant le Christianisme* (Lille, 1854).
Dr A. Baderot, 'L'Influence du Milieu sur le Développement du Délire Religieux en Bretagne. (Etude Statistique faite à l'Asile de Rennes en 1897) (Paris University, medical thesis, 1897).
Dr J. G. F. Baillarger, *Recherches sur les Maladies Mentales et sur Quelques Points d'Anatomie et de Physiologie du Système Nerveux* (Paris, 1890), 2 vols.
— *Note sur la Folie à la suite des Fièvres Intermittantes* (Paris, 1843).
J. Baissac, *Les Grands Jours de la Folie* (Paris, 1890).
B. Ball, 'La Folie Religieuse', *Revue Scientifique de la France et de l'Etranger* (9 September 1882), pp.336ff.
— *La Médecine Mentale à Travers les Siècles* (Paris, 1880).
— *Leçons sur les Maladies Mentales* (Paris, 1883).
— *L'Aliéné devant la Société* (Paris, 1882).
— *Le Délire des Persécutions* (Paris, 1889).
G. Ballot, 'La Sorcellerie et les Sorciers', *Bulletin de l'Institut Général Psychologique* (1906), pp.3–23.
L. Bargain, 'Contribution à l'Etude du Suicide chez les Persécutés' (Paris University, medical thesis, 1905).
S. Baring-Gould, *Curious Myths of the Middle Ages*, ed. E. Hardy (abr. edn, London, 1977).
A. de Barrac, 'Le Grimoire de Levroux et le Trésor de la Garenne', *Revue du Centre* (1886), VIII, pp.380–92.
Dr J. B. Barth, *Rapport sur les Epidémies du Choléra-Morbus qui ont régné en France pendant les années 1854–5* (Paris, 1874).
M. Barthéty, *La Sorcellerie en Béarn et dans le Pays Basque* (Pau, 1879).

Dr M. Bastié, *Le Languedoc: Description complète du Département du Tarn* (Albi, 1875), 2 vols.
Dr Bataille (pseud. C. Hacks), *Le Diable au* XIXe *Siècle* (Paris, 1892–5), 2 vols bound in one.
E. Baudot, *Etudes Historiques sur la Pharmacie en Bourgogne* (Paris, 1905).
C. Beauquier, *Traditions Populaires. Les Mois en Franche-Comté* (Paris, 1900).
T. Beaurain, *Monts de Piété* (Rouen, 1893).
A. Beauvais, 'Une oraison de ma grand 'mère', *RTP* (1886), p.199.
F. Béchard, *De L'Etat du Paupérisme en France et des Moyens d'y Rémédier* (Paris, 1852).
R. Béchon, *La Divination et sa Répression dans l'Histoire* (Riom, 1896).
R. Belbèze, *La Neurasthénie Rurale* (Paris, 1911).
Dr J. E. Belhomme, *Influence des Evénements et des Commotions Politiques sur le développement de la folie* (Paris, 1849).
Bérenger-Féraud, *Superstitions et Survivances* (Paris, 1896), 5 vols.
A. V. C. Berbiguer de Terreneuve du Thym, *Les Farfadets ou Tous les Démons ne sont pas de l'autre monde* (Paris, 1821), 3 vols.
Dr G. H. Bergmann, ed., 'Réflexions d'une Personne qui avait été atteinte d'alienation mentale, sur sa propre maladie', *Annales d'Hygiène Publique et de Médecine Légale* (1836), XVI, pp.172–96.
Bernard, 'Encore les Empiriques: Accidents Mortels observés sur deux chevaux . . .', *Journal des Vétérinaires du Midi* (January 1850), pp.18–24.
C. Bernard, *Cahier de Notes, 1850–1860*, ed. M. Grmek (Paris, 1965).
Dr H. Bernheim, *De la Suggestion et des ses Applications à la Thérapeutique* (Paris, 1886).
— *Hypnotisme, Suggestion et Psychothérapie* (Paris, 1891).
— *Automatisme et Suggestion* (Paris, 1917).
Dom G. Bernoni, *Preghiere Popolari Veneziane* (Venice, 1873).
Abbé N. Béronie, *Dictionnaire du Patois Bas-Limousin (Corrèze) et plus particulièrement des environs de Tulle* (Tulle, n.d.).
J. Berriat-Saint-Prix, *Vieilles Prières (d'Auvergne)* (Clermond-Ferrand, 1906).
S. H. Berthoud, *Chroniques et Traditions Surnaturels de la Flandre* (Paris, 1831–4 3 vols.
Abbé V. G. Berthoumieu, *Fêtes et Dévotions Populaires. Tableau des Us et Coutumes Religieux des Patronages, des Saints et Pèlerinages Célèbres* (Paris, 1873).
Dr E. Bertulus, *Marseille et son Intendance Sanitaire à propos du choléra* (Marseille, 1864).
— *Hygiène Publique. De la Réforme Sanitaire des Evénements Providentiels qui l'ont amenée, des causes humaines qui en retardent l'application* (Montpellier, 1867).
A. F. E. Bessières, 'Etude sur les Erreurs et les Préjugés Populaires en Médecine' (Paris University, medical thesis, 1860).
A. Bez, *Les Miracles de Nos Jours ou les Manifestations Extraordinaires Obtenues par intermédiaire de Jean Hillaire, cultivateur à Sonnac (Charente-Inférieure)* (Paris, Bordeaux, 1864).
Dr P. Bidault, 'Superstitions Médicales du Morvan' (Paris University, medical thesis, 1889).

Dr E. Biéchy, *D'Une Révolution dans la Constitution Médicale et de la Méthode Thérapeutique durant le cours du siècle actuel* (Paris, 1880).

L. F. Bigeon, *Notice sur le choléra qui s'est manifesté à Saint-Cast (Côtes-du-Nord)* (Dinan, 1832).

Dr Billot, *Rapport à l'Académie de Médecine sur l'Epidémie de Choléra... (Jura 1854)* (Poligny, 1854).

Dr A. Binet, *La Suggestibilité* (Paris, 1900).

— *Les Altérations de la Personnalité* (Paris, 1891).

W. G. Black, *Folk Medicine. A Chapter in the History of Culture* (London, 1883).

J. F. Bladé, 'Seize Superstitions Populaires de la Gascogne', *Revue de l'Agenais* (March–April 1881), pp.114–59; (May–June 1881), pp.255–63.

— 'Quatorze Superstitions Populaires de la Gascogne', *Revue de l'Agenais* (Jan.–Feb. 1883), pp.17–31.

— *Contes Populaires recueillis en Agenais* (Paris, 1874).

— *Poésies Populaires de la Gascogne* (Paris, 1881).

— *Trois Contes Populaires recueillis à Lecouture* (Bordeaux, Agen, 1877).

— 'Quatre Superstitions Populaires de la Gascogne', *Revue de l'Agenais* (Nov.–Dec. 1884), pp.457–61.

H. Blanc, *Le Merveilleux dans le Jansénisme, le Magnétisme... Recherches Nouvelles* (Paris, 1865).

Dr R. Blanchard, 'Traditions et Superstitions de la Touraine. II. Petit Guide Médical', RTP (1890), pp.741–9.

— 'Sorcellerie dans les Hautes-Alpes', RTP (1891), pp.248–9.

A.-J. Blanqui, *Des Classes Ouvrières en France Pendant l'Année 1848* (Paris, 1849).

— *Tableau des Populations Rurales de la France en 1850* (Paris, 1850).

— 'Rapport sur la Situation Générale des classes ouvrières en 1848', *Journal des Economistes* (15 December 1848), pp.51–60.

Dr. A. Blum, *De l'Hystéro-Neurasthénie Traumatique* (Paris, 1869).

Dr J. Bocamy, *Rapport sur le Choléra Epidémique... dans les Pyrénées Orientales. (1835/7 & 1854)* (Perpignan, 1856).

J. Bodin, *Démonomanie des Sorciers* (Paris, 1580).

H. Boguet, *Discours des Sorciers avec six advis en faict de sorcelerie...* (3rd edn, Lyon, 1610).

J. Bois, *Le Satanisme et la Magie* (Paris, 1895).

Dr Boismoreau, *Coutumes Médicales et Superstitions Populaires du Bocage Vendéen* (Paris, 1911).

Dr H. Bon, *Essai Historique sur les Epidémies en Bourgogne* (Dijon, 1912).

M. J. F. Bonnafoux, *Légendes et Croyances Superstitieuses Conservées dans le Département de la Creuse* (Le Guéret, 1867).

L. Bonnemère, 'Les Superstitions du Canton de Gennes et Maine-et-Loire', RTP (1890), pp.673–9.

— 'Superstitions du Département de l'Indre', RTP (1890), p.440.

J. Bonneton, *Légendes et Nouvelles Bourbonnaises. Archéologie-Histoire-Etude des Moeurs* (Paris, 1877).

J. Borienne, 'Essai sur les Erreurs en Médecine répandues dans le Département de la Haute-Vienne' (Paris University, medical thesis, 1831).

E. Bosc, *Glossaire raisonné de la Divination etc.* (Paris, 1910).
— *Diabolisme et Occultisme* (Nice, 1896).
R. L. M. Botmiliau, *Du Paupérisme et de l'Assistance Publique en France* (Paris, 1856).
Dr H. Bouchet, 'Relation sur l'Epidémie de Morzine' (Lyon University, medical thesis, 1899).
A. Bouët, *Breiz Izel ou la Vie des Bretons dans l'Armorique* (Paris, Quimper, Brest, 1918). Written in 1835.
R. Bouiller, ed., *La Chronique de Madame Bonnard* (Cahiers du Musée Forézien, 1976).
Dr. A. Cabanès, *La Peste dans l'Imagination Populaire* (Paris, 1901).
Dr A. Cabanès and Dr Nass, *Poisons et Sortilèges* (Paris, 1903).
H. Calhiat, 'Pèlerinages Thérapeutiques dans le Tarn-et-Garonne', *Bulletin Catholique du Diocèse de Montauban* (3 June 1899), pp.365–8; (10 June 1899), pp.383–4.
Dr Calmeil, Art. 'Lycanthropie', in *Dictionnaire Encyclopédique des Sciences Médicales* (Paris, 1870), 2nd series, III, pp.359–71.
— *De la Folie considérée sous le point de vue pathologique, philosophique, historique et judiciaire, depuis la Renaissance des sciences en Europe jusqu'au XIXe siècle* (Paris, 1845), 2 vols.
— *Traité de Maladies Inflammatoires du Système Nerveux* (Paris, 1859).
— Art. 'Hallucinations', in *Dictionnaire de Médecine et de Chirugie*, ed. G. Andral (Paris, 1829–36), 15 vols.
Dom. Calmet, *Dissertation sur les Apparitions et les Revenants et Vampires de Bohème, de Moravie et de Silésie* (Paris, 1751), 2 vols.
J. Cambry, *Voyage dans le Finistère* (Paris, 1838). Written in 1794.
— *Description de l'Oise* (Paris, 1803). 2 vols and atlas.
J. M. Caméliat, 'Deux Poèmes Religieux des Pyrénées', *Mélusine* (1900–1), X, pp.79–83.
— 'Prières Populaires et Formules Magiques des Pyrénées', *Mélusine* (1899–1900), IX, pp.49–60.
Dr R. Cantaloube, 'L'Exercice Illégale de la Médecine et les Médicastres des Cévennes' (Montpellier University, medical thesis, 1904).
Dr G. Cany, 'La Médecine Populaire. L'Empirisme à Toulouse et dans les Environs' (Toulouse University, medical thesis, 1899).
E. F. Carey, 'The Chevauchée de S. Michel', *Folklore* (December 1914), pp.411–27.
A. Carlier, 'L'Homme Sauvage', *Revue de Folklore Français et Colonial* (1935), V, p.378.
D. Carnel, 'Proverbes et Locutions Proverbiales chez les Flamands de France', *Annales du Comité Flamand de France* (1858–9), 4, pp.132–45.
E. H. Carnoy, *Littérature Orale de la Picardie* (Paris, 1883).
— *Contes Français recueillis par E. H. C.* (Paris, /Le Puy, 1885).
— 'Les Fêtes de Février', *La Tradition* (1892), VI, pp.38–42.
Carré de Busserole, *Notice sur la fête des ânes et des fous qui se célébraient au moyen âge ... à Rouen, à Beauvais et à Autun* (Rouen, 1859).
Dr G. Carrier, *Contribution à l'étude des folies par contagion* (Evreux, 1903).
E. Castan, *Déviations et Maladies du Sentiment Religieux* (Paris, 1913).
A. de Caston, *Les Vendeurs de Bonne Aventure* (Paris, 1886).

Dr G. Cauvin, 'La Médecine Populaire en Provence' (Lyon University, medical thesis, 1930).
T. de Cauzons, *La Magie et la Sorcellerie en France. Les Sorciers d'Autrefois: le Sabbat: la Guerre aux Sorciers de Nos Jours* (Paris, 1910–12), 4 vols.
Dr C. Cavalier, *Etude Médico-Psychologique sur la Croyance aux Sortilèges* (Montpellier, 1868).
Dr J. B. Cazauvielh, *Du Suicide, de l'Aliénation Mentale et des Crimes Contre les Personnes... chez les Habitans des Campagnes* (Paris, 1840).
J. Cazotte, *Le Diable Amoureux* (Paris, 1960).
J. Cazeneuve, 'La Peur du Sorcier', *Le Monde Nouveau* (Feb.–March 1957), pp.90–100.
P. Cazin, 'L'Homme Sauvage, coutume de la Pentecôte, *Revue de Folkore Français et Colonial* (1835), v, p.310.
J. Cénac-Moncaut, *Littérature Populaire de la Gascogne* (Paris, 1868).
P. Cère, *Les Populations Dangereuses et les Misères Sociales* (Paris, 1872).
J.-F. Cerquand, *L'Imagerie et la Littérature Populaire dans le Comtat Venaissin (1600–1830)* (Avignon, 1883).
C. Chaffard, 'Etude Critique sur les Agents Provocateurs de la Chorée', (Montpellier University, medical thesis, 1894).
M. de Champfleury (pseud. J. F. Fleury-Husson), *Recherches sur les Variations du Bonhomme Misère* (Paris, 1861).
— Histoire de l'Imagerie Populaire (Paris, 1869).
Dr A. Chapelle, *De L'Epidémie de Choléra qui a régné dans le Département de Charente pendant l'année 1855* (Paris, 1856).
Dr L. J. Charcellay, *Histoire Médicale et Topographique des Epidémies de Choléra qui ont régné en 1832, 1849 et 1854 dans la ville de Tours et le Département d'Indre-et-Loire* (Tours, 1856).
Drs J. M. Charcot and P. Richer, *Les Démoniaques dans l'Art* (Paris, 1887).
Dr J. M. Charcot, *Leçons sur les Maladies du Système Nerveux* (Paris, 1875–87), 3 vols.
— *Lectures on Diseases of the Nervous System* (trans. of above, London, 1877–89), 3 vols.
— *La Foi qui Guérit* (Paris, 1897).
Charente 1966, Terre de Chretienté? Terre de Mission? (n.d.p.).
Dr R. Charpentier, *Dégénerescence Mentale et Hystérie. Les Empoisonneuses* (Paris, 1906).
C. Chastenet, 'Essai sur les Mélancoliques Anxieux' (Paris University, medical thesis, 1850).
P. Chavigny, 'Du Délire Fébrile' (Lyon University, medical thesis, 1892).
J. Chênedolent, *Souvenirs de la Vieille Bretagne* (Dijon, 1912).
A. Chéruel, *Dictionnaire Historique des Institutions, Moeurs et Coutumes de la France* (Paris, 1835), 2 vols.
A. Chervin, *Traditions Populaires Relatives à la Parole* (Paris, n.d.).
A. de Chesnel, *Usages, Coutumes et Superstitions des Habitants de la Montagne Noire* (Paris, 1839).
Chesnel de la Charbonnais (pseud. A. de Nore), *Coutumes, Mythes et Traditions des Provinces de France* (Paris, 1846).
M. Chevalier, 'Médecine Superstitieuse', *RTP* (1905), p.122.

Dr C. Chiara, *Les Diables de Morzine en 1861, ou les Nouvelles Possédés* (Lyon, 1861). Extract from *Gazette Médicale de Lyon*.

A. F. Chomel, *Des Fièvres et des Maladies Pestilentielles* (Paris, 1821).

F. Claudon, *Journal d'un Bourgeois de Moulins, dans la deuxième moitié du XVIIIe siècle* (Moulins, 1898).

A. Clausse, 'Contribution à l'Etude de la Neurasthénie' (Paris University, medical thesis, 1891).

Mme Clément-Héméry, *Histoire des Fêtes Civiles et Religieuses, des Usages Anciens et Modernes, du Département du Nord* (2nd edn, Cambrai, 1836).

Clément-Janin, 'Notice on Popular Prayers', RTP (1887), p.234.

J. R. Coignet, *Mémoires d'un Officier de l'Empire* (Plon edn, Paris, 1934). Written in 1850.

Dr H. Colin, 'Essai sur l'Etat Mental des Hystériques' (Paris University, medical thesis, 1890).

Collin de Plancy (pseud. Baron C. A. de Walckenauer), *Dictionnaire Critique des Reliques et des Images Miraculeuses* (Paris, 1821–2), 3 vols.

P. P. Colon, 'Essai sur la Médecine Populaire et ses Dangers' (Paris University, medical thesis, 1824).

C. Colson, 'Saints et Idoles Châtiés', *La Tradition* (1892), pp.115–16.

Dr A. Constans, *Relation sur une Epidémie d'Hystéro-Démonopathie en 1861* (Paris, 1862).

E. Corbière, *Trois Jours d'une Mission à Brest* (Paris, 1819).

A. Corbon, *Le Secret du Peuple de Paris* (2nd edn, Paris, 1865).

E. Cortet, *Essai sur les Fêtes Religieuses et les Traditions qui s'y rattachent* (Paris, 1867).

E. Cosquin, *Contes Populaires de Lorraine Comparés avec les Contes des Autres Provinces de France et des Pays Etrangers* (Paris, 1886), 2 vols.

Canon L. Côte, *En Montagne Bourbonnaise au Bon Vieux Temps* (S. Etienne, 1958).

Dr H. Coulon, 'Erreurs et Superstitions Médicales', *Mémoires de la Société d'Emulation de Cambrai* (1911), LXV, pp.1–51.

A. Court de Gébelin, *Le Monde Primitif Analysé et Comparé avec le Monde Moderne, Vol. IV Le Monde Primitif considéré dans l'Histoire Civile, Religieuse et Allégorique du Calendrier ou Almanach* (Paris, 1884).

Dr. A. Cullerre, *Traité Pratique des Maladies Mentales* (Paris, 1890).

— *Les Frontières de la Folie* (Paris, 1888).

R. Cusacq, *Le Folklore des Landes: la Littérature Orale et Populaire* (Bayonne, 1949).

Dr H. Dagonet, 'Traditions, Croyances et Superstitions de la Gironde', *Bulletin de la Société d'Anthropologie de Bordeaux et du Sud-Ouest* (1886), pp.13–110.

— *Questionnaire pour recueillir les Coutumes, les Croyances, les Dictions, les Légendes, les formulettes, les Remèdes Populaires, les Superstitions et les Usages Existant encore à la campagne ou à la ville, suivi de l'Ethnologie Traditionnelle* (Bordeaux, n.d.).

Abbé Dambielle, *La Sorcellerie en Gascogne* (Auch, 1907).

Abbé J.-L. Daniel, *Mission de Coutances* (Coutances, 1821).

Abbé L. Dardy, *Anthologie Populaire de l'Albret* (Agen, 1891), 2 vols.

Dr A. J. Darmezin, *Superstitions et Remèdes Populaires en Touraine* (Bordeaux University, medical thesis, 1904).

E. Debäcker, 'Lecture en bas: formulaire d'un Guérisseur Mystico-Empirique de la campagne au XIXe siècle', *Mémoires de la Société Dunquerquoise* (1907), XLVI, pp.215–42.
D. Defoe, *Essay on the History and Reality of Apparitions* (2nd edn, London, 1735).
A. Delacour, 'Les Sorciers de Brie', *Bulletin de la Société Littéraire et Historique de la Brie* (1894–7), pp.69–74.
C. Delaigne, 'Dans la Montagne Bourbonnaise. Ce que l'on pouvait voir et entendre au début du siècle', *Le Pays Gannatais, Société Culturelle et de Recherches* (July 1978), pp.4–9.
F. Delarue, *De la Peur et de la Folie des Gouvernements de l'Europe au sujet du Choléra* (Paris, 1831).
P. Delarue, *Recueil de Chants Populaires du Nivernais* (Nevers, Paris, 1947).
— *Le Conte Populaire Français: Catalogue des Contes Populaires Français* (Paris, 1957–64), 2 vols.
— 'Les Contes Merveilleuses de Perrault et la Tradition Populaire', *Bull. Folk. Ile de France* (Jan.–March 1951), pp.195–201.
P. Delarue and A. Millien, *Contes du Nivernais et du Morvan* (Paris, 1953).
C. Delpech, 'Contribution à l'Etude de la Folie Héréditaire' (Montpellier University, medical thesis, 1884).
M. Delpech de Fraysinnet, *Mémoire sur le Choléra-Morbus* (Lyon, 1833).
A. Delvau, *Bibliothèque Bleue* (Paris, 1859–60), I, VII, VIII, IX, XXI, XXIII.
A. Denis, *Recherches Bibliographiques et Historiques sur les Almanachs de la Champagne et de la Brie* (Châlons-sur-Marne, 1880).
J.-B. Demangeon, *Du Pouvoir de l'Imagination sur le Physique et le Moral de l'Homme* (Paris, 1834).
L. Desaivre, *Les Chants Populaires des Rois, ou l'Epiphanie en Poitou au* XIXe *siècle* (Saint-Maixent, 1888).
A. Desforges, 'L'Exorcisme des Chenilles', *Revue de Folklore Français et Colonial* (1935), 5, p.87.
— 'Le Sorcier de Saint Georges', *Revue de Folklore Français et Colonial* (1935), 5, p.90.
— 'Le Danger des Trésors dans le Nivernais', *Revue de Folklore Français et Colonial* (1935), 5, p.314.
Dr F. Desjars, 'Les Récits Imaginaires chez les Hystériques' (Paris University, medical thesis, 1899).
A. Devoille, *Mémoires d'un Curé de Campagne* (Paris, 1854). Devoille was a prolific writer of improving novels.
Dr P. Diday, *Examen Médical des Miracles de Lourdes* (Paris, 1873).
D. Diderot, *Oeuvres*, ed. A. Billy (Paris, 1951).
— *Oeuvres de Denis Diderot* (Paris, Year VI, 1798).
Dr P. Dignat, *Remarques sur L'Epidémie de Choléra* (Clermont, 1893).
A. Diot, *Le Patois Briard, dont, plus particulièrement, le patois parlé dans la région de Provins* (Coulumiers, 1930).
Documents sur le Département des Basses-Pyrénées, de 1803 à 1848. Ière Partie. 1803 à 1830 (Pau, 1850).
A. Dominique, *Le Choléra à Toulon, Etude Historique, Statistique et Comparative des Epidémies de 1835, 1849, 1865 et 1884* (Toulon, 1885).
G. Doncieux, *Le Romancéro Populaire de la France. Choix de Chansons Populaires Françaises* (Paris, 1904).

Donnadieu (pseud. Abbé Déléon), *Salette-Fallavaux, ou la Vallée du Mensonge* (Grenoble, 1852–3), 2 vols.

P. Donostia, 'Quelques Notes au sujet des médecins et médecines populaires au Pays Basque', *Gure Herria* (1961), I, pp.14–31.

Le Double Almanach de Liège (Paris, Tournai, 1858).

Y. Dou Perbos, 'Drin de Tout', *Escole de Gaston Phebus. Réclams de Biarn et de Gascougne* (1903), p.243–4.

V. E. Doyen, 'Quelques considérations sur les terreurs morbides et le délire émotif' (Paris University, medical thesis, 1885).

Le Dragon Noir, ou les Forces Infernales Soumises à l'Homme (Paris, 1896).

Le Dragon Rouge, ou l'Art de Commander les Esprits Celestes ets. (Nîmes, 1823/1849).

Dralet, *Description des Pyrénées* (Paris, 1813), 2 vols.

L. Dreneau, 'Contribution à l'Etude du Délire Alcoolique' (Bordeaux University, medical thesis, 1905).

M. Droüart, *Les Saints Guérisseurs, Les Saints Protecteurs et les Saints qui regardent de travers Haute-Bretagne* (Rennes, 1939).

J. Drouillet, *Folklore du Nivernais et du Morvan. Vol.* IV. *Etres Fantastiques, Sorcellerie et Médecine Populaire* (Paris, Nevers, 1964).

Dr G. Drouineau, *De l'Assistance aux Nomades* (Rouen, 1898).

Dr L. Druhen, *Des Causes de l'Indigence et des Moyens d'y Remédier* (Paris, 1850).

Dr P. Dubalen, 'Pratiques Médicales Populaires dans les Landes' (Lyon University, medical thesis, 1907).

D. Dubois, *Une Page d'Histoire Locale, à Propos des Epidémies... Traitées dans les Hôpitaux de Douai de 1832 à 1885* (Douai, 1886).

H. Dubois, 'Des Atrophies Musculaires d'Origine Hystérique' (Paris University, medical thesis, 1898).

J. L. Dubourdieu, 'Des Idées de Grandeur dans la Mélancolie' (Bordeaux University, medical thesis, 1895).

Drs Dubreuil and Rech, *Rapport sur le Choléra-Morbus...qui a régné dans le Midi de la France en 1835* (Montpellier, 1836).

L. Du Broc de Segange, *Les Saints Patrons des Corporations et Protecteurs spé cialement invoqués dans les maladies et circonstances critiques de la vie* (Paris, 1887).

C. Ducange, *Glossarium ad Scriptores Mediae et Infimae Latinatis* (Paris, 1733–6), 6 vols.

P. L. Duchartre and R. Saulnier, *L'Imagerie Populaire. Les Images de Toutes les Provinces Françaises du* XVe *siècle au Second Empire* (Paris, 1925).

N. Duclos, *De L'Extinction de la Mendicité dans la Nièvre* (Nevers, 1843).

P. Ducourtieux, *Les Almanachs Populaires et les Livres de Colportage de Limoges* (Paris, Limoges, 1921).

Abbé P. Duffard, *L'Armagnac Noir ou Bas Armagnac* (Auch, 1902).

G. Dugaston, *Magie et Sorcellerie* (Paris, 1922).

Abbé Duhaut, *Traité des Démons... Terreur des Démons* (Paris, 1915).

B. Duhourceau *et al.*, *La Vierge dans l'Art et la Tradition Populaire des Pyrénées* (Montpellier, 1958).

Dr Dupain, 'Etude Clinique sur le Délire Religieux' (Paris University, medical thesis, 1888).

F. Dupanloup, *Lettre sur les Prophéties Contemporaines* (Paris, 1874).
E. Dupouy, *Psychologie Morbide* (Paris, 1907).
G. L. Duprat, *Le Mensonge, Etude de Sociologie Pathologique et Normale* (Paris, 1903).
— *Les Causes Sociales de la Folie* (Paris, 1900).
— *L'Instabilité Mentale* (Paris, 1898).
E. Dupré, *La Mythomanie, Etude Psychologique et Médico-Légale du Mensonge et de la Fabulation Morbides* (Paris, 1905).
C. F. Durand, *Le Guérisseurs* (Paris, 1884).
Durand-Fardel, Art. 'Fièvre', *Supplément au Dictionnaire des Dictionnaires de Médecine* (Paris, 1851).
J. Durandeau, 'Prières de Guérisseurs', *RTP* (1887), p.165.
A. Durieux, 'Sorciers et Sorcières à Cambrai', *Mémoires de la Société d'Emulation de Cambrai* (1891), XLVI, pp.119–42.
Dr M. Ellensberger, 'Le Monde Fantastique dans le Folklore de la Vienne', *Nouvelle Revue des Traditions Populaires* (1949), I, pp.407–35; (1950), II, pp.3–26.
Enchiridion Leonis Papae Serenissimo Imperatori Carlo Magno (Lille, 1813).
In Hoc Enchiridion Manuale Pie Lecto Orationes Devotae Leonis Papae. (Le Veritable Clavicule de l'Enchiridion) (Ancona, 1649).
'Une Enquête: La Forge de Village', *AHES* (1935), p.603–14.
M. E. Escandre de Messières, 'Les Rêves ches les Hystériques' (Bordeaux University, medical thesis, 1895).
G. Esnault, 'L'Imagination Populaire. Métaphores Occidentales. Essai sur les Valeurs Imaginatives Concrètes du Français Parlé en Basse-Bretagne' (Paris University, medical thesis, 1925).
Dr E. Esquirol, *Des Maladies Mentales Considérées sous le rapport médical, hygiénique, et médico-légal* (Paris, 1838), 2 vols.
— *Des Etablissements des Aliénés en France* (Paris, 1819).
— *Mémoire Historique et Statistique sur la Maison de Charenton* (Paris, 1835).
— 'Des Passions Considérées comme Causes, Symptômes et Moyens Curatifs de l'Aliénation Mentale' (Paris University, medical thesis, 1805).
L'Explication des Songes et des Visions Nocturnes, selon la Doctrine des Anciens et leurs Significations (Deckherr, Montbéliard, n.d.).
B. Eygun, 'Superstitions Basques', *RTP* (1890), p.174.
Factums et Arrests du Parlement de Paris Contre les Bergers Sorciers Executez depuis peu dans la Province de Brie (Amsterdam, 1733–4).
P. Fagot, 'Formules de Conjuration Contre le Mal dans les pays de Languedoc', *Revue des Pyrénées* (1891), pp.170–77, 516–22.
J. P. Falret, *Des Maladies Mentales et des Asiles d'Aliénés* (Paris, 1864).
J. Falret, *Les Maladies Mentales* (1890).
— *Les Aliénés et les Asiles d'Aliénés. Assitance, Législation et Médecine Légale* (Paris, 1890).
Mme L. Fanguin, *La Chair de sa Chair, ou Journal d'une Sage-Femme de Campagne* (Rodez, 1964).
Dr Fanjoux, 'Aperçu Médico-Légal sur la Magie et la Sorcellerie avec leurs influences actuelles sur le développement des maladies mentales' (Lyon University, medical thesis, 1909).

A. Favraud, 'Prières Populaires du Poitou', *Mélusine* (1884), pp.286–7.
J. Favret-Saada, *Les Mots, La Mort et les Sorts* (Paris, 1977).
E. D. N. Fayard *Du Dépôt Mendicité Départemental d'Albigny* (Lyon, 1860).
— *Essai sur l'Assistance Publique et L'Extinction de la Mendicité à Lyon* (Lyon, 1862).
A. Fenayroux, 'Contribution à l'Etude des Folies Rurales' (Toulouse University, medical thesis, 1894).
J. Fleury, *La Littérature Orale de la Basse-Normandie* (Paris, 1883).
F. Fodéré, *Traité du Délire, appliqué à la Médecine, à la Morale et à la Législation* (Paris, 1817), 2 vols.
Abbé V. Foix, *Sorcières et Loups-Garous dans les Landes* (Auch, 1904).
— *Poésie Populaire Landaise* (Dax, 1890). Very difficult to read without proper glossary.
Fontenelle, 'De l'Origine des Fables', in *Oeuvres de Fontenelle* (Paris, 1825), vol. IV.
G. Foucart, *Des Erreurs et des Préjugés Populaires en Médecine* (Paris, 1893).
A. Fourcade, *Album Pittoresque et Historique des Pyrénées* (Paris, 1835).
M. Fournail, 'Essai sur la Psychologie des Foules' (Lyon University, medical thesis, 1892).
Dr Fournier, 'Les Sorciers et leurs Pratiques Médicales dans les Vosges',*Bulletin Médical des Vosges* (1890), pp.16, 57–60.
Fraisse *et al.*, *Rapport sur le Choléra-Morbus à Paris... Epidémie de 1849* (Lyon, 1849).
— *Des Classes Dangereuses de la Population dans les Grandes Villes et des Moyens de les Rendre Meilleures* (Paris, 1840), 2 vols.
French Popular Imagery, Five Centuries of Prints (London, 1774). Exhibition catalogue.
D. Friedmann, 'Magnétiseur: une Vocation, un don de soi', *Panseurs de Secret & de Douleurs*. Special No. of *Autrement* (Sep. 1978), XV, pp.20–29.
— 'Je ne fais jamais de diagnostic', *ibid*, pp.30–35.
J. Frison, 'Traditions et Superstitions en Basse-Bretagne', *RTP* (1908), XXIII, p.394.
Dr P. F. Gachet, *Etude sur la Mélancolie* (Paris, 1858).
C. Gagnon, *Folklore du Bourbonnais* (Moulins, 1947–68), 3 vols.
— *Légendes, Contes et Goguenettes en Bourbonnais* (Moulins, 1976).
M. Gaidoz, *Un Vieux Rite Médical* (Paris, 1892). Written in 1842.
L. Ganachaud, *Souvenirs et Espoirs d'un Paysan Charentais* (Angoulême, 1946).
M. C. Gandrille-Ourcel, 'La Médecine Populaire en Bourgogne' (Paris University, medical thesis, 1957).
E. Garay de Montglave (pseud. M. Dufresne), *Histoire des Missionaires dans le Midi et l'Ouest de la France* (Paris, 1819–20), 3 vols.
J. A. Garde, 'Folklore Libournais', *Revue Historique et Archéologique du Libournais* (1950), pp.21–8, 63–76, 95–100.
E. Garnier, 'Essai sur les Ecrits des Aliénés' (Paris University, medical thesis, 1894).
J. M. Garnier, *Histoire de l'Imagerie Populaire et des Cartes à Jouer à Chartres* (Chartres, 1869).
E. de Gasparin, *Rapport au Roi sur les Hôpitaux, les Hospices et les Services de Bienfaisance* (1971). (Reprint of 1837 edn).

E. Genab, 'Messes Singulières', *Revue des Traditions Populaires* (1895), v, p.231).
C. Géniaux, *La Bretagne Vivante* (2nd edn, Paris, 1912).
C. Genoux, *Mémoires d'un Enfant de la Savoie, écrits par lui-même* (Paris, 1844).
Dr E. J. Georget, *De la Folie* (Paris, 1820).
E. Gilbert, *Les Sorciers en Bourbonnais* (Moulins, 1877).
— *Autrefois, aujourd'hui. Sorciers et Magiciens* (Moulins, 1895).
L. Gilbert, 'La Sorcellerie au Pays Messin', *Pays Lorrain* (1907), pp.33–6.
Gilbert-Villeneuve, *Itinéraire Descriptif du Finistère* (Paris, 1828).
Dr Gilles de la Tourette, *L'Hypnotisme et les Etats Analogues au Point de Vue Médico-Légale ...* (Paris, 1887).
— *Traité Clinique et Thérapeutique de l'Hystérie* (Paris, 1891, 1895), 2 vols.
Dr A. Giraud, *Fragments d'Histoire de la Folie. La Sorcellerie au Moyen-Âge. Une Epidémie de Délire de Nos Jours* (Bar-le-Duc, 1883). Deals with Morzines.
A. Giroudin, 'Contribution à l'Etude des Caractères du Délire dans leurs Rapports avec l'Intelligence du Délirant' (Lyon University, medical thesis, 1895).
Abbé J. Goudret, *Moeurs et Coutumes des Habitants du Quéras au* XIXe *siècle* (Nyons, 1974). Goudret's manuscript dates from 1858.
M. R. Gougenot des Mousseaux, *La Magie au* XIXe *siècle* (Paris, 1860).
Grand Almanach des Jacques Bonhomme, Annuaire des Villageois et des Cultivateurs pour 1861 (Paris, 1860).
Le Grand Almanach du Cultivateur, pour l'année bissextile 1836, Contenant l'Agriculture Populaire (Niort, n.d.).
Le Grand Calendrier et Compost des Bergers. Composé par le Berger de la Grande Montagne, avec le Compost. Manuel, réformé selon le retranchement des dix jours, réformé par nostre sainct père le Pape Grégoire Treizième (Troyes, Oudot, 1618).
Le Grand Diable Bleu pour 1859 (Paris, n.d.).
Le Grand Grimore, ou l'Art de Commander les Esprits Célestes etc. (Paris, 1849).
Le Grand Calendrier et Compost des Bergiers avec leur Astrologie et Plusieurs Autres Choses (Paris, 1925 rpr. of Troyes edition of Nicolas le Rouge).
Le Grand Sorcier, Recueil de Nouveaux Tours de Société (Epinal, Pellerin, 1851).
J. Grand-Carteret, *Les Almanachs Français. Bibliographie-Iconographie, 1600–1895* (Paris, 1896).
— *Vieux Papiers, Vieilles Images* (Paris, 1896).
H. Graulle, 'Traditions et Médecine Populaire en Bourbonnais. (Etude des Croyances, Coutumes et Superstitions Traditionnelles, ainsi que des Phénomènes para-religieux actuels)' (Montpellier University, PhD thesis, 1963).
— 'Médecine Populaire et Guérison Magico-Religieuse dans le Bourbonnais Occidental', *Arts et Traditions Populaire* (1963), II, pp.99–118.
Abbé H.-B. Grégoire, *Promenade dans les Vosges* (Epinal, 1895). The text dates from the end of the eighteenth century.
— *Rapport sur la Nécessité et les Moyens d'Anéantir les Patois et d'Universaliser l'Usage de la Langue Française* (Paris, 4 June 1794).

Dom P. N. Grenier, *Introduction à l'Histoire Générale de la Province de Picardie* (Amiens, 1856). Text was written in 18th century – Grenier died in 1789.
Grimoire (Nalognes, 1860).
Grimoire ou Magie Naturelle (The Hague, n.d. – late 17th century).
A. Guéraud, *Etude sur les Chants Populaires en Français et en Patois, de la Bretagne et du Poitou* (Nantes, 1859).
A. N. Guerry de Champneuf, *Essai sur la Statistique Morale de la France* (Paris, 1833).
Dr H. Guiard and Dr Clérambault, *Contribution à l'Etude de la Folie Communiquée* (Evreux, 1903).
E. Guignot, *Le Paupérisme en France suivi de Moyens aussi simples qu'infaillibles d'en Restreindre considérablement l'Etendue* (Strasbourg, 1859).
E. Guillaumin, *Tableaux Champêtres* (Moulins, 1901).
— *La Vie d'un Simple* (reprinted Paris, 1971).
C. Guillon, 'Prières Populaires de l'Ain', RTP (1886), I, pp.35–9.
Rev. Guyard, *Analyse des Sermons du P. Guyon, Précédée de l'Histoire de la Mission du Mans pendant le Jubilé de 1826* (2nd edn, Le Mans, 1829).
— *Nouvelles Lectures et Méditations pour le Temps des Missions* (Montpellier, 1821).
C. E. Guyot, *Variations de l'Etat Mental et la Responsabilité* (Bordeaux, 1896).
F. M. G. Habasque, *Notions Historiques, Géographiques, Statistiques et Agronomiques sur le Littoral du Département des Côtes-du-Nord* (Saint-Brieuc, 1832–6), 3 vols.
D. Halévy, *Visites aux Paysans du Centre* (Paris, 1978, reprint of 1921 edn).
Dr L. Hamon, *Testament Médical d'un Médecin de Campagne* (Paris, 1863).
E. Harmonic, 'Adjurations et Conjurations. I. A Saint Yves', RTP (1888), III, pp.139–41.
A. Harou, 'L'Imagerie Populaire Flamande', RTP (1890), pp.281–3.
— 'Sorciers et Sorcières, *La Tradition* (1892), pp.266–7.
— 'Le Bon Dieu et S. Pierre: Conte Wallon', RTP (1892), pp.316–18.
P. Hartenberger, 'De l'Elément Psychique dans les Maladies', (Nancy University, medical thesis, 1895).
P. Hauser, *Le Choléra en Europe depuis son Origine jusqu'à nos Jours* (Paris 1976).
P. J. Hélias, *Le Cheval d'Orgueil. Mémoires d'un Breton du Pays Bigouden* (Paris, 1976).
P. J. Hélias and J. Markale, *La Sagesse de la Terre* (Paris, 1978).
Dr C. E. Hellis, *Souvenirs du Choléra en 1832* (Paris, 1833).
Dr C. Hélot, *Névroses et Possessions Diaboliques* (Paris, 1897).
R. Hélot, *Canards et Canardiers en France et Principalement en Normandie* (Paris, n.d.).
— *La Bibliothèque Bleue de Normandie* (Rouen, 1928).
C. Helvétius, *De L'Esprit* (Paris, 1959 edn).
P. Henri, called La Rigueur, 'Tout ce que je me rappelle de ma vie depuis 1801', *Magasin Pittoresque* (1850, in instalments).
G. Hérelle, *Etudes sur le Théâtre Basque. Le Théâtre Comique . . .* (Paris, 1925).
— *Les Pastorales Basques* (Bayonne, 1903).
— *Les Farces Charivariques Basques* (n.d.p.).
— *Les Parades Charivariques de la Vallée de la Nive* (n.d.p.).

P. Hermant and D. Boomans, *La Médecine Populaire* (Brussels, 1928).
J. V. Von Hildenbrand, *Du Typhus Contagieux* (Paris, 1811).
J.-F. Hirsch, 'Sur les Confins de Viadène – Aubrac: un Prêtre Radiésthésiste', *Panseurs de Secrets et de Douleurs*. Special No. of *Autrement* (September 1978), pp.35–52.
— 'La Magie et les Hommes en Noir', *Autrement* (September, 1978), pp.53–62.
Histoire de Cartouche, suivie de son Procès (Paris, 1843).
Histoire de Richard sand Peur, Duc de Normandie, fils de Robert le Diable (Montbéliard, Deckherr, n.d.).
Histoire du Célèbre Mandrin, Chef de Bandits, Suivie de Plusieurs Autres Chefs de Voleurs et Brigands etc. (Paris, 1857).
Histoire du Fameux Gargantua (Montbéliard, Deckherr, 1848).
Histoire du Juif Errant (Clermont-Ferrand, 1850).
Histoire Terrible et Epouvantable de Robert le Diable (Montbéliard, Deckherr, n.d.).
Baron P. H. D. Holbach, *La Morale Universelle ou les Devoirs de l'Homme Fondés sur la Nature* (Paris, year IV).
— *Système de la Nature, ou les Loix du Monde Physique & du Monde Moral* (New edn, London, 1775).
— *L'Enfer Détruit* (London, 1769).
— *La Contagion Sacrée ou Histoire Naturelle de la Superstition* (London, 1768).
— *Essai sur les Préjugés* (London, 1770).
M. Hugo, *France Pittoresque ou Description Pittoresque, Topographique et Statistique des Départements et Colonies de la France* (Paris, 1835), 3 vols.
J. Huyttens, *Etudes sur les Moeurs, Les Superstitions et le Langage de nos Ancêtres Comparés avec les Usages existant de nos Jours dans la Flandre Orientale* (Gand, 1861).
R. Hyvert, 'Contribution à l'Etude Historique et Séméliogique des Délires Religieux' (Paris University, medical thesis, 1899).
Dr M. Igert, *Le Problème des Guérisseurs* (Paris, 1931).
— 'Les Guérisseurs Mystiques. Etude Psychopathologique' (Toulouse University, medical thesis, 1928).
Dr I. M. Itard, *De l'Education d'un Homme Sauvage ou des Premiers Développements Physiques et Mentaux du Jeune Sauvage de l'Aveyron* (Paris, Year X, 1801).
— *Rapport fait à S. E. Ministre de l'Intérieur sur les Nouveaux Développements et l'Etat Actuel du Sauvage de l'Aveyron* (Paris, 1807).
Dr P. Janet, *De l'Angoisse à l'Extase* (Paris, 1926–8), 2 vols.
— *Névroses et Idées Fixes* (Paris, 1926–8), 2 vols.
— *L'Etat Mental des Hystériques* (2nd edn, Paris, 1911).
— *Les Obsessions & la Psychasthénie* (Paris, 1903).
— 'L'Hallucination dans le délire des persécutions', *Revue Philosophique* (Jan. 1932), pp.61–98.
— 'Les Croyances et les Hallucinations', *Revue Philosophique* (Jan. 1932), pp.279–331.
T. Janvrais, 'Les Offrandes Aux Saints', RTP (1895), X, pp.173–9.
Jayet de Fontenay, *Mission à Grenoble* (Grenoble, 1818).

E. Jobbé-Duval, *Les Idées Primitives dans la Bretagne Contemporaine* (Paris 1911–14, 1930).
F.-G.-T.-B. de Jolimont, *L'Allier Pittoresque* (Paris, 1974, rpr. of 1852 edn).
J. J. Juge Saint Martin, *Changements Survenus dans les Moeurs des Habitans de Limoges* (Limoges, 1817).
Abbé Julio, *Prières Merveilleuses pour la Guérison de Toutes les Maladies Physiques et Morales* (Paris, 1896).
R. Kaufmann, 'Pratiques Superstitieuses et Médicales en Poitou' (Paris University, medical thesis, 1906).
F. J. M. Kérambrun, 'Les Rebouteurs et les Guérisseurs en Bretagne. Croyances Populaires' (Bordeaux University, medical thesis, 1898).
L. Kerbirou, 'Sorcellerie et Diableries en Bretagne', *Nouvelle Revue de Bretagne* (1947), III, pp.161–8.
M. Kessel, 'Obsessions et Impulsions' (Montpellier University, medical thesis, 1895).
D. Kuhn, 'De l'Epidémie d'Hystéro-Démonopathie de Morzine', *Annales Médico-Psychologiques* (Jan.–June 1865), V, pp.400–13; (July–Dec. 1865), VI, pp.20–41.
Dr Labadie, *Lettre sur le Choléra-Morbus Epidémie... à Narbonne (Aude) en 1854* (Narbonne, 1854).
J. B. Laborde, 'La Grêle et les conjurations ce Fléau', *Revue Historique et Archéologique du Béarn et du Pays Basque* (1935), pp.14–22, 83–95.
— 'Les *Brouches* (sorcières) en Béarn, Gascogne et le Pays Basque', *Revue Historique et Archéologique du Béarn et du Pays Basque* (Jan.–March 1935), pp.4–23; (April–June 1935), pp.104–30; (July–Sep. 1935), pp.230–49; (Oct.–Dec. 1935), pp.285–309.
P. La Boulinière, *Itinéraire Descriptif et Pittoresque des Hautes Pyrénées Françoises* (Paris, 1825), 3 vols.
Abbé B. Labrune, *Mystères des Campagnes* (Limoges, 1858).
L. Lacouture, 'La Sorcellerie dans le Béarn', *Réclams de Biarn et Gascounhe* (1913), VIII, pp.45–8, 65–8.
J. M. Ladevèze, *Mémoire sur la Question Suivante ... Quelles sont les Maladies qui règnent le plus communément dans le Département de la Gironde?* (Bordeaux, 1824).
J. C. F. Ladoucette, *Histoire, Topographie, Antiquités, Usages, Dialectes des Hautes Alpes* (3rd edn, Paris, 1848).
J. U. F. Lafforgue, 'Contribution à l'Etude Médico-Légale de l'Hypnotisme' (Bordeaux University, medical thesis, 1887).
C. M. Lafon du Cujula, 'Notice sur le Langage et les Usages Particuliers des Habitans du Département de Lot-et-Garonne', *Second Recueil des Travaux de la Société d'Agriculture, Sciences et Arts d'Agen* (Agen, 1812), pp.154–79.
— *Annuaire ou Description Statistique du Département de Lot-et-Garonne* (1806).
R. De La Grasserie, *Essai Scientifique sur l'Argot et le Parler Populaire* (Paris 1907).
— *Des Parlers des Différentes Classes Sociales* (Paris, 1909).
A. Lailler, *Assistance aux Indigents de la Campagne* (Rouen, 1898).
Laisnel de la Salle, *Croyances et Légendes du Centre de la France* (Paris, 1875–81), 2 vols.

— *Souvenirs du Vieux Temps. Le Berry: Moeurs et Coutumes* (Paris, 1902).

J. Lalanne, 'Les Persécutés Mélancoliques' (Bordeaux University, medical thesis, 1897).

L. Lallement, 'Médecine Superstitieuse. Prière pour le Mal des Dents', RTP (1912), p.327.

Abbé P. Lamazouade, 'La Sorcellerie à Corneillan, Lauraët, Mirande et Plaisance', *Bulletin de la Société Archéologique du Gers* (1909), pp.145–9.

J. O. de La Mettrie, *L'Homme Machine*, ed. G. Delaloye (n.p., 1966).

M. L. Lamiaud, 'Le Souper des Anciens Morts', *Etudes Locales. Bulletin de la Société Charentaise des Etudes Locales* (1922), pp.26–9.

A. Lamoureux, 'Essai Critique sur le Merveilleux en Médecine' (Paris University, medical thesis, 1865).

C. Lancelin, *La Sorcellerie des Campagnes* (Paris, 1911).

— *Ternaire Magique de Satan* (Paris, 1904).

H. Landouzy, *Traité Complet de l'Hystérie* (Paris, 1846).

J. de Laporterie, 'Les Vieilles Coutumes de Chalosse', *Bulletin de la Société de Borda* (1887), XII, pp.137–46.

A. Lamarque de Plaisance, *Usages et Chansons Populaires de l'Ancien Bazadais, Baptêmes, Noces, Moissons, Enterremens* (Bordeaux, 1845).

— *Le Club de Village* (Paris, 1849).

Comte de Lapparent, 'Pratiques Conjuratoires', *Revue de Folklore Française et Colonial* (1936), VI, pp.226–7.

Drs Lasègue and J. Falret, 'De la Folie à Deux ou Folie Communiquée', *Annales Médico-Psychologiques* (July–Dec. 1877), 5th series, XVIII, pp.321–55.

G. de Launay, 'Des Apparitions en Vendée', RTP (1809), pp.353–4.

— 'Médecine Superstitieuse en Anjou', RTP (1891), p.422.

L. Laurand, 'Sorcellerie en Armagnac Noir', *Bulletin de la Société Archéologique du Gers* (1955), p.325.

E. Laurant, *Le Paupérisme et les Associations de Prévoyance* (Paris, 1865), 2 vols.

Abbé R. Laurentin, *Lourdes, Dossiers des Documents Authentiques* (2nd edn, Paris, 1957–9), 5 vols.

M. Lauvergne, *Le Choléra-Morbus en Provence* (Toulon, 1836).

L. Lavigne, *Le Patois de Cumières et du Verdunois* (Verdun, 1939–40).

G. Le Bon, *Les Lois Psychologiques* (Paris, 1894).

— *The Crowd* (London, 1896).

A. Le Braz, *Pâques d'Islande* (Paris, 1897).

— *Le Théâtre Celtique* (Paris, 1906).

— *La Légende de la Mort en Basse Bretagne* (Paris, 1893).

— *Au Pays des Pardons* (Paris, 1901).

— 'Les Saints Bretons d'après la Tradition Populaire', *Annales de Bretagne* (1893–6), VIII–XIII.

Rev. P. Le Brun, *L'Histoire Critique des Pratiques Superstitieuses qui ont séduit les Peuples et Embarrassé les Sçavans* (Amsterdam, 1733–6), 2 vols.

Dr A. A. Lecadre, *Une Panique, Souvenir du Choléra en 1832* (Le Havre 1878).

— *Histoire de Trois Invasions Epidémiques de Choléra-Morbus au Havre* (Le Havre, 1863).

H. Le Carguet, 'Superstitions et Légendes du Cap Sizun: Le Mauvais Oeil', RTP (1889), pp.465–7; RTP (1890), pp.169–70.

A. L. Lecocq, *Les Sorciers de la Beauce* (Chartres, 1861).
— *Empiriques, Somnambules et Rebouteurs Beaucerons* (Chartres, 1862).
— *Les Loups dans la Beauce* (Chartres, 1860).
J. Lecoeur, *Esquisses du Bocage Normand* (Condé-sur-Noireau, 1883–7), 2 vols.
Dr P. Ledru, *Du Paupérisme dans les Campagnes* (Paris, 1846).
L. F. Lélut, *L'Amulette de Pascal, pour servir à l'Histoire des Hallucinations* (Paris, 1846).
— *Le Démon de Socrate* (Paris, 1836).
J. Lemoine, 'La Sorcellerie Contemporaire dans l'Entre-Sambre et la Meuse', *La Tradition* (1892), pp.103–12, 151–60.
Abbé N. Lenglet-Dufresnoy, *Recueil des Dissertations Anciennes et Nouvelles sur les Apparitions, les Visions et les Songes* (Avignon, 1752), 2 vols.
G. de Lépinay, 'Prières Populaires de la Corrèze', *Mélusine* (1884), pp.218–24.
M. Leproux, *Médecine, Magie et Sorcellerie* (Paris, 1954).
— *Dévotions et Saints Guérisseurs* (Paris, 1957).
A. J. F. Le Roux de Lincy, *Le Livre des Proverbes Français, Précédé d'un essai sur la Philosophie de Sancho Pança* (Paris, 1842).
F. Leuret, *Fragmens Psychologiques sur la Folie* (Paris, 1834).
Dr Leveillé, 'Mémoire sur la Folie des Ivrognes ou le Délire Tremblant', *Mémoires de l'Académie Royale de Médecine* (1828), I, pp.181–220.
Dr A. A. Liébeault, *Du Sommeil et des Etats Analogues Considérés surtout au Point de Vue de l'Action du Moral sur le Physique* (Paris, 1866).
— *Le Sommeil Provoqué et les Etats Analogues* (Paris, 1889).
C. Lombroso, *L'Anthropologie Criminelle et ses Progrès Récents* (2nd edn, Paris, 1891).
C. Londe, Arts. 'Délire' and 'Délire Tremblant', in *Dictionnaire de Médecine et de Chirugie Pratiques*, ed. G. Andral *et al.* (Paris, 1831), VI.
B. Lunel, *Relation de l'Epidémie Cholérique de Montbréhain (Aisne)*, (Saint-Quentin, 1854).
F. M. Luzel, *Légendes Chrétiennes de la Basse-Bretagne* (Paris, 1881), 2 vols.
— 'Les Contes Populaires du Moyen-Âge. II. L'Horrible Exemple de l'Envêque Hugues', *RTP* (1890), pp.355–66.
— 'L'Imagerie Populaire de la Basse-Bretagne', *RTP* (1890), pp.629–31.
— 'Sermon pour la Fête de la Toussaint, le premier Novembre', *Annales de Bretagne* (Nov. 1893), pp.120–136.
Dr J. Mabit, *Rapport sur le Choléra-Morbus Asiatique, Qui a été observé à Bordeaux*... (Bordeaux, 1832).
Dr M. A. A. Macario, *Etudes Cliniques sur la Démonomanie* (Paris, 1843).
— *Des Hallucinations* (Paris, 1846).
— *Du Sommeil, des Rêves et du Somnambulisme dans l'Etat de Santé et de Maladie* (Paris, 1857).
— *Topographie Médicale du Canton de Sancergues* (Bourges, 1850).
— 'Du Traitement Moral de la Folie', (Paris University, medical thesis, 1843).
V. Magnan, *Des Dégénérés* (Paris, 1895).
— *Leçons Cliniques sur les Maladies Mentales* (Paris, 1887–97), 3 vols.
A. Magnin, *Recherches Géologiques, Botaniques, et Statistiques sur l'Impaludisme dans les Dombes et le Miasme Paludéen* (Paris, 1876).
Abbé J. Mahé, *Essai sur les Antiquités du Morbihan* (Vannes, 1825).

Dr M. Maingault, *Des Causes de la Fréquence des Fièvres dans le Département d'Indre-et-Loire* (n.p., 1838).
L. Maître, 'Le Sorcier de Pierrec', *Bulletin de la Société Archéologique de Nantes et du Département de la Loire-Inférieure* (1905), XLVI, pp.5–39.
H. Mallard, *Les Miracles de N.D. de Chappes* (Paris, 1946).
Dr Marnadon de Montyel, 'Des Conditions de la Contagion Mentale Morbide', *Annales Médico-Psychologiques* (Jan.–June 1894), XIX, pp.266–93; 467–87.
Dr Marc, *De la Folie* (Paris, 1840).
Dr A. Marie, *Mysticisme et Folie* (Paris, 1907).
— *Vagabondage et Folie* (Rouen, 1898).
Dr A. Marie and Dr Frièse, *Asile de la Roche-Gandon. Rapport sur le Service Médical et Administratif, 1889–90* (Mayenne, 1891).
Dr A. Marie and J. Violet, 'L'Envoûtement Moderne: Ses Rapports avec l'Aliénation Mentale', *Journal de Psychologie* (1906), III, pp.211–25.
L. Marin, *Les Contes Traditionnels en Lorraine. Institutions de Transfert des Valeurs Morales et Spirituelles* (Paris, 1964).
J. Markale, 'En forêt Perseigne, sorciers et guérisseurs blancs', *Autrement* (September 1978), p.94–7.
P.-F.-X. Marrel, 'Les Phobies: Essai sur la Psychologie Pathologique de la Peur' (Paris University, medical thesis, 1895).
Dr F. Martin, *Du Choléra Epidemique... Observé dans la Ville d'Arles, en Provence, en 1832, 1835, 1849* (Arles, 1850).
M. A. Martin, *L'Imagerie Orléannaise* (Paris, 1928).
Dr L. Martinecq, *Choléra de Toulon* (Paris, 1848).
— *Appendice au Choléra de Toulon à Propos de l'Epidémie de Marseille de 1865* (Grasse, 1866).
J. Marucchi, 'Psychologie Paysanne, Empirisme et Médecine Vétérinaire' (Paris University, thesis in vet. medicine, 1950).
M. Massol, *Description du Département du Tarn, Suivie de l'Histoire de l'Ancien Pays d'Albigeois* (Albi, 1818).
Dr. C. Mathieu, 'Médecine Populaire et Médecine Rurale dans la Région de la Grésigne en Haut-Albigeois' (Toulouse University, medical thesis, 1946).
L. Mazaret, 'Notes sur la Sorcellerie en Gascogne', *RTP* (1909), pp.267–72; *RTP* (1910), XXV, pp.316–18.
Le Médecin de la Ville et de la Campagne (Lyon, 1865).
Le Médecin des Pauvres (Armentières, Cadot-Petit, c.1868).
Le Médecin des Pauvres, ou Recueil de Prières pour le Soulagement des Maux d'Estomac... (Troyes, 1858).
Le Médecin des Pauvres. En Dieu la Confiance. (n.p., 1832).
Le Médecin des Pauvres (n.p., 1858).
Le Médecin des Pauvres (n.d.p.).
Le Médecin des Pauvres (Coulommiers, 1821).
Le Médecin des Pauvres (Rouen, 1851).
Le Médecin du Village (Amiens, 1851). A modern, sensible work, unlike the *Médecins des Pauvres* above, which are traditional.
Le Médecin des Pauvres (Noirt, 1904).
De la Mendicité en Bretagne et des Moyens Propres à l'éteindre (Châteaulin, 1860).

De la Mendicité et des Moyens d'y Rémédier (Lyon, 1828).

C. de Mensignac, *Notice sur les Superstitions, Dictions, Proverbes, Devinettes et Chansons Populaires de la Gironde* (Bordeaux, 1888).

Le Messager Boîteux (n.p., 1851).

P. Meyer and C. Joret, 'Recettes Médicales en Français, Publiées d'après le ms 23 d'Evreux', *Romania* (1889), XVIII, pp.571–82.

A. Meyrac, *Traditions, Coutumes, Légendes et Contes des Ardennes* (Charleville, 1890).

C. F. Michéa, *Du Délire des Sensations* (Paris, 1846).

Abbé J. P. Migne, *Nouvelle Encyclopédie Théologique* (Paris, 1851–64), 52 vols. Some articles are relevant.

Dr A. Mignot, 'Topographie Médicale de l'Arrondissement de Gannat', *Congrès Scientifique de France* (Moulins, 1872), pp.31–66.

J. Milin, 'Prières Populaires de l'Ile de Batz', RTP (1886), pp.112–13.

A. Millien, 'La Messe de Tourmentation', RTP (1913), pp.84–5.

A. Millien and P. Delarue, *Contes du Nivernais et du Morvan* (Paris, 1953).

— *Recueil des Chants Populaires du Nivernais* (Nevers, 1947).

A. S. Miron (pseud. Morin), *Le Prêtre et le Sorcier. Statistique de la Superstition* (Paris, 1872).

La Mission. Épître à M. M. Les Missionaires (Toulouse, 1819).

Mission à Aiguemortes (Nîmes, 1860).

Mission à Montjean. Avent 1892 (Angers, 1893).

Mission à Nancy (Nancy, 1912).

Mission à S. Maurille de Chalonnes (Angers, 1899).

Mission à Toulon (Toulon, 1853).

Mission d'Arles (1817) (Grenoble, n.d.).

Mission d'Azay-le-Rideau (Tours, n.d.).

Mission de Besançon (Besançon, 1825).

Mission de Châtillon-sur-Loing (Paris, 1892).

Mission Diocésaine de Clermont. Manuel du Fidèle (Clermont-Ferrand, 1912).

Mission d'Ebrueil (Clermond-Ferrand, 1845).

Mission de Grenoble (Grenoble, 1818).

Mission de Nantes à l'Occasion du Jubilé, 1827 (Nantes, 1827).

Mission des RR. PP. Franciscains à S. Michel du Havre (Balbec, 1860).

Mission de Vaucluse (Vaison-la-Romaine, n.d.).

Mission donnée à Revel en 1839 (Castelnaudary, n.d.).

Mission donnée à Romans... en Novembre et Décembre 1820 (Valence, 1821).

Mission du Diois (Lyon, 1866).

Mission du Mans (Le Mans, 1818).

Mission Intérieure du Gard (Nîmes, 1874).

Mission Prêchée à Angoulême... par les RR. PP. Capucins (Carême, 1887) Angoulême, 1887).

Missions en France et Etrangères 1818–20 (n.p.d.) Collection of brochures condemning Restoration missions throughout France.

F. Mistral, *Memoirs of Mistral, rendered into English by C. E. Maud* (London, 1907).

V. Modeste, *De la Cherté des Grains et des Préjugés Populaires qui déterminent des Volences dans les Temps de Disette* (3rd edn, Paris, 1862).

Dr J. B. Monfalcon, *Histoire Médicale des Marais et Traité des Fièvres Intermittentes* (Paris, 1824).
D. Monnier, *Traditions Populaires Comparées: Mythologie: Règnes de l'Air et la Terre* (Paris, 1854).
D. Monnier and A. Vingtrinier, *Croyances et Traditions Populaires recueillies dans la Franche-Comté, le Lyonnais, la Bresse et le Bugey* (2nd edn, Lyon, 1874: a re-edition of Monnier's work of 1854).
J. Moreau de Tours, *Du Hachisch et de l'Aliénation Mentale* (Paris, 1974, rpr. of 1845 edn).
— 'De l'Influence du Physique relativement au désordre des Facultés Intellectuelles' (Paris University, medical thesis, 1830).
— *La Psychologie Morbide dans ses Rapports avec la Philosophie et l'Histoire* (Paris, 1859).
P. Moreau de Tours, *De la Deménce, dans ses Rapports avec l'Etat Normal des Facultés Intellectuelles et Affectives* (Paris, 1878).
— *Les Excentriques* (Paris, 1894).
— *De la Contagion du Suicide* (Paris, 1875).
B. A. Morel, *Traité de Dégénérescences Physiques, Intellectuelles et Morales de l'Espèce Humaine et des Causes qui produisent ces variétés maladives* (Paris, 1857).
— *Traité des Maladies Mentales* (Paris, 1859).
Canon J. J. Moret, *Devins et Sorciers dans le Département de l'Allier, 1840–1909* (Moulins, 1909).
J. Morin, *Hystérie et les Superstitions Religieuses* (Paris, 1901).
L. Morin, 'Le Calendrier des Illettrés. L'Almanach des Bergers', RTP (1890), p.146.
— 'La Bonne Femme qui Tire les Saints', RTP (1895), pp.599–600.
— 'Essai de Catalogue du Culte des Fontaines dans l'Aube', RTP (1901), p.184.
— 'Les Sorciers dans la Région Troyenne' RTP (1901), pp.153–61, 267–73, 487–501.
J. Moriot, 'Sorciers et Rebouteux', *Revue Scientifique du Bourbonnais* (1901), pp.169–73.
A. Moulis, *Vieux Sanctuaires Ariégeois* (Verniolle, 1967).
— *Traditions, Coutumes de Mon Terroir* (Verniolle, 1972).
M. Nadaud, *Mémoires de Léonard, Ancien Garçon Maçon*, ed. M. Agulhon (5th edn, Paris, 1976).
Nagaty, 'Contribution à l'Etude de la Folie' (Paris University, medical thesis, 1886).
A. Niceforo, *Le Génie de l'Argot. Essai sur les Langages Spèciaux, Les Argots et les Parlers Magiques* (Paris, 1912).
N. de Nicolay, *Générale Description du Bourbonnais* (Paris, 1974; reprod. of 1889 edn). Work dates from 1569.
M. de Nimal, 'Histoires Contemporaines des Sorciers', RTP (1889), pp.295–7.
C. Nisard, *Histoire des Livres Populaires ou de la Littérature de Colportage, depuis l'Origine de l'Imprimerie jusqu'à l'Etablissement de la Commission d'Examen des Livres de Colportage* (2nd edn, Paris, 1964), 2 vols.
Dr V. Nivet, *Documents sur les Epidémies qui ont Regné dans l'arrondissement de Clermont-Ferrand de 1849 à 1864* (Paris, 1865).

L

— *Essai sur les Erreurs Populaires Relatives à la Médecine* (Clermont-Ferrand, 1841).
C. Nodier, *Du Fantastique en Litterature* (Paris, 1852).
— *De Quelques Phenomènes du Sommeil*, in *Oeuvres Complètes* (Paris, 1832–7), v.
Abbé J. L. M. Noguès, *Moeurs d'Autrefois en Saintonge et Aunis* (Saintes, 1891).
C. Noiret, *Mémoires d'un Ouvrier Rouennais* (Rouen, 1836).
A. de Nore (pseud. Chesnel de la Charbonnais), *Coutumes, Mythes et Traditions des Provinces de France* (Paris, 1846).
M. Nozot, 'Usages et Superstitions Populaires des Ardennes', *Revue des Sociétés Savantes de la France et de l'Etranger* (July–Dec 1872), pp.122–33.
Dr J. P. Odenthal, 'Etude sur la Sorcellerie Médicale en Dordogne' (Bordeaux University, medical thesis, 1923).
Ogée, *Dictionnaire Historique et Géographique de la Province de Bretagne* (Rennes, 1843). Text dates from previous century.
A. Orain, 'Prières du soir', *Mélusine* (1884), *c*. p.250.
— 'Prières Populaires de l'Ile-et-Vilaine', *Mélusine* (1884), *c*. p.500.
E. Orcurto-Joany, *Recueil des Usages Locaux Constatés dans le Département des Basses-Pyrénées* (Pau, 1868).
H. Paillard, *Histoire Statistique du Choléra-Morbus qui a régné en France en 1832* (Paris, 1832).
Passeport pour l'Eternité (Aurillac, 1821).
E. Pauc, 'Des Erreurs et des Préjugés Populaires en Médecine' (Montpellier University, medical thesis, 1882).
E. F. Peignot, *Histoire Morale, Critique, Politique et Littéraire du Charivari, depuis son origine vers le* XIV*e* *siècle* (Paris, 1833).
M. Pellisson, 'Superstitions Béarnaises', RTP (1891), p.154.
P. V. A. Penon, *Contribution à l'Etude Post-Opératoire* (Bordeaux, 1893).
A. Perdiguier, *Mémoires d'un Compagnon* (Paris, 1977, re-edition of 1854 edn).
F. Pérot, 'Contributions au Folklore Bourbonnais. Légendes, Contes Populaires. Noëls et Chansons', *Les Cahiers du Centre* (April–May 1912), pp.7–135.
— 'Prières, Invocations, Formules Sacrées, Incantations en Bourbonnais', RTP (1903), XVIII, pp.297–306.
— *Du Caractère Ethnique du Bourbonnais* (Montluçon, 1897).
— *Folklore du Bourbonnais* (Paris, 1908).
C. Perrault, *Oeuvres Choisies*, ed. Collin de Plancy (Baron C. A. de Walckenauer) (Paris, 1826).
Dr L. Perret, *Erreurs, Superstitions Doctrines Médicales* (Paris, 1879).
L. Petit, 'Une Epidémie d'Hystéro-Démonopathie en 1878 à Verzegnis, Province de Frioul, Italie', *Revue Scientifique* (10 April 1880), pp.973–8.
Le Petit Albert (Paris, 1865).
Le Petit Almanach de l'Est (Bar-le-Duc, 1871).
Petit Almanach des Ardennes (Charleville, 1874–5), 2 vols.
Petit Manuel des Arts d'Utilité et d'Agrément (Paris, 1839).
Le Petit Savoyard (Lille, 1839). Sentimental chapbook novel.
Le Petit Sorcier (Paris, 1843).
Petit Astrologie Populaire. Théorie des Eclipses. Eclipse du 8 Juillet 1842 (Paris, 1842).

Dr C. Pézet, *Contribution à L'Etude de la Démonomanie* (Montpellier, 1909).
Z.-J. Piérart, *Guide Complet du Touriste, de l'Archéologue, de l'Industriel... sur le Chemin de fer de S. Quentin à Mauberge* (Paris, 1862).
Pierson and Loiseau, *Géographie Historique, Statistique, et Administrative du Département de la Meuse* (2nd edn, Verdun, 1862).
A. Pitres and E. Régis, *Les Obsessions et les Impulsions* (Paris, 1902).
Plouvain, *Souvenirs à l'Usage des Habitants de Douai* (Douai, 1843).
A. Pommerel, *Les Sorcelleries Lorraines* (Metz, 1853). Tales.
A. Ponsard, 'Essai sur les Préjugés en Médecine et sur leurs Dangers' (Paris University, medical thesis, 1822).
A. de Ponthieu, *Les Fêtes Légendaires* (Paris, 1866).
F. Pouy, *Recherches sur les Almanachs et les Calendriers Historiés du* XVIe *au* XIXe *Siècle* (Amiens, 1874).
C. Pris, 'Carnet de Prières Magiques de Gennevilliers (Seine)', *Bulletin Folklorique de l'Ile-de-France* (1935), pp.488–90.
R. A. Proust, 'Etude sur la Folie à Deux' (Paris University, medical thesis, 1895).
Dr Prouvost, 'Le Délire Prophétique' (Bordeaux University, medical thesis, 1896).
J. O. Pugo, 'Quelques Considérations Contre les Doutes et les Préjugés du Monde, relatifs à la Médecine' (Paris University, medical thesis, 1834).
J. P. Quénot, *Statistique du Département de la Charente* (Paris, Angoulême, 1818).
R. de Quirielle, ed., *Le Livre de Raison des Boyard, Bourgeois-Agriculteurs de Bert, 1611–1780* (Moulins, 1899).
C. Rabaud, *Phénomènes Psychiques et Superstitions Populaires* (Castres, 1908).
Rapport sur la Dépopulation en Eure-et-Loir, ses causes et le Remède (Chartres, 1875).
N. U. Raulin, 'Essai sur les Dangers de la Médecine Exercée par les Charlatans et les Gens à Secrets' (Paris University, medical thesis, 1818).
Reboul de Neyrol, *Paupérisme et Bienfaisance dans le Bas-Rhin* (Paris, Strasbourg, 1858).
Dr E. Régis, *La Médecine et le Pessimisme Contemporain* (Bordeaux, 1898).
— *La Folie à Deux ou Folie Simultanée* (Paris, 1880).
P. Regnard, 'Les Sorcières', *La Revue Scientifique de la France et de l'Etranger* (1 April 1882), XXIX, pp.385–97.
Dr P. Regnard, *Les Maladies Epidémiques de l'Esprit. Sorcellerie, Magnétisme, Morphinisme* (Paris, 1887).
Dr J. Regnault, *La Sorcellerie, Ses Rapports avec les Sciences Biologiques* (Bordeaux, 1896).
Dr J. Remize, *Contribution à l'Etude de la Médecine Somatique. – La Médecine sur le Plateau de l'Aubrac – 'Pierrounet' de Nasbinals* (Aurillac, 1949).
Rétif de la Bretonne, *La Vie de Mon Père*, ed. G. Rouger (Paris, 1970).
Comte de Résie, *Histoire et Traité des Sciences Occultes ou Examen des Croyances Populaires sur les Êtres Surnaturels, la Magie, La Sorcellerie* (Paris, 1857), 2 vols.
M. Revault d'Allonès, 'Le sentiment du mystère les Aliénés', *Journal de Psychologie* (1906), III, pp.193–210.
Drs Reverchon and Pagès, *La Famille Lochin* (Paris, 1882).

C. Richelet, ed., *Noëls Nouveaux* (n.d.p.).
P. Richer, *Etudes Cliniques sur l'Hystéro-Epilepsie ou Grand Hystérie* (Paris, 1881).
— *Etudes Cliniques sur l'Hystérie* (Paris, 1889).
P. Ristelhuber, 'S. Antoine en Alsace', *La Tradition* (1892), VI, p.92.
J. A. Robert-Guyard, *Essai sur l'Etat du Paupérisme en France et sur le Moyen d'y Rémédier* (Paris, 1847).
Abbé G. Rocal, *Le Vieux Périgord* (Toulouse, 1927).
Dr N. Rodrigues, 'La Folie des Foules. Nouvelle Contribution à l'Etude des Folies epidémiques du Bresil', *Annales Médico-Psychologiques* (1901), XIII, pp.19–32, 187–99, 372–81; XIV, 5–18, 202–9.
E. Rolland, 'Prières Populaires', *Mélusine* (1884), pp.142–4.
— *Devinettes ou Enigmes Populaires de la France* (Paris, 1877).
— 'Une Epidémie de Démonomanie en 1878', *Revue Scientifique* (17 March 1883), pp.339–40.
R. Romain, *Souvenirs d'une Enfant Pauvre* (Paris, 1886).
U. Rouchon, *La Vie Paysanne dans la Haute-Loire* (Paris, 1977, reprod. of 1933 1st edn), 3 vols.
Dr A. Roujon, 'Le Buis sur le Feu', *Revue Scientifique du Bourbonnais* (1900), p.252.
C. Rouleau, *Essai de Folklore de la Sologne Bourbonnaise* (Moulins, 1935).
C. Rousset, *Traité du Choléra-Morbus de 1849* (Paris, 1851).
J. B. Rouvellat de Cussac, *Mémoire sur la Situation des Paysannes dans le Département de l'Aveyron et dans celui du Tarn en janvier 1853, et les Moyens de l'améliorer* (Albi, 1853).
Dr F. Rozier, *Les Inondations en 1910 et les Prophéties* (Paris, 1910). An eccentric theory of prophecy.
J. Sabbatier, *Affaire de la Salette* (Paris, 1857).
Marquis D. A. F. de Sade, *Idée sur les Romans* (Paris, 1878).
— *Français, Encore un Effort* (n.p., 1965).
C. Sadoul, 'Les Guérisseurs et la Médecine Populaire en Lorrain', *Pays Lorrain* (1934), XXXVI, and pp.1–82.
L. Saint-Michel, 'Un petit formulaire de Médecine Occulte découvert en Berry est [sic] toujours en usage' *Connaître, Cahiers de l'Humanisme Médical* (Jan.–Feb. 1948), pp.21–4.
Dr A. Sallet, 'Une rancune de Saint dans le diocèse de Toulouse', *Revue de Folklore Français et Colonial* (1935), V, p. 42.).
— 'Un contre-envoûtement en Haute-Garonne', *ibid*, p.35.
E. Salverte, *Des Sciences Occultes, ou Essai sur la Magie, les Prodiges et les Miracles* (Paris, 1850). Inspired by Comte.
J. F. Samazeuilh, *Dictionnaire Géographique, Historique et Archéologique de l'Arrondissement de Nérac* (Nérac, 1881).
G. Sand, *Légendes Rustiques* (Verviers, 1975).
S. Sandras, Art. 'Délire', :*Supplément au Dictionnaire des Dictionnaires de Médecine* (Paris, 1851).
J. Saugnieux, *Les Danses Macabres de France et d'Espagne et leurs Prolongements Littéraires* (Paris, 1972).
L. F. Sauvé, *Lavorou Koz a Vreiz-Izel... Proverbes et Dictions de la Basse-Bretagne* (Paris, 1878).

— *Le Folklore des Hautes Vosges* (Paris, 1889).
— 'Charmes, Oraisons et Conjurations Magiques de la Basse Bretagne', *Revue Celtique* (1883–5), VI, pp.67–85.
H. E. Say, *Des Monts de Piété* (Paris, 1848).
L. Shély, 'L'Envoûtement par la Statuette en Lorraine', *Revue de Folklore Français et Colonial* (1935), V, pp.32–3.
— 'L'Envoûtement en Alsace', *ibid*, p.35.
M. Schwob and G. Guieysse, 'Etude sur l'Argot Français', *Mémoires de la Société Linguistique de Paris* (1889), VII.
P. Sébillot, 'L'Imagerie Populaire en Haute et Basse-Bretagne', extr. from RTP (1888).
— *Le Folklore des Pêcheurs* (Paris, 1901).
— *Le Paganisme Contemporain* (Paris, 1908).
— *Gargantua dans les Traditions Populaires* (Paris, 1883).
— *Contes des Provinces de France* (Paris, 1884).
— *Le Folklore de France* (Paris, 1904–7), 4 vols.
— *Petite Légende Dorée de la Haute-Bretagne* (Nantes, 1897).
— *Le Peuple et l'Histoire* (Vannes, 1899).
— 'L'Enfer et le Diable dans l'Iconographie', RTP (1890), p.20; *ibid* (1889), pp.129–32, 509–11.
— 'Traditions et Superstitions du Languedoc', RTP (1891), pp.548–50.
— 'Superstitions Iconographiques: I Les Portraits. II Les Statues', RTP (1886), pp.34–54; (1887), pp.16–23.
— *Le Folklore: Littérature Orale et Ethnographie Traditionnelle* (Paris, 1913).
— *Contes de la Haute-Bretagne qui Présentent quelques Ressemblances avec le Contes Imprimés* (Paris, 1894).
P. Sébillot *et al.*, *Livres et Images Populaires* (Paris, 1894).
J. P. Séguin, *Canards du Siècle Passé, Presentés par J. P. Séguin* (Paris, 1969).
C. Seignolle, *Le Folklore du Languedoc* (Paris, 1960).
H. Sentoux, *De la Surexcitation des Facultés Intellectuelles dans la Folie* (Paris, 1867).
S. Sighele, *La Foule Criminelle* (Paris, 1900).
L. Silvy, *Relation concernant les Evénements qui sont arrivés à un Laboureur de la Beauce dans les Premiers mois de 1816* (Paris, 1817). Concerns the visionary, Martin.
Dr Sirus-Pirondi, *Relation Historique et Médicale de l'Epidémie Cholérique qui à régné à Marseille pendant 1854* (Paris, 1859).
A. Socard, *Livres Populaires: Noëls et Cantiques Imprimés à Troyes depuis le XVIIe siècle jusqu'à nos Jours* (Paris, Troyes, 1865).
— *Livres Populaires imprimés à Troyes de 1600 à 1800 Hagiographie* (Paris, 1864).
J. Socquet, 'Contribution á l'Etude Statistique de la Criminalité en France, de 1826 à 1880' (Paris University, law thesis, 1883).
Ch. E. Sol, 'Remèdes d'Autrefois dans le Département du Lot', *Revue de Folklore Français et Colonial* (1936), VI, pp.16–17.
E. Souvestre, *La Bretagne Pittoresque* (Nantes, n.d.).
— *Les Derniers Bretons* (Paris, 1971, facs. of 1854 edn and Paris, 1836).
J. Sprenger *et al.*, *Malleus Maleficarum*, trans. M. Summers (London, 1928).
Dr V. Stefani, *Les Délires Hystériques* (Bordeaux, 1912).

C. Steib, 'Copie d'un Livret et Remèdes du 8 avril 1824, redigé par G. Perret, Habitant Etoban, Village Protestant du Pays de Montbéliard', *Revue de Folklore Français et Colonial* (1939), x, pp.24–8.
Abbé P. Sutter, *Le Diable, ses Paroles, son Action dans les Possédés d'Ilfurt* (9th edn, Arrac, 1934).
L. R. Szafkowski, *Recherches sur les Hallucinations au point de vue de la Psychologie de l'Histoire et de la Médecine Légale* (Paris, 1849).
Abbé T., 'Une Possession Diabolique Compliquée de Magie en Auvergne', *Revue du Monde Invisible* (Jan.–April 1901), pp.495–512, 556–71, 623–9, 687–96.
Abbé L. Tabonnier, *Les Dévotions Populaires du Perche, en Particulier dans le Bellemois* (Bellême, 1923).
G. Tarde, *La Criminalité Comparée* (Paris, 1886).
A. Tardieu, *Etude Médico-Légale sur la Folie* (Paris, 1872).
A. Tavarne, *Médecine Populaire et Sorcellerie en Rouannais et Forez: Enquêtes* (Ambierle, 1976).
Dr F. Terrien, *L'Hystérie et la Neurasthénie chez le Paysan* (Anvers, 1906).
— *De l'Hystérie en Vendée* (extr. from *Archives de Neurologie)* (n.p.d).
Abbé J. B. Thiers, *Traité des Superstitions Selon l'Ecriture Sainte, les Décrêts des Conciles et les Sentiments des Saints Pères et des Théologiens* (Amsterdam, 1733–6, in 1 vol.), 1st pub. 1679.
C. Thuriet, 'Les Sorciers devant la Législation au Moyen Age et la Législation Moderne', *Mémoires de la Société d'Emulation du Doubs* (1874), 4th series, IX, pp.515–32.
Dr Tiffaud, 'L'Exercice Illégale de la Médecine dans le Bas-Poitou' (Paris University, medical thesis, 1899).
P. A. Tissié, 'Les Aliénés Voyageurs' (Bordeaux University, medical thesis, 1887).
M. J. Tissot, *Les Possédés de Morzine ou le Diable qui n'y voit goutte* (Paris 1865).
V. Tixier, 'De l'Exercice Illégale de la Médecine et l'Etude du Caractère de la Paysanne au point de vue de l'Education dans les Campagnes', *Congrès Scientifique de France* (1871), pp.337–59.
Dr E. Toulouse, *Les Causes de la Folie* (Paris, 1896).
G. Tourdes, *Histoire de l'Epidémie de Ménigite Cérébro-Spinale* (Strasbourg, 1842).
— *Exercice Illégale de la Médecine et de la Pharmacie à Strasbourg* (Strasbourg, 1844).
A. Tranier, *Dictionnaire Historique et Géographique du Département du Tarn* (Albi, 1862).
S. Trébucq, *La Chanson Populaire et la Vie Rurale des Pyrénées à la Vendée* (Bordeaux, 1912), 2 vols.
Dr U. Trélat, *Recherches Historiques sur la Folie* (Paris, 1839).
Dr. P. Trélaün, 'Paraoïas avec Hallucinations' (Toulouse University, medical thesis, 1905).
Dr A. Trousseau, *Rapport sur les Epidémies qui on régné en France en 1856* (Paris, 1858).
N. Truquin, *Mémoires et Aventures d'un Prolétaire à travers la Révolution* (Paris, 1977). Dates from late 19th century.

Dr Tueffard, *Mémoire sur l'Epidémie de Choléra* (Montbéliard, n.d.).
C. Vallon and A. Marie, *Des Psychoses Religieuses* (Evreux, 1896–7).
A. Van Gennep, 'Un cas de Possession', *Archives de Psychologie* (Paris, 1911), x, pp.88–92.
— *Folklore de la Flandre et du Hainaut Français, Département du Nord* (Paris, 1935–6), 2 vols.
— *Le Folklore des Hautes-Alpes* (Paris, 1846–8), 2 vols.
— *Le Folklore du Dauphiné* (Paris, 1932–3), 2 vols.
— *Le Folklore de l'Auvergne et du Velay* (Paris, 1942).
— *La Formation des Légendes* (Paris, 1910).
— *Le Culte Populaire des Saints en Savoie* (Paris, 1973).
— *Manuel de Folklore Français Contemporain* (Paris, 1943), 7 vols.
E. Van Heurck and G. J. Boekenoogen, *Histoire de l'Imagerie Populaire Flamande* (Brussels, 1910).
A. Vée, *Du Paupérisme et des Secours Publics dans la Ville de Paris* (Paris, 1849).
L. Vène, 'Etude sur les Délires Post-Operatoires' (Paris University, medical thesis, 1891).
Dr H. Verdalle and Dr E. Mauriac, *Etude Médicale sur l'Extatique de Fontet* (Paris, 1875).
Le Véritable Messager Boîteux de Bâle en Suisse (n.p., 1788).
Le Véritable Messager Boîteux de Bâle en Suisse (Montbéliard, Deckherr, 1850).
La Vérité sur la Mort de T. Martin de Gallardon (Paris, 1834).
La Vérité sur le Choléra à Lyon (Lyon, 1849).
A. Vernière, 'Prière Populaire de la Haute-Loire', *Mélusine* (1884), p.499.
J. Vézian, 'Les Contre-Envoûtements dans l'Ariège', *Revue de Folklore Français et Colonial* (1935), v, pp.31–2.
— 'Une Prière de Guérison', *ibid*, p.119.
L. de V. M. 'Les Enfants Morts sans Baptême', RTP (1901), pp.526–7.
Dr F. Vidalin, *Mémoire sur les Fièvres Intermittentes du Département de la Corrèze* (Paris, Tulle, 1825).
Dr J. C. Villain, *Remarques sur les Maladies qui ont été Observées le plus communement sous le climat de Poitiers* (Paris, 1848).
L. R. Villermé, 'Mémoire sur la Mortalité en France, dans la classe aisée et dans la classe indigente', *Mémoires de l'Académie Royale de Médecine* (1828), I, pp.51–98.
J. Vinçard, *Mémoires Episodiques d'un Vieux Chansonnier Saint Simonien* (Paris, 1878).
P. Vinçard, *Les Ouvriers de Paris, Alimentation* (Paris, 1863).
Dr. J. Vinchon, 'Du Rôle de la Suggestion dans les Succès obtenus par les Guérisseurs', *Revue Anthropologique* (1928), XXXVIII, pp.49–58).
— 'Les Dangers de la Sorcellerie Moderne', *Revue de Médecine Légale* (1914), XXI.
J. Vinson, *Folklore du Pays Basque* (Paris, 1883).
E. Violet, *Le Patois de Clessé en Mâconnais* (Paris, Macon, 1932).
Mme Vion-Pigalle, *De la Peur du Choléra et de l'Influence Pernicieuse que ce Sentiment Exerce sur la Santé* (Paris, 1865).
J. Voisin, *Histoire de ma Vie et 55 Ans de Compagnonnage* (Tours, 1931).
Voyage à Bordeaux et dans les Landes, où sont décrits les Moeurs, Usages et Coûtumes du Pays (Paris, Year VI).

Vrais Textes de Prières Destinées au Pansement pour toutes les Maladies et au Pansement du Charbon. (Found on 4/11/1972 at S. Ouin-de-la-Pent des Bois, Nièvre). A. D. Allier, Series G, XI, 1972.
G. Vuillier, 'Chez les Magiciens et les Sorciers de la Corrèze', *Le Tour du Monde* (1899), pp.505–40.
A. Watteville du Grabe, *Statistique des Etablissements de Bienfaisance. Rapport à M. Le Ministre de l'Intérieur sur l'Administration des Hospices et des Hôpitaux* (Paris, 1851).
— *Statistique sur la Situation du Paupérisme en France et des Secours à Domicile* (Paris, 1855).
— *Essai Statistique sur les Etablissements de Bienfaisance* (2nd edn, Paris, 1847).
Dr R. Westphalen, *Petit Dictionnaire des Traditions Populaires Messines* (Metz, 1934).
Dr E. Wickersheimer, *Formules de Prières à dire en cas de Maladie*, extr. from *Bulletin de la Société Française d'Histoire de la Médecine* (Paris, 1910).
J. Wier, *Histoires, Disputes et Discours, des Illusions et Impostures des Diables . . .* (Paris, 1885, rpr. of 1579 edn), 2 vols.
Dr Witry, 'Les Grands Exorcismes du XIXe Siècle', *Revue de l'Hypnotisme et de Psychologie Physiologique* (Paris, 1905–6), XX, pp.163ff., 196ff., 305ff.
Dr A. A. F. Wormser, 'Des Hallucinations Unilatérales' (Paris University, medical thesis, 1895).

Secondary Sources

J. Aboudrar, 'Contribution à l'Etude des Guérisons Inattendues au cours des Maladies Mentales' (Paris University, medical thesis, 1964).
R. D. Abrahams, 'Proverbs and Proverbial Expressions', in *Folklore and Folklife*, ed. R. Dorson (Chicago, 1972), pp.117–26.
E. H. Ackerknecht, *Short History of Psychiatry* (2nd edn, New York and London, 1968).
— *A Short History of Medicine* (New York, 1955).
— *Medicine at the Paris Hospital, 1724–1848* (Baltimore, 1967).
— 'Hygiene in France, 1815–1848', *Bulletin of Medical History* (1948), 22, pp.117–55.
J. Adhémar, *Imagerie Populaire Française* (Milan, 1968).
M. Agulhon, *Pénitents et Francs-Maçons dans l'Ancienne Provence* (Paris, 1968).
— *Le Cercle dans la France Bourgeoise, 1810–1848* (Paris, 1977).
— *1848 ou l'Apprentissage de la République* (Paris, 1973).
— *La République au Village* (Paris, 1970).
M. Agulhon *et al.*, *Apogée et Crise la Civilistion Paysanne, 1789–1914* (vol. III of *Histoire de la France Rurale*), eds G. Duby and A. Wallon (Paris, 1976).
F. Alexander and S. T. Selesnick, *The History of Psychiatry* (London, 1967).
P. Alfonsi and P. Pesnot, *L'Oeil du Sorcier* (Paris, 1973).
J. Ambrosi, 'Quelque part en Corse, des "secrets"', *Autrement* (1978), 15, pp.89–93.
R. D. Anderson, *Education in France, 1848–1870* (Oxford, 1975).

R. Andree, *Votiv- und Weihegabe des katolischen Volks in Süddeutschland. Ein Beitrag zur Volkskunde* (Braunschweig, 1904).
'Approches de Nos Traditions Orales', *Arts et Traditions Populaires*, Special Number, 1970.
R. Aramborou, 'L'arrondissement de la Réole au Début de la IIIe République', *Revue Historique de Bordeaux* (1963), pp.211–36.
Arbellot, 'Les Prédicateurs du Carême et de l'Avent à Limoges', *Bulletin de la Société Archéologique et Historique du Limousin* (1900), XLVIII, p.515.
P. Ariès, *Histoire des Populations Françaises* (Paris, 1971).
— *L'Enfant et la Vie Familiale sous l'Ancien Régime* (2nd edn, Paris, 1975).
— *Essais sur l'Histoire de la Mort en Occident* (Paris, 1975).
— *L'Homme devant la Mort* (Paris, 1978).
L. Armand *et al.*, *Histoire des Chemins de Fer en France* (Paris, 1963).
F. Arnaudin, ed., *Recueil des Proverbes de la Grande Lande* (Bordeaux, 1965).
L'Art Populaire en France (Strasbourg, 1960).
F. Baby, *La Guerre des Demoiselles en Ariège (1829–1872)* (Toulouse-Carcassonne, 1972).
E. L. Backman, *Religious Dances in the Christian Church and in Popular Medicine* (London, 1952).
R. Baehrel, 'Epidémie et Terreur: Histoire et Sociologie', *Annales Historiques de la Révolution Française* (April–June 1951), pp.113–46.
— 'La haine des classes en temps d'épidémie', *AESC* (1952), VII.
M. Bakhtine, *L'Oeuvre de François Rabelais et la Culture Populaire au Moyen Age et sous le Renaissance* (Paris, 1970).
M. A. Baleydier, *A Propos d'un Mal Mystérieux à Morzine, sous le Second Empire* (Chambéry, 1949).
A. Bardet, 'La Vie en Bourbonnais il y a 50 ans. Moeurs et Coutumes', *Notre Bourbonnais* (1925), II, pp.35–48.
M. Barthes, 'Recherches sur le Recul de l'Analphabétisme et sur la Fréquentatation scolaire dans la population masculine du Département de la Loire-Inférieure, de 1848 à 1885', *Actes du 95e Congrès National des Savants* (1974), I, pp.447–60.
R. Barthes *et al.*, *Poétique de Récit* (Paris, 1977).
F. C. Bartlett, 'Psychology in Relation to the Popular Story', *Folklore* (December 1920), pp.264–94.
— 'Some experiments on the reproduction of folk-stories', *Folklore* (March 1920), pp.30–48.
H. Baruk, *La Psychiatrie Française de Pinel à Nos Jours* (Paris, 1967).
— *L'Hypnose* (15th edn, Paris, 1981).
A. Baruzzi, *Aufklärung und Materialismus im Frankreich des 18ten Jahrhunderts* (Munich 1968).
Bassette, *Le Fait de la Salette, 1846–1854* (Paris, 1965).
R. Bastide, *Sociologie des Maladies Mentales* (Paris, 1965).
— Le Rêve, La Transe et la Folie (Paris, 1972).
G. Bataille, *L'Experience Intérieure* (Paris, 1943).
— *La Littérature et le Mal* (Paris, 1957).
J. Baumel, *Le 'Masque-Cheval' et Quelques Autres Animaux Fantastiques. Etude de Folklore, d'Ethnographie et d'Histoire* (Paris, Montpellier, 1954).
N. Bayon, *Miracles Chez les Guérisseurs* (Paris, 1952).

A. Beaufrère, 'Un Aspect de l'Art Populaire, les Croix de Chemin', *Revue de la Haute-Auvergne* (1952), pp.83–90, 176–83, 383–91, 460–66.
N. Beaurieux, 'Le Prix du Blé en France au XIXe Siècle', (Paris University, law thesis, 1908).
N. Belmont, *Mythes et Croyances dans l'Ancienne France* (Paris, 1973).
R. Benedict, *Patterns of Culture* (London, 1971).
J. Bennet, *Les Sociétés de Secours Mutuels et la Fourniture des Médicaments au Siècle Dernier* (Etampes, 1959).
Y. M. Bercé, *Fête et Révolte* (Paris, 1976).
— *Croquants et Nus-Pieds* (Paris, 1974).
R. Berland, *Les Cultures et la Vie Paysanne dans la Vienne à l'Epoque Napoléonienne* (Paris, 1937).
E. Besson, *Colporteurs de l'Oisans en XIXe Siècle* (Grenoble, 1975).
Bienvenu, 'Les Semeurs de Peste', *La Médecine Internationale* (March 1911), pp.75–81.
C. Bila, *La Croyance à la Magie au XIIIe siècle en France* (Paris, 1925).
M. Bloch, 'Mémoire collective, traditions et coutumes', *Revue de Synthèse Historique* (1925), XL, pp.74–83.
— *French Rural History*, trans. J. Sondheimer (London, 1978).
R. E. Blum, *The Dangerous Hour: The Lore of Crisis and Mystery in Rural Greece* (London, 1970).
F. Boas, *Race, Language & Culture* (New York, London, 1966, rpr. of 1940 edn).
— 'The Mind of Primitive Man', *Annual Report of the Smithsonian Institution* (1901), p, pp.451–61.
M. Boîteux, 'Carnaval annexé: essai de lecture d'une fête romaine', *AESC* (March–April 1977), pp.356–80.
G. Bollème, *La Bibliothèque Bleue: La Littérature Populaire en France du XVIe au XIXe siècles* (Paris, 1971).
— 'Littérature Populaire et Littérature de Colportage au XVIIIe siècle', in F. Furet, ed., *Livre et Société dans la France du XVIIIe siècle* (Paris, 1965).
— *Les Almanachs Populaires au XVIIIe siècle* (Paris, 1969).
R. Bonnain-Moerdyk and D. Moerdyk, 'A Propos du Charivari: discours bourgeois et coutumes populaires', *AESC* (March–April 1977), pp.381–98.
J. Bossy, 'The Counter-Reformation and the People of Catholic Europe', *Past and Present* (May 1970), pp.51–70.
G. Bouchard, *Le Vllage Immobile, Sennely-en-Sologne au XVIIIe Siècle* (Paris, 1972).
M. Boudet and R. Grand, 'Etude Historique sur les Epidémies de peste en Haute-Auvergne du XVe au XVIIIe siècles', *Revue de la Haute-Auvergne* (1902), pp.44–71, 129–81, 267–99.
F. Boulard, *Premiers Itinéraires en Sociologie Religieuse* (Paris, 1966).
— *La Pratique Religeuse Urbaine* (Paris, 1968).
— La Pratique Religieuse, *Annales E. S. C.* (July–August, 1976), pp.000–0.
F. Braudel, *Capitalism and Material Life, 1400–1800*, trans. M. Kochan (London, 1977, rpr. of 1st English edn 1973).
P. Brochon, *Le Livre de Colportage en France depuis le XVIe Siècle* (Paris, 1954).
M. Bouteiller, *La Médecine Populaire* (Paris, 1966).
— *Sorciers et Jeteurs de Sort* (Paris, 1958).

P. Burke, *Popular Culture in Early Modern Europe* (Paperback edn, London, 1979).
C. Cahier, *Caractéristiques de Saints dans l'Art Populaire* (Paris, 1867), 2 vols.
A. Caillet, *Manuel Bibliographique des Sciences Psychiques et Occultes, Science des Mages, Hermétique, Astrologie: Kaballe, Franc-maçonnerie, Médecine ancienne* (Paris, 1932), 3 vols.
R. Caillos, *L'Homme et le Sacré* (3rd edn, Paris, 1963).
— *Le Mythe et l'Homme* (re-edn, Paris, 1972).
G. Callon, 'Le Mouvement de la Population dans le Département de Lot-et-Garonne au cours de le période 1821–1920', *Revue de l'Agenais* (1929), 56, pp.13–42).
G. Canguilhem, 'La Monstruosité et le Monstrueux', *La Connaissance de la Vie* (2nd edn, Paris, 1965), pp.171–84.
W. B. Cannon, *Bodily Changes in Pain, Hunger, Fear and Rage* (New York, 1929).
Cantaloube, *La Réforme en France vue d'un Village Cévenol* (Paris, 1951).
J. Capré, *Histoire du Véritable Messager Boîteux de Berne et de Vevey* (Vevey, 1884).
P.-J. Carle, *Du Dogme Catholique sur l'Enfer* (Paris, 1942).
E. Caro, *Du Mysticisme du* XVIIIe *Siècle. Essai sur la vie et la doctrine de St Martin* (Paris, 1852).
J. Caro Baroja, *Le Carnaval* (Paris, 1979).
Dr A. Castan, *Coup d'Oeil sur l'Histoire de la Faculté de Médecine de Montpellier* (Paris, 1875).
N. Castan, 'Caractéristiques criminelles des hautes régions du Languedoc oriental de 1780 à 1790', *Vivarais et Languedoc* (Montpellier, 1972).
Y. Castan, *Honnetêté et Relations Sociales en Languedoc* (Paris, 1974).
R. Castel, *L'Ordre Psychiatrique* (Paris, 1976).
E. Castelli, *Il Problema della Demitizzazione* (Rome, 1961).
— *Demitizzazione e Immagine* (Rome, 1962).
— ed., *Cristanesimo e Ragion di Stato: L'Umanesimo e il Demoniaco nell 'arte* (Rome, 1952).
Marquis de Castelnau, 'Une famille fermière au même domaine depuis 145 ans', *La Réforme Sociale* (January, 1884), pp.94–6.
P. Castex, *Histoire du Conte Fantastique Français* (Paris, 1951).
— ed., *Anthologie du Conte Fantastique Français* (Paris, 1947).
M. de Certeau, *La Culture au Pluriel* (Paris, 1974).
— *La Possession de Loudon* (Paris, 1978).
A. Certeux, *Les Calendriers à Emblèmes Hieroglyphiques* (Paris, 1891).
A. Chabert, *Essai sur le Mouvement des Prix et des Revenus en France de 1789 à 1820* (Paris, 1945).
Charente, Population par Commune, 1821–1968 (n.d.p).
F. L. Charpin, *Pratique Religieuse et Formation d'un Grande Ville: le Geste de Baptême et sa Signification en Sociologie Religieuse. (Marseille, 1806–1958)* (Paris, 1964).
R. Chartier, M. M. Compère, D. Julia, *L'Education en France du* XVIe *Siècle* (Paris, 1976).
R. Chartier, 'Représentations des Elites et des Gueux', *Revue d'Histoire Moderne et Contemporaine* (July–Sep. 1974), pp.376–88.

— 'Les Almanachs Populaires', *Revue Histoique* (1970), pp.193–7.
R. Chastel, *La Haute-Lozère Jadis et Naguère* (Paris, 1976).
P. Chaunu, 'De la Violence au Vol; en Marche vers l'Escroquerie', *Annales de Normandie* (1962), pp.235–7.
A. Chervel, *Et il fallut apprendre à lire à tous les petits Français* (Paris, 1977).
L. Chevalier, ed., *Le Choléra: La Première Epidémie du XIXe siècle* (La Roche-sur-Yon, 1958).
— *Classes Laborieuses, Classes Dangereuses à Paris pendant la Première moitié du XIXe Siècle* (Livre de Poche edn, Paris, 1978).
P. Chevalier, B. Grosperin, J. Maillet, *L'Enseignement du Français de la Révolution à nos jours* (Paris, The Hague, 1968).
G. Cholvy, *Géographie Religieuse de l'Hérault* (Paris, 1968).
G. E. Clancier, *La Vie Quotidienne en Limousin au XIXe Siècle* (Paris, 1976).
B. Clarke, *Mental Disorder in Early Britain. Exploratory Studies* (Cardiff, 1975). Includes interestiong early 16th-century account of miracles attributed to Henry VI.
R. Cobb, *Death in Paris, 1795–1801* (Oxford, 1978).
— *The Police and the People* (London, 1970).
G. Cocchiara, *Storia del Folklore in Europa* (Turin, 1952).
F. P. Codaccioni, 'Le Textile Lillois durant la Crise, 1856–51', *Revue du Nord* (January–March 1956), pp.29–63.
R. H. Codrington, *The Melanesians* (New Yor, 1972, rpr. of 1891 1st edn).
N. Cohn, *Europe's Inner Demons* (St Alban's, 1977, rpr. of 1975 1st edn).
— *The Pursuit of the Millennium* (rpr. London, 1970).
P. Coirault, *Formation de Nos Chansons Populaires* (Paris, 1953).
A. Collomp, 'Alliance et Filiation en Haute-Provence au XVIIIe Siècle' (May–June 1977), pp.445–77.
J. Combelles, *Le Travet, Petite Commune du Tarn* (Toulouse, 1954).
A. Corbin, *Archaïsme et Modernité en Limousin au XIXe Siècle 1845–1880* (Paris, 1975), 2 vols.
A. Costedoat, 'La criminalité mystique dans les sociétés modernes', *Annales de Médecine Légale* (1930), pp.125–99.
E. Coulon, 'Les apparitions en Franche-Comté', *Revue de Folklore Français et Colonial* (1935), V, p.317.
H. Cox, *The Feast of Fools, a Theological Essay on Festivity and Fantasy* (New York, 1970).
M. R. Cox, *Cinderella. 345 Variants of Cinderella, Catskin and Cap O'Rushes, abstracted and tabulated* (London, 1893).
R. Cranston, *The Mystery of Lourdes* (London, 1956).
J. Cuisenier, *French Folk Art* (Tokyo, New York, 1977).
C. de Danilowicz, *L'Art Rustique Français, L'Art Provençal* (Nancy, 1913).
J. J. Darmon, *Le Colportage de Librairie en France sous le Second Empire* (Paris, 1972).
A. Dauzat, *Le Village et le Paysan de France* (Paris, 1941).
R. David, *La IIIe République. De 1871 à Nos Jours* (Paris, 1934).
N. Z. Davis, *Society and Culture in Early Modern France* (Stanford, 1975).
V.-H. Debidour, *La Sculpture Bretonne, Etude d'Iconographie Populaire Religieuse* (Rennes, 1953).
P. Delarue and M.-L. Tenèze, *Le Conte Populaire Français, Catalogue Raisonné*

des Versions de France et des pays de Langue Française d'Outre-Mer (Paris, 1957–76), 3 vols.
J. Décréau, Review of *Histoire de la Dévotion au Sacré Coeur* by A. Hamon (Paris, 1939 in RHEF (Jan.–June 1941), XXVII, pp.102–3.
H. Decugis, *Les Etapes du Droit des Origines à Nos Jours* (2nd edn, Paris, 1946), 2 vols.
Rev. J. Deery, *Our Lady of Lourdes* (Dublin, 1958).
L. Dégh, *Folktales and Society: Story-Telling in a Hungarian Peasant Community* (Blommington, 1969).
— 'Folk Narrative', in *Folklore and Folklife*, ed. R. Dorson (Chicago, 1972), pp.53–84.
P. Degrully, 'Le Droit de Glanage: Grapillage, Patelage, Chaumage et Sarclage: Patrimoine des Pauvres' (Paris University, law thesis, 1912).
E. Delcambre, *Le Concept de Sorcellerie dans le Duché de Lorraine* (Nancy, 1948–51), 3 vols.
— *L'Initiation à la Sorcellerie et le Sabbat* (Nancy, 1948).
— *Maléfices et Vie Supranaturelle des Sorciers* (Nancy, 1949).
— *Les Devins Guérisseurs dans la Lorraine Ducale. Leur Activité et leurs Méthodes* (Nancy, 1951).
H. Delehaye, 'Note sur la Légende de la Lettre du Christ tombée du ciel', *Académie Royale de Belgique. Bulletin de la Classe des Lettres* (Brussels, 1899), pp.171–213.
— *Les Légendes Hagiographiques* (Brussels, 1905).
J. O. Delepierre, *L'Enfer: Essai Philosophique et Historique sur les Légendes de la Vie Future* (London, 1876).
— *Le Livre des Visions, ou l'Enfer et le Ciel décrits par ceux qui les ont vus* (London, *c.* 1870).
— *Essai biographique sur l'Histoire littéraire des Fous* (London, 1857–8).
J. Delumeau, *La Peur en Occident (XIVe–XVIIe siècles). Une Cité Assiégée* (Paris, 1978).
— *Le Catholicisme de Luther à Voltaire* (Paris, 1971).
— *La Mort des Pays de Cocagne. Comportements Collectifs de la Renaissance à l'Age Classique* (Paris, 1976).
W. C. Dément, 'La Psychophysiologie du Rêve', *Le Rêve et les Sociétés Humaines*, eds. R. Caillos and G. E. von Grünebaum (Paris, 1967), pp.64–91.
H. Demonet, P. Dumont, E. Le Roy Ladurie, 'Anthropologie du Conscrit: Une Cartographie Cantonale (1819–1830)', AESC (July–August 1976), pp.700–760.
A. Denis, *Recherches Bibliographiques et Historiques sur les Almanachs de la Champagne et de la Brie* (Paris, Châlons-sur-Marne, 1880).
J. Deprun, 'L'Inquiétude et l'Histoire' *AHRF* (1969), 41, pp.1–27.
E. Dermenghem, *Le Culte des Saints dans l'Islam Maghrébin* (5th edn, Paris, 1954).
R. Desné, *Les Matérialistes Français* (Paris, 1965).
H. Desroches, *Jacob and the Angel: An Essay in the Sociology of Religion* (Cambridge Massachusets, 1973).
— *Sociologie de l'Espérance* (Paris, 1973).
J.-F. Détrée, *Sorciers et Possédés en Cotentin* (Coutances, 1975).
G. Devereux, 'Rêves Pathogènes dans les sociétés non-occidentales', *Le Rëve et*

les Sociétés Humaines, ed. R. Caillos, Grünebaum (Paris, 1967), pp.189–204.
P. Deyon, 'Mentalités Populaires: un sondage à Amiens au XVIIe siècle', *AESC* (1962), pp.448–58.
P. Diel, *La Peur et l'Angoisse* (Paris, 1973).
E. R. Dodds, *The Greeks and the Irrational* (8th rpr, London, Berkeley, 1973).
R. Dorson, ed., *Folklore and Folklife* (Chicago, 1972).
E. Doutté, *Magie et Religion dans l'Afrique du Nord* (Alger, 1909).
A. Dubois, *Les Anciens Livres de Colportage en Sologne* (Romorantin, 1936).
P.-L. Duchartre, 'Imageries Populaires. Les Origines de l'Imagerie et des Imagiers. Leurs Sources d'Inspiration et la Couleur Locale', introduction to H. Martin, *L'Imagerie Populaire* (Paris, 1928), pp.ix–xxxi.
E. Duché, 'Le Crime d'Incendie (Paris University, law thesis, 1913).
G. Dumas, *Le Surnaturel et les Dieux dans les Maladies* (Paris, 1946).
— 'Contagion Mentale. Epidémies Mentales. Folies Collectives. Folies Grégaires', *Revue Philosophique* (1916), I.
G. Dumézil, *Heur et Malheur du Guerrier* (Paris, 1969).
G. Dupeux, *La Société Française, 1789–1960* (Paris, 1964).
G. Durand, *Structures Anthropologiques de l'Imaginaire* (Grenoble, 1960).
P. Durand, *La Politique Contemporaine de Sécurité Sociale* (Paris, 1953).
E. Durkheim, *Les Formes Elémentaires de la Vie Religieuse* (4th edn, Paris, 1960).
— *Le Suicide* (Paris, 1897).
R. Dussaud, 'La Matérialisation de la Prière en Orient', extr. from *Bulletins et Mémoires de la Société d'Anthropologie de Paris* (Paris, 1906).
H. Dussourd, *Au même Pot, et au même Feu: Etude sur les Communautés Agricoles du Centre de la France* (Moulins, 1962).
E. Dubal, *Monts-de-Piéte* (Rouen, 1898).
J. Duvignard, *Spectacle et Société. Du Théâtre Grec au Happening. La Fonction de l'Imagination dans les Sociétés* (Paris, 1970).
— *Les Ombres Collectives, Sociologie du Théâtre* (Paris, 1973).
M. Eck, 'Naissance de la Clinique. A Propos du Livre de Michel Foucault', *La Nouvelle Presse Médicale* (23 Sep. 1972), pp.2189–94.
J. Ehrard, 'Opinions Médicales en France au XVIIIe siècle. La Peste et l'Idée de Contagion', *AESC* (Jan.–March 1957), pp.46–59.
— *L'Idée de la Nature en France à l'Aube des Lumières* (Paris, 1970, 1st pub. 1963).
M. Eliade, *The Quest. History and Meaning in Religion* (Chicago, London, 1969).
— *Occultism, Witchcraft and Cultural Fashions* (Chicago, London, 1976).
— *Aspects du Mythe* (Paris, 1963).
— *Myths, Dreams and Mysteries* (London, 1979, 1st pub. Paris, 1957).
— *The Sacred and the Profane* (New Yor, 1959).
— *Images et Symboles* (Paris, 1952).
N. Elias, *La Civilisation et les Moeurs* (Paris, 1973), 2nd edn of 1st vol. of *Über das Prozess der Zivilisation* (1939).
T. Evans-Pritchard, *Witchcraft, Oracles and Magic among the Azande* (abr. edn, Oxford, 1976).
— *Anthopology and History* (Manchester, 1961).

D. Fabre and J. Lacrois, *La Vie Quotidienne des Paysans du Languedoc au XIXe Siècle* (Paris, 1973).
J. A. Farrer, *Primitive Manners and Customs* (London, 1879).
M. Faugeras, *Le Diocèse de Nantes sous la Monarchie Censitaire (1813–1822–1849)* (Fontenay-le-Comte, 1964), 2 vols.
H. Faure, *Hallucinations et Réalité Perceptive* (Paris, 1969).
— *Les Objets de la Folie: les Appartenances du Délirant* (Paris, 1971).
P. Favre, *Sade Utopiste* (Paris, 1967).
L. Febvre, 'La Sensibilité et l'Histoire', *Annales d'Histoire Sociale* (1941), I, p.18.
— *Le Problème de l'Incroyance au Seizième Siècle* (Paris, 1968).
— *Combats pour l'Histoire* (Paris, 1953).
— *Amour Sacré, Amour Profane. Autour de l'Heptaméron* (Paris, 1971).
— *Pour une Histoire à Part Entière* (Paris, 1962).
P. de Felice, *Foules en Délire: Extases Collectives* (Paris, 1947).
G. Ferraud, 'Prières et Invocations Magiques en Malgache Sud Oriental', extr. from *Actes du XIVe Congrès International des Orientalistes* (Paris, 1906), II.
J. Ferté, *La Vie Religieuse dans les Campagnes Parisiennes 1622–1694* (Paris, 1962).
O. Festy, *Les Délits Ruraux et leur Répression sous la Révolution et le Consultat* (Paris, 1956).
L. Figuier, *Histoire du Merveilleux dans les Temps Modernes* (Paris, 1859–62), 4 vols.
J.-L. Flandrin, *Familles-Parenté, Maison, Sexualité dans l'Ancienne Société* (Paris, 1976).
Florian-Parmentier, *La Sorcellerie dans les Temps Modernes* (n.p.d. –*c*.1911).
H. Fortmann, 'Le Primitif, le Poète, le Croyant. Notes Relatives à la Psychologie de la Sécularisation', *Concilium* (1969), 47, pp.25–9.
G. M. Foster, *Traditional Societies and Technological Change* (2nd edn, London, New York, 1973).
M. Foucault, *Histoire de la Folie à l'Âge Classique* (Paris, 1964).
— *Naissance de la Clinique* (2nd edn, Paris, 1972).
— *Moi, Pierre Rivière ayant égorgé ma mère...* (Paris, 1973).
— *Discipline and Punish. The Birth of the Prison* (London, 1979, 1st pub. 1975).
A. de Foville, 'Variations du Bien-Être dans les Campagnes Lorraines depuis le Moyen Age', *Journal de la Société de Statistique de Paris* (October 1888), pp.333–42.
— 'Le Budget de l'Ouvrier au XIXe et au XXe Siècle', *Le Correspondant* (10 Feb. 1905), pp.425–52.
— 'Les Variations de Prix en France: les Salariés Agricoles', *L'Economiste Français* (8 Jan. 1876), pp.35–7; (22 Jan. 1876), pp.100–101.
C. Fraysse, 'Les Lettres d'Origine Céleste au Pays de Baugé', *Revue de Folklore Français et Colonial* (1935), V, p.112.
— 'Au Pays de Baugé. Deux Sorciers en Justice', *RTP* (1906), pp.255–7.
J. G. Frazer, *The Golden Bough* (abr. edn, London, 1974).
— *Man, God and Immortality* (London, 1927).
S. Freud, *Totem and Taboo* (re-edn, London, 1960).
— *The Interpretation of Dreams*, ed. A. Richards (Aylesbury, 1978).

G. Friedmann, 'Communautés Rurales et Milieux Naturels', *AESC* (1954), pp.227–35.
G. Friedman, ed., *Villes et Campagnes* (Paris, 1953).
W. Frijhoff and D. Julia, *Ecole et Société dans la France d'Ancien Régime* (Paris, 1975).
M. H. Froeschle, Chopard, 'Univers Sacré et Iconographie au XVIIe Siècle: Eglises et Chapelles des Diocèses de Vence et Grasse', *AESC* (May–June 1976), pp.489–519.
E. Fromm, *The Forgotten Language* (New York, 1978).
F. Funck-Brentano, 'La Grande Peur en Angoumois', *Etudes Locales, Bulletin de la Société Charentaise des Etudes Locales* (1920), XXVI, pp.329–32.
Funk and Wagnall, *Standard Dictionary of Folklore, Mythology and Legend*, ed. M. Leach (New York, 1949–50), 2 vols.
C. Gagnon, *Histoire du Métayage en Bourbonnais depuis 1789* (Paris, 1920).
C. Gagnon and M.-L. Florentin, *Le Carnaval. Essais de Mythologie Populaire* (Paris, 1974). An interesting, if not always convincing work.
C. Gaignebet, 'Une Coutume de Folklore Juridique dans l'Oeuvre de Rabelais. La Redevance du Pet', *Arts et Traditions Populaires* (1970), pp.183–94.
M. Garçon and J. Vinchon, *Le Diable, Etude Historique, Critique, Médicale* (Paris, 1926).
Garinet, *Histoire de la Magie en France* (Paris, 1818).
Garsonnin, 'Notice sur l'Imagerie Orlénnaise', in H. Martin, *L'Imagerie Orléannaise* (Paris, 1928), pp.1–18.
L. and J. Gayral, 'Les Délires de Possession Diabolique' (Toulouse University, medical thesis, 1944).
E. Germain, *Parler du Salut. Aux Origines d'Une Mentalité Religieuse* (Paris, 1968).
C. Ginzburg, *I Benandanti; Stregoneria e Culti Agrari tra Cinquecento e Seicento* (Turin, 1966).
— *Il Formaggio e I Vermi. Il cosmo di un mugnaio del '500* (Turin, 1976).
C. Girard, 'La Catastrophe Agricole de 1816 dans le Département de la Meurthe', *Annales de l'Est* (1954),V, pp.133–57.
— 'La Disette de 1816–17 dans la Meurthe', *Annales de l'Est* (1955), VI, pp.333–62.
M. Godin and Y. Daniel, *La France, Pays de Mission?* (Paris, 1962, rpr. of 1943 edn).
F. Goguel, *La Politique des Partis sous la IIIe République* (Paris, 1946).
L. Goldmann, *The Philosophy of the Enlightenment. The Christian Burgess and the Enlightenment* (London, 1973).
I. Goldziher, 'La Prière Naïve du Berger', *Revue des Etudes Juives* (1902), XLV, pp.11ff.
P. Gonnet, 'Esquisse de la Crise Economique en France de 1827 à 1832', *Revue d'Histoire Economique et Sociale* (1955), XXXIII, pp.249–91.
M. Gontard, *L'Enseignement Primaire en France de la Révolution à la Loi Guizot* (Paris, 1959).
— *Les Ecoles Primaires de la France Bourgeois (1833–75)* (Toulouse, 1957).
J. Goody and Watt, 'The Consequences of Literacy', *Comparative Studies in History and Anthropology* (1962–3), pp.304–45.
G. Gorer, *Death, Grief and Mourning in Contemporary Britain* (London, 1974).

J. P. Goubert, *Maladies et Médecine en Bretagne: 1770–1790* (Paris, 1974).

J. Goubert and L. Cristiani, *Messages et Apparitions de la Sainte Vierge, de 1830 à nos Jours* (Paris, 1952). Uncritical.

P. Goubert, *Cent Mille Provinciaux au* XVII*e siècle* (2nd edn, Paris, 1968).

P. Goulème, *Evolution des Pouvoirs d'Achat en France: 1880–1972* (Paris, 1974).

A. Goursand, *La Société Rurale Traditionnelle en Limousin* (Paris, 1976), vol. I.

Mgr. P. Gouyon, *La Pratique Religieuse dans l'Agglomération Bordelaise* (Bordeaux, 1957).

— *L'Introduction de la Réforme Disciplinaire du Concile de Trente dans le Diocèse de Bordeaux, 1582–1624* (Bordeaux, 1945).

V. W. Gras, ed., *European Literary Theory and Practice from Existential Phenomenology to Structuralism* (New York, 1973).

G. Grassoreille, 'Un Procès de Sorcellerie à Moulins en 1623', *Revue Bourbonnais* (1886), pp.196–202.

P. Gratton, *Les Luttes des Classes dans les Campagnes* (Paris, 1971).

A. Grenet and C. Jodry, *La Littérature de Sentiment au* XVIII*e siècle* (Paris, 1971), 2 vols.

G. E. von Grünebaum and R. Caillos, eds, *Le Rêve et des Sociétés Humaines* (Paris, 1967).

H. Guégo, *Etude Statistique sur la Criminalité en France de 1826 à 1900* (Paris, 1902).

S. Guercherg, 'La Controverse sur les Prétendus Semeurs de la Peste Noire d'après les Traités de Peste de l'Epoque', *Revue des Etudes Juives* (1948), pp.3–40.

L. Guibert, 'La Famille Limousine d'autrefois d'après les Testaments et la Coutume', *La Réforme Sociale* (April 1883), pp.341–57, 388–400.

G. Guillain, *J. M. Charcot 1825–1893. His Life and Work*, trans. and ed. P. Bailey (London, 1959).

Abbé P. Giullaume, *Essai sur la Vie Religieuse dans l'Orléannais. 3rd Series. 1801–1878* (Orléans, 1959).

L. Guyon, *Un Médecin de Campagne d'Autrefois... Notes et Souvenirs (1795–1865)* (Le Mans, 1902).

J. A. Hadfield, *Dreams and Nightmares* (London, 1954).

M. Halbwachs, *Classe Ouvrière, et les Niveaux de Vie Recherches sur l'Hiérarchie des Besoins dans Les Sociétés Industrielles Contemporaines* (Paris, 1913).

— *Les Cadres Sociaux de la Mémoire* (Paris, 1925).

— *Les Causes du Suicide* (Paris, 1930).

— *La Mémoire Collective* (Paris, 1950).

G. Hardy, 'L'Ardennais', *Revue de Psychologie des Peuples* (1950), pp.156–88.

J. D. Hardy *et al.*, *Pain, Sensation and Reactions* (Baltimore, 1952).

M. J. Harner, ed., *Hallucinogens and Shamanism* (London, Oxford, New York, 1976).

E. S. Hartland, *The Science of Fairy-Tales* (London, 1891).

H. Hastings, *Man and Beast in French Thought of the Eighteenth Century* (Baltimore, London, Paris, 1936).

P. Hauser, *Le* XIX*e Siècle au Point de Vue Médico-Social* (Paris, 1905).

O. d'Haussonville, 'La Vie et les Salaires à Paris', *Revue des Deux Mondes* (15 April 1883), pp.815–67.
— 'La Misère à Paris', *Revue des Deux Mondes* (15 June 1881), pp.814–49; (1 October, 1881), pp.611–51.
E. D'Hauterive, *Le Mervilleux au* XVIIIe *Siècle* (Paris, 1902).
A. Hayter, *Opium and the Romantic Imagination* (London, 1971).
J. Hellé, *Miracles* (London, 1953).
M. Henle, J. Jaynes, J. J. Sullivan, eds, *Historical Conceptions of Psychology* (New York, 1973).
C. Herzlich, *Santé et Maladie, Analyse d'un Représentation Sociale* (Paris, 1969).
Y. H. Hilaire, 'La Pratique Religieuse en France de 1815 à 1878', *L'Information Historique* (March–April 1963), pp.57–69.
E. J. Hobsbawm, *Primitive Rebels. Studies in Archaic Forms of Social Movement in the Nineteenth and Twentieth Centuries* (Manchester, 1974, rpr. of 1959 edn).
— *Bandits* (London, 1972).
E. J. Hobsbawm and G. Rudé, *Captain Swing* (London, 1973).
A. M. Hocart, *The Life Giving Myth and Other Essays* (London, 1970, rpr. of 1952 1st edn).
— 'Psychology and Ethnology', *Folklore* (June 1915), pp.115–37.
H. Hubert, *Etude Sommarie de la Représentation du Temps dans la Religion et la Magie* (Paris, 1905).
H. Hubert and M. Mauss, *Mélange d'Histoire des Religions* (Paris, 1909).
— 'Esquisse d'Une Théorie Générale de la Magie', orig. pub. in *l'Année Sociologique* (1902–3) (Paris, 1904).
O. Hufton, *The Poor of 18th Century France, 1750–1789* (Oxford, 1974).
P. Huot-Pleuroux, *La Vie Chrétienne dans le Doubs et la Haute-Saône, 1860–1900* (Besançon, 1966).
E. Ilvonen, *Parodies de Thèmes Pieux dans la Poésie Française du Moyen Age* (Paris, 1914).
R. Jakobson, 'Le Folklore, Forme Spécifique de Création', *Questions de Poétique* (Paris, 1973), pp.59–72).
R. Jalby, *Sorcellerie, Médecine Populaire et Pratique Médico-Magiques en Languedoc* (Nyons, 1974).
E. O. James, *Seasonal Feasts and Festivals* (London, 1961).
L. James, *Fiction for the Working Man 1830–1850* (London, 1963).
W. James, *The Varieties of Religious Experience* (London, 1977, 1st pub. 1903).
H. W. Janson, *Apes and Ape-lore in the Middle Ages and Renaissance* (London, 1952).
C. Joisten, 'De Quelques Sources d'Influence dans la Formation des Récits Légendaires Alpestres', *Arts et Traditions Populaires* (1970), pp.141–58.
G. Jourdanne, *Contribution au Folklore de l'Aude* (Paris, 1899–1900).
C. G. Jung, *Psychology and Religion* (New Haven, London, 1974, 1st edn 1938).
— *Psychology and the Occult*, trans. R. Hull (London, 1982).
— *Psychological Reflections, An Anthology of His Writing 1905–1961*, ed. J. Jacobi (2nd edn, London, 1973).

M. Keen, *The Outlaws of Medieval Legend* (London, 1961).
H. A. Kelly, *Towards the Death of Satan, the Growth and Decline of Christian Demonology* (London, 1968).
H. de Kerbeuzac, 'Les Esprits forts à la Campagne', RTP (1906), pp.403.
A. Kiev, ed., *Magic, Faith and Healing* (New York, London, 1964).
A. M. Killen, *Le Roman 'Terrifiant' ou Roman 'Noir' de Walpole à Anne Radcliffe et son Influence sur la Littérature Française Jusqu' en 1840* (Paris, 1915).
T. Kselman, *Miracles and Prophecies in 19th-Century France* (New Brunswick, 1983).
T. S. Kuhn, *The Structure of Scientific Revolutions* (2nd edn, Chicago, 1975).
Dr E. Labat, *L'Âme Paysanne, La Terre, La Race, L'Ecole* (Paris, 1919).
E. Labrousse, ed., *Aspects de la Crise et de la Dépression de l'Economic Française au Milieu du XIXe siècle (1845–51)* (La Roche-sur-Yon, 1956).
F. Labrousse, 'Quelques Notes sur un Médecin Philosophe. P. J. G. Cabanis (1757–1808)' (Paris University, medical thesis, 1903).
A. Laccassagne and E. Martin, *Précis de Médecine Légale* (3rd edn, Paris, 1921).
P. Lacroix, *Curiosités Infernales* (Paris, 1886).
M. Lagrée, *Mentalités, Religion et Histoire en Haute Bretagne au XIXe Siècle. Le Diocèse de Rennes, 1815–1848* (Paris, 1977).
J. La Harpe, *L'Abbé Laurent Bordelon et la Lutte contre la Superstition en France entre 1680 et 1730* (Berkeley, Los Angeles, 1942).
H. Lalou, 'Des Charivaris et de leur Répression dans le Midi de la France', *Revue des Pyrénées* (1904), XVI, pp.493–514.
F. A. Lamiaud, 'L'Instruction Publique à Aunac sous la Restauration', *Etudes Locales. Bulletin de la Société Charentaise des Etudes Locales* (1922), XX, pp.120–22.
A. Langlade, 'Le Personnel d'une Ferme en Bas-Languedoc', RTP (1886), pp.52–3.
C. Langlois, *Le Diocèse de Vannes au XIXe siècle, 1800–1830* (Paris, 1974).
Mme B. Lardant, 'Un Curé de Champagne-Mouton accusé de Sorcellerie', *Etudes Locales. Bulletin de la Société Charentaise des Etudes Locales* (1922), XIXp.23–4.
P. Laslett, *The World We Have Lost* (London, 1965).
G. Latour, *Les Dépôts de Mendicité. Les Monts-de-Piété* (Paris, 1872).
E. Laurain, *Querelles et Procès de nos Aïeux en Bas-Maine* (Laval, 1921).
F. Laurentie, *Le Délire Prophétique* (Paris, 1914).
Dr V. Leblond, *Notes pour servir à l'Histoire des Possessions Démoniaques* (Paris, 1910).
G. Le Bras, *L'Eglise et le Village* (Paris, 1976).
— 'Les Missions en France au XIXe siècle', RHEF (1905), XXVI, pp.70–74.
— *Etudes de Sociologie Religieuse* (Paris, 1955).
— 'Religion Legale et Religion Vécue', *Annales de Sociologie Religieuse* (Jan.–June 1970), 29, pp.15–20.
— 'Les Transformations Religieuses des Campagnes Françaises depuis la fin du XVIIIe', *Annales Sociologiques* (1937), series E, fasc. 2, pp.15–70.
R. Lecotté, *Cultes Populaires* (Paris, 1953).
— *Au Village de France* (Paris, 1945).

M. Leiris, *La Possession et ses Aspects Théâtraux chez les Ethiopiens de Gondrar* (Paris, 1958).
F. Lentacker, 'Les Ouvriers Belges dans le Département du Nord au Milieu du XIXe Siècle', *Revue du Nord* (Jan.–March 1956), pp.5–15.
P. Léon, ed., *Structures Economiques et Problèmes Sociaux du Monde Rural dans la France du Sud-Est, (fin XIIIe–1835)* (Paris, 1966).
J. Léonard, *La France Médicale au XIXe Siècle* (Paris, 1978).
F. Le Play, *Les Ouvriers Européens* (Paris, 1855).
E. Le Roy Ladurie, *Montaillou, Village Occitan de 1294 à 1324* (Paris, 1975).
— *Les Paysans de Languedoc* (2nd edn, Paris, 1969).
— *Love, Death and Money in the Pays d'Oc*, trans. A. Sheridan (London, 1980).
— *Carnival. A People's Uprising at Romans, 1579–1580*, trans. M. Feeney (London, 1980).
— 'Out of the Blue', *AESC* (1973), XXVIII, pp.146–51.
J. Lestocquoy, *La Vie Religieuse en France du VIIe au XIXe Siècle* (Paris, 1964).
P. Leuillot, *L'Alsace au Debut du XIXe Siècle. III. Religions et Culture* (Paris, 1960).
C. Lévi-Strauss, *Race et Histoire* (Paris, 1916).
— *Tristes Tropiques* (Paris, 1976, rpr. of 1955 edn).
— *Anthropologie Structurale* (Paris, 1974, rpr. of 1958 1st edn).
— *La Pensée Sauvage* (Paris, 1962).
J. Levron, *Le Diable dans l'Art* (Paris, 1935).
R. Lévy, 'La Disette de 1812 au Havre', *Revue des Etudes Napoléoniennes* (1915), VIII, pp.5–43.
L. Lévy-Bruhl, *La Morale et la Science des Moeurs* (5th edn, Paris, 1953).
— *Le Surnaturel et la Nature dans la Mentalité Primitive* (Paris, 1931).
— *Les Fonctions Mentales dans les Société Inférieures* (Paris, 1910).
— *La Mentalité Primitive* (Paris, 1976, rpr. of 1922 edn).
I. M. Lewis, *Ecstatic Religion* (London, 1975).
Dr J. Lhermitte, *Le Problème des Miracles* (Paris, 1956).
— *Vrais et Faux Possédés* (Paris, 1956).
— *Les Hallucinations: Clinique et Physiopathologie* (Paris, 1951).
— 'Les Pseudo-Possessions Diaboliques', in *Satan, Etudes Carmélitaines* (Bruges, 1948), pp.472–92.
E. L'Hommédé, 'Un Procès de sorcellerie au village sous le Consultat', *Revue des Etudes Historiques* (July–Sep. 1931), pp.261–80.
Libert, *Les Sorciers de la Haye du Puis* (Rouen, 1911).
A. Lille, *The Worship of Satan in Modern France* (London, 1896).
S. Lo Nigro, *Tradizione e Invenzione nel Pacconto Popolare* (Florence, 1964).
C. Louandre, *La Sorcellerie* (Paris, 1853).
R. Lowie, *Primitive Religion* (New York, rpr. of 1924 1st edn).
J. Lucas-Dubreton, *La Grand Peur de 1832* (Paris, 1932).
A. Macfarlane, *Witchcraft in Tudor and Stuart England* (London, 1970).
F. Macler, 'Correspondance épistolaire avec le ciel. Lettres Addressées par les Juifs d'Hébron et des environs aux patriarches', *RTP* (Feb.–March 1905), pp.65–82.

J. Maho, *L'Image des Autres chez les Paysans* (Paris, 1974).
R. Mandrou, *De la Culture Populaire aux* XVII*e* *et* XVIII*e* *siècles. La Bibliothèque Bleue de Troyes* (2nd edn, Paris, 1975).
— *Introduction à la France Moderne 1500–1640* (Paris, 1974, rpr. of 1961 edn).
C. Mannoni, *Clefs pour l'Imaginaire* (Paris, 1969).
L. Manzoni, *Libro di Carnevale dei Secoli* XV*o* *e* XVI*o* (Bologna, 1881).
B. Malinowsky, *Magic, Science and Religion and Other Essays* (London, 1974, rpr. of 1948 1st edn). Includes 'Myth in Primitive Psychology' (1926).
C. Marcilhacy, *Le Diocèse d'Orléans sous l'Episcopat de Mgr Dupanloup, 1849–1878* (Paris, 1962).
— *Le Diocèse d'Orléans au Milieu du* XIX*e* *Siècle* (Paris, 1964).
H. Martin, *L'Imagerie Orléannaise* (Paris, 1928).
M. Marwick, ed., *Witchcraft and Sorcery* (London, 1975 rpr.).
Abbé J. Masce, *La Provence et L'Ame Provençale* (Aix, 1911).
G. Massignon, *Contes de l'Ouest* (Paris, 1953).
H. Matthey, *Essai sur le Merveilleux dans la Littérature Française depuis 1800* (Lausanne, Paris, 1915).
A. Maury, *Les Fées du Moyen Age. Recherches sur leurs Origines... pour servir à la connaissance de la mythologie Gauloise* (Paris, 1843).
— *Essai sur les Légendes Pieuses du Moyen Age* (Paris, 1843).
— *Le Sommeil et Les Rêves* (Paris, 1861).
— *La Magie et l'Astrologie dans l'Antiquité et au Moyen Age. Etude sur les Superstitions Païennes qui se sont perpétuées jusqu à nos jours* (Paris, 1864).
M. Mauss, *Sociologie et Anthropologie* (3rd edn, Paris, 1966).
— *Les Fonctions Sociales du Sacré* (Paris, 1968).
— *La Prière* (Paris, n.d.).
R. Mauzi, *L'Idée du Bonheur dans la Littérature et la Pensée Françaises au* XVIII*e* *Siècle* (Paris, 1960).
Médecine et Merveilleux (Paris, 1957).
R. Mehl, *Le Vieillissement et la Mort* (Paris, 1966).
H. Mendras, *Sociétés Paysannes* (Paris, 1976).
P. L. Menon and R. Lecotté, *Au Village de France, La Vie Traditionnelle des Paysans* (Paris, 1945).
Dr Merland, 'Singulière Affaire de Simulation, Deux Accusés Traduits devant trois Juridictions', *Annales d'Hygiène Publique et de Médecine Légale* (July–Oct. 1864), pp.141–56.
R. Mesuret, 'Essai sur les Sources Iconologiques de l'Imagerie Toulousaine', *Arts et Traditions Populaire* (1953), pp.145–9.
— 'L'Imagerie Populaire', *Arts et Traditions Populaires* (1952).
E. Meletinski, *L'Etude Structurale et Typologique du Conte* (Paris, 1973).
J. Meyer, 'Alphabétisation, Lecture et Écriture. Essai sur l'Instruction Populaire en Bretagne du XVIe au XIXe siècle', *Histoire de l'Enseignement de 1810 à nos Jours. Actes du 95e Congrés National des Savants* (1974), I, pp.333–54.
F. Michel, *Histoire des Races Maudits* (Paris, 1847), 2 vols.
J. Michelet, *La Sorcière* (Paris, 1964).
— *Pages Choises*, ed. C. Seignebos (Paris, 1935).

J. B. Millet Saint-Pierre, *Recherches sur le Dernier Sorcier et la Dernière Ecole de Magie* (Le Havre, 1859).
M. Milner, *Entretiens sur l'Homme et le Diable* (Paris, The Hague, 1965).
R. Miquel, *Les Métamorphoses du Diable* (Paris, 1968).
E. de Mirville, *Pneumatologie des Esprits et de leurs Manifestations diverses* (Paris, 1863–4), 8 vols.
Abbé A. Monnin, *Vie du Curé d'Ars J. M. F. Vianney* (Paris, 1861), 2 vols.
A. Moreau de Jonnès, 'Travail et Salaire Agricoles en France', *Journal des Economistes* (15 Oct. 1850), pp.201–15.
— *Réponse à une Réfutation de la Statistique des Aliénés. Institute de France: Académie Royale des Sciences* (Paris, 1843).
A. Morel, 'Power and Ideology in the village community of Picardy. Past and Present', in *Rural Society in France*, eds Forster and Ranum (Baltimore, London, 1977), pp.107–25.
Canon J. J. Moret, *Histoire de Saint Menoux* (Moulins, 1907).
A. Morin, *Catalogue Descriptif de la Bibliothèque de Troyes, Almanachs Exclus* (Geneva, 1974).
E. Morin, *La Rumeur d'Orléans* (Paris, 1909).
— *Commune en France. La Métamorphose de Plodémet* (Paris, 1967).
A. Mosso, *Fear, A Psycho-Physiological Study* (London, New York, Bombay, 1896).
R. Muchembled, 'Sorcellerie, Culture Populaire et Christianisme au XVIe siècle', *AESC* (Jan.–Feb. 1973), pp.264–84.
— *Culture Populaire et Culture des Elites* (Paris, 1978).
M. A. Murray, *The Witch-cult in Western Europe* (Oxford, London, 1971, rpr. of 1921 1st edn).
H. Najean, *Le Diable et Les Sorcières chez les Vosgiens* (S. Dié, 1970). Work of Popularization.
V. E. Neuberg, *Popular Literature. A History and Guide* (London, 1977).
M. P. Nillson, *Primitive Time Reckoning* (London, 1920).
F. Novati, *La Parodia Sacra nelle letterature moderne. Studi Critici e Litterari* (Turin, 1889).
Dr H. Nux, *S. Appoline. Patronne de ceux qui souffrent des dents. Etude Historique, Folklorique et Ethnologique* (Paris, 1947).
T. K. Oesterreich, *ossession Demoniacal and Other among Primitive Races in Antiquity, the Middle Ages and Modern Times* (London, 1930).
R. Otto, *La Sacré* (18th edn, Paris, 1969).
M. Ozouf, *L'Ecole, L'Eglise et la République, 1871–1914* (Paris, 1963).
J. Palous, *La Sorcellerie* (Paris, 1957).
— *La Peur dans l'Histoire* (Paris, 1958).
J. Paquet, *La Santé Publique et Conditions de Vie dans le Département de l'Isère du XIXe siècle* (Grenoble, 1964).
P. Parfait, *Le Dossier des Pèlerinages* (Paris, 1877).
G. Parrinder, *Witchcraft, European and African* (London, 1963).
J. Pataut, *Sociologie Electorale de la Nièvre au XXe siècle. (1902–1951)* (Paris, 1956).
L. Pérouas, *Le Diocèse de la Rochelle de 1648 à 1724. Sociologie et Pastorale* (Paris, 1964).

R. de la Perraudière, 'La lettre de Dieu', *Mémoires de la Société Nat. d'Agriculture, Science, Arts d'Angers* (1905), VIII, pp.131–6.
R. Perrin, 'L'Esprit Public dans le Département de la Meurthe de 1814 à 1816', *Annales de l'Est* (1913), pp.9–119).
J. C. Peyronnet, 'Famille Elargie ou Famille Nucléaire. L'Exemple du Limousin au début du XIXe siècle', *Revue d'Histoire Moderne et Contemporaine* (Oct.–Dec. 1975), XXII, pp.568–82.
J. Piaget, *The Child's Conception of the World*, trans. J. and A. Tomlinson (London, 1977, 1st pub. in English 1929).
Abbé M. X. Pic, *La Bête qui Mangeait le Monde en Pays de Gévaudan et d'Auvergne* (Paris, 1962).
P. Pierrard, *Le Prêtre Français* (Brussels, 1969).
— *La Vie Ouvrière à Lille sous le Second Empire* (Paris, 1965).
E. Pin, 'La Religion et le Passage d'une Civilisation Pré-Industrielle à une Civilisation Industrielle', *Essais de Sociologie Religieuse* (Paris, 1966).
P. Pinchemel, *Géographie de la France* (Paris, 1964), 2 vols.
H. Platelle, *Les Chrétiens devant le Miracle, Lille au XVIIe Siècle* (Paris, 1968).
C. Ploix, *Le Surnaturel dans les Contes Populaires* (Paris, 1891).
B. Plongeron, *Conscience Religieuse et Révolution* (Paris, 1969).
J. H. Plumb, 'The New World of Children in 18th Century England', *Past and Present* (May 1975), LXVIII, pp.64–95.
H. Poussat, *Les Sorciers du Canton* (Paris, 1933). Fanciful and popular, but based on conversations held in central France.
C. Pouthas, *La Population de la France pendant la première moitié du XIXe siècle* (Paris, 1956).
G. A. Prévost, *L'Eglise et les Campagnes au Moyen-Âge* (Paris, 1892).
V. Propp, *Morphologie du Conte* (Paris, 1973, trans. of 12th Russian edn).
— *Les Transformations des Contes Merveilleux* (Paris, 1973).
A. Prost, *L'Enseignement en France 1800–1967* (Paris, 1968).
Quénot, 'Les Ravages de la Grêle en 1812', *Etudes Locales Bulletin de la Société Charentaise des Etudes Locales* (1923), pp.340–41).
A. J. Ratcliff, *A History of Dreams* (London, 1923).
R. Redfield, *The Little Community, Peasant Society and Culture* (London, 1973).
G. Reicher, 'Le sens du Sacré chez les Basques', *Gure Herria* (1961), pp.55–64, 146–52, 282–86.
S. Reinach, *Cultes, Mythes et Religions* (Paris, 1912), IV.
P. J. Richard, *Histoire des Institutions d'Assurance en France* (Paris, 1956).
N. Robine and R. Escarpit, *Atlas de la Lecture à Bordeaux* (Bordeaux, 1963).
A. Rousselle, 'Du Sanctuaire du Thaumaturge. La Guérison en Gaule au IVe siècle', AESC (Nov.–Dec. 1976), pp.1085–1107.
G. Rudé, *The Crowd in the French Revolution* (2nd edn, Oxford, 1977).
— *Paris and London in the 18th Century. Studies in Popular Protest* (London, 1974, rpr. of 1952 edn).
A. Sabatier, *Religion et Politique au XIXe siècle (en Ardèche). Le Canton de Vernoux-en-Vivarais* (Nancy, 1975).
M. de Saint-Pierre, *Bernadette and Lourdes*, trans. E. FitzGerald (London, 1954).
P. Saintyves (pseud. E. Nourry), *Reliques et Images Légendaires* (Paris, 1912).

— *L'Astrologie Populaire* (Paris, 1937).
— 'La Foi à l'Envoûtement dans les Landes', *Revue de Folklore Français et Colonial* (1935),V, pp.35–6.
— *En Marge de la Légende Dorée* (Paris, 1930).
— *Le Manuel du Folklore* (Paris, 1936).
— *Les Contes de Perrault. Leurs Origines. (Coutumes Primitives et Liturgies Populaires)* (Paris, 1923).
— *La Guérison des Verrues: De la Magie Médicale à la Psychothérapie* (Paris, 1913).
— *Les Origines de la Médecine: Empirisme ou Magie?* (Paris, 1920).
— *Le Simulation du Merveilleux* (Paris, 1912).
Satan: Etudes Carmélitaines (Bruges, 1948).
R. Saulnier and A. Aynaud, 'Prototypes de l'Imagerie Populaire', *Arts et Traditions Populaires* (1953), pp.59–69.
R. Schenda, *Volk ohne Buch, Studien zur Sozialgeschichte der populären Lesestoffe, 1770–1910* (Frankfurt 1970).
G. Schindelholz, *Grimores, Secrets* (2nd edn, Portentruy, 1973). A popular anthology of spells and oral traditions, written in mystifying vein.
W. Scott, *Letters on Demonology and Witchcraft* (London, 1830). Written to keep the wolf from the door.
M. A. Sèchehaye, *Journal d'une Schizophrène* (Paris, 1950).
J. P. Séguin, *Nouvelles à Sensation, les Canards du XIXe Siècle* (Paris, 1959).
C. Seignolle, *Les Evangiles du Diable selon La Croyance Populaire* (Paris, 1964). Popular.
Dr. R. Semelaigne, *Les Grands Aliénistes Français* (Paris, 1894), 2 vols.
E. Sevrin, 'La Pratique des Sacrements et des Observances au diocèse de Chartres sous l'épiscopat de Mgr Clausel de Montais (1824–52)', *RHEF* (1939), pp.316–44.
— *Les Missions Religieuses en France sous la Restauration* (Paris, 1948, 1959), 2 vols.
— 'Croyances Populaires et Médecine Supranaturelle en Eure-et-Loir au XIXe Siècle', *RHEF* (1946), XXXII, pp.265–308.
E. Shorter, *The Making of the Modern Family* (London, 1979, rpr. of 1975 edn).
A. Siegfried, *Tableau des Partis Politiques en France* (Paris, 1930).
— *Tableau Politique de la France de l'Ouest sous la IIIe République* (Paris, 1913).
P. S. Sigal, 'Maladie, Pélèrinage et Guérison au XIIe siècle: Les Miracles de S. Gobrien à Reims', *AESC* (1969), pp.1522–1239.
F. J. Simiand, *Le Salaire, L'Evolution Sociale et la Monnaie* (Paris, 1932), 3 vols).
— 'La Psychologie Sociale des Crises et les Fluctuations économiques de courte durée', *Annales Sociologiques* (Paris, 1936), series D, fasc. 2, 1937), pp.3–22.
A. Soboul, 'The Persistence of "Feudalism" in the Rural Society of Nineteenth Century France', in *Rural Society in France*, eds Forster and Ranum (Baltimore, London, 1977), pp.50–71).
— *Sans-Culottes et Jacobins* (Paris, 1966).
M. Sonnenscher, 'La Révolte des Masques Armés en 1783 en Vivarais', *Vivarais*

et Languedoc, XLIVe Congrès de la Féderation Historique du Languedoc Méditérraneen et du Roussillon (Montpellier, 1972).
M. Soriano, 'Quelques Travaux Récents sur la Littérature Populaire', *AESC* (May–August 1971), XXVI, pp.771–781.
— *Les Contes de Perrault, Culture Savante et Traditions Populaires* (Paris, 1977, rpr. of 1968 edn).
J. Stany-Gauthier, 'Les Saints Bretons, Protecteurs des Récoltes et des Jardins', *Arts et Traditions Populaires* (1953), p, pp.307–21.
L. Stone, *The Family, Sex and Marriage in England 1900–1800* (Abridged edn, London, 1979).
— *The Past and The Present* (London, 1981).
S. Strowski, 'Le Caractère Breton dans le Culte des Morts et de la Religion des Saints', *Revue de Psychologie des Peuples* (Nov. 1948), pp.366–78.
M. Sudré, 'La Criminalité dans la Paroisse de S. Michel de Bordeaux 1676–9', *Revue Historique de Bordeaux et du Département de la Gironde* (Bordeaux, 1975), pp.87–106.
F. Sulloway, *Freud, Biologist of the Mind* (London, 1979).
M. Summers, *The Geography of Witchcraft* (New York, 1927).
Dr G. Surbled, *Le Diable et les Sorciers* (Arras, 1898).
— *Le Diable et les Médecins* (Paris, 1899). Not very good.
T. Szasz, *The Myth of Mental Illness* (new edn, London, New York, 1974). Argues that mental illness is a social rather than medical problem.
— *The Manufacture of Madness* (London, 1971).
J. L. Talmon, *The Origins of Totalitarian Democracy* (London, 1970).
V. L. Tapié *et al.*, *Rétables Baroques de Bretagne et Spiritualité au XVIIIe siècle* (Paris, 1972).
M. L. Tenèze, 'Introduction à l'Etude de la Littérature Orale: le Conte', *AESC* (1969), pp.1104–1120.
— 'Du Conte Merveilleux comme genre', *Arts et Traditions Populaires* (1970), pp.11–65.
M. L. Tenèze and P. Delarue, *Le Conte Populaire Français* (Paris, 1976). Vol. III of Delarue's *Magnum opus*.
F. Ténot, *La Province en Décembre 1851* (3rd edn, Paris, 1868).
— *Le Suffrage Universel et les Paysans* (Paris, 1865).
R. Thabault, *1848–1914. L'Ascension d'un Peuple. Mon Village (Mazières-en-Gâtine). Ses hommes, ses routes, son école* (Paris, 1944).
K. Thomas, *Religion and the Decline of Magic. Studies in Popular Belief in 16th and 17th Century England* (London, 1973).
— *Man and the Natural World* (Paperback edn, London, 1984).
E. P. Thompson, *The Making of the English Working Class* (London, 1979, rpr. of 1963 edn).
S. Thompson, *The Folktale* (Berkeley, London, 1977, rpr. of 1946 edn).
— *Motif-Index of Folk-Literature* (Bloomington, Indiana, 1932–6), 6 vols.
L. Thorndike, *History of Magic and Experimental Science: The 17th Century* (New York, 1958), vol. VIII.
A. Thuillier, *Economie et Société Nivernaises au Début du XIXe Siècle* (Paris, 1974).
T. Todorov, *Introduction à la Littérature Fantastique* (Paris, 1970).
J. de Tonquéduc, *Merveilleux Métapsychique et Miracle Chrétien* (Paris, 1955).

H. R. Trevor-Roper, *The European Witch-Craze of the 16th and 17th Centuries* (London, 1969).
L. E. Troclet, *La Première Expérience de Sécurité Sociale* (Brussels, 1953).
A. Tuetey, *La Sorcellerie dans le Pays de Montbéliard au* XVIIe *siècle* (Dôle, 1886).
E. Tylor, *Anthropology. An Introduction to the Study of Man and Civilisation* (London, 1881).
— *Primitive Culture* (London, 1871).
M. Van Haudenard, 'Le Juif errant', *Le Folklore Brabançon* (April 1929), pp.319–26.
A. Varagnac, *Civilisation Traditionnelle et Genres de Vie* (Paris, 1948). Overrated.
J. Vartier, *Sabbat, Juges et Sorciers. Quatre Siècles de Superstitions dans la France de l'Est* (Paris, 1968).
Verscheure *et al.*, *Aspects Sociologiques de la Pratique Dominicale, Diocèse de Lille* (Lille, 1961).
P. Viard, 'Les Subsistences en Îlle-et-Vilaine sous le Consultat et le Premier Empire', *Annales de Bretagne* (1917), pp.328–52; (1918), pp.131–54.
— 'La Disette de 1816–1817, particulièrement en Côte-d'Or', *Revue Historique* (1928), pp.95–117.
A. Viatte, *Les Sources Occultes du Romantisme. Illuminisme, Théosophie, 1770–1820* (Paris, 1928).
Vidal de la Blache, *La Personnalité Géographique de la France* (Manchester, London, 1952).
J. Vidalenc, *Le Peuple des Campagnes* (Paris, 1970).
R. Villeneuve, *Le Diable dans l'Art. Essai d'Iconographie Comparée, à propos des rapports entre l'art et le Satanisme* (Paris, 1957).
J. Viplé, *Devant le Tribunal Correctionnel de l'Allier, (1792–1811)* (Moulins, 1946).
J. F. Viplé, 'La Politique et les Elections dans l'Allier pendant la IIIe République' (Paris University, law thesis, 1967).
O. Voillard *et al.*, *Statistique d'Histoire Economique* (Strasbourg, Paris, 1964).
F.-X. Vollet, *De La Sorcellerie* (Caen, 1971).
M. Vovelle, *Mourir Autrefois* (Paris, 1974).
— *Piété Baroque et Déchristianisation en Provence au* XVIIIe *siècle* (Paris, 1973).
Wakefield, 'Some Unorthodox Popular Ideas', *Medievalis Humanistica* (1971), pp.25–36.
D. Walker, *The Decline of Hell, 17th Century Discussions of Eternal Torment* (London, Chicago, 1964).
E. Weber, *Peasants into Frenchmen. The Modernisation of Rural France* (London, 1977).
W. Y. E. Wentz, *The Fairy Faith in Celtic Countries* (London, 1979, rpr. of 1911 edn).
E. Westermarck, *Magic and Social Relations* (London, 1905).
B. Wilson, *Magic and the Millenium* (London, 1975).
L. Wylie, 'Demographic Change in Roussillon', in *Mediterranean Countrymen*, ed. J. Pitt-Rivers (Paris, The Hague, 1963), pp.215–36.
— *Village in the Vaucluse* (Cambridge Mass., 1957).

R. Yves-Pessis, *Essai d'une Bibliographie Française Méthodique de la Sorcellerie et Possessions Démoniaques...* (Paris, 1900).
T. Zeldin, *France, 1848–1945* (Oxford, 1973–7), 2 vols.
— ed., *Conflicts in French Society. Anticlericalism, Education and Morals in the Nineteenth Century* (London, 1970).
— *The French* (London, 1983).
M. Zeraffa, *Roman et Société* (Paris, 1971).
J. Zipes, *Breaking the Magic Spell* (London, 1979). Theoretical Marxist approach.
E. Zolla, *Storia del Fantasticare* (Milan, 1964).

Index

Index

Index